abril, 1995

**Literary Bondage**

*Slavery in Cuban Narrative*

Para Carlos: Gracias por las atenciones que has tenido conmigo.

The Texas Pan American Series

# Literary Bondage

## SLAVERY IN CUBAN NARRATIVE

# WILLIAM LUIS

 University of Texas Press   Austin

First edition, 1990

Requests for permission to reproduce material from this work should be
sent to Permissions, University of Texas Press, Box 7819, Austin, TX
78713-7819.

∞ The paper used in this publication meets the minimum requirements
of American National Standard for Information Sciences—Permanence of
Paper for Printed Library Materials, ANSI Z39.48-1984.

LIBRARY OF CONGRESS CATALOGING-IN-PUBLICATION DATA

Luis, William.
    Literary bondage : slavery in Cuban narrative / by William Luis. — 1st ed.
        p.   cm. — (Texas Pan American series)
    Includes bibliographical references.
    ISBN 0-292-72463-2 (alk. paper)
        1. Cuban fiction—History and criticism.   2. Cuban prose literature—
History and criticism.   3. Slavery and slaves in literature.   4. Blacks in
literature.   I. Title.   II. Series.
PQ7382.L85   1990
863—dc20                                                          89-37603
                                                                      CIP

The Texas Pan American Series is published with the assistance of a
revolving publication fund established by the Pan American Sulphur
Company.

Reprinted by permission of Centro Nacional de Derecho de Autor: "Sol de
domingo" by Nicolás Guillén; quotations from Francisco Estévez, *Diario
de un rancheador*, ed. Roberto Friol, *Revista de la Biblioteca Nacional
José Martí* 64, no. 1 (1973): 47–148; quotations from "Los cobreros y los
palenques de negros cimarrones," *Revista de la Biblioteca Nacional José
Martí*, 64, no. 1 (1973): 37–46.

Reprinted by permission of Three Continents Press: quotations from *So
Spoke the Uncle* by Jean Price-Mars.

Reprinted by permission of Pantheon Books: excerpts from *The
Autobiography of a Runaway Slave*, by Esteban Montejo, edited
by Miguel Barnet, translated by Jocasta Innes.

*Para Linda*

# CONTENTS

# PREFACE

This study proposes to show the unity, coherence, and continuity of the theme of slavery in Cuban narrative. Although there have been works published in and outside of Cuba pertaining to slavery, they are either limited to the early antislavery narrative or focus on one particular nineteenth- or twentieth-century author such as Cirilo Villaverde, Juan Francisco Manzano, Miguel Barnet, or Alejo Carpentier. There are other studies which treat the theme of blacks in Cuban, Caribbean, and Latin American literatures, but none has attempted to trace the theme of slavery from its inception to the contemporary period and understand it as a past and present literary concern.

From a broader perspective, this study strives to redefine the canon of Spanish American literature which has systematically relegated themes related to blacks to the margins of literary discourse. Leading scholars have successfully identified and classified important movements, trends, and authors and included them in the canon, but few have paid attention to slavery and blacks as a fundamental component of literature, history, and culture. For example, Villaverde's *Cecilia Valdés*, which I consider to be one of the most important, if not the most important, novel in nineteenth-century Spanish American literature, continues to receive little attention outside of Cuba. *Cecilia Valdés* should be read alongside José Mármol's *Amalia* and Jorge Isaacs's *María*, thus forming a nineteenth-century literary triangle between Cuba, Colombia, and Argentina and a trilogy of works whose titles contain the names of women.

Now that we are well into the postboom period or approaching the boundaries of a new Latin American discourse, other types of narratives and genres will gain the attention of readers. The novel of the boom period and the circumstances associated with its development fulfilled an important mission; that is, to bring Spanish America and its literature to the attention of the world, particularly the

works of writers such as Gabriel García Márquez, Guillermo Cabrera
Infante, Carlos Fuentes, Mario Vargas Llosa, and Julio Cortázar. As
we enter a new period in Spanish American literature, we can look
forward to exploring other writers and aspects of the literature which
I believe are as important as those of the boom period. I am referring,
for example, to feminist literature and the theme of blacks. From
my perspective, *Cecilia Valdés* as well as Anselmo Suárez y Romero's
*Francisco*, Alejo Carpentier's *The Kingdom of This World*, and Miguel Barnet's *The Autobiography of a Runaway Slave*, among others,
and the themes they represent should be familiar to students of Spanish and Latin American literatures. Other works such as Lino Novás
Calvo's *El negrero* and Manzano's *Autobiografía* are essential for the
study of slavery but also for understanding the strategies of writing
biography and autobiography, respectively. I hope this study will
raise questions about canon and canon formation in general and
blacks and slavery in particular and inspire a fruitful dialogue among
scholars regarding the value of the themes addressed in this book.
Ultimately, I hope it will serve as an example for the study of slavery
and blacks in nineteenth- and twentieth-century Spanish American
literature.

This book could not have been written without the help and support of colleagues and friends. I owe special gratitude to Roberto
González Echevarría and Antonio Benítez Rojo for their invaluable
suggestions throughout the various stages of this manuscript. I have
learned much from their ideas and suggestions. Their dedication,
discipline, and work have provided me with a model I have attempted
to follow. Many of their writings are reflected in mine.

I would also like to thank Sara Castro Klarén, Aníbal González,
Bob Russell, Enrique Pupo Walker, Sylvia Molloy, Bob Márquez, and
Randolph Pope, who have directly or indirectly supported this project. Their faith in my work gave me the energy and enthusiasm to
overcome adverse circumstances and complete the manuscript. At
Dartmouth, I was given invaluable assistance by the interlibrary
loan officer, Patsy Carter, who helped to track down many obscure
and difficult to obtain books. In addition, I received financial support
in the form of a Dartmouth Junior Faculty Fellowship for the fall
term of 1983 which allowed me to complete portions of the manuscript. I want to recognize Fred Berthold and Jim Tatum, members of
the Committee Advisory to the President, for reading the manuscript and recognizing the value of its content. At Washington University in St. Louis, I would like to thank Randolph Pope, Horacio
Xaubert, John Garganigo, Antonio Vera-León, Joseph Schraibman,

and Nancy Schauum for taking me in as one of their own and creating a friendly and intellectual environment. I am also grateful to the graduate students in the Department of Romance Languages and Literatures for their valor in taking a seminar on Slavery in Cuban Narrative and allowing me a forum to express many of the ideas contained herein; they were patient but also challenging and asked many probing questions. I also owe much gratitude to my copy editor, Mary Hill, for her patience in reading the manuscript and her suggestions, and to Rae O'Connor for her help in preparing the index.

Finally, I would like to recognize members of my immediate family, Linda, Stephanie, and Gabriel, and my mother, Petra, for their sacrifice and support; above all, Linda for her trust and faith in me and her personal dedication in helping me complete the manuscript. I also owe special recognition to my close friends Peter and Nancy Beck for their unwavering support during difficult moments and for allowing me to use their home in Alburg Springs, along the shores of Lake Champlain, where I was able to edit portions of the manuscript.

W.L.

# Literary Bondage
*Slavery in Cuban Narrative*

# INTRODUCTION

## *Fiction and Fact*
### The Antislavery Narrative and Blacks as Counter-Discourse in Cuban History

*Discursive practices are not purely and simply ways of producing discourse. They are embodied in technical processes, in institutions, in patterns for general behavior, in forms for transmission and diffusion, and in pedagogical forms which, at once, impose and maintain them.*

*And when the prisoners began to speak, they possessed an individual theory of prisons, the penal system, and justice. It is this form of discourse which ultimately matters, a discourse against power, the counter-discourse of prisoners and those we call delinquents—and not a theory about delinquency.*

     —FOUCAULT, *LANGUAGE, COUNTER-MEMORY, PRACTICE*

FICTION Antislavery narrative refers to a group of works written mainly during the 1830s, an incipient and prolific moment in Cuban literature. They include ex-slave Juan Francisco Manzano's *Autobiografía* (written in 1835, published in England in 1840 and in Cuba in 1937), Anselmo Suárez y Romero's *Francisco* (written in 1839, published in 1880), and Félix Tanco y Bosmeniel's *Escenas de la vida privada en la isla de Cuba* (written in 1838, published in 1925) and "Un niño en la Habana" (written in 1837, published in 1986).[1] These early works were requested by Domingo del Monte, Cuba's most influential literary critic, and reflect the literary and historical circumstances of the times.[2] They provide a sympathetic view of blacks and slaves during a period in which slavery was at its peak and Cuba was the most important sugar-producing country in the world.

Fiction in the antislavery works is not part of a creative or inventive process intended to entertain or delight the reader. On the contrary, it is a carefully constructed system whose purpose is to reveal a reality not often seen, accepted, or understood by the reader; one intended to alter a socioeconomic system based on sugar, slavery, and the slave trade. By creating a verisimilar narrative system, fiction takes on a special meaning; it becomes a way of rewriting other fiction and, most importantly, history. There is an intrinsic relationship between the antislavery narrative and history: The antislavery works are based on a historical reality which allows them to challenge history and rewrite in narrative discourse a different version of the same history. The dominant discourse in Cuba during the early part of the nineteenth century centered on slavery and the cultivation of sugar, as represented, for example, in Francisco Arango y Parreño's *Discurso sobre la agricultura de la Habana* (1792). In his *Discurso*, Arango encouraged Havana sugar growers to take advantage of the insurrection in Saint Domingue by filling the sugar void in the international market and promoting their own agricultural prosperity.[3] The antislavery narrative, on the other hand, is a counter-discourse to power whose immediate aim is to question and ultimately dismantle nineteenth-century colonial and slave society.[4]

Any sympathetic presentation of blacks in nineteenth-century Cuban literature represents a counter-discourse to power and is subversive to a Western form of rule. If the fabric of colonial Cuba was based on sugar and slavery, the antislavery narrative questioned the very strength that motivated the society by resorting to an image that challenged and undermined it. In the antislavery works, blacks are not described as mere accidents of history but as an indispensable element of Cuban culture and nationality.

The antislavery works were written during the emergence of Cuban narrative and, therefore, make a daring attempt to include blacks as an integral part of the island's culture. In effect, they create a permanent space for blacks in a literature of foundation. This narrative represents the first cohesive movement to describe blacks and slaves as a dominant element in Cuban and Latin American literatures and broadens the margins of literary discourse.[5] The antislavery writers inserted a different voice into an undifferentiating and hermetic discourse to produce a dialogue on slavery. Although the dialogue was initiated, it was not totally realized. Even though the antislavery works were written for the most part by white intellectuals with a European-style education, they did not form part of a dialogue on slavery but rather fell outside of it. By questioning the slavery system, the narrations inevitably complemented other historical events which undermined the power of sugar and slavery, in particular those surrounding the rebellion in Saint Domingue (1791) and the Aponte Conspiracy in Cuba (1812), two movements intending to create a power space for blacks within their respective countries. In Cuba, the antislavery works were considered a threat by the Spanish authorities, were censored, and were not published on the island until slaves ceased to represent an imminent danger to whites.

As counter-discourse to power, the antislavery narrative represents a counter-writing of fiction and history and proposes a counter-reading of narrative discourse. Writing is a conscious manipulation of language and a careful structuring of story and plot.[6] The author of the antislavery narrative (re)orders commonplaces produced by the dominant discourse and writes and rewrites the roles of characters in history and literature. The author creates a counter-world in which he is another participant. Writing is a commitment to and a reliving of the events narrated.

The reader is an important part of the writing process. The author strives to persuade the reader into understanding and accepting the life of the slave, someone antagonistic to his own interest and existence. In other words, the narrative strategy reduces the distance between the master's quarters and the slave's barracoon, between the oppressor and the oppressed, the white and the black. The space traditionally occupied by master and slave is also inverted and the interested reader is persuaded to view slavery no longer from the master's perspective but from the slave's. With the change in space, the signs are also inverted; black as negative and white as positive are revealed not as absolute categories inherent in Western language or culture but as an arbitrary system of signs subject to textual manipulation. If blacks and slaves represented a threat to whites, as the Haitian example suggests, they are now portrayed as the victims of a society which exploits them without apparent justification. Likewise, if the familiar slave master and overseer are the protectors of slavery and the livelihood of whites, they are transformed into morally corrupt individuals whose interest is to satisfy their own libidinal needs.

As a form of protest against the slavery system, the antislavery narrative did not end with the emancipation of slaves in 1886 but continues well into the twentieth century.[7] The abolition of slaves in Cuban history has not altered a concern for the antislavery theme, which up to the present study has been limited to the early nineteenth-century works. From their inception to the present, the antislavery works can be divided into four historical moments: slavery, post-slavery, the republic, and the Cuban revolutionary periods. This chronology suggests two different but complementary patterns. The antislavery works are both a beginning regarding the four synchronic moments surrounding the specific circumstances in which the works were written and a continuum reflecting the conditions of slaves who lived tied to an economic and racial system based on sugar. Yet an investigation into the literature shows that a structure based on discourse and counter-discourse, oppression and rebellion which allowed the antislavery narrative as a form of protest to emerge is reflected in the lives of blacks in nineteenth- and twentieth-century Cuban history. In this introductory chapter, I will propose a periodization of the antislavery narrative and then show how the same stages are also present in the history of blacks in Cuba. I divide the antislavery narrative into four historical periods: the first, from its beginning in 1835 to emancipation in 1886; the second, from emancipation to 1902, the founding of the Republic of Cuba; the third, from 1902 to the triumph of the Cuban Revolution in 1959; and the fourth, from the Cuban Revolution to the present.

Not until the beginning of the nineteenth century did the tension between the white oppressor and the black slave peak in Cuba. This was due mainly to the rapid increase in the number of blacks on the island, an increase directly related to the growth of the sugar industry. The success of the Haitian rebellion, which created a vacuum in the world sugar market that Cuba filled, precipitated this growth.[8] As a result of sugar, the Cuban census indicates that the number of slaves grew along with the number of all colored people. Blacks for the first time outnumbered whites during the first half of the nineteenth century. The fear of the rising number of blacks and the recent Haitian rebellion led white slave owners to become more oppressive, thus increasing pressure within the system and causing a higher number of slaves to attempt to flee.

In response to an alarming concern regarding the number of slaves and their treatment in Cuba, Del Monte commissioned antislavery narratives from Tanco y Bosmeniel, Suárez y Romero, and the slave Manzano. These works represent a political-literary discourse and were written with an immediate purpose in mind: to bring an end to slavery and the slave trade. To the early antislavery works, I add another group that was written or completed and published abroad: Gertrudis Gómez de Avellaneda's *Sab* (Madrid, 1841), Antonio Zambrana's *El negro Francisco* (Santiago de Chile, 1873), and Cirilo Villaverde's *Cecilia Valdés* (New York, 1882). Villaverde belonged to the Del Monte literary circle and wrote and published two earlier versions of his *Cecilia Valdés* in 1839, but I have decided not to include them among the early antislavery works. There are substantive differences between the short story and volume 1 and the last edition of *Cecilia Valdés*. The first two narrations were not antislavery works; they passed the censors and were published in Cuba.

The last version reflected the sentiments of the early antislavery works and was completed not in Cuba but while Villaverde lived in exile in New York.[9]

Gómez de Avellaneda did not belong to the Del Monte circle, but her knowledge of the slavery system in Cuba, her compassion, and a liberal political climate under Regent María Cristina in Spain allowed her to write and publish her novel. And although Zambrana was not born until after the writing of the first antislavery works, he attended at the home of the abolitionist Nicolás de Azcárate a reading of Suárez y Romero's manuscript. Zambrana's *El negro Francisco* is a rewriting of *Francisco*. His novel was not requested by Del Monte but by another patrician, doña Ascensión Rodríguez de Necochea, a Chilean who wanted to read a novel written by the Cuban writer. Zambrana seized the opportunity to express his political views regarding blacks on the island. Like Villaverde and Gómez de Avellaneda, Zambrana wrote and published his novel while living abroad.[10]

With the exception of Silvestre de Balboa's epic *Espejo de paciencia*, an early seventeenth-century poem whose protagonists include an Ethiopian slave,[11] the antislavery narratives were the first works to introduce blacks and mulattoes as protagonists in Cuban narrative. In these early works, the authors describe the tragic lives of passive and defenseless slaves who are ruthlessly abused by their masters. But the incipient Cuban narrative also includes works which describe slavery not from the slave's but from the slaver's point of view, as represented by the slave hunter. Written in the same period as the antislavery literature, Francisco Estévez's *Diario de un rancheador* (written between 1837 and 1842) documents his periodic trips to hunt fugitive slaves, and José Morillas's short story "El ranchador" (written in 1839 and published in 1852) narrates the life of another slave hunter, Valentín Páez. Recently, Adriana Lewis Galanes discovered the content of the album Del Monte gave to Madden for his antislavery cause. According to her, it included an earlier version of Morilla's "El ranchador."[12] Even though the short story formed part of the early antislavery works, because of its theme and development I have decided to read it alongside Estévez's diary. From a different perspective, the short story and the diary also describe the sufferings of slaves and the brutalities of proslavers. The slavery and antislavery works depict the same historical moment, the first third of the nineteenth century, a time in which uprisings were commonplace and the tension between whites and blacks was increasing.

Antislavery works written and published after the emancipation of slaves, the founding of the republic, and the triumph of the Cuban

Revolution continued to highlight the same slavery period and the plight of the Cuban slave, but with some important differences. The works of the early authors contained a direct correspondence between the time of the narration and the time in which the works were written; they described a condition that was present during the time of the writing and turned history into a narrative discourse. Later, writers continued to narrate the same slavery period but from a different point of view, one that reflected the conditions of the society in which they lived, a contemporary period familiar to them and their readers. The passage of time has allowed these writers a privileged perspective into a historico-literary process of which their works became an integral part.

Francisco Calcagno is an example of a writer who published his novels during a crucial moment of transition in Cuban history, from slavery to emancipation. He wrote some works before the abolition of slavery; because of the censors he suppressed them and published them many years later. For example, *Los crímenes de Concha* was written in 1863 and published in 1887, and *Romualdo, uno de tantos* was written in 1869 and published in 1881.[13] These works capture the historical period of the early antislavery narratives but incorporate a contemporary understanding of slavery, one present during the time in which the works were written, when the slave trade was coming to an end and the abolition of slavery was an inevitable course of history. A correlation between the time of the narration and the one in which the works were written allowed for the reader and author to understand that little had changed between the two periods. Equally important, nothing will have changed, as the prologue, written during the time in which the work was published, indicates.

As slavery came to an end, the antislavery works were no longer a direct threat to the colonial government and were published; the postslavery works moved from the space outside the dominant discourse on slavery to a space within it. They entered into a dialogue on slavery, one which now coincided with the shift in society, away from slavery but where sugar continued to be the dominant discourse and blacks, though inside the dialogue, remained at the margins of it.

Just as the emancipation of slaves represented another stage in the lives of blacks and the theme of slavery in Cuba, the period after the founding of the republic and during the first decades of the twentieth century marked a new beginning for the black protagonist beyond the geographic boundaries of the island. Leo Frobenius's *The Black Decameron* (1910), Spengler's *Decline of the West* (1917),

Vachel Lindsay's *The Congo and Other Poems* (1914), and Blaise
Cendrars's *Anthologie nègre* (1927), among other works, signaled a
change from dominant Western images to black or African ones.[14]
During this period, blacks in the United States were experiencing
their own cultural revival in the Harlem Renaissance. In Europe, Africa was seen as an exotic place and blacks became a theme of avant-
garde art. This process of simultaneous subversion and expansion of
African culture was captured, for example, by Apollinaire's sculp-
tures and Picasso's paintings. Furthermore, the surrealists' emphasis
on the subconscious made for an easier return to the primitive stage
that Africa was assumed to represent. They and other white artists
and writers brought blacks as subject matter into the mainstream of
the European intellectual community.[15]

Europe's rediscovery of Africa also gave new meaning to the black
theme in countries with black culture in Latin America and the
Caribbean.[16] Cuban intellectuals who participated in the surrealist
movement, such as Wifredo Lam, began to look not to Africa but to
their own country for a black expression.[17] Others, like Fernando
Ortiz, continued a study of blacks begun by José Antonio Saco,
Del Monte, and the antislavery writers. Ortiz's investigation dates
as early as 1906 with his *Hampa afro-cubana: Los negros brujos
(Apuntes para un estudio de etnología criminal)*. Ortiz altered his
external perspective, as embodied in his first book, when he realized
through his investigation the importance of the black segment of
the population for an overall explanation of Cuban culture. In subsequent studies, Ortiz used information from the early antislavery
novels for his investigation.[18] The presence of blacks in the contemporary period exhibited other characteristics. The black image would
be expressed in *negrismo*, an Afro-Cuban poetic movement of the
1920s and 1930s. Ramón Guirao's "Bailadora de rumba" and José
Tallet's "La rumba" in 1928 gave popularity to certain cultural and
aesthetic images they attributed to blacks.[19] Nicolás Guillén, Mar-
celino Arozarena, and Regino Pedroso shared similar concerns but
added a social dimension to this thematic.[20] The *negrismo* movement became a phenomenon experienced simultaneously in the Antilles and other Latin American countries.[21]

Unlike French negritude and its conventional use of language for
self-expression, the Afro-Cuban movement was to deform the European language to express African folklore and rhythms. This particular linguistic or literary use conveyed what was lost by the falsification of one culture through the use of language.[22] Gabriel Coulthard
states that, for Cuban writers, Africanism was more than just a European novelty; it became part of the Cuban being and Cuba's contri-

bution to a universal literature.²³ The Afro-Cuban movement would
confirm the contribution made by the early antislavery writers
and continued to introduce blacks into the mainstream of Cuban
literature.

Although the antislavery writers continued to narrate the history
of the early part of the nineteenth century, the novels of the republic
period went beyond exposing a racial-economic problem based on
sugar. They also uncovered a deeper social concern as well. Works
like Lino Novás Calvo's *El negrero* (1933), José Antonio Ramos's
*Caniquí* (1936), and Alejo Carpentier's *The Kingdom of This World*
(1949) adopted the earlier antislavery form of expression but transcended the temporal limitations of those novels to comment on a
contemporary social setting, one present during the time in which
the works were published. Moreover, both Carpentier and Novás
Calvo take advantage of a broader interest in blacks and explore
their literary discourse outside the island; *El negrero* takes place in
Europe, Africa, and the Caribbean and *The Kingdom of This World*
develops mainly in Haiti but also in Cuba and Italy.

Like the antislavery and postantislavery works, the novels written in the republic continued a counter-discourse of social and political protest, not only for black characters but for whites as well.
This idea is best excmplified by Ramos's *Caniquí*, which used the
theme of slavery to set forth other contemporary concerns. Although
its plot unfolds in the historical Trinidad (Cuba) of the 1830s, it alludes transparently to the existing political conditions one century
later, during the time in which the novel was written and published—the Machado and post-Machado eras of the 1920s and
1930s. Ramos used the slavery period as an allegory of his own times
and thereby transcended the issue of race. What is implicit in the
novel is explicit in the prologue, where Ramos explains his intentions, knowing that his work, as Suárez y Romero and others realized during the early nineteenth century, would only be completely
understood in the future.²⁴

*Caniquí*'s contemporary view of slavery focuses upon the specific
economic and racial preoccupations of that system but serves as a
metaphor for the existing slavelike conditions to which blacks and
whites were subjected during the early part of the twentieth century.
*Caniquí*'s message is a contemporary call for rebellion, a rebellion
that will emancipate not only blacks but the entire society. With
*Caniquí*, we discern how the passage of time has allowed the incor-
poration of a discourse of rebellion that was present in the nineteenth century, as represented, for example, by José Antonio Aponte

and later David Turnbull but not included in the early novels of the slavery period.

Social commentary takes on still a different meaning in a society that is attempting to rewrite its own history, such as today's Cuba. With the triumph of the Cuban Revolution in 1959, another dimension of the nineteenth-century antislavery novel was brought forth. The novels written during this period show a thematic development from those published after the postemancipation period and follow closely the political events reflecting the time in which the works were written. The reevaluation of the roles of blacks in revolutionary Cuba, for example, became a significant issue for the new revolutionary government, and the elimination of prerevolutionary structural inequities led to a questioning of social and cultural values. From the outset of the revolution, Castro affirmed his goal. In his March 22, 1959, speech, he addressed the race issue: "Let white and black unite to end racial discrimination. And thus we shall proceed, step by step, to create our new homeland."[25] By altering the socioeconomic structures, the present Cuban government appears to have incorporated blacks into mainstream society.

Castro's initiative set the tone for what was to come.[26] Blacks, and the African element of Cuban culture, became the concern of many, and there has been a literary upsurge on the subject. The studies of writers interested in a black theme, including those of Ortiz, were reprinted. Many of the works published in today's Cuba which promote the black image received international recognition, such as Guillén's writings, Miguel Barnet's *The Autobiography of a Runaway Slave* (1966), César Leante's *Los guerrilleros negros* (1976), and Moreno Fraginal's monumental *The Sugar Mill* (1978). Afro-Cuban culture has been officially recognized by the government. In affirming Cuban solidarity with African countries, Castro has acknowledged that Cubans are an Afro-Latin people.[27]

For many, the Cuban Revolution represents a counter-discourse to the Batista dictatorship and to the dominant discourse of capitalist society. The revolution's counter-discourse, however, is no longer marginal to Cuban society but central to its own survival. It has now become the dominant discourse. Similarly, from the government's point of view, marginal elements in Cuban society, such as blacks, women, and poor people, have been "integrated" into a revolutionary discourse. With the revolution, the counter-discourse of the antislavery narrative has moved from the margins to the center, though, in spite of the economic changes and as in the nineteenth century, sugar continues to determine the lives of blacks and

whites on the island. Like the antislavery narrative, the Cuban
Revolution is both a beginning and a continuum. It is a beginning
insofar as the Castro forces overthrew an existing order and a continuum as the government views its own revolution not as a recent
event which started with the attack on the Moncada Barracks in July
26, 1953, but with the uprising of Carlos Manuel de Céspedes nearly
a century before in 1868.

Unlike the earlier works, the antislavery novels of this period are
written not from a point of transition but, like the Cuban revolutionary process, from the point of arrival. Writers can now look back
to the nineteenth and early twentieth centuries, understand the long
historical and literary process which culminated in the present, and
write from a vantage point of view. Leante's *Los guerrilleros negros* is
perhaps the best example of a contemporary version of a nineteenth-
century antislavery novel. By closely following the historical accounts of a runaway slave community in the mountains, the Gran
Palenque de Moa, Leante uncovers a series of events that were not
documented by earlier writers. Leante's novel does not represent a
desire to break with the past but rather embodies a communion
with it. By adhering closely to the patterns of history, Leante incorporates works that were based on a similar history. His narration rewrites scenes that have become familiar in earlier antislavery novels
in order to correct their shortcomings. The characters and scenes of
his work recall those of others but with significant changes. Leante
brings them into his work to give them a different context, life, and
meaning.

However, some may argue that a rebellious slave image had already been described effectively in previous works and, in particular,
by Carpentier in *The Kingdom of This World*. After all, Leante's
character embodies the same rebel spirit as Ti Noel, Mackandal,
Bouckman, and others. A close reading reveals that Leante's novel
goes beyond the historical limitations of other novels, including *The
Kingdom of This World*. Carpentier's second novel proposes a historical process, one which begins with Mackandal in the 1850s and
ends after the Boyer government almost a century later. Whereas
Carpentier exemplified Afro-Cuban culture in *¡Ecue Yamba-O!*
(1933), in *The Kingdom of This World* he presents a historical rebellion as a novelistic theme. He associates events with the Haitian
rebellion and, more importantly, the characters' own awakening to
history, a process that would liberate them from their destinies.

Yet an alternate reading of *The Kingdom of This World* reveals
that it does not offer a chronology of historical events that would
liberate its characters. What in Carpentier's second novel appears to

be a linearity of events is undermined by a cycle of rebellion motivated not by history but by African gods and religion. Leante's *Los guerrilleros negros*, in comparison, reflects the same concern for historical change seen in the Cuban government and provides a historical linearity, a chronological sequence of events.

The theme of blacks and slavery culminates in the works written during the Cuban Revolution. The increased temporal distance from the past century has allowed writers to introduce new perspectives when writing about the nineteenth century. History has given contemporary writers a more complete picture of the slavery issue. But Leante's reevaluation of the slavery theme is not preconditioned only by the need to document the history of blacks before the abolition of slavery. Like *Caniquí, Los guerrilleros negros* also reponds to a present time; that is, to the political reality of the time in which the work was written. One must look to the Cuban Revolution to understand Leante's thematic concerns when writing his novel. Revolution and revolutionary activity are no longer considered marginal and incidental but are factors essential for change. Like the current Cuban government, Leante will analyze the past from a revolutionary present. As political leaders and historians have reevaluated history, so too will Leante, Barnet, and other writers introduce into literature the slave rebellions as an origin of modern Cuban history.

By developing the theme of antislavery, like the Cuban Revolution, both Barnet and Leante have appropriated a counter-discourse and made it their own. In this respect, the antislavery novels written during the revolution exhibit a shift in narrative structure; they no longer challenge the society in which the works were written but conform to it. However, this is not to say that the counter-discourse is not present in society and in their works. For example, Barnet's testimonial novel incorporates an opposition between the ex-slave Montejo's voice and Barnet's writing; that is, between discourse and counter-discourse. This relationship is also present in Leante's novel, which physically reproduces fragments of the early antislavery works. Both Leante and Barnet attempt to control and reshape the counter-discourse so that it conforms to the ideas of the revolutionary government. The antislavery works written during the revolution describe the theme of slavery from a counter-discourse but also submit it to the discourse of power. Nevertheless, there is a questioning, if slight, of the dominant discourse. Within the context of the antislavery works, the Castro revolution can be traced not to the Ten Years' War but to slave rebellions during the first part of the nineteenth century.

Within the same revolutionary period, it will be Reinaldo Arenas's
*Graveyard of the Angels,* a novel written and published outside of
Cuba, which will return to the counter-discourse of the early antislavery works and challenge Cuban society during the time in which
the work was written.

The events after 1959 have opened up a different avenue from
which to analyze the antislavery narrative. The perspective offered
now is no longer written from a marginal but a privileged moment
in Cuban history. Leante's, Barnet's, and Arenas's novels look back
to the nineteenth century and the origin of the antislavery narrative
to see this genre culminate within their own pages.

| FACT | The antislavery works contain and reflect a historical
process, and the same fictional patterns they represent
are embodied in history. Although social conventions
have attributed marked differences to history and fiction, writing as
textuality has allowed them to be read side by side. Fiction has provided me with a reading of history and history with a reading of fiction, thus privileging a simultaneous reading of blacks and slavery
in Cuban history and fiction. Both fact and fiction are conditioned
by a "deep structure" based on discourse and counter-discourse, oppression and rebellion, which motivates them to unfold in a similar
manner. Thus the patterns which allow me to view the antislavery
narrative as both a historical continuum and a beginning are also
evident in the experiences of blacks in Cuban history. Throughout
their history, the subjugation of slaves and free blacks conforms to a
historical pattern, one which the antislavery literature addresses
eloquently. The history of blacks as counter-discourse has challenged white dominance over them, as seen by numerous black
uprisings and rebellions since Africans were brought to the New
World. And, if we continue the parallel between fact and fiction, we
discover that the oppression of blacks under the Spaniards did not
end with the emancipation of slaves but continued into the founding
of the republic in 1902 and well into the twentieth century.

In literature, the counter-discourse is defined by the antislavery
narratives; in history, the same counter-discourse of blacks and
slaves is represented by their attempt to undermine and subvert the
white power structure based on sugar, slavery, and the oppression of
blacks. The actions of slaves to flee slavery and live in Maroon communities in the mountains denoted a total rejection of the white
power structure, which intended to define their roles, though central to sugar production, as subordinate and expendable within the
society at large. The escape of slaves to the mountains represents a

counter-discourse to power with an inherent power of its own. However, so long as the ex-slaves remain in mountain communities, their discourse falls outside the dominant one. But once the fugitive slaves come into contact with proslavers, the dominant discourse, their interaction produces a dialogue on slavery, one questioning the other, one attempting to undo the other, and, in their struggle, one remaining marginal to the other.

As with the antislavery narrative, the history of blacks and slaves in the slavery, postslavery, republic, and revolutionary periods reflects the passage of time. What may be understood as synchronic periods separated by transformations in Cuban history taken together offer insight into a diachronic history of blacks in Cuba. The continuous oppression of blacks has been interrupted by their struggles to gain liberation and political freedom. Thus a meta-historical reading of the lives of blacks in Cuba would inevitably recount over and over again a struggle for liberation, freedom, and self-determination.

In literature, the antislavery narrative represents a moment in which the black theme asserts itself, but it always responds to the patterns of history. In history, the oppression and marginality of slaves and blacks and their rebellion against whites are evident especially in three distinct events—during the Aponte Conspiracy of 1812, the Ladder Conspiracy of 1844, and the Race War of 1912—and propose to continue into the Cuban revolutionary period.

Although a Caribbean counter-discourse may have started with the coming together of Africa and Europe, the black and white races, it became more evident during the nineteenth century. The Haitian rebellion, certainly the most important event in Caribbean history and in the history of blacks in the Americas, had a profound impact on the lives of blacks in Cuba. The revolt gave free blacks and slaves the incentive to fight a dominant power to gain their freedom and inspired independence movements throughout Latin America and the Caribbean. It also put Spanish officials and slavers on guard to prevent a similar occurrence on the island of Cuba. Thus proslavers resorted to more oppressive measures to control the ever-increasing black and slave population, often imprisoning, whipping, or killing them.[28]

The Haitian rebellion caused a general unrest among blacks in Cuba and would be used by Spanish officials and slavers to justify oppressing slaves and free blacks on the island.[29] At the beginning of the nineteenth century, the colonial authorities feared Dessalines, whose emissaries were sent to organize black and slave rebellions in Cuba and other countries.[30] But not until 1812 did a unified move-

ment form on the island to gain independence from Spain and emancipate slaves. In many ways, the free black José Antonio Aponte became Cuba's Toussaint Louverture. The 1812 Aponte Conspiracy in
Cuba echoed the neighboring rebellion, but it had its origin two years
earlier in another uprising, organized by Román de la Luz and Luis
Francisco Bassave y Cárdenas.[31] Like Bassave, Toussaint, and others,
Aponte was a well-known figure. A successful carpenter and a first
corporal of the prestigious Havana militia of the Batallón de Morenos, Aponte was also important among members of his community.
He was the leader of the religious chapter Shangó-Teddun; an *ogboni*,
or member of a powerful Nigerian secret society; and, within his religious order, an Oni-Shangó, a position that recognized his civil and
spiritual powers.[32]

Aponte used his religious and civil leadership to unite blacks and
mulattoes throughout the island by organizing the various tribes and
black and mulatto émigrés living in Cuba. The black leader used his
broad appeal to gather into his movement whites who participated in
the 1810 conspiracy and others who were influenced by the separatist
movements in Mexico, Venezuela, and Colombia. Aponte's goal was
to abolish slavery and the slave trade and replace the colonial status
with a just government. His plan included setting fire to sugarcane
fields in the provinces of Havana and Matanzas and taking over the
Atares fortress and the Cuartel de Dragones to arm rebels. In Havana,
Aponte visited Gil Narciso, one of Dessaline's generals, who, en
route from Central America to Saint Domingue, enlisted his participation and learned first-hand about the Haitian uprising. The black
rebel was also familiar with Henri Christophe's triumph in the
northern part of Haiti and considered the possibility of receiving
help from the black leader.[33]

However, unlike the Haitian rebellion, Aponte's plan failed. There
was dissension among the rebels. Unity was not based totally on
race; some blacks and mulattoes preferred to defend the colonial system.[34] There was a successful assault on the sugar mill Peñas Altas
in the province of Havana on March 15, 1812, but the attack on Trinidad the following day proved fatal. Slave Pedro María Chacón, who
had been in Bayamo, another rebel city, warned his master, and a
priest, Manuel Donoso, convinced slaves not to rebel.[35] Captain
General Someruelos intervened with his forces and detained Aponte
and other leaders in the Cuartel de Dragones. On April 7, Aponte
was condemned to die, and two days later he and his followers were
hanged. That same day, Aponte's severed head was displayed in a
cage for all to see.

The Aponte Conspiracy, in which blacks and mulattoes rebelled but were then killed or punished severely, would be repeated in the Ladder Conspiracy of 1844. By the time Richard Madden, the arbiter in Mixed Court, published Manzano's *Poems by a Slave in the Island of Cuba* in 1840, the British had abolished slavery in the Anglophone Caribbean. Sugar islands like Jamaica were at a distinct disadvantage; they depended on wage laborers, while Cuba still counted on a large slave population to work the sugar plantations. Unlike the sugar islands, Cuba's sugar was comparatively less expensive since the island had the capacity to refine it.[36] Through British pressure, Captain General Valdés received orders from Spain to execute a plan to emancipate slaves taken to Cuba after 1820. However, once the order reached the island, it was suppressed and never carried out. With the increasing black and slave populations and conspiracies for the political independence of Cuba, as promoted, for example, by the society Sol y Rayos de Bolívar,[37] many feared a racial confrontation provoked by abolitionists.

By 1841, the British appeared to be winning the emancipation battle. In July, the *Anti-Slavery Report of London* gave encouraging news: "It is my pleasure to inform you that the abolitionists principles are beginning to take root in this city and in Matanzas. The present moment is full of the best hopes for favorable results for humanity and liberty. . . . The abolitionists of this city . . . although few in numbers are influential in means."[38] In that same year there were numerous rebellions, including those in the sugar mill of Arratea in Macurijes and the coffee plantation of Perseverancia in Lagunilla and in the construction of the Palace of Aldama belonging to relatives of Del Monte.

With Conservatives coming to power in England, the more conciliatory Lord Aberdeen replaced the relentless and unyielding abolitionist Lord Palmerston. Consequently, in 1842 Joseph Tucker Crawford replaced Turnbull in Cuba, thus forcing him to leave the island. Nevertheless, Turnbull's name and ideas were a cause for alarm in the Spanish colony. Turnbull resided on the nearby island of Jamaica and became head of the Luso-British Mixed Court in Kingston. Hysteria about the possibility of slave uprisings and black invasion from abroad plagued Cuba.[39]

Instead of the sporadic rebellions of previous years in the Matanzas-Cárdenas regions, in 1843 there were successive uprisings in the sugar mills of Alcancía, La Luisa, La Trinidad, Las Nieves, and the ranch Ranchuelo, as well as in the railroad construction line from Cárdenas to Jucaro. Like the others, these rebellions were suppressed.

Although the uprisings were not a part of the Turnbull conspiracy, some hoped that they had aborted the larger one which was still to come.[40]

Rebellions continued after Valdés left office and into the interim government of Francisco Javier de Ulloa, who governed from October to November 1843. Under his administration, a major rebellion erupted in the sugar mill Triunvirato, where whites were killed. When Leopoldo O'Donnell (1843–1848) took over as the next captain general, rumors of Cuba becoming another Haiti were widespread. In another uprising at the Santísima Trinidad sugar mill, a slave told her master, Esteban Santa Cruz de Oviedo, of a major slave uprising planned for December 25, 1843, which would include the massacre of many whites.[41] O'Donnell seized this opportunity to put his ruthless plans into action and terrorized the slave and free black populations. His actions were known as the Ladder Conspiracy of 1844, which Hugh Thomas describes in the following manner: "In early 1844, about 4,000 people (in Matanzas) were suddenly arrested, including over 2,000 free negroes, over 1,000 slaves, and at least 70 whites. Negroes believed to be guilty of plotting were tied to ladders and whipped to confess—the name La Escalera thus becoming notorious, though this has been for a long time the name of a recognized type of punishment. Seventy-eight were shot, and perhaps one hundred more whipped to death."[42] Thomas also points out that the authorities used this opportune time to "disembarrass themselves of all troublemakers, real and potential," and entertains the idea of a contrived conspiracy to raise the price of slaves.[43] José Luciano Franco's sources place the whipping fatality at over seven thousand and suggest that the "conspiracy" was provoked by Captain General O'Donnell with the cooperation of traffickers in slavery. Their intentions included suppressing the growing black bourgeoisie,[44] some of whom appear in Villaverde's Cecilia Valdés. Those who were not killed were jailed or forced into exile.

The conspiracy, which delivered a strong blow to a growing black professional class, also destroyed the environment which had produced such antislavery works as Suárez y Romero's Francisco and Tanco y Bosmeniel's "Petrona y Rosalía" and forced other writers, like Juan Francisco Manzano, into permanent silence. The mulatto poet Gabriel de la Concepción Valdés, better known as Plácido, a frequent visitor at the Del Monte tertulia, or literary salon, was accused of leading the uprising in Matanzas. Plácido in turn accused Del Monte, Tanco y Bosmeniel, and Manzano, among others, of participating in the rebellion. Del Monte left the island in 1843 and died in exile in 1853. Plácido and other free blacks were shot in the back on June 24, 1844; Plácido's accusation against Del Monte may have been contrived since he never signed the confession.[45]

As in the antislavery narrative, the emancipation of slaves in 1886 brought an end to the old order and the start of a new one. But this beginning and the next one, during the founding of the republic, did not signal a radical change for blacks in Cuba. The Race War of May 20, 1912, recalled the uprising and brutal massacre of blacks during the Ladder and Aponte conspiracies. Blacks belonging to the Partido Independiente de Color, under Evaristo Estenoz, organized massive demonstrations and strikes throughout the island. Blacks protested their unrewarded participation in the War of Independence and in the Liberal party's campaign against Estrada Palma in 1906. Another point of contention was the Morúa Amendment to the electoral law, forbidding the formation of political parties on the basis of race. Thomas compares the existing atmosphere on the part of whites to that of the "great fear" during the French Revolution. The protest was strongest in Oriente Province, where General Monteagudo, who suspended constitutional rights, defeated four thousand black insurgents and claimed to have killed three thousand himself.[46] Carlos Moore, who considers the white action similar to that of slavers, believes that some fifteen thousand Afro-Cubans were killed, many shot and lynched without trials.[47]

The most comprehensive reports of this period come from a collection of newspaper articles by Rafael Conte and José M. Capmany entitled *Guerra de razas (Negros contra blancos en Cuba)*. This collection is of value not only for the information it contains but also for the way in which it is written, embodying the racial tension it describes. Both Conte and Capmany wrote a series of reports about blacks in Oriente, the province chosen by the rebels for their uprising. Oriente was also the province which had the largest number of runaway slaves. Composed of separate articles, the text as a whole contains detailed accounts of the War of the Races and the overwhelming victory of the Cuban soldiers over the black rebels. Conte and Capmany place the war not only within its contemporary setting but, more importantly, within the context of slavery and support the white dominant discourse. For them, history has not evolved but has remained the same, and it is interpreted along racial lines.[48]

The rebellion was to have erupted simultaneously in the six provinces but failed. Estenoz made a tactical error. Better known in the west than in the east, Estenoz decided to take charge of Oriente, where his other commanders, Lacoste and Ivonet, were more popular. Lacoste, considered the mastermind of the rebellion, thought that the government, fearing a U.S. invasion, would enter into a compromise. Lacoste was thinking about another rebellion, that of the copper miners of Santiago del Cobre, who rose against the Spanish authorities and won their freedom in 1800.[49] However, because of the fear of the United States, the rebellion was suppressed immediately. On May 31, U.S. marines landed at Daiquirí in Oriente; many believed that Americans would never allow Cuba to become a black republic.

The plan was to create uprisings in both the eastern and western parts of the island, giving the impression that the rebellion had spread throughout the island and thus dividing Cuban forces. But the plan failed. Although there were small uprisings in the western provinces, they were short-lived. Others became discouraged when Estenoz remained in Oriente instead of going to Las Villas and Havana as he had promised. This tactical error allowed the government to concentrate its forces in the east.[50]

As in the Ladder Conspiracy, the War of Races destroyed black political movements. From that time, and up to the next historical transition in 1959, no major political black figure emerged to press for relief of the plight of Afro-Cubans. Juan Gualberto Gómez and other blacks who had been involved in supporting black rights during the early part of the twentieth century faded into the background of Cuban politics.[51] The only major black figure to emerge was the leader of the Labor Federation, Lázaro Peña, who demanded rights not just for blacks but for all workers.

If we note the patterns established by history, we see a continuation of the same oppression of blacks which, for the purpose of this study, started at the beginning of the nineteenth century, continued toward the middle of the same century and the start of the twentieth century, and proposes to be repeated, as with the Ladder Conspiracy, toward the middle of the current century.

One can claim that the Castro Revolution has given Cuban history a chance to overcome the obstacles of the past and produce a true beginning. As a first impression, the Cuban Revolution appears to represent a significant change in the lives of blacks insofar as it marks a historic moment which, unlike previous ones, brought blacks into the mainstream of Cuban society. Harry Ring and others who visited Cuba have testified to the nondiscriminatory policies of the new government, Ring going so far as to claim that "in less than three years the revolution has wiped out racial discrimination almost completely."[52]

However, if the patterns of oppression and marginality of blacks have not been extricated from the past and continue, the next cycle would occur contemporaneous to the Cuban Revolution.[53] Although it is too early to ascertain, further investigation into the modern period uncovers the suppression of black rights during the early stages of the revolution, even though no known massacres of blacks have taken place. Thomas, among others, believes that blacks have not fared well under Castro. He writes: "The advantages gained by the Cuban Negroes since 1959 at Castro's hands have certainly been less far-reaching than those obtained in the last ten years of Spanish colonial rule by mulatto publicists such as Juan Gualberto Gómez or Martín Morúa Delgado."[54]

The success of the Cuban Revolution has produced a shift in historical discourse. If the antislavery narrative represented a counter-discourse, as did the Cuban Revolution before it gained power, once the rebel forces triumphed its own counter-discourse became the dominant discourse. The movement from the margins to the center privileged the discourse of those coming to power. However, once a counter-discourse becomes dominant, it ceases to be counter and becomes central to maintaining itself in power. And as we have seen, any dominant discourse will produce its own counter-discourse. Since blacks as a group have not reached any significant position of power within the revolutionary government, they still represent a counter-discourse to power or a counter-counter-discourse to a counter-discourse.[55] In this sense, little has changed in Cuban history. As in the past, and in spite of the radical changes in the social and political structure, today's Cuba continues to be a country based on sugar and blacks continue to be at the margins of power.

During the first years of the revolution and for the first time since the Race War of 1912, the concept of black power in Cuba gained momentum. Black awareness was due both to its presence in Cuban history, as demonstrated by the platform of the Partido Independiente de Color, and, in recent times, to the international appeal of the civil rights and the black power movements in the United States. The mistreatment and struggle of blacks in the United States received much publicity in Cuba.[56] Black militants such as Eldridge Cleaver, Andrew Ferrell, and Robert Williams, among others, were attracted to the revolution and emigrated to the island. Surprisingly, it was not long before they denounced the same revolutionary government which they had embraced. They, individually and collectively, spoke out against the persistence of racism in Cuba and were eager to abandon Castro and his revolution.[57] The testimony of Cleaver, Ferrell, and Williams may be suspect, perhaps due to an idealization of the revolution, or to discontent with the treatment they received, or even to their attempt to impose familiar concepts onto the new society; nevertheless, others have exposed racism in Cuba from the inside.

Juan René Betancourt, former secretary-general of the Sociedad "Victoria" in Camagüey and cultural secretary of the Federación Provincial de Sociedades Negras de Camagüey, has accused the revolutionary government of racial discrimination. As a supervising delegate of the Federación de Sociedades Negras de Cuba during the first months of the revolution, he met with opposition from Communist supporters who wanted to prevent a reorganization of blacks. Betancourt points out that since 1959, all of the 256 black societies founded in the republic have been eliminated. With the exception of the Cuban Communist party, Afro-Cuban societies were the best-organized groups on the island and represented a threat to any group seeking power. Within the context of the ideas expressed by Conte and Capmany, government officials have made sure that another Estenoz does not emerge. In effect, by suppressing any black movement emerging from the masses, history not only has stood still but, in some respects, has repeated the past. Betancourt demystifies official pronouncements regarding the elimination of racism in Cuba in the following manner:

> The Communist regime in Cuba has declared over and over again, with typical insistence and boring emphasis, that racial discrimination has been eliminated on the island. Public announcements of the Castro regime would make it appear that racial discrimination is something to be established or eliminated on the basis of a governmental decree. Castro's regime ignores the historical, economic, and social factors which are the genesis of discrimination and which continue to perpetuate it. Nor does the government seem aware of the truth that a government may, by its policies and practices, create an *ambiance* favorable to racial equality. A mere governmental fiat, however, does not meet the problem. Hence Sr. Castro's assertion that his government has eradicated racial discrimination in Cuba is not only false but is bleating demagoguery.[58]

In addition to Betancourt, Walterio Carbonel and Carlos Moore, both black Communists, have become two of the most outspoken critics of the Castro government's policies toward blacks in Cuba.

In his "Le peuple noir a-t-il sa place dans la révolution cubaine?"[59] Moore, like Betancourt and Carbonel, believes that there have been no substantive changes for blacks in the revolution. On the contrary, in a recounting of history from a black perspective, he shows that, as in the past, nothing has really changed. Moore observes that the leaders in present-day Cuba continue to be white. Dismissing the opening of hotels and beaches to blacks as paternalistic and insignificant vis-à-vis real issues, Moore goes to the heart of the problem:

> The Afro-Cuban population has taken up arms and shed its blood— throughout Cuban history—not for the meager crumbs of "access to the beaches," but for something totally different. It was done for the right to govern, to participate in an effective manner in the power which directs the destination of the Cuban nation, a nation constructed on the free work of the black slaves, their ancestors, liberated from the Spanish colonial domination thanks to the blood shed by their grandparents and liberated from North American imperialism, thanks to the *indispensable* and *decisive* participation of its black population.[60]

Moore, who situates himself not within the counter-discourse of the counter-revolutionary forces but within those antagonistic to U.S. imperialism, believes that Cuban officials have refused to recognize any racial problems in the new society. I should note that historically oppressed and disenfranchised groups such as women, workers, students, and writers have been allowed to organize under their respective banners to insure the protection of individual rights; however, no organization has been created for blacks as an oppressed group in today's Cuba.[61] Rather, the ones that did exist, as Betancourt states, have been dismantled.

Moore's argument takes on a broader significance when he suggests that racism today, unlike previous times, is not open but subtle. In this sense, the structures of history, which led to the massacres of blacks in slavery and the republic, have been slightly altered, though blacks continue to be at the margins of Western history. He associates racism with *Weltanschauung,* the Western world's need to assimilate all different and therefore presumably inferior Third World cultures to its own. If Conte and Capmany believed at the beginning of the century that ethnic and racial assimilation as a means of making blacks disappear was not viable, Moore sees it as an acceptable contemporary strategy for whites. Moore elevates the dialectic of Marx's class struggle to a global level, here between the white and nonwhite countries. And in the Marxist regime in Cuba, he perceives the continual emasculation of black culture.[62] Moore considers the new Cuban government a national bourgeoisie which has conveniently turned Marxist to survive against imperialism. As in the past, it is a white minority dictating the lives of a nonwhite majority, pressuring them to assimilate and become "white Latins." (According to Moore, those Afro-Cubans who assert their black history are accused of being "counter-revolutionaries," similar to charges made during the sixteenth century.) Castro's unwillingness to draw distinctions between black and white Cubans, his suggestion that all are Cubans, recall policies from the early part of the twentieth century, in particular the Morúa Amendment, which was used to deny the organization of blacks on the basis of race. As before, the current policies of the revolutionary government do not allow blacks to gather as a political group and obtain political power.[63] The repetitions continue, and the Cuban Revolution does not seem to offer any substantive alternative for the betterment of blacks.[64]

Moore is unyielding in his views of blacks in the revolution. In a recent article, "Congo or Carabalí," from a forthcoming two-volume work on *Cuban Race Politics*, Moore expands and updates his views of actions taken against blacks in Cuba. The present government has attempted to suppress and eliminate black identity and aspects of Cuban culture which he identifies as originating in slavery and continued by Afro-Cubans. He enumerates government actions against Afro-Cubans in the following manner: "Assaults on the Afro-Cuban cults; abolition of the Afro-Cuban mutual aid Sociedades de Color; brutal persecution of the secret male brotherhood, or Sociedad de Abakuá; unofficial offensive against Afro-Cuban language patterns (Afro-Spanish) and black Cuban creole, or Kalo; attempts to discredit the Afro religious outlook as 'primitive,' 'irrational' and 'superstitious'; the banning of the secular, village happenings known as *fiestas de solar*, during which *guaguancó* music is spontaneously derived."[65]

In his latest assertion, Moore even suggests that the race situation is worse than in the prerevolutionary period. He sees Marxism as a white European imported ideology and just another white system of government which proposes a racial democracy without altering white supremacy and black oppression; Cuban blacks are asked to give up their black or African identity in order to integrate themselves into the revolution. Moore looks for support of his accusations in Castro's recent actions to seek reconciliation with Catholics in Cuba and the Vatican but not with Afro-Cuban religions. In his speech before the Third Congress of the Communist party of Cuba, Castro even admitted that blacks are not reflected in the party's leadership, suggesting that, as in the past, they continue to suffer discrimination in present-day Cuba.[66] However, and paradoxically, because of the suppression of black rights and the government's internationalist position with regard to Africa and Caribbean countries, a black awareness is emerging among younger Afro-Cubans which may prove to be problematical for the government's "non-racial" position.

The slavery, postslavery, republic, and contemporary periods which we have been analyzing in both fact and fiction, although appearing to repeat themselves, are part of a structure in history and literature in which slavery is a central issue which has determined the lives of blacks and mulattoes. In the present, as in the past, they continue to demand their rights and liberty.

There is no doubt that the antislavery literature written during the revolution provides a new way of looking at the past, even though Moore's testimony, for example, denies any substantive change in the lives of blacks. But if we were to simultaneously compare the antislavery literature with the dominant white point of view regarding blacks in any given period, fiction as counter-discourse would consistently offer a more aggressive look at history insofar as it represents a significant variation of the dominant discourse. Even though in the antislavery works fact and fiction are interrelated, fiction questions and even undermines facts by providing an alternative understanding of both the past and the present. The course which the Cuban nation follows repeats itself but with no signs of historical redemption, yet it is fiction which rewrites history and provides its salvation by extricating present events from the past. Throughout the different periods in both fact and fiction, fiction and the antislavery narrative have assumed a different position, one which represents the direction in which history should unfold.

In this study, I provide periodization of the slavery and antislavery narrative and divide the book into four historical periods. Chapters 1 and 2 are devoted to the slavery and antislavery narratives written in the slavery period; chapter 3 is devoted to those works written in the postslavery period; chapter 4 to those in the period of the republic; chapter 5 to those in the Cuban revolutionary period; and chapter 6, the conclusion, to a period concurrent with the Cuban Revolution which takes into account a recent novel written and published outside of Cuba. However, I have not resisted the temptation of grouping these works according to specific literary concerns and exploring literary critical concepts that stem from but are not limited to a textual reading of the works themselves. In some ways I am drawn to the diacritical problems of textuality proposed by contemporary criticism while recognizing the shortcomings of this methodology. Thus I also value a textual interplay with history.

My primary interest is to analyze the theme of slavery in Cuban narrative and to show how the historical or contextual referentiality is implicit in these works. In this historical space, textuality attempts to define itself, in many ways challenging and opposing the unfolding of history. In a more general manner, I believe that these works are a representation of a concern in Latin American literature regarding the impact history has on literature and literature's attempt to influence history by creating its own succession of events. Although I attempt to focus my attention on the relationship between history and fiction in Cuban literature, the same analysis can be applied to the workings of Latin American narrative. From this perspective, the book shows the interrelationship between history and fiction either explicit or implicit in Latin American literature.

In this introduction, I have proposed a periodization of the antislavery novel, dividing fiction into historical stages such as the slavery, postslavery, republic, and Cuban revolutionary periods. I then show how these same periods are present in the lives of blacks in Cuban history. I depart from the assumption that each historical moment of transformation will change the outcome of the past, but the history of blacks in Cuba and the antislavery narrative in any given period reveal a different reality. To some degree, there has been no historical relief for blacks but a continuation of what existed before.

In the first chapter, I explore the emergence of the antislavery narrative and how it helped to define a Cuban national culture which unavoidably had to include blacks. The antislavery narrative represents a means of combating the slave trade and broadening the definition of culture and literature in Cuba. I attempt to show how the literature consciously manipulates the reader and forces him to sympathize with and accept the black tragic protagonist. This is done in part by developing a narrative strategy which appeals to the reader and is designed to create a specific reader response. In this chapter, for chronological reasons that pertain to the founding of narrative discourse, I also include an analysis of the narrative of the slave hunter which was written in the same period as the antislavery works and forgotten by many critics. Estévez's diary and Morilla's short story contain two discourses, one dominant, which forces the reader to sympathize with the slave hunter, and one underlying, which questions the first to produce a dialogue on slavery.

In the second chapter, I study the various editions of Juan Francisco Manzano's *Autobiografía*, the only nineteenth-century slave autobiography written in Spanish America, and of Cirilo Villaverde's masterpiece *Cecilia Valdés*. I have decided not to compare Manzano's autobiography with Novás Calvo's biography of Pedro Blanco or Barnet's biography of Esteban Montejo. Such a study would violate our periodization, since the first was written in the slavery period, the second in the republic period, and the third in the Cuban revolutionary period. Instead, I have opted to explore the concept of textuality and the manifestation of the text as represented by the various editions of the autobiography. This also allows me to look at the various editions of Villaverde's *Cecilia Valdés*. In the first part of this chapter, I analyze a tension in Manzano's autobiography, one which entraps the slave between the privileges he receives under one mistress and the punishment under another, or between his privileged position as a slave who could read and write and his status as a common slave, which he refused to be. I also show how the "original" text differs from the other editions, in particular the English one, which Richard Madden translated and published in 1840. Madden, in part, restructured the autobiography to make Manzano's denunciation of slavery stronger. In the second part I compare the three versions of *Cecilia Valdés* to show that the first two, published in 1839, and the definitive one, published in 1882, are not the same and only the last one can be considered an antislavery novel.

In the third chapter, I explore Francisco Calcagno's *Los crímenes de Concha, Romulado, uno de tantos,* and *Aponte* and Martín Morúa Delgado's *Sofía* and *La familia Unzúazu.* "Time in fiction" refers to the relationship between the time of the narration and the time in which the works were written and published. By researching the history of these different periods, I show how these writers imposed a contemporary perspective onto the narrative past.

In the fourth chapter, I study Novás Calvo's *El negrero* and Carpentier's *The Kingdom of This World,* two works which have a detailed historical base. With Novás Calvo's novel, I explore the life of the slave trader Pedro Blanco and other biographies with a similar theme. With Carpentier's novel, I study his use of history and religion. *The Kingdom of This World* covers a broad time span, more than one century, which allows me to read the unfolding of history in the novel. Moreover, Carpentier's description of pre- and post-Haitian society does not offer one but two interpretations of events, both of which are antagonistic to each other, one corresponding to the white world and the other to African religion.

In the fifth chapter, I focus on two works published in the Cuban Revolution: Barnet's *The Autobiography of a Runaway Slave* and Leante's *Los guerrilleros negros.* With Barnet's work, I demonstrate how Montejo's life has not changed throughout the different periods of the narration: slavery, postslavery, and the republic. But here I explore how Montejo's narration is not so much a reconstruction of history, as the text attempts to show, but of memory. In part, what is being commemorated is a present time as defined by the end of the narration, during the founding of the Cuban Republic in 1902, and the time in which the work was written, during the revolution. Moreover, as ethnographer and transcriber of Montejo's speech, Barnet also writes the "autobiography" insofar as he imposes his own understanding of history and fiction onto the narration. With Leante's novel, I show how the revolution's attempt to rewrite history allows him to do the same in fiction. Yet his use of history as narrative discourse suggests that his novel is as veridical as a text of history and that the history texts used to analyze fiction are as fictional as his novel. This leads me to uncover the very fiber which motivates Latin American and Caribbean history and literature, one which is composed of both fact and fiction.

In the final chapter, I analyze Reinaldo Arenas's *Graveyard of the Angels*, a novel written during the Cuban revolutionary period but published outside the island. Arenas's novel suggests both a communion with and a rewriting of Villaverde's *Cecilia Valdés*. Although Arenas's novel shares the same historical moment as Barnet's and Leante's works, it departs from their textual strategies and recalls those employed in the earlier antislavery works; it is critical of the Castro government and its interpretation of history and fiction. For Arenas, Cuban culture is not based on unity but on fragmentation with history and the mother country. *Graveyard of the Angels* represents another stage in the development and continuity of the antislavery narrative in Cuban literature.

# ONE

# The Antislavery Narrative
## Writing and the European Aesthetic

*Que nunca escuchar yo pude*
*sin que hirviera en ira el alma,*
*el bárbaro y atroz chasquido*
*del látigo en carne esclava.*

*Y mas preferí orgulloso*
*pobre vivir, mas sin mancha,*
*que o en opulencia infame*
*a infame precio comprada.*

—DEL MONTE, *Romances cubanos*

Now as I know no atrocity so likely to render men
"feros" as stealing men, or buying stolen men—I
state to you, that I considered—where that monstrous
Incubus the slave trader hung over the morals of any land—
no permanence for prosperity no field for pure religion—
while "undefiled before God" means charity, and, no
extensive influence to be hoped for Literature where it was
not permitted to grapple with a Monster that rears aloft its
many headed iniquity and for all evil is omnipotent.

—RICHARD MADDEN TO DEL MONTE

I   The antislavery narrative developed as part of a movement
to abolish slavery and the slave trade.[1] Domingo del Monte
gave rise to this form of protest by encouraging friends in his
literary circle to write about slavery and the plight of the slave.
These early works describe the abuses of the slavery system and the
unjust and cruel punishment of the slave protagonist. By making
blacks and slaves dominant elements of the emerging Cuban narrative, the antislavery works reflect a historical and literary counter-
discourse which directly challenged the colonial and slavery systems.

Del Monte and the authors of the antislavery narrative were among the first to define Cuban culture, which, by its very nature, developed in opposition to the Spanish colonial discourse. Del Monte, who was born in Venezuela, was interested in promoting a Cuban type of education and culture on the island. With the Spanish writer J. Villarino, Del Monte founded and published the weekly *La Moda o Recreo Semanal del Bello Sexo* (1829 to 1831), a magazine about culture which included articles on fashion, music, and literature.[2] Del Monte gave publicity not only to Lord Byron, Goethe, and other European writers but to young native-born authors. As a member of the prestigious and powerful Sociedad Económica de Amigos del País, Del Monte was in charge of the education section, a position he held from 1830 to 1834. He was also named secretary and, in 1842, president of the Comisión de Literatura of the Sociedad Económica. With editor José Antonio Saco and others, Del Monte helped to make the Sociedad Económica's *Revista Bimestre Cubana* (1831 to 1834) one of the most important publications in the Spanish language. Del Monte was an active participant in the society and joined Cuban-born liberals in developing and defending a national culture.

Saco was the first to write about the emerging national culture. He used Arango y Parreño's distinction between *madre patria,* Spain, and *patria,* Havana, and applied them to the idea of nation, not to a region, like Havana, but to the entire island. Saco, who neither was from Havana nor had ties to the dominant sugar interest, was an exponent not of the *Cuba grande,* of sugar planters, but of the *Cuba pequeña.* According to the program of the *intendente* Alejandro Ramírez, supporters of the latter favored eliminating the slave trade, diversifying agriculture, and importing white workers.[3] Saco defined Cuban nationality in the following manner: "That all people who live in the same land, have the same origin, the same language, the same usage and customs, those people have the same *nationality* . . . To negate Cuban nationality is to negate the sun's rays of the tropics in the afternoon."[4] Saco, in effect, had conceived of a Cuban nationality without independence. Although Saco added that Cuban nationality was only composed of the white race, Eduardo Torres-Cuevas and Arturo Sorhegui suggest that his idea of nationalism differed radically from that of slavers. According to them, Saco believed that there could be no nation with slavery. Saco wanted to eliminate slavery because it was an impediment to forging a Cuban nationality.[5] For Del Monte and antislavery writers, the Cuban nationality also included blacks.

With intellectuals such as Saco and José de la Luz y Caballero, Del

Monte promoted a spirit of "Cubanness" by transforming the Comisión de Literatura into the Academia Cubana de Literatura; literature became a weapon for expressing a national culture and changing society. Fernando VII's death in 1833 provided some optimism for Del Monte and his supporters. They successfully sought approval of the newly governing regent, María Cristina, and succeeded in making the Comisión an independent academy. However, Del Monte's efforts to promote a national culture met with resistance and touched upon existing tensions between sugar planters and liberal Cubans. Slavers and others hostile to Cuban-born nationals considered a Cuban academy to be subversive. Juan Bernardo O'Gavan, director of the Sociedad Económica de Amigos del País, and Claudio Martínez de Pinillos, *intendente* and count of Villanueva, both proslavers, were the most outspoken opponents of the independent character of the newly formed academy. The powerful Sociedad Económica refused to recognize the academy, and Captain General Tacón suppressed it.[6]

In spite of the failure to create an Academia Cubana de Literatura, Del Monte pursued his literary and cultural interests. Del Monte was better known for his famous literary circle, which he began in his hometown of Matanzas in 1834, where young writers gathered and consulted his vast library and knowledge and looked to him for inspiration and guidance. To some extent, Del Monte continued the goals of the defunct academy with his *tertulia*. By 1835, Del Monte had moved his prestigious circle to Havana, where young and progressive authors continued to attend until he left the island in 1843. Del Monte indeed had an impact on the writers who gathered in his home and on their vision of a national literature. Many of the participants reached prominence in Cuban literature, including Cirilo Villaverde, Félix Tanco y Bosmeniel, Anselmo Suárez y Romero, José Zacarías González del Valle, Ramón de Palma, José Jacinto Milanés, Emilio Blanchet, and the ex-slave Juan Francisco Manzano. During their gatherings, Del Monte, a belated neoclassicist, encouraged his writer friends to abandon Romanticism and write a more realistic type of literature, which included portraying the evils of slavery. The group was not only literary and social in nature but political as well. For critic Mario Cabrera Saqui, the *tertulia* was of political importance: "The slavery question and its enormous consequence of injustice and horrendous crime was the preferred conversation in the Del Monte athenaeum. Inculcated in philanthropic and liberal ideas, Domingo del Monte and his select group of friends devoted themselves with enthusiasm to the dangerous task of combating the degrading and wretched secular institution. They advocated the total

reform of customs as a means of obtaining a just social equilibrium."[7] Literature became a way of defining a national culture which
included blacks and changing society.

The years surrounding the founding of Del Monte's literary circle
coincided with a series of events, both in Cuba and Spain, which
help to explain the reasons for the *tertulia*'s existence. These events
pertain, in part, to the tension on the island between the ruthless
Captain General Tacón and liberal *criollo* intellectuals. Ramiro
Guerra suggests that even influential Cuban patricians clashed with
the Tacón government.

The objectives of sugar, coffee, and tobacco growers, cattle owners, and supporters of Spanish sovereignty were even incompatible
with Tacón's dictatorial policies. Tacón set out to destroy these supporters of Spain with the same energy as he did "ambitious youths,"
whom he considered to be enemies of Spain.[8] Nonetheless, Tacón
was an ally of large sugar planters. Del Monte, who was interested in
promoting a Cuban national culture, opposed the Tacón government
and its suppression of liberties on the island. In some respects, the
Del Monte literary circle can be viewed both as a continuation of his
interest in Cuban culture and as a challenge to and a defiance of the
Tacón government, which represented the interests of slavers.

Del Monte's ideas regarding slavery are explained in his "Estado
de la población blanca y de color de la isla de Cuba, en 1839." If Del
Monte looked to France and Great Britain for literary models, he
also sought in their policies political direction. By the time Del
Monte wrote his essay, France and Great Britain had ended slavery in
their Caribbean colonies; for him slavery held back Cuba's progress
into the modern era. Del Monte argued that slavery and slave masters were a thing of the past, characteristics of an uncivilized country. Furthermore, Cuba was violating the law. The slave trade was
illegal and corruption permeated Cuban society. Here and elsewhere
Del Monte accuses the captain general and governors of corruption
and of receiving half an ounce of gold for every slave that entered the
country.[9] Del Monte proposed that Cuba could maintain its agricultural prominence without slaves and claimed that Cuba's success
would be lost if the growing black population rebelled.[10] The uncertainty of Cuba's future was a real concern for Del Monte and writers
who would represent it as the figure of a child.

Del Monte's ideas form part of a counter-discourse on slavery
which dates back to slave rebellions in Cuba, perhaps to the successful miners' rebellion from 1724 to 1800 and certainly to the uprising
in Saint Domingue in 1791.[11] However, his text echos Félix Varela's
"Memorias que demuestran la necesidad de extinguir la esclavitud

de los negros en la Isla de Cuba, atendiendo a los intereses de sus propietarios, por el Presbítero don Félix Varela, Diputado a Cortes." Varela, in his capacity as an elected representative from 1822 to 1823, was the first native-born creole to propose an end to slavery in Cuba.[12] Varela, like Del Monte, Saco, and others who participated in a counter-discourse to slavery, was responding to Arango y Parreño's *Discurso sobre la agricultura de la Habana y medios de fomentarla* (1792), which proposed a plan to expand sugar production in Havana. Arango was the representative of the town council of Havana to the courts and spokesman for the sugarocracy, and he effectively lobbied for agricultural prominence. Three years before, in his *Primer papel sobre el comercio de negros* (1789), he had requested and the courts had granted the free importation of slaves to Cuba, starting a new stage of slavery and the slave trade. The royal decree of February 28, 1789, opened Cuba (but also Puerto Rico and the province of Caracas) for a period of two years to the slave trade. The decree did away with special permissions and contracts and allowed any resident of Spain or the Indies to engage in the free traffic in slaves. Arango was able to further his cause when the rebellion in Saint Domingue erupted. While negotiating the extension of the slave trade, Arango utilized the rebellion as a means of justifying the benefits to agriculture. His *Oficio acompañando copia de la representación sobre la introducción de negros y corroborándola con razones muy sólidas* led to the royal decree of 1791, which stated that in 1792 the free slave trade would be extended for another six years. In reality it would last until 1820.[13]

Speaking to the same audience Arango did, Varela wanted to show a different reality. He addressed the same concern for agriculture but, unlike Arango, concluded that Cuba's agricultural prominence could be ruined by the increasing number of blacks on the island. Varela believed that blacks did not accept their inferiority and resented being treated as incompetent. Moreover, they could rebel and obtain their "liberty and right to be happy." For this, blacks in Cuba could receive help from independent countries, in particular Haiti. A black rebellion would not only ruin agriculture, but Spain could lose the island. Valera believed that he was proposing what people in Cuba wanted; that is, an end to slavery, an idea counterposed to the interest of powerful slavers.[14]

Varela was a professor at the Colegio-Seminario de San Carlos, which, under the direction of Bishop Díaz de Espada, became a center of change from scholasticism to rationalism. Varela supported the Constitution of Cádiz of 1812, which was based on the "natural rights of man" and the "social contract." Its triumph in 1820 pro-

duced in Spain a shift from the slave to the commercial bourgeoisie,
from loyalists of Fernando VII to supporters of liberal ideas. Although the shift was not reproduced to the same degree in Cuba, creole and Spanish intellectuals began to express their dissatisfaction
and found encouragement in the political situation in the peninsula.[15]

Del Monte's ideas are more directly influenced by Saco's "Análisis por don José Antonio Saco de una obra sobre el Brazil, intitulada, *Notices of Brazil in 1828 and 1829, by Rev. R. Walsh, Author
of a Journey from Constantinople, etc."* (1832) and, in particular, his
elaboration in "Mi primera pregunta. La abolición del comercio de
esclavos africanos arruinará o atrasará la agricultura cubana? De-
dícala a los hacendados de la isla de Cuba su compatriota José Antonio Saco" (1837).[16] Del Monte admired Saco's patriotic valor for
proposing that, in a society governed by the slave trade, the increased number of blacks caused a danger to whites. Although Saco's
and Del Monte's ideas were antithetical to the antislavery cause,
they were aware of the discourse of power and chose to challenge it
not by going outside of the rhetoric of slavers but by appropriating
their ideas and showing the fallacy of the sugar discourse. Like
Varela, Saco and Del Monte employed the same strategy used by
those who supported slavery and the slave trade to reveal a different
truth. They were not revolutionaries by today's standards but, in the
period in which they lived, they were at the vanguard of a counter-
discourse on slavery. Any questioning of the hegemonic discourse
was interpreted as a threat to the slaver's power. In effect, Saco and
Del Monte were important agents in breaking the monopoly of a
sugar discourse and attempting to create a dialogue on slavery.

In "Mi primera pregunta," Saco was aware that anyone who opposed the slave trade was considered an abolitionist of Cuban slavery, even though the slave trade was prohibited by law and the "en-
lightenment of the century resisted it." Saco argued two points: (1)
Cuban agriculture could survive without the slave trade and (2) a continued slave trade would endanger the lives of whites on the island.
Saco relied on his broad knowledge of history to demonstrate that
whites are just as capable as blacks of working in labor-intensive
jobs, including sugarcane fields and mills; he also disputed the accepted notion for keeping only slaves on plantations. In place of the
slave, Saco proposed importing free wage laborers, who he believed
would be advantageous for growers. White workers would do away
with inefficient, sick, and runaway slaves and costly uprisings. Saco
supported smaller sugar mills, pointing out that in 1838 there were
many more mills run by smaller groups of slaves. He argued that big
mills did not necessarily produce more sugar and the smaller ones

could diversify their agricultural production. Such propositions addressed the continuing conflict between large sugar planters and small agriculturists.

Saco's text confronts the concerns of the dominant discourse. In what appears to be an attempt to gain support among slavers and drive a wedge between large and small planters,[17] Saco reassures readers that his position is not to emancipate slaves but to end the slave trade. He disarms the central issue that sugar production will decline if the slave trade is eliminated. Saco's impressive research shows that after the slave trade ended in British and French Caribbean islands, sugar production increased with the same slave population, which also had increased.

After appealing to the reason of his readers, in the second part of his essay Saco continued to cite statistics but also incorporated an emotional component. He argued, like Del Monte would, that the increase in slave population in Cuba would put at risk everything whites owned, including their lives and the country. Saco cites rebellions in Saint Domingue and Jamaica, the latter having five major uprisings in the early part of the nineteenth century, the last one in 1832 in which two hundred whites and five hundred blacks died. Winning battles did not reveal the entire picture. Any battle which whites won would still mean the destruction of the island and pointed to a conspiracy among the growing free black population of the British islands which could threaten slave countries, including the southern United States.

Like Del Monte, Saco considered Cuba backward in comparison to most enlightened nations such as France, Great Britain, Denmark, Holland, and the United States, all of which had growing abolitionist movements that sought emancipation of slaves. Saco believed that it was in Spain's interest to preserve Cuba for its favorable trade with the island and for its geographic position, controlling access to other countries in the Americas. However, Cuba's geographic position also made the island vulnerable to foreign power struggles which would find help among the black population.

Saco ends his counter-discourse by appropriating the law into his essay and referring to Spain's treaty with Great Britain to end the slave trade in 1820. The illegal slave trade leaves open the possibility, sooner or later, of some retaliation by the British government. Saco reassures his readers that he is on their side and is defending their interests. Although Saco does not argue for the emancipation of slaves in Cuba, this proposition is clearly implicit in his essay. Importing white workers meant stopping the slave trade. For slavers, ending the slave trade was as threatening as ending slavery. But Saco also supported a black free labor force, thus further suggesting an emancipation of sorts.

By the time Del Monte established his literary circle, Saco was a known enemy of the captain general and slave traders. Arango, who by this time had abandoned his proslavery position, saved Saco from exile for proposing the elimination of the slave traffic when reviewing, in the *Revista Bimestre Cubana,* Walsh's article on Brazil. However, two years later, in 1834, Tacón exiled Saco to Trinidad (in Cuba) and later forced him to leave the island for his defense of the Academia Cubana and his attacks on O'Gavan, published in the pamphlet *Justa defensa de la Academia Cubana de Literatura contra los violentos ataques que se le han dado en el Diario de la Habana desde el 12 hasta el 23 de abril del presente año, escrita por don José Antonio Saco y publicada por un amigo de la Academia.* In reality, Saco was expelled by Spaniards and sugarocrats. O'Gavan and Martínez de Pinillos were instrumental in denouncing Saco. Tacón, who had subsequently dissolved the academy, also closed the important *Revista Bimestre Cubana.*

Saco believed that he was being punished not so much for defending the academy but for attacking the slave trade two years before. In his autobiography he writes: "The article to which I allude, in spite of it having been published with the expressed approval of the first authority of the island, was the fundamental cause of my expatriation in 1834; and if this one was not verified since 1832, it was due to the utmost respect of the distinguished don Francisco Arango who, manifesting my honorable intentions to General Ricafort, who then governed Cuba, undid the plot formed against me by many Cubans and Europeans of great importance."[18] For Del Monte, literature and culture became a more effective means of combating slavery and the slave trade. Saco, Luz y Caballero, Nicolás Manuel Escobedo, and Del Monte were recognized as the most influential figures among young intellectuals.

The year 1835 appears to be pivotal for an overall understanding of politics and literature in Cuba. It was the year in which Del Monte moved his literary circle to Havana, and another confrontation between Tacón and liberal *criollos* took place in the May election of deputies for the Estamento de Procuradores. In spite of Tacón's opposition, and with the support of Gen. Manuel Lorenzo, governor of the province of Oriente, Luz y Caballero, Saco (in absentia), Andrés de Arango, and Juan Montalvo were elected deputies. The election was interpreted as a victory for Saco and Luz y Caballero and a defeat for Tacón. However, political changes in Spain did not allow the new deputies to assume their responsibilities. Istúriz, who took power in

Spain on May 15, dissolved the courts and convoked new elections. At the end of the second election period, Montalvo, Saco, and Arango again triumphed, but they were prevented from carrying out their representation a second time by an uprising of sergeants in August who demanded a reinstatement of the Constitution of 1812.[19]

Reinstating the constitution in Spain had other ramifications in Cuba. In spite of opposition from the Tacón administration, many liberals were encouraged by the creation of a constitutional monarchy. During the Guerra Carlista (1834 to 1838), Lorenzo was a staunch supporter of María Cristina, the young Isabel, and constitutional Spain, and as governor of Oriente he made efforts to implement the constitution on the island. Tacón opposed the constitution and took measures to suppress it. He marched against Lorenzo, forcing him to leave Cuba in December 1836.[20] The victory gave Tacón more strength to continue his oppressive rule over the colony. However, in spite of Tacón's success or because of it, opposition to his government continued.

Del Monte and other liberal Cubans received encouragement to promote their ideas not only from the constitution and Lorenzo's actions but also from British activities in Cuba and Spain. The same year Del Monte transferred his literary circle to Havana, the British on June 28, 1835, strengthened their 1817 treaty with Spain, pressuring the more conciliatory Cristina government to end the slave trade. One year before, in 1834, the British had abolished slavery in their Caribbean possessions. As a result, British commerce became more costly than that of the Spanish colonies. For economic, moral, and religious reasons,[21] British abolitionists pressed for an end to slavery and the slave trade in Cuba and other Spanish colonies. Provisions had been made for ending the slave trade. The 1817 treaty established a Mixed Commission to judge ships and crews caught trafficking in slaves.[22] In return, the British government paid Fernando VII 400,000 pounds sterling to terminate the slave traffic. But the agreement did little to curtail the slave trade.[23] The much stronger 1835 treaty allowed both Spanish and British navies on the open sea to search ships suspected of trafficking in slaves. Unlike the 1817 treaty, that of 1835 did not require the presence of slaves on board but allowed the use of other evidence to find slavers guilty. Slave ships caught in the slave traffic were dismantled and sold in pieces and their slave cargo was set free. In spite of the power and vigilance of the British navy, the profitable slave trade persisted and the most recognized Spanish slaver, Pedro Blanco, continued sending slaves to Cuba until he retired a few years before he died in 1854. The 1835 treaty made provisions for the creation of a mixed Anglo-Spanish tribunal to be established in Havana.[24] The British government also obtained permission to dock one of its ships, the *Rodney*, in Havana Bay. The Spanish authorities viewed the *Rodney* as a threat and its black crew a provocation.

One year after Britain strengthened its treaty with Spain, Richard Madden arrived in Cuba. Madden, an abolitionist and arbiter in Mixed Court, played an important role in supporting Del Monte's antislavery activities and publicizing the antislavery cause in Europe and the Americas. In his *Memoirs*, Thomas More Madden described the reasons for his father's trip to Havana:

> At that time, this magnificently situated city was not only the flourishing capital of the finest of all the Spanish colonies, but was also the chief commercial center of the West Indian slave-trade, the extinction of which was the object of Dr. Madden's mission. Here, for upwards of three years, he continued to devote all the energies of his character to the battle of right against might, in the vindication of the cause of humanity and liberty which it was his privilege to maintain almost single-handed with the Cuban slave traders, then supported by the Spanish authorities. At the time of Dr. Madden's arrival in the Havana [*sic*], the predominant evil influence of the slave-trade was painfully evinced not only in the miserable condition of the oppressed negro race, but also in the demoralization of their masters, and the irreparable evils thereby effected in the social life as well as in the political affairs of that fair, but ill-governed island.[25]

Richard Madden was superintendent of Liberated Africans and judge of the Mixed Court until 1840. He was a known enemy of slavers and a friend of the Del Monte group.

By 1835, the slave Manzano was a visitor of the Del Monte literary circle and celebrated by its members for reading his autobiographical poem "Treinta años." Manzano, while still a slave and with the help of Del Monte, published his *Poesías líricas* in 1821 and *Flores pasageras* [*sic*] in 1830. The dates of these publications suggest that Del Monte's attitude toward slavery and national culture had been formed before founding *La Moda o Recreo Semanal del Bello Sexo* and indeed before he became one of the editors of the *Revista Bimestre Cubana*. In 1835, Del Monte requested that Manzano write his autobiography and, in that same year, collected money to purchase his freedom. Del Monte also commissioned antislavery narratives of Tanco y Bosmeniel and Suárez y Romero.[26] Adriana Lewis Galanes has determined that Del Monte gave Madden for his antislavery portfolio the following items:

1. Manzano's *Apuntes autobiográficos.*
2. Thirteen poems contained in "Poesías de J. F. Manzano, esclavo en la isla de Cuba."
3. Suárez y Romero's *El ingenio o las delicias del campo.*
4. Del Monte's glossary to explain Cuban words contained in *Francisco* under the title "Definición de voces cubanas."
5. Tanco's "El hombre misterioso," which he later entitled "El cura," considered to be the second of three included in his *Escenas de la vida privada en la isla de Cuba.*
6. Pedro José Morilla's "El ranchador." Lewis Galanes considers this short story to be an earlier version of the one Morilla published in *La Piragua* in 1856.
7. "Cartas," written by one or more authors. Lewis Galanes suspects they belong to Suárez y Romero.
8. A group of prose and verse compositions, one of them belonging to José Zacarías González del Valle, and a short narration, "Un niño en la Habana."
9. Interviews entitled "Interrogatorio de Mr. R. R. Madden, Absuelto el 17 de septiembre de 1839, por Domingo del Monte."
10. Interviews entitled "Interrogatorio de 120 preguntas que sobre el estado eclesiástico de la Isla de Cuba me ha hecho Mr. R. Madden, Juez de la Comisión Mixta por Inglaterra. Noviembre 1838, por Domingo del Monte."
11. Rafael Matamorros y Téllez's five long compositions entitled "Elejías cubanas."[27]
Of the antislavery information given to him by Del Monte, Madden translated and published Manzano's autobiography, poems, and interviews with Del Monte, along with two of his own poems, under the title *Poems of a Slave in the Island of Cuba* (1840) in England.

Del Monte was aware of the different discourses of the time. Just as Del Monte employed one type of discourse with slavers in his "Estado de la población blanca y de color de la isla de Cuba, en 1839," he used a different one when discussing slavery with British officials. Del Monte's other position is clear in his interviews with Madden which the judge translated and included in *Poems by a Slave in the Island of Cuba.* Del Monte's answers coincided to some extent with the judge's abolitionist position to document violations in the Cuban slave trade. Whereas Del Monte's and Saco's essays pertained to the survival of agriculture in Cuba without slavery and pointed to the fear of a possible slave uprising, Del Monte's interview, like his essay, implicated Tacón in the slave trade. It also made reference to the enslavement of emancipated blacks and requested British intervention to remove them from the island. Del Monte shaped his discourse to reach another audience. If Saco in his "Mi primera pregunta" proposed that terminating the slave trade would not produce a significant change in Cuban slavery, Del Monte, who used in his essay Saco's statistics, provided a different response when Madden asked the same crucial question: "If the slave-trade were stopped, in how many years would the slave-population be extinct, provided the system of management remained unaltered?" Del Monte answered: "In twenty years, or thereabouts; but the ordinary mortality is calculated at 5 per cent., although it is certain that on the sugar plantations the mortality is much greater; while in the towns, on coffee properties, and other farms, the deaths are much less."[28] Saco too employed a different discourse with abolitionists like Madden. In a letter he wrote to Del Monte regarding a reading of Suárez y Romero's *Francisco*, Madden makes reference to Saco's intentions: "How in God's name could Saco say that slavery was a bland servitude in Cuba!" "Why should a man like Saco say any thing he did not think *for the sake of disarming the hostility of the planters to his enlightened views.*"[29] Madden's correspondence with Del Monte and perhaps with Saco as well points to a certain complicity between the judge and them. For example, upon his departure, Madden wrote to Del Monte: "Whether we meet again or not—we must not cease to be friends—claiming kindred with your tastes—and a relationship though in a very far degree with our talents I look upon myself as one of your literary cousin germains but 'something more than kith though less than kin' with your opinions and principles in all their bearings on 'the iniquity of iniquities' the slave trade."[30] For Madden, Saco, and Del Monte, an end of the slave trade was tantamount to an end of slavery.

   Both Madden and Del Monte agreed that their antislavery cause could be better achieved through literature for its "humanizing" effect. Like Del Monte, Madden had a strong interest in literature and recognized its importance in altering the existing evils of society; namely, slavery and the slave trade. In his capacity as judge, Madden was obligated to respect laws sanctioned by the colonial government but did find refuge in a higher religious order. In a letter to Del Monte dated July 2, 1838, he wrote: "*He that shall steal a Man and sell him being convicted of the guilt shall be put to death.!!!*" In the same letter, Madden looked to literature for expressing his ideas: "And I have only to repeat that I love Literature too well to be indifferent to its success in any country and that its successful cultivation here so much the result of the dedication of your own valuable talents to its pursuit is in my opinion worthy of the highest praise—and to you and those like you—permit me to say in all sincerity Go on and prosper!"[31] In the same letter, Madden conveyed to Del Monte his successful efforts to establish in Jamaica, some years before the end of slavery, a literary institution.

Like Madden, Del Monte believed that literature should reflect reality and, in the interest of promoting "Cubanness," the incipient narrative had to describe life on the island. By depicting aspects of Cuban life, Del Monte in effect was asking his author friends to combine literature and slavery or, in a contemporary language, literature and politics. Del Monte felt that a realistic narration should explore the theme of slavery. In an 1832 study of the historical novel, published in the *Revista Bimestre Cubana*, Del Monte proposed that a successful writer must possess three qualities: he must be a poet, a philosopher, and an antiquarian.[32] For Del Monte, the change in literary focus from romanticism to realism represented a possible means of altering the Cuban slave society; that is, to bring an end to slavery and the slave trade.

II — In 1835 Juan Francisco Manzano, at the request of Del Monte, wrote the first antislavery narrative and one of the first works in Cuban narrative. In his autobiography, Manzano describes vividly his unjust punishment by the cruel marquesa de Prado Ameno. Manzano tells us that on many occasions he was punished for no apparent reason. With some variation, Manzano's life became a model for and a generator of narrative production. In some way, the emerging Cuban narrative was based on slavery; Manzano's life and writings would be repeated by other antislavery writers who would describe many of Manzano's characteristics in their works: a docile house servant; transference from the master's house to the sugar mill, which allows the narrator to describe the evils of slavery; and the unfair punishment of the slave protagonist. Manzano's life was known to members of the literary circle, and in 1839 Suárez y Romero corrected the numerous grammatical mistakes of the autobiography. I believe that Suárez y Romero's copy was the one Madden translated and published in England in 1840. Manzano's text influenced Suárez y Romero's novel and certainly the creation of his protagonist, Francisco, named after the slave he knew so well. It is also possible that Manzano was an inspiration for Tanco when he wrote his "Historia de Francisco" even though it pertains to a twelve-year-old slave taken from the barracoons located in front of the *alameda*.[33] My intention is to explore the text, the context, and the intertextual connection of the first antislavery works which emerged from the Del Monte circle.[34] I will also make reference to Zambrana's *El negro Francisco*, since this novel is indebted to Suárez y Romero's work

and contains important literary and historical variants. I contend
that the antislavery theme of the early work was written in a crucial
moment in which writers attempted to introduce a new image into a
language already codified by European values. These works represent a first effort at broadening literary discourse in Spanish American literature.

Even though Manzano's autobiography determined the direction
in which the antislavery narrative would unfold, there were other
writers and works important to Del Monte and his friends. In spite
of Del Monte's insistence on a realistic tradition, the antislavery
narrative also incorporated a romantic vision which Pablo Veglia, an
Italian writer and counsel, had introduced in Cuba.[35] There were
other romantic writers known to Del Monte and members of his salon; Victor Hugo's *Bug-Jargal* (1826), a novel which describes slavery and uprisings on the nearby island of Saint Domingue, was of
particular importance to them. Hugo, who himself was influenced
by Chateaubriand and Walter Scott, not only reflected in his works
the local conditions in the ex–French colony but also reacted to a
spirit which fueled the French, American, and even Haitian revolutions, the same spirit which supported independence and roman-
ticized those living at the margins of society. The French ideals and
*Bug-Jargal* were known to Del Monte and members of his group. In a
letter dated February 13, 1836, Tanco tells Del Monte of having received Hugo's eight-volume collection printed in Brussels which included *Bug-Jargal*. Tanco makes reference to Hugo's novel, suggesting that a similar project be undertaken in Cuba:

> And what shall you say about *Bug-Jargal?* I would want that among
> us a novel be written in the same style as that one. Think about it.
> Blacks on the Island of Cuba are our Poetry and we do not have to
> think about anything else; not only blacks, but the blacks with the
> whites, all mixed, and then develop the descriptions, scenes, which
> by necessity ought to be infernal and diabolical; but truthful and evi-
> dent. Let our Victor Hugo be born and let us learn once and for all what
> we are, described with the truth of Poetry, since we know by the num-
> bers and the philosophical analysis the sad misery in which we live.[36]

Creole writers did not have to look outside of the island for the
themes Hugo sought on Saint Domingue. The slave conditions on
the nearby island were, in varying degrees, present in Cuba. For the
most part, antislavery narrative is a phenomenon which developed
in Cuba without external literary models, though Hugo's novel
should be considered an inspiration. Tanco and other writers sup-

ported Hugo's project, but no one dared to write about the actions of a rebel slave. Instead, writers extracted a working model for narrative discourse from Cuban colonial and slave society, based on the suffering of slaves on the island. Nevertheless, the antislavery narrative does incorporate a progressive spirit which the French and Haitian revolutions represented. Creole intellectuals like Del Monte looked toward France and Great Britain as examples of civilized societies. In two letters dated April and May 1836, González del Valle, Suárez y Romero's copy editor, addresses the importance the author of *Francisco* gives to Rousseau and his *Social Contract*, although not without certain criticism.[37]

Rousseau's ideas and the primacy of the French Revolution were widespread. As we have mentioned, they were incorporated into the liberal Constitution of 1812. The ideas also had a special impact in resolving the copper miners' rebellion of Santiago del Prado in 1800. After the mines were closed in 1670, the Spanish crown gave land to the slaves to work for their freedom. Their descendants were enslaved one century later when the land was reclaimed by heirs of Juan de Eguiluz and Francisco Salazar. Simón de Echenique's defense of the copper miners in March 1793 was based on Rousseau's *Social Contract* and the *Declaration of the Rights of Man and the Citizen*.[38] Freedom and liberty as natural rights of man are also embodied in the antislavery narrative and, in particular, in Suárez y Romero's black protagonist. Francisco's natural rights have been denied him. After all, slavery is against natural law.

The romantic theme Suárez y Romero developed between the slaves Francisco and Dorotea may not have been totally original and appears to follow a similar one Juan Padrines, a Spanish writer residing in Matanzas, selected for his story two years before the writing of *Francisco*. Encouraged to finish his composition by Tanco in a letter dated July 23, 1836, Padrines had already proposed his subject matter to Del Monte:

> The argument of my work is as follows: Tubero, lover of Cora, tries to ask his master, owner of a coffee plantation, for her hand in marriage. Under the title *Exposition*, I describe the plantation and inform the reader of the love of my two lovers: Tubero finally asks his lover for her hand in marriage, written in some *décimas* which I entitle *Supplication*. They get married at the church of Pueblo-Nuevo, and here you have *The Engagement*. The slaves of the plantation celebrate the wedding with *A Tango*. Some of the youth of the nearby hacienda go to it and will be preceded by an old black which they call *zajoria* or *zahorí* who prognosticates the future and takes pride in uncovering

the most hidden secrets of the heart. Immediately following, under
the epigraph of *The Overseer*, I am thinking of describing this unique
man of our countryside with his long sideburns, his whip and his dogs,
finding pleasure in punishing the miserable Africans whom he scares
with only a stare. I will outline equally his corruption, his ignorance,
and his malice, opposed to simple innocence, which appears to belong
to the honorable patrimony of the country people. This overseer will
fall in love with Cora, already the wife of Tubero; and one stormy
night when the hurricane roars, when it downpours, when destruc-
tive lightning splits and fells the proud crest of the palm trees to the
brightness of a thousand lightnings, then he assaults Cora's hut and
tries to satisfy his brutal needs. But she resists and protects *The Fidelity* owed to her dear Tubero. In despair, the overseer invents a crime,
and the following day the unfortunate slave presents the horrible
scene of *The Punishment:* naked, stretched out, and tied to four rings,
she will receive a whipping. The overseer will force her husband to be
the executioner of the sentence. This unfortunate soul will be obligated to punish the fidelity of his wife. He will want to cry, he will
want to free himself from the barbarous order, but the whip of the
overseer will threaten him, and if he is weak, if he does not unleash
the strikes with vigor, if his tears dare to appear in his eyes . . . I pity
him! There is nothing he can do: he has to resign himself and in
whipping his object of affection, he has to hear her painful moans
and he has to show indifference, insensibility, when his heart lies
destroyed by the rage and the pain: his strength fails him; his numbed
arm does not let itself unleash more strikes, nor does the African
woman yell . . . what has happened? A dirty trick, the overseer would
say and will ask for a flaming half-burnt stick to apply it for the purpose of making her yell. But at the moment of doing it, of touching
her . . . O God! She is cold, she does not exist . . . Her husband, her
unfortunate husband Tubero, will withdraw desperately and resolves
to hang himself. *The Song of Slave* will be intoned by Tubero before
he dies, in the dense woodland. In it he will remember his work, his
grief, his misfortune. He will cry the miseries and horrors of slavery
and the tragic end of his unfortunate lover. But he finally regains his
composure, consoles himself, his eyes sparkle with a ray similar to
the sudden glow of a dying lamp . . . he is going to commit suicide
and the suicide will return him to his country! There, in the desert,
free of oppressors, without fright, without worry he will again hold
in his arms his beloved wife at the banks of the river which will
bathe her at birth and under the rustic ceiling which re-echoes her
first cry of life. Who knows if they will even find there their parents!
This song will prepare the *Suicide* which was the finishing touch of

my work. Of course, you would have understood that each one of these titles which I underline will be the object of a separate composition and in a different versification.[39]

With the letter, Padrines sent Del Monte a copy of the composition which he considered to be inspirations without any rhyme scheme. The theme of the frustrated romance between Tubero, Cora, and the white overseer, Tubero's and Cora's suffering, and Tubero's suicide by hanging is the same one repeated in *Francisco*. Tubero, Cora, and the old slave in Padrines's composition are Francisco, Dorotea, and taita Pedro in Suárez y Romero's novel. Like that of Padrines, Suárez y Romero's intricate narrative creates a tension by allowing an unjust and cruel situation to exist and, in some ways, to triumph. However, this apparent triumph on the part of the overseer is undermined by the reader's reaction. The nonrebellious black protagonist elicits sympathy and the white overseer hatred.

Padrines counterbalances the death of the slaves by ending his composition with Tubero's awakening and communion with the past. Before committing suicide, Tubero understands how slavery had oppressed him, a strategy which allows both poet and narrator to summarize the tragedy and reaffirm what had been described throughout the work. Yet, just as the slave dies and wakes up to a meaningful reality, so too will the reader die metaphorically and experience a metamorphosis of sorts which will allow him to question slavery and the slave trade.

There are some differences between Padrines's and Suárez y Romero's works. Unlike Padrines, who was interested in poetry and described a coffee plantation, Suárez y Romero wrote a novel and his story develops in a sugar mill, where slavery was even more oppressive. Padrines's master is benevolent and allows the slaves to marry, while Suárez y Romero's narration is more daring and attributes the ruthless qualities to the *mayoral* and, most importantly, to the master himself (that is, Mendizábal's son Ricardo). But in Padrines's composition, the overseer's character is further destroyed when he violates the sanctity of the slaves' marriage and forces Tubero to whip Cora to death.

Padrines incorporates African ideas and religion into the composition. In his *El cántico del esclavo*, death, even though tragic, is associated not with the Christian concept of burial and resurrection but with the African belief that after death slaves return to their native home. The return is equated with origin, peace, and harmony during a time before the arrival of the Europeans and the start of the slave trade. In a similar manner, before taking his life, Francisco recalls his African past. After his suicide, he is taken down from the tree by four slaves who sing African songs.

Perhaps the most important contribution of Padrines's story, which is also repeated in Suárez y Romero's, is the presence of the black slave protagonist, perhaps a Manzano type. Villaverde's and Gómez de Avellaneda's protagonists were mulattoes, but Padrines's Tubero and Suárez y Romero's and Zambrana's Franciscos were black slaves attracted not to whites but to their own blackness. The presence of blacks cannot be emphasized enough. In Tanco's reading of *Francisco*, he praises Suárez y Romero for including blacks in his narration. He states: "Let us abandon the ridiculous habit or error of painting a chosen society: society, white alone, isolated, because *blacks discolor* and dirty that society. It is essential to see it with the grime left by their touch; that is, it is necessary, indispensable to see the blacks." [40] As we shall later see, the presence of blacks is an important detail included to create a reader response to the slave's suffering.

There are other factors that help to explain the type of character Suárez y Romero chose for his novel. Like Manzano, Suárez y Romero's and Zambrana's protagonists were intentionally house slaves. In comparison to the field slave, the house or domestic slave was better treated. House and rural slaves were known to the distinguished members of the Del Monte group. The contrast in the reader's mind between the two would force him to realize that the protagonist, a house slave, was not any better off than a rural one and was subjected to the same intensive labor and punishment as his counterpart.

The domestic slave in general and the calèche driver in particular were common figures in Havana of the early and mid nineteenth century and were appropriated as the objects of literary discourse. The calèche driver became the central theme of *Francisco* and *El negro Francisco* and was also present in the works of Manzano, Villaverde, and Martín Morúa Delgado. Even Sab worked as a coach driver for a few years. Like the other writers, José E. Triay expressed interest in the calèche driver and provided a valuable picture of this historical figure. In his "El calesero," Triay considers the calèche and the slave coach driver to be typically Cuban, thus continuing to document aspects of Cuban life. Triay begins his portrait by describing the *quitrín*, or the *volante*, a two-wheeled open carriage, believing that it originated in Cuba. He then proceeds to describe a *calesero*; that is, a Francisco type. According to him, this kind of slave was known to everyone and was considered to be a hard-working and privileged slave. He offers a stereotypical description of a *calesero* as someone black by the name of José, born in the master's house of unknown origins. The *calesero* was well dressed and his formal attire included calfskin shoes, metal or gold buckles, tall boots with silver decorations, and spurs with large stars. He wore a jacket with stripes, a shirt of cretonne thread with three gold buttons, a black ribbon for a tie, white drill pants fastened at the waist by a big silver buckle, and a top hat. Triay also tells us that the calèche driver had many privileges. When he got older, he was retired and looked after. And because of his looks, he was envied by common servants, admired by others, and became the object of desire of female servants.[41]

Suárez y Romero describes his *calesero* with characteristics similar to Triay's protagonist. But unlike Triay's José, who merits a book about his love affairs, Suárez y Romero's Francisco is a tragic figure:

> A black—by now my mom should have opened up her eyes—, a black she took out of the barracoons as a child, raised him like a son, and grew up to be a man by her side; he never received a whipping nor a scolding, and if not, let him show his body, let him confess it himself; a black who has dressed like a prince, good trousers, a good shirt, good shoes; he always had something to spend, because once in a while he was given a peseta, four reales, or a peso. And for what type of work, don Antonio? Cleaning the *quitrín* and the harness, taking care of the horse, preparing the carriage once in a great while, from Corpus to San Blando.[42]

There are similarities and differences between Triay's stereotype and Suárez y Romero's character. For example, Suárez y Romero's *calesero* was named not José but Francisco. Both Triay's and Suárez y Romero's narrations suggest that José and Francisco are good looking don Juan types. In this regard, Suárez y Romero's novel narrates the aftermath of the love relationship between Francisco and Dorotea and the mistress's objection to their coming together. However, we do not have any indication that Francisco had more than one lover, perhaps purposely breaking with this common stereotype and the negative connotations that were attached to it. Nevertheless, Francisco was sent to the sugar plantation and punished for impregnating Mrs. Mendizábal's favorite slave. Within the context of Triay's description, Suárez y Romero's narration confirms that the calèche driver was a well-known character and a familiar sight in the Havana of the Del Monte literary circle. Furthermore, it was widely known that the calèche driver was the most privileged male slave and had more to lose than any other slave. Toward the end of his description, Triay tells us that as the calèche driver got older and saved some money, he would ask for the *papel*, a license which would enable him to work for others, earn enough money, and eventually buy his own freedom. As the novel unfolds, Suárez y Romero's readers are exposed to the sufferings of a privileged slave, a common figure in early nineteenth-century slave society.

Most importantly, Francisco is a black slave. The desire to be white that Richard Jackson attributes to Sab and Cecilia Valdés is not present in *Francisco* and *El negro Francisco*.[43] On the contrary, they identify with their own black race. Unlike the protagonists of *Sab* and *Cecilia Valdés*, the female character in *Francisco* is attracted not to someone white, as research into the historical period would suggest, but to someone of darker skin. The same observation is evident in Zambrana's Camila, a mulatto who, like Cecilia Valdés, had embraced white culture but, unlike her, realizes that she can no longer delude herself and accepts her blackness. She chooses not to escape her own condition and identifies not with the master but with the slave; that is, with Francisco's culture and race. Contrary to Cecilia Valdés, both Zambrana's Camila and Suárez y Romero's Dorotea reject their white suitors and the privileges extended them in favor of their black lovers who are slaves. Suárez y Romero has challenged the values of Western society; money, racial betterment, and even freedom from slavery are not as important as love and black identity. In nineteenth-century society, it was acceptable for the master to have sexual relations with his slave. In Suárez y Romero's and Zambrana's novels, the sexual image is taken one step further and inverted: the master falls in love with his slave, thus ironically becoming a slave to his own slave. Suárez y Romero's Ricardo wants to transform himself into a black to appeal to Dorotea. He even promises her freedom, a furnished apartment, and slaves if she agrees to become his mistress. Zambrana's Carlos chooses Camila over Rosalía, a white and rich but ugly woman. Beauty, in this case, is not defined by whiteness.

By altering or inverting the values of nineteenth-century Western slave society, the powerful master is rendered powerless; regardless of his race or economic position, neither Ricardo nor Carlos is able to force the female slave to fall in love with him. In *Francisco*, the confrontation between the slave and the slavery system is intensified not by narrating a presumably realistic situation but by describing situations which are diametrically opposed, allowing the slavery drama and the reader's response to be heightened. If supporters of slavery accept white as good and black as bad, for Suárez y Romero black and white do not have a natural referent and are arbitrary terminologies. For him, the dark Francisco and Dorotea are good and both Ricardo and don Antonio, the overseer, are ruthless without end. By questioning certain beliefs of the slavery system, Suárez y Romero raises moral, ethical, legal, and religious issues with which the reader must come to terms. For example, as the plot unfolds, Mendizábal's objection to Dorotea's and Francisco's love and marriage forces the slaves to hide their relationship from her. However, the slaves experience a contradiction which they and the reader must resolve. Love, in this context, has serious ramifications for the master and slave relationship. The narration juxtaposes the slaves' loyalty to their master and the slaves' love for each other. Lying to the mistress is justified and equated with the slaves' desire to be true to their own feelings. The slaves' love, as an expression of their natural right, is a threat to the master and subversive to his power. Although the reader understands that the slave must obey his master, he is forced to look beyond slavery and identify with the protagonists' frustrated love relationship, a condition the reader may have also experienced.

The interaction between the master and slaves is based on racial and economic power but also responds to a structure of desire which transcends and complements both the slaves' and master's will to power. When reading René Girard's "Triangular Desire" with *Francisco* and *El negro Francisco* and other antislavery novels, we uncover other reasons which motivate the master and slave relationship. The "triangular desire" develops between Dorotea, Francisco, and Ricardo or Camila, Francisco, and Carlos. From the point of view of the master, in which Francisco is the mediator and Dorotea is the object, the slaves' attraction for each other arouses the master's desire to possess the female slave. Francisco is severely punished because he impregnates Dorotea and is an obstacle to Carlos's love for the slave. The closer Francisco gets to his companion, the more hatred Ricardo feels for him. The intense hatred is complemented by an increased desire on the part of the master for the female slave. Carlos and Ricardo control and punish Francisco as a means of acquiring and controlling the object of desire. Ironically, the master's desire to possess the female slave forces him to identify with Francisco insofar as he wants to become the mediator; that is, a slave. The closer Dorotea and Francisco are, the more the master wants Dorotea and the more he wishes to be Francisco.

As in the antislavery narrative, in a triangular relationship the signs are inverted and the mediator and subject change positions. In this analysis, the slave is privileged and the master is the victim. Girard states the following:

The subject would like to think of himself as the victim of an atrocious injustice but in his anguish he wonders whether perhaps he does not deserve his apparent condemnation. Rivalry therefore only aggravates mediation; it increases the mediator's prestige and strengthens the bond which links the object to this mediator by forcing him to affirm openly his right or desire of possession. Thus the subject is less capable than ever of giving up the inaccessible object: it is on this object and it alone that the mediator confers his prestige, by possessing or wanting to possess it.[44]

Within the context of slavery, the master realizes he lacks the power to force the slave to be his, causing him to be even more ruthless to gain control of his object. The symbiotic relationship between the master and the mediator can be taken one step further. The pain the master inflicts on Francisco is a reflection of the suffering the master feels for the female slave. Only after he is able to alleviate his own psychological, physical, and emotional pain is the master willing to end Francisco's punishment. The pain between one character and another also suggests that the master wants to and in effect does substitute Francisco; that is, the master transforms himself into a "slave." Like Francisco, Ricardo possesses Dorotea.

Dorotea also reacts to the shift in position between Francisco and Ricardo. Once the distance between Ricardo and Dorotea is closed, she refuses her old lover as she once did her master. Claiming that she is no longer worthy of his love, Dorotea rejects Francisco and tells him to forget her.

Francisco also changes position. Excluded from his relationship with Dorotea, Francisco ceases to be a victim and assumes the position of the subject; that is, the master. The helpless slave imitates the master and like him suffers in his desire for the slave. But in shifting positions with the master, Francisco also acquires his power. As the subject and the "master," Francisco is no longer passive and obedient. He is transformed into an active character. Francisco uses his power to punish his lover, his master, and himself. He is decisive and commits suicide. By committing suicide, Francisco punishes Dorotea, who is stricken with grief and dies within a few years. Equally important, Francisco punishes his master. Francisco's suicide dissolves the triangle and Ricardo lacks a means to oppress the female slave and loses interest in her.

In both *Francisco* and *El negro Francisco*, the slave masters follow the same pattern: They want to please their female slaves in exchange for their love. The female slaves show more strength and pride than the white masters and remain loyal to their black companions. They give in to their masters only after they discover that the oppressive slavery system has been used, in its most extreme form, against their lovers. The weakness of both slave owners, as male and white, is shown in the very power they possess to avenge themselves against the female slaves. In spite of their race and power, neither Carlos nor Ricardo is able to achieve the pure love relationships attributed only to the slaves.

The passage of time between the writing of *Francisco* and *El negro Francisco* allowed Zambrana to use themes and characters present in the first work but also to take their resolution one step further. In *El negro Francisco* there is a political development toward greater militancy, as the adjective *negro* in the title suggests. Zambrana's Francisco, for example, twice contemplates killing his master, even though this would be a crime of passion, not of rebellion. Such an act is more definitive than Sab's desire to kill whites to possess Carlota. Not surprisingly, Francisco does not carry out his plan because this would have meant an end to his and Camila's sacred love. In a manner common to the novels of the nineteenth century, Camila explained her sentiments to Francisco in a letter she never sent him. The letter serves as an intertextual connection between Zambrana's and Suárez y Romero's novels. In a letter dated November 17, 1838, González del Valle, Suárez y Romero's editor, advises his friend to omit from his manuscript an unrealistic letter between Francisco and Dorotea. Those who were present at the private reading agreed.[45] The letter deleted from Suárez y Romero's manuscript appears in chapter 12 of *El negro Francisco*. Including Suárez y Romero's letter gives Zambrana's novel a sense of authenticity in regard to the earlier text at the expense of offsetting his own narrative construction since Francisco was illiterate and could not have read the letter. However, the reader is told that even though Francisco never saw the letter, he understood Camila's character and, before committing suicide, forgave her for giving in to the master.

In Zambrana's novel there is also a politicization on the part of the master. Ricardo, a spoiled child, resigns himself to Dorotea's rejection. After Francisco's death, he lacks the means to force her will. Unlike Suárez y Romero's novel, Zambrana's rewriting takes a stronger stand against slavery. Carlos experiences a conversion. The death of both Camila and Francisco moves him to fight for the abolition of slavery. Carlos conveys this information to Enrique Delmonte, whose surname recalls that of Domingo del Monte. A converted abolitionist, Carlos feels that the liberation of black slaves should take precedence over the struggle against Spain's hegemony. Carlos has chosen to devote his life to the emancipation of slaves. In this sense, the name Carlos recalls the famous Carlos Manuel de Céspedes, who in 1868 freed his own slaves, an act associated with the start of the Ten Years' War against Spain. Zambrana himself was a member of the rebel group.

Antislavery sentiments are also present in Tanco's *Escenas de la vida privada en la isla de Cuba*, in which only "Petrona y Rosalía" and "Un niño en la Habana" have been found. We suspect that the latter story, discovered recently by Adriana Lewis Galanes, is part of Tanco's collection of short stories.[46] Like Suárez y Romero, Tanco was a member of the Del Monte group and later suffered imprisonment for his alleged participation in the Ladder Conspiracy of 1844. His stories were written in the same antislavery spirit as *Francisco* but also *El negro Francisco*. In fact, Fernández de Castro believed Tanco described the slavery issue better than Villaverde or Suárez y Romero. In his *Tema negro*, Fernández de Castro cites a letter which leaves no doubt about Tanco's antislavery sentiment:

> What hopes Mr. d. Domingo that our land will be better with statute, nor with new town halls, nor with civil governors, nor with provincial deputations, nor with assemblies, nor with foolishness and more foolishness while they are packing us in all over with blacks? What sinful civilization, nor what progress will there be among us if this is a barbarous place, the most abominable region on earth? God would allow for these dumb blacks to be all transformed into tigers, bears, serpents, and into every carnivorous and fattened animal and would not leave alive anyone of the cursed Caucasian race who lives on the island. I am writing with such anger that I do not know what I am writing.[47]

Tanco's letter, like the positions held by Del Monte and Saco, alludes to a fear that a black rebellion would be to the detriment of whites. However, the rebellion is providential and associated with the corrupt legal and moral system of the present-day society. In a letter dated August 20, 1838, Tanco attacked Ramón de Palma and his novel *Una pascua en San Marcos* for criticizing Cuban society without including descriptions about the corrupt slavery system, often avoiding the usage of words associated with blacks and slavery. Although Palma's novel was criticized by conservative elements and Del Monte went to his defense claiming, among other things, that the author was describing customs, Tanco nevertheless found objections to Palma's novel because he did not go far enough and avoided the slavery issue.[48] Tanco's antislavery stand contained in his letters are present in his short stories.

Tanco's "Un niño en la Habana" is concerned with the decadence of Cuban society, for which slavery is responsible. The story, which evinces a strong moral conviction, is divided into two narrations. The first contains the narrator's monologue and the second a dialogue between the narrator and a child, supporting the impression conveyed by the monologue. The child is a recurring theme in many of the antislavery narratives and a symbol of the country's future. The story is obsessed with slavery and the treatment of slaves in Cuba. The boy, who represents innocence, the young Cuba, internalizes the beliefs of the dominant discourse, his father, who is a member of the sugarocracy: Blacks should be whipped because they are bad and lazy. In effect, slaves are not human but animals. The narrator, as a symbol of knowledge and authority, challenges the boy's acquired belief. When speaking to him, the narrator makes a correlation between the sugar mill and hell; in the former, slaves are punished, and in the latter, the boy will be punished. The message is clear: The black hell is on earth and the white hell is after death, in eternity. It is unusual that the narrator is a woman; she is the first woman narrator in Cuban literature. One is tempted here to read that a woman narrator's antislavery stand may not be taken as seriously as a man's and what she says will be less offensive to the reader. But in relation to the boy, she as a woman and perhaps as a mother, a symbol of the nation, the mother country, does not have control over his actions, the future. Therefore, her criticism is a desire to correct the boy, Cuba's future, before the society is put at risk beyond repair. The story, moreover, takes exception to parents, who do not assume responsibility for educating their children and conspire with the slave society. Slavery is not only an economic problem; it is also a moral and familial one that can and must be changed.

Tanco develops his ideas on women or motherhood further in "Petrona y Rosalía," a story about mothers.[49] Tanco situates this story in the sugar mill and foreshadows the brutal punishment Francisco received. In a way which recalls Ricardo's and Carlos's actions, the masters, Antonio and Fernando, show their power by raping and impregnating their slaves Petrona and Rosalía (mother and daughter), respectively. Unlike the other antislavery novels, the love relationship is less romantic and the narration exposes more directly the oppressive slavery system. Petrona's mistress, as in Suárez y Romero's novel, discovers her slave's pregnancy. This time not the culprit, as in Suárez y Romero's novel, but the female house slave is sent to the sugar mill, where she, like Francisco, is severely beaten. Tanco, who was familiar with Padrines's composition, may have deemed it strategically useful to include the punishment of the fe-

male slave over that of her male counterpart. Petrona's daughter
Rosalía meets a similar fate. But Tanco's description of the slave society goes beyond exposing the brutality of the master-slave relationship and, like his "Un niño en la Habana," includes a commentary about whites who support and profit from slavery. The reader is
thus confronted with problems which many nineteenth-century
writers or readers may have attributed solely to slaves. More em-
phatically than the other antislavery writers, Tanco points the finger
at the masters and shows white society to be ruled by lies and deception. Whereas the other writers protect the sanctity of white women,
Tanco reveals that just as the male slave owner takes sexual advantage of his slaves, the mistress also participates in deception. (From
this perspective, Tanco's short story may contain the first feminist
protagonist in Cuban literature.) Petrona's mistress, for example,
allows her son to rape the slave because of her own guilt regarding
her son's true father, not Antonio but the marqués de Casanueva.[50]
Similarly, Antonio does not interfere in Consuelo's treatment of the
slave because of his secretive relationship with Petrona. The deaths
of Petrona and Rosalía (who dies while giving birth) represent a hermetic structure which has condemned the slaves.

The child image of "Un niño en la Habana" is repeated in the
death of Rosalía's child, who symbolically offers no possibility of
change in the lives of blacks within the morally decaying colonial
system. If in the previous story the future of the island was represented by a white child, in this story it is more accurately portrayed
by an offspring of the white and black races. Under these conditions,
Cuba's future, that is, the future of black slaves but also of whites, is
hopeless. The child could only live within a changing society. Suárez
y Romero's novel conveys a similar concern. After Francisco's and
Dorotea's death, Lutgarda's future is uncertain. Tanco's story suggests that the suffering of blacks is generational and it is better for
the child to die than to live under slave conditions. Zambrana's story
provides a different solution to the same problem. Unlike Dorotea,
Camila abstains from having sexual relations with Francisco. Her
intention is political and represents her own personal challenge
to slavery: she refuses to become pregnant because she does not
want to perpetuate slavery. Although she made a personal decision,
Camila's actions will have political and economic ramifications for
slavery. If the future generations of slaves die or are not born, she
alleviates her suffering by contributing to the collapse of the slavery
system.

As counter-discourse, the antislavery works force the reader to
side with the protagonist. *Francisco* and *El negro Francisco*, specifi-

cally, portray impossible love. Invariably, the reader is forced to sympathize and even identify with and hail the black slaves. The reader is then subjected to reading not only about the cruelty of the slavery system but the application of that system to its tragic protagonists. These characters are shown as passive and more ethical than their white counterparts. Thus they are nonthreatening and acceptable to white readers. The psychological impact of the novels on the reader could not have been more effective. In a letter to Suárez y Romero dated September 25, 1838, González del Valle provides a nineteenth-century reading of *Francisco.* He indicates to his friend that even though he had never visited a sugar mill he was disenchanted with what he considered an inconceivable situation.[51] Similarly, Luz y Caballero cried profusely after reading certain passages of Suárez y Romero's novel.[52] The emotional reaction was not limited to a few and included foreigners. In a letter to Del Monte, Madden reveals his reading of some chapters he received.

> I read the little piece thro last night The "Ingenio o las Delicias del campo"—Byron said "Truth was stranger than fiction" I understand the saying now. Tho there is literary merit of but small amount in this piece, there is life and truth in every line of it. . . . In this little piece of the Ingenio there is a minuteness of description and closeness of observation and a rightness of feeling that I have not often seen surpassed. Ah my good friend what intelligence what talents and what virtues are not doomed here "to waste their sweetness on the desert air."[53]

When Suárez y Romero wrote his novel, he certainly had the reader in mind and was conscious of how his reader would react to the slave's docility. In a letter to Del Monte dated April 11, 1839, Suárez y Romero made his intentions clear:

> In effect, I was trying to describe a black slave, and who mourning under the terrible and annoying yoke of servitude could be so gentle, so peaceful, of so angelic and holy customs like him . . . ? Francisco is a phenomenon, a unique exception, not the man tied to the sad consequences of slavery, not the good book where the whites, seeing their error, can learn to be humans. The truth is that I tried to describe the overseers, stewards, etc. like they are; but I have demonstrated that if the blacks are bad, is it because the masters are also bad? Not so— Afflicted, I, Mr. Del Monte, by the miseries of the slaves more than you can imagine, I was determined to write a novel where I could relieve my heart's sentiments, where I would demonstrate that if there were whites, staunch enemies of the Ethiopian race, there are others

who will cry blood tears for their calamities: a friend for all times, I
want that in my surroundings I will never hear a sob, or a sigh of pain,
that everyone's life slip so serene and calm like the moon travels across
the Sky courted by shining stars: I would want reciprocal love, charity,
peace, laughter, Sir, and not bitter cries. So it was, from the moment I
started to write, I started to sadden: I became angrier and angrier against
whites as I described their lost ways; and since my character, let us
say it once and for all, tolerates with patience the misfortunes of this
poor Valley of tears, I attributed to Francisco that Christian resignation and meekness, flowers that do not sprout, but like the miracle,
among the dirty mire, where slavery places men. In my sadness I said—
whites, sir, you are tyrants with blacks, be ashamed to see here one of
those unfortunate men, a better man than you. Here is the reason for
my error. But will this forgive me? No—The novelist should imitate
nature, what takes place in the world; not to let him drift to imaginary
regions. In order for it to fly, talent needs equilibrium and not feathers,
which is something we all know about. It is a golden principle which
we should always keep in mind—Let us change the subject.[54]

Suárez y Romero attributed his own characteristics to the slaves
and, therefore, identified with their sufferings, condemning white
slave owners for their actions. In essence, for him the black was
more noble than the white.

González de Valle's reaction to "Petrona y Rosalía" is similar to
those who read *Francisco*. González del Valle recognizes the story's
veracity and considers slavery a cancer. He concludes his reading in
the following manner: "If the author of *Petrona y Rosalía* sins for
any reason, it is because he is too loyal to events. No one can doubt
that the things he describes actually take place in our society. I believe that his work should be circulated as much as possible. Because if we see our own portraits, we will begin to hate the picture
and end up bettering ourselves."[55]

A description which insists on the slaves' docility must be looked
upon as the author's contrived scheme to heighten the drama of punishment. Just as important, the novels refer to specific *códigos*, or
codes of law, to create a determined response from the reader. The
*códigos* employed refer to law, the family, and religion, as we shall
see later. Suárez y Romero's and Zambrana's slaves are punished for
no real reason, for their only "crime" is to have loved each other.
The punishment the slaves receive is excessive, as is evident in
the abusive use of the whip. In one incident, Mendizábal punishes
Francisco with fifty lashes, shackles for two years, and perpetual
exile to the farm. In another, Francisco received 305 lashes in ten

days, leaving him immobilized for two weeks.[56] Francisco's punishment exceeded that prescribed by law. The royal decree of May 31, 1789, chapter 8, states that a slave should not receive more than twenty-five lashes and this should be done with an instrument that will not cause him/her any serious injuries.[57] More likely than not, the readers of the manuscripts were familiar with such ordinances and they would have condemned the violations.

The dominant frustrated love theme in *Francisco* and *El negro Francisco* and the desire of the slaves to be happy also have legal and moral implications, evinced by the *Declaration of the Rights of Man and the Citizen*, which states that "men are born and remain free and equal in rights." The concept of natural happiness contained in the declaration, as we have seen, was echoed by Echenique in his defense of the copper miners and is also present in Varela's speech to the courts regarding the abolition of slavery. Varela opened his speech with the statement, "The irresistible voice of nature claims that the island of Cuba should be happy."[58] Like the slaves, Cuban society could not be happy so long as slavery existed. The narration clearly blames the slave master for denying slaves a basic "natural" right to happiness. The slaves may be guilty of disobeying their master, but they are in compliance with a higher religious, moral, and legal order, which, as individuals, allows them to be happy.

The tension and violence which result from the master-slave relationship, whether real or metaphorical, is a strategy employed in the antislavery novel, from *Francisco* to *Cecilia Valdés*. The violence against the slaves is also a violence against the Cuban family, to which whites and blacks belong. Slavery is ultimately responsible for the decomposition of family structure. The rage that both Carlos and Ricardo feel goes beyond "biological" and "social" dimensions. Neither Carlos nor Ricardo care nor have respect for what has been described as a "milk sister" by Suárez y Romero and as a "play sister" by Zambrana. These descriptions highlight the makeup of the Cuban family, which includes both whites and blacks. However, from the point of view of the narrations, there is no peace and harmony in this family, only hatred and violence.

Current criticism offers another level of interpretation to the early nineteenth-century narrative. From a feminist perspective, the violence against the family is accomplished by raping the slave. Unlike Cecilia Valdés, who wanted to marry Leonardo Gamboa to "improve her race," Dorotea, Camila, Petrona, and Rosalía are unwilling sexual participants, even if it meant giving birth to lighter-colored offspring. The master's violation of the slave's body symbolically is also a rape of Cuban culture, which the female slaves represent.

From this perspective, Cuban culture emerges not out of synthesis of the various elements present on the island but as a rape, a sexual violation, by the white male of the black and mulatto female slave. Cuban culture is based on the systematic and generational rape of one culture by the other.

The violence against the Cuban family may appear only to affect the lives of blacks, the victims of the slavery system. But a narrative which exempts the slave master from any physical punishment must be considered as a strategy to draw the reader into the story. We should keep in mind that the novels were requested by well-to-do whites for a public like themselves. Thus they conform to the sensibilities of the readers and elicit their sympathetic reactions. In a letter dated November 17, González del Valle answers Suárez y Romero's inquiry regarding Del Monte's objections to "subversive" language in the manuscript. He believed that the novelist should not put unrealistic speeches in the characters' dialogue. But Del Monte also intended that Suárez y Romero's manuscript circulate with little difficulty, perhaps to avoid resistance from readers.[59] Del Monte's interest in a broad reading public may also explain why he insisted on changing the title of *Francisco* to the deceptive but enticing "El ingenio o las delicias del campo." Others, such as Villaverde and González del Valle, have expressed concern for their readers,[60] just as Zambrana did for doña Asensión Rodríguez de Necochea. The impact of the antislavery narrative as counter-discourse on a contemporary reader is not any less dramatic. When reading *Francisco*, Gabriel Coulthard, like González del Valle, Luz y Caballero, and Madden, was appalled at the cruelties of the slavery system and those who perpetuated it. He interprets the novel as a condemnation of slavery.[61]

Some contemporary readers may question the effectiveness of the novels; that is, the authenticity of their denunciation. But the much-criticized suicide by Francisco suggests, above all, a romantic theme. It also represents a realistic manner of escaping slavery and is deemed credible by González del Valle's standards.[62] This method of escape was also used by Chinese indentured servants taken to Cuba to supplement slave labor after 1847. The other feasible alternative was to escape to the mountains or the city or to join pirates and other adventurers.[63] Because of its suggestive threat to readers, the escape to the mountains is a theme not available in literature until after the emancipation of slaves in 1886; it was first used by Francisco Calcagno in his *Romualdo, uno de tantos* and later by José Antonio Ramos in his *Caniquí*. Furthermore, in the literature written during the Cuban Revolution, escape to the mountains became not only a real but the only alternative for runaway slaves, as we shall see in chapter 6.

The controversial and "docile nature" of the Franciscos is effective, in my opinion, because it provokes a human and religious response with which the reader must come to terms. Within a religious context, the slaves' passivity suggests the sacrifice of Christ and thus harks back to the Bible. There is an intertextual link between *Francisco* and the Bible. Intentionally, Easter is the day Dorotea confesses to Francisco her own sacrifice to save the slave. This day is equated with Francisco's loss of innocence; that is, with Adam's and Eve's eating from the tree of knowledge and their ejection from paradise. For the first time, Francisco understands not only his isolation from his family but, more importantly, his alienation from Africa and his race. If in the past he deluded himself, now he is no longer willing to do so.

However, Easter is not the day of resurrection but of death without salvation. In slavery the signs continue to be inverted. Time flows backwards and the Christian images do not correspond to their traditional referents. Francisco is the crucified black Christ figure. The day after Francisco's disappearance and death, don Antonio finds him on his cross; that is, hung from the tallest branch, partly decomposed and pecked by vultures. As in Padrines's composition, in the novel the events are narrated toward the beginning, that is, an origin; the day after Easter is not a Monday but Good Friday, the day Christ died for mankind. Similar to Christ and consistent with an awareness of his blackness, Francisco is taken down from his "cross" by four African *minas*. The African element recalls Tubero's death and his return to Africa. In the tradition of *his land*, the African-born slaves sing songs as they carry Francisco to the cemetery and bury him in his grave.

As in any other Spanish-speaking country, religion was important in Cuba, as the Christianization of native Americans and Africans would suggest. Thus the reader is manipulated by religious symbolism insofar as he associates Francisco with the sacrificial Christ figure. Religion is also present in Manzano's autobiography, in which Manzano confesses to his belief in God. He even attributed his wrongdoings to either a lukewarm or a forgotten prayer. By incorporating religion into his autobiography, Manzano cannot avoid relying on European and Christian descriptions to narrate his life. In some cases he establishes a link with other well-known ideas and images familiar to the reader. In one incident, Manzano is punished for taking a geranium leaf. The slave compares his punishment to that of Christ: "My hands were tied behind like a criminal [the origi-

nal states: "They were tied like those of Christ"] and my feet se-
cured in an aperture of the board. O my God! Let me not speak of
this frightful scene! When I recovered I found myself [at the doorstep
of the oratory] in the arms of my mother, bathed in tears, and dis-
consolate."[64] Through his association with Christ, Manzano conveys his experiences to the reader and, like Christ after the crucifix-
ion, Manzano found himself in the arms of his own mother.

III · Contemporary critics both in and outside of Cuba have
questioned the way in which slavery was denounced in the
antislavery narratives and the motives of intellectuals wanting to abolish slavery and the slave trade. In *The Island of Cuba*
(1849), Madden reveals that his interest is not limited to humanistic
concerns but to economics as well.[65] Critics such as Salvador Bueno
suggest that Del Monte and members of his literary circle were re-
formists.[66] Ileana Rodríguez proposes that writers of the Del Monte
group, like Suárez y Romero and Villaverde, wrote antislavery works
because they felt a need to repay sugarocrats like Del Monte for the
education they received.[67] And Ivan Schulman points out that Del
Monte and other members of the literary circle, in view of their own
economic interest, wished for a gradual end to slavery.[68] But Walterio
Carbonel rejects the bourgeois position of many critics in the revolution who consider Saco, Luz y Caballero, and others as representative of Spanish colonialism.[69] Others, such as José Luciano Franco,
suggest that men like Del Monte reacted to the existing fear of slave
rebellions which permeated the island.[70] Government officials in
Cuba suspected the abolitionist David Turnbull of protecting and
liberating slaves and inciting them to rebel.[71] We should recall that
Madden, Del Monte, Tanco, and others were supplying Turnbull
with antislavery information for a forthcoming volume of the parlia-
mentary papers to further the antislavery cause.[72] Marrero believes
that Turnbull's abolitionist plans to end slavery in Cuba were real.
According to Marrero, Turnbull felt betrayed when, at the request of
the Spanish court, Lord Aberdeen sought his replacement. Turnbull,
who was willing to go beyond Madden's respect for law in Cuba, was
convinced that the slavery issue on the island would not be resolved
through diplomatic channels. Turnbull hoped to use his influence
among whites, blacks, and mulattoes and the support of British abolitionists to gain Cuba's independence. In the end, Turnbull wanted
to establish a republic through a joint insurrection of whites, free
blacks and mulattoes, and slaves. After Turnbull's departure, U.S.
influence on the island increased. General Campbell had replaced

Calhoun and the U.S. position directly challenged British plans to control Cuba's future. In fact, U.S. government officials also wanted to annex the island. As early as March 23, 1837, the *Herald*'s editorial proposed a U.S. annexation of Cuba for fear of British takeover of the island. If necessary the United States would employ the same violent means the Texans had used to occupy Mexican territory. For liberal creoles, a U.S. nonviolent alternative became more acceptable than a British plan to incite rebellion. But whereas the British favored independence and abolition, the United States discouraged emancipation.[73] Some believed that the British were willing to support independence if the creoles accepted emancipation, but that the English would carry this plan with or without their help.[74] To ensure the success of his ideas, Del Monte continued to use multiple discourses. He supported Turnbull's abolitionist plans but also courted Americans residing on the island and, as with Turnbull, provided them with information regarding the Cuban political situation.[75] Del Monte's shift was in response to Turnbull's liberation plans to establish a black republic which went beyond the interest of liberals who supported an end to the slave trade. Aware that Spain could not stop a Turnbull attempt to free the slaves and establish a black military republic under British protection and conscious of U.S. opposition to British control of the island, Del Monte warned his friend, diplomat Alexander H. Everett, of the dangers for both Cuba and the United States.[76] According to Everett's reply to Del Monte, Webster and Cushing did not take seriously Del Monte's alarming news. Del Monte's request for help was based less on his acceptance of U.S. policies toward Cuba than on his fear of a black takeover of the island. It is possible, as an Everett letter suggests, that even though Del Monte continued to oppose the slave trade he wanted to dissociate himself from Turnbull. But Betancourt Cisneros did not believe that Del Monte was happy among Yankees.[77]

Del Monte's ideas and actions can be understood by Saco's *Paralelo entre la Isla de Cuba y algunas colonias inglesas,* in which he explains the creation of Consejos Coloniales so that Cubans from Cuba could dictate their own laws, thus proposing autonomy for Cuba. Saco, an antiannexationist, viewed annexation as a last resort:

> If the Spanish government decided to cut the political ties that unite Cuba with Spain, I could not be so criminal as to propose to unite my country to Great Britain. Give it then its own existence, an independent existence, and possibly if it were so isolated in the political as it is in nature; in my opinion here is the target to which we ought to direct

the efforts of all good Cubans. But if dragged by circumstances it had
to find shelter in foreign arms, it could not fall with honor and more
glory than into those of the great North American confederation.[78]

For Del Monte, the circumstances were the rumors of a British-
supported slave rebellion.

Throughout the nineteenth century, the Haitian Revolution and
its repercussions in Cuba and the rest of the Caribbean were persuasive arguments which discouraged violent emancipation of slaves as
well as independence movements. The latter position is expressed
eloquently by Arango, who, in his "Reflexiones de un habanero
sobre la independencia de esta Isla" (1824), argued against independence. Arango had expressed similar ideas in 1816, believing that
the composition of the island, in which blacks outnumbered whites,
made independence impossible. He discouraged revolutionary movements, claiming that any uprising would inevitably produce a slave
rebellion, the destruction of whites, and the transformation of Cuba
into another Haiti.[79] Although the fear of blacks was a real concern,
there is no doubt that members of the literary circle agreed with the
British in bringing an end to the slave trade, which also meant an
end to slavery. How to accomplish this end, however, was a point of
contention. Creoles in effect proposed to change the character of the
Cuban economy by replacing slave labor with white workers.[80] Like
Saco and Del Monte, in a letter dated July 24, 1843, Miguel de Aldama y Alfonso, Del Monte's brother-in-law, makes clear that the
importation of white workers was under way. Of the first three-
hundred workers, his father, Domingo de Aldama y Arechaga, would
receive fifty. He adds that public opinion was condemning the slave
trade and few if any plantation owners had bought slaves in the current month.[81]

The fear of blacks continued and became a reality on November 7,
1843, the day slaves of the Triumvirato plantation rebelled and attacked the nearby Acana sugar mill, killing six whites (three women,
two men, and one child). The runaway slaves continued to the Concepción, San Miguel, San Lorenzo, and San Rafael de Felipillo Mena
plantations, where they had uneven victories, winning some slaves
to their cause but finding resistance from others.[82] According to Domingo Andrés, casualties included sixty to seventy Africans and ten
to twelve whites.[83] During this period, even some landowners dis-
agreed with the indiscriminate massacre and punishment of free
blacks and slaves. Miguel de Aldama condemned the white repression, believing that the punishment by whites was worse than slave
rebellions. He even considered slaves martyrs of liberty.[84] For Al-

dama, blacks were fighting for their "holy" liberty and the seventeen sentenced to death "were all men, real heroes."[85] On a separate occasion, Miguel de Aldama condemned the slave trade and called the black rebellions a just cause.[86] Aldama's reaction was not an isolated case and was shared by other creole slave owners. In a letter dated December of the same year (1843), José Luis Alfonso, marqués of Montelo, reveals that he and his brother-in-law, Domingo de Aldama, signed a protest against the slave trade and, with Pepe Ofarrill, he proposed to initiate another one favoring the destruction of the slave trade. For it to have a strong impact, Alfonso intended to gather some sixty signatures comprising the most respected *hacendados*. Moreover, recognizing that the representations were only manifestations of opinions, he offered to take stronger measures. He agreed with Juan Poey's "legal opposition" and created an anonymous society which would denounce ships illegally disembarking slaves on Cuban shores. Alfonso believed that the mere existence of the society would destroy the slave trade and its membership would constitute a protest against it. Alfonso's position regarding the slave trade is not purely humanistic but is based on the fear of blacks and a concern for their treatment in light of the continual arrival of slave ships to the island.[87]

Members of Del Monte's literary circle and their writings, as represented by the antislavery narrative, were at the forefront of a movement which opposed slavery and directly challenged the slave trade. It appears that this opposition movement was gathering momentum and gaining a following among some landowners who shared Saco's ideas and favored replacing slaves by importing white workers. But this counter-discourse was undermined by the more powerful slave traders and Spanish colonial officials and resulted in the Ladder Conspiracy of 1844.

Del Monte, his writer friends, and the antislavery narrative represented one side of a dialogue on slavery which directly threatened slavers and Spanish officials in Cuba. Letters to Del Monte provide information regarding the official reaction toward blacks. In one dated March 19, 1843, Saco writes, with reference to the Sociedad Patriótica de La Habana: "The fault of being a *negrophile* there is worse than that of *independent*. This one at least has the sympathy of a party; but the other one stirs up hatred from all whites."[88] Betancourt Cisneros offers a similar understanding regarding Joaquín de Aguero, who was called before the captain general to explain his actions to free his slaves and his abolitionist position. Betancourt Cisneros advised him to go to the United States as soon as possible. The reason was, of course, his support of blacks: "Today it is a crime

to have or to express compassion for slaves: humanity, good treatment, none of this can be recommended, because they are synonymous with abolitionism."[89] Betancourt is also in jeopardy. As I have
mentioned, any opposition to the slave trade was considered a threat
to the government. He states: "The censor [Antonio Herrera] does
not allow me to write a single word regarding the white colonization. He has strict orders: A friend has told me that my words and
actions are being watched and I know that it is true that they are
watching me." In the same letter, Betancourt mentions the continual fear regarding Turnbull's plans and, like Aldama, he too has
received white workers from the Canary Islands. According to him,
they seem to mix well with the blacks and without distinction.

In his literary circle, Del Monte was daring enough to promote
the slavery theme and the works of the slave Manzano, and he became an enemy of the Spanish authorities. He was implicated by
Plácido, along with Luz y Caballero, Manzano, and others, in the
slave revolt, La Escalera. Considered a friend of Turnbull, Del Monte
left the island in 1843 and refused to present himself before the military tribunal. In 1845, Del Monte requested permission to return to
the island, but Captain General O'Donnell, a known supporter of
slavers who, like other officials, profited from the clandestine slave
trade, rejected his petition. Consequently, Del Monte died in exile in
Madrid in 1853.

Intellectuals such as Del Monte represented one end of the spec-
trum of the bourgeois dialogue; the other, the dominant discourse,
supported slavery and the slave trade. Fernández de Castro explains
the two prevalent positions before the writing of the antislavery narrative. For him, O'Gavan represented one extreme and Del Monte
the other:

> In 1821, don Bernardo O'Gavan published in Madrid a brief polemical
> essay against the dispositions destined to bring an end to the slave
> trade since 1817. This O'Gavan was an accomplished representative
> in the intellectual sector of criollo plutocratic supporters of the estab-
> lishment of slavery, which attempted to justify affirming that all Af-
> rican slaves of the Antilles were happier in this state than when they
> enjoyed their liberty in their native continent. Del Monte, who within
> the same sector as O'Gavan represented the opposite side, in his inter-
> esting bibliographic work *Biblioteca cubana*, said that this work of
> O'Gavan entitled *Observaciones sobre la suerte de los negros de Af-
> rica considerados en su propia patria y transplantados a las Antillas
> Españolas*, etc. was refuted in another one of the interesting English

erudite John Batturin[?], famous supporter of free trade and an ardent abolitionist.[90]

Even if we continue to question the position of Del Monte and his group regarding slavery, there is no question but that fiction, as a counter-discourse on slavery, is firm about its antislavery stance. Like Fernández de Castro, Zambrana writes a slavery debate between proslavers and abolitionists. The narrator in *El negro Francisco* traces the history of slavery and sides not with whites but with the slave:

> There have been those who have written that slavery is not a disgrace for the black. A Spanish newspaper, which classified as hollow phrases the laments of the abolitionist, took the trouble of investigating the origin of the slave trade and thought itself a winner, and thought it had won its cause, when it found out that the savage king of Dahomey sold to whites its prisoners of wars who were destined to be sacrificed. Slavery came to be a type of redemption. The black, who in the remote corner of his rustic country would have died by the knife and the shadow of barbarism, was tied like a bundle, given in exchange for an iron knife or barrel of rum, submerged in the bottom of the hold of the ship, transported, not as one transports men, but as one transports merchandise. If he was fortunate enough not to run into the British cruiser, he was not thrown into the sea; if he had enough vital strength he would not starve or die of neglect on the arid beach while they waited for the buyers or evaded the authorities, he then would live without a country, without a family, without dignity, without rest, without hope, and usually whipped to death: all of this when they were enlightened enough so that they would understand it well. The Spanish reporter opted for the proceedings known as civilization; we prefer those of the savage Dahomey king.[91]

The above quotation takes issue with the then popular idea that blacks lived as savages in Africa and any "civilization" attempt made by whites would be an improvement over their conditions. On the contrary, the narrator considers the African way of life to be superior to the "savagery" committed by slave traders.

The antislavery novels make political statements which can be attributed to author intentionality as contained in the text. Suárez y Romero felt an intrinsic relationship between his life and the characters in his work. Suárez y Romero inserts himself into his story by attributing his personality traits to his characters and his mother's name, Lutgarda, to Francisco's and Dorotea's daughter. In some ways, their child was also a member of his own family. Zambrana, who attended a reading of *Francisco* in Nicolás de Azcárte's literary circle, carried his independence and antislavery stance into the Ten Years' War. A known revolutionary, he participated in the Guáimaro Assembly and, with Ignacio Agramonte, wrote the new constitution which proclaimed all Cubans free. In 1873, Zambrana traveled to Chile as a representative of the revolutionary government and it was there that he wrote his antislavery novel. The ending of Zambrana's novel is unambiguous about its antislavery position. After Francisco's death, the now enlightened Carlos joins the antislavery cause; he fights on the side of the Federal troops to emancipate slaves in the United States. This ending is consistent with the historical time of the narration. Zambrana wrote his novel after the start of the Ten Years' War, but his narration develops between 1861 and 1862, when he recalled hearing a reading of *Francisco*.[92] Although the slave traffic was diminishing and Chinese and Canary Islanders were brought to supplement slave labor, it was not until 1868 that there was a cohesive movement to emancipate slaves. To comply with historical events, Zambrana transfers the antislavery cause to the United States, where, at the time of the narration, abolition was an important issue for the North. In so doing, Zambrana makes the strongest antislavery statement possible. He goes beyond other antislavery works and makes the fight against slavery not a local issue pertinent to one region or a single country but an international one. The cause for emancipation was in progress in the United States, and Carlos willingly risked his life for the emancipation of the black race.

The problem of focus and perspective is important for understanding the antislavery novel. Some critics both in Cuba and the United States, reflecting a contemporary intellectual perspective present in their own society, impose a personal view on a particular work without understanding the nature and implication of their observations. It is dangerous for critics to claim that many of the early writers did not go far enough, omitting from consideration the position the early writers represented within the society in which they lived. These contemporary critics do not see or understand that their reading of a text communicates, in many cases, more about their own personal and contemporary ideology than the novels that they pretend to analyze. Few are willing to reconstruct history and situate narrative discourse within the context of the past. Even so, it is tempting to assume that the lack of a revolutionary perspective can be attributed to a "white" point of view, which the works implicitly embody, not only because the authors are white but because the works are also part of a Western tradition. This statement can be revealing only if we do not take into account the problems of language and writing. Although the mulatto characters Sab and Cecilia Valdés are described as having white features and Zambrana described his protagonist as the "Apolo de ébano," it stands to reason that antislavery, as a concept or as a literary, political, or economic movement in Cuba, could only exist as a white movement. The white dominant perspective, whether British or Spanish, which helped to formulate the antislavery narrative could only be expressed by using the mechanism available to white or Western culture. Language and writing, as a bourgeois means of expression, can only be in the form of a dominant white aesthetic. A slave or a black described as having white characteristics may suggest, for a contemporary reader, assimilation. But within a different context, the same description was, in fact, aggressive and daring and challenged the slavery system. The repression of blacks as a dominant literary character offended the sensibility of many readers and attempted to push back the boundaries of Western literature. These early works attribute the dominant white sacred values to blacks and slaves who, within the context of the period, were treated like animals. The descriptions put the slaves on a higher moral and ethical level than the whites.

The antislavery discourse incorporates an unfamiliar situation into Western language and describes it from a bourgeois point of view. It is unequivocal that another position was not possible, at least not before the middle of the nineteenth century and certainly not during the writing of the first antislavery works. After Turnbull was expelled from Cuba, his position regarding armed insurrection became less plausible among creoles, and his alternative was reduced to a theoretical possibility and fell outside the Spanish bourgeois dialogue. The antislavery novel as counter-discourse inserted blacks and slaves within the dialogue. For blacks, the transition from outside the discourse to within it required a metamorphosis of sorts. Some blacks who escaped slavery, like Juan Francisco Manzano, moved up on the social scale and learned to read and write. To do so, Manzano had to abandon his own frame of reference, of Africa and slavery, and accept a different one. When writing his autobiography, Manzano had to become psychologically someone else to write about his condition within a white aesthetic, the only aesthetic of his time. In so doing, Manzano joined and therefore accepted one part of the bourgeois discourse. Manzano's *Autobiografía* does not propose any radical alternative from the views of Suárez y Romero's and Zambrana's novels. Moreover, his tone and plot development are similar to theirs.[93] We should recall that even though Manzano does escape the brutal punishment of his master, he flees not into the mountains, like the true rebel slave, but to the city, seeking protection from the law. An educated slave, Manzano was aware of slavery laws and the aid he might receive from Spanish authorities. In his autobiography, Manzano attributes this information to a slave friend who suggested he run away. The royal decree of November 14, 1693, empowered the captain general to take actions against slave owners who excessively punished their slaves, though it was not until the royal decree of 1789 that specific fines were imposed on violators. Section 10 of the decree states that immoderate punishment would lead to the confiscation of the slave. But these and other laws were difficult to enforce until the Slave Ordinance of 1842. Not until the royal decree of November 27, 1883, after the publication of both *Francisco* and *El negro Francisco,* was the punishment of slaves substantially reduced.[94] The law nevertheless represented a glimmer of hope for the slave Manzano.

Zambrana's characters also contemplate Manzano's actions. In effect, their attempted escape follows closely the actual life of the slave poet. However, unlike Manzano, they do not seek the aid of the captain general but of "Delmonte," someone more reliable and trustworthy. In fact as in fiction, these characters, independent of the perspective offered, choose to solve their problems from within the slavery system. It should therefore be no surprise that Afro–Latin American writers like José Vasconcelos, Gabriel de la Concepción Valdés, Candelario Obeso, and Gaspar Octavio Hernández, among others, were not able, for reasons already explained, to portray the image of the rebellious black.[95]

In reality, there is no insider perspective, only the one dictated by language and writing. Even though Manzano is a black, his life is already mediated by writing. Thus he appeals not to black but to white readers by divorcing himself from others like him. Manzano was not typical but privileged. On a number of occasions he states that his family considered him to be different from the rest of the other blacks, a belief he also internalized: "Remembering don Saturnino's previous warnings, I saw myself without parents in the sugar mill, not even one, in other words, mulatto among blacks. My father was somewhat arrogant and never allowed cliques in his house nor that any of his children play with the darkies of the hacienda."[96] Manzano was not able to narrate the image of the rebel slave.[97] The "real" black rebellious slave could not tell his story from his own point of view. Those who revolted and fled into the mountains or died for their freedom rejected the white system in all its manifestations, whether cultural, economic, or literary. His refusal to be a part of slavery or Western society meant the absence of his discourse and his literature. Those blacks or whites who did not rebel, whether consciously or not, participated in a Western bourgeois dialogue and partook of writing as a legitimate form of self-expression. However, they chose to participate in one aspect of a dialogue which continued to be a threat to the dominant slavery perspective.

As literature within a Western tradition, the antislavery works narrate the image of blacks in a way which conforms to the problematics of writing. The descriptions of characters cannot go beyond and are limited to the strategies of the text. Through their perspective, the antislavery works produce a rupture in writing, however slight, in which a standard *código* is turned on itself to offer in the same language a counter-discourse on slavery. In this regard, by participating and remaining in Western culture, these works have undermined traditional language by widening the margins of a political and literary discourse. This literature represented an important segment within society which could not be easily dismissed. The antislavery works were written to promote a specific understanding of slaves and slavery in nineteenth-century Cuban society. The works were written for a particular audience and successfully engaged that audience in a dialogue on slavery.

With the passage of time, the patterns of the first half of the nineteenth century began to shift. But only a historical conversion will cause writers to go beyond these early works and write about what has always been present but marginal in fact and fiction. In the twentieth century, writers like Alejo Carpentier, Miguel Barnet, and César Leante will write about the rebel slave as protagonist, a character little known in nineteenth-century Cuban narrative. One important factor for this conversion is the manumission of slaves in 1886. Another one would be the Cuban Revolution. Contemporary authors narrate the slavery system in retrospect, from the point of view of another uprising, thus providing the reader with a more complete understanding of this literary historical theme.

| IV | The incipient Cuban literature narrates the life of the tragic slave protagonist who is unjustly punished by the slave master and the slavery system. The early narrative also includes a different type of literature; unlike the antislavery narrative, this one portrays slavery not from the slave's point of view but from that of his counterpart, the slave hunter. Like the antislavery narrative, the proslavery works insert themselves in the same dialogue on slavery and describe the slave society of the first part of the nineteenth century. If the antislavery narrative represented a counter-discourse

to slavery and the slave trade, the proslavery literature was *the* discourse insofar as it supported slavery by highlighting the life of the slave hunter. While Del Monte asked his author friends to denounce the abuses of slavery, others were documenting runaway slave attacks against the white segment of the Cuban population. The whites present in antislavery narratives are depicted as merciless, immoral characters whose ultimate aim is to profit from the slave's suffering; the proslavery narrative depicts whites as victims of slave uprisings and challenges the passive slave image portrayed in the antislavery works. The antislavery and proslavery literatures have more than a theme in common; they were written during the same crucial moment in Cuban history, during the first half of the nineteenth century. Francisco Estévez's *Diario de un rancheador* was written between 1837 and 1842, and José Morilla's "El ranchador" was written in 1839 but published in 1856. As I have mentioned above, Morilla's short story may have been written for and included in the antislavery portfolio Del Monte gave Madden before the abolitionist returned to England in 1839. Although this action may provide a privileged reading of Morilla's story, its theme and perspective have allowed us to read it alongside Estevez's diary, each offering a different dimension of slave hunters during the first half of the nineteenth century in Cuba.

There is also a personal relationship between the pro- and antislavery narratives. It was Cirilo Villaverde who copied Estévez's diary in 1843 and later wrote an introduction to it. Villaverde's father, an inspector of slave hunters, owned the diary. In an 1884 letter to Julio Rosas, the young Villaverde provides a background to the diary:

> I possess the diary (copied by me) of a captain slave hunter of black fugitives, of Vuelta Abajo, which spans two consecutive years and it contains the official history of mountain slave communities and the atrocities they committed in the frequent and bloody battles which they conducted with dogs, machetes, and firearms. I was thinking about publishing it without adding either a period or a comma. They are a series of tasks written by the chief slave hunter's daughter according to the oral descriptions that he told of his pursuits and finding of groups of runaway slaves,—and given to my father in San Diego de Núñez, who was a delegate member of the Junta de Fomento to form and inspect the band of slave hunters.[98]

Villaverde's introduction to the diary in part describes the western part of the Cuban countryside known to both the narrator of the diary and the author of *Cecilia Valdés*. His description recalls his

*Excursión a Vuelta Abajo,* a travel book about the countryside and customs of a region in which Villaverde was born. Villaverde's travel book and introduction conform to a literature documenting aspects of Cuban life. The book was published in two parts, the first in 1838 and the second in 1842; that is, during the approximate years in which the diary was written.[99] More importantly, Villaverde copied Estévez's *Diario de un rancheador,* published it, and later included this historical figure in the definitive version of his *Cecilia Valdés,* completed in 1879. Parts of his novel unfold in the same region of Vuelta Abajo. To include Estévez in his novel, Villaverde broke with the chronology of *Cecilia Valdés* and the *Diario.* The narrative time of the novel is between 1812 and 1832; however, Estévez worked as a slave hunter between 1837 and 1842. Villaverde fused both historical periods into one to bring this important figure into his work. *Cecilia Valdés* narrates the exploitation of blacks by whites and the severe punishment inflicted upon runaway slaves; the *Diario* describes the other side of the slavery issue, the "brave" slave hunter who, against great odds, captured fugitive slaves.

Both the diary and the short story have more in common than a time of writing and a historical theme; they also describe the same western region in Cuba, Vuelta Abajo, in the province of Pinar del Río. A brief discussion of demography in Cuba helps to understand why the proslavery narrative described the Vuelta Abajo region. During the time of writing, sugar and slavery were on the increase. The 1827 census shows the total black population outnumbered that of whites, though the slave population did not. The total breakdown is as follows: slaves, 40.6 percent; free blacks, 15.2 percent; and whites, 44.2 percent. That same census indicates that a disproportionate number of slaves as compared to whites was concentrated in the west. The composition by department was as follows: west, 28.02 percent slave, 6.54 percent free black, and 23.43 percent white; center, 5.96 percent slave, 3.44 percent free black, and 13.94 percent white; east, 6.74 percent slave, 5.14 percent free black, and 6.78 percent white. The high percentage of slaves in the west reflects the presence of slaves in or near the region of Havana, which contained a large number of sugar mills, including some of the most important ones on the island. In spite of the preponderance of slaves in the west, the area in which the proslavery literature unfolds, the westernmost region in the jurisdiction of Pinar del Río contained the lowest percentage of slaves and the highest one of free blacks: 27 percent slave, 23 percent free black, and 50 percent white.[100] The statistics reveal that, as in many colonies, most of the population lived in or near the capital (the highest percentages were in Havana, Matanzas, Santiago

de las Vegas, and Güines). The important sugar mills were located in
the area, suggesting that slavery was more severe in the western part
of the island than in the eastern part. However, of the western regions, Pinar del Río had the smallest number of sugar mills. According to the census of 1860, the westernmost jurisdiction of Pinar del
Río, San Cristóbal, Bahía Honda, and Guanajay contained a total of
102 sugar mills, producing 38,643 metric tons. By comparison, the
Matanzas, Cárdenas, and Colón jurisdictions contained 401 sugar
mills, producing 241,753 metric tons.[101] In fact, since its settlement,
the province of Pinar del Río was better known for cattle and, especially, tobacco.[102] In his introduction to the diary, Villaverde describes the area in which it unfolds in the following manner:

> Indeed, around the period which encompasses the diary's narration
> all of the mentioned region, from the Mariel to Bahía-Honda, was
> populated by large sugar plantations in the lower or septentrional part
> of the woodlands; the opposite part or southern plains of vast horse
> land and tobacco plantations; and the central or rugged land of some
> ranches for the raising of minor cattle and of beautiful flowering coffee
> plantations, crowning high mountains or hanging from their hurried
> slopes like the Babylonian gardens.[103]

The rural area and its mountainous terrain, where sugar production
was not as intense as in other jurisdictions, made the region of
Vuelta Abajo attractive for slaves to flee to with relative success.
This was also the case in the province of Oriente, where sugar production was less intense. The same 1860 census shows that the 198
sugar mills in the eastern region produced 31,950 metric tons, less
than that produced in the province of Pinar del Río. Like in the west,
Oriente is covered with mountainous terrain, making it easier for
slaves to escape and hide in the sierra. The many slave communities
in Oriente co-existed with plantations. Runaway slaves even traded
regularly with whites of the region, as Leante's *Los guerrilleros negros* reveals. Moreover, all major movements for independence, including Castro's 26th of July Movement, had their origin in Oriente.
Bahía Honda and Oriente had a high concentration of fugitive slaves.
Unlike Oriente, Bahía Honda is closer to Havana, the center of cultural and literary activities, giving the slavery narrative importance
among intellectual circles. Villaverde, Morilla, and others became
interested in fugitive slaves in an area close to the center of political and cultural activities. Both Estévez's and Morilla's narrations
document slavery in a region close to Havana and known to have
relatively high numbers of runaway slaves.

The increased number of runaway slaves forced owners to make efforts to recover their property, and slave hunters were hired to capture runaway slaves. The slave hunter's profession dates back to the conquest, first to capture Amerindians and later Africans brought to the Caribbean to supplement and substitute for the rapidly dying native population. The high number of runaway slaves led to Article 62 of the Cáceres Ordinance of 1641, which made provisions for the hunting of slaves: "We order and command that anyone can capture the black fugitive slaves and that the cattle raiser, the cattle hand or foreman or any other person who captured a black fugitive outside his village up to 8 miles, the slave owner pay him 4 ducados, and if he were captured farther than 80 miles and up to 160 miles, he be given 12 ducados, and if he were captured from more than 160 miles, he be given 15 ducados."[104] Between 1796 and 1815, a reported 15,971 runaway slaves were captured throughout the island. In the region of Cuzco in Pinar del Río, an area known to slave hunters Francisco Estévez and Valentín Páez, the fifty to sixty families with more than three thousand slaves lived in fear of the continual threat posed by runaway slaves. In Vuelta Abajo, of which the Cuzco region is a part, a proponent of slavery estimated that in 1819 there were more than five hundred fugitive slaves.[105]

There were two types of slave hunters: one was hired by slave masters to capture fugitive slaves for a particular plantation, and the other was commissioned by the government to capture and eliminate all fugitive slave threats. Of the two, the commissioned hunter was the cruelest; he received a fixed salary and was not financially motivated to return live slaves, often bringing back the slave's ear as proof of his task.[106] The slave and slave hunter entered into a symbiotic relationship in which one survived at the expense of the other.

Most slave hunters abused their power, often killing slaves indiscriminately. In an uprising in 1827, a well-known slave hunter, Domingo Armona, killed the first eighteen blacks he encountered without asking if they belonged to the rebel group.[107] The hatred of the slave hunter went beyond the slave and included free blacks, who were often accused of harboring fugitive slaves. From the beginning, slave hunters took advantage of their legal and physical powers, and slave hunting became synonymous with mistreating all blacks, whether slaves or free. Franco describes the origins of the slave hunters and the atrocities they committed:

> To hunt runaway slaves before 1530—aborigines as well as black Africans—the colonizers formed a fraternity in Santiago de Cuba. Later the groups called *rancheadores* or *arranchadores* were formed.

The band was first used by the mayor of Santiago de Cuba, Bartolomé Ortiz, in 1538 to combat Indian and black slaves who escaped to the mountains. But the barbarity and cruelty of the slave hunters with runaway slaves and the constant offenses to which free black farmers were victims under the pretext of asking for cooperation for their bloody hunts were to the extreme that King Felipe IV, by means of a royal decree—Madrid, July 21, 1623—ordered the governors "that they provide convenient remedies to the referred wrongs and do justices to blacks so that they are no longer bothered."[108]

In a similar manner, under the guise of complying with his objectives, Estévez harassed free blacks in the region of Vuelta Abajo.

Often there was a disproportionately higher number of fugitive slaves to whites and, at times, the slave hunter fought against greater odds. A decisive factor was the slave hunter's dogs. Ortiz tells us dogs were highly regarded and were used during the U.S. Civil War to fight against blacks who sought refuge with Seminole Indians. In Central America, only twelve Cuban hunters with thirty-five dogs were enough to fight the Mesquito Indians of Nicaragua, who had decimated three Spanish regiments. Hunting dogs were also used in other parts of the Caribbean, including Jamaica and Haiti.[109]

Slave hunters were poor and uneducated whites who left their lands to profit from the slavery system. In providing a profile of the slave hunter, Francisco Calcagno says those who became hunters were good-natured but were corrupted by the slavery environment, which turned them into ruthless individuals. In his *Romualdo, uno de tantos,* Calcagno describes this historic figure in the following manner:

> And where do slave hunters come from? Here is why we have said habit or custom hardens our souls. They come from the same candid and hospitable hillbillies who give everything to friends, who sacrifice everything to do good, and if they are habitual gamblers, it is because there have always been in our countryside more valleys than schools. The hillbilly is cruel by ignorance, the foreman by necessity: this proves nothing against him, nor against the African race; nor is it a result of the extreme degradation to which he has fallen, one more argument against the slavery institution.[110]

Villaverde describes Estévez as a "semi-civilized hillbilly with a family, a slave owner who owned land for growing coffee in the rugged mountains of San Blas."[111]

Estévez's *Diario de un rancheador* and Morilla's short story "El ranchador" are the only narrative samples which focus on the life of a defender of slavery in nineteenth-century Spanish American literature. They are unknown to many critics and recently have been re-edited in Cuba, the diary in 1973 and the short story in 1976. The publication of these works and the antislavery narrative represents an effort in revolutionary Cuba to document a certain aspect of the country's past.[112] Although the proslavery discourse provides valuable information about the life and activities of the slave hunter, I propose to show that the *Diario* is a contrived narration which intends to hide the brutalities committed by Estévez and that the short story's ambiguous ending is an attempt to question the evils of the slavery system. The antislavery narrative and the literature of the slave hunter together provide a dialogue on slavery.

Francisco Estévez, a coffee grower and slave owner, was commissioned by government inspectors to capture slaves in the region of Vuelta Abajo. An illiterate, Estévez dictated his *Diario* to his daughter, who then wrote the accounts of her father's actions. In the diary, Estévez documents a variety of information, such as slave masters' requests to seek and return fugitive slaves, complaints of fugitive slave raids, slave thefts, encounters with runaway slaves, number of captured and killed slaves, and location and date of each expedition. Time has allowed a different perspective into Estévez's document. The *Diario* also reveals the bravery of runaway slaves, who often chose to fight and die rather than be returned to slavery; the aid Maroons received from plantation slaves and free blacks; valuable descriptions of slave communities in the mountains and their trade with both blacks and whites; and the relative success of runaway slaves like Julián, who had remained free in the mountains for thirty-seven years. Contrary to popular belief, the *Diario* reports that attacks on plantations were also carried out by blacks who were not runaway slaves. These slavelike raids were encouraged by whites whose plantations lacked food. The diary is written in a statistical and bureaucratic language.

A typical entry shows that on July 15, 1837, Estévez and his men discovered a runaway slave community containing sixteen ranches and seven more under construction, sheltering fifty to sixty fugitive slaves. Estévez reports: "We found spears, many horns of fine gunpowder, sharp knives, an undetermined number of rifle shots, the kind that are sold in taverns, seven or eight bundles of hemp for stoppers in different ranches. From what I can gather, they have six or seven firearms. We also found fourteen or fifteen crates of ba-

nanas, pork, and beef, forty old blankets, men's and women's clothing, pieces of pots and kettles which we gathered and burned with
the ranch."[113]

Morilla's "El ranchador" differs from Estévez's *Diario* insofar as
we do not get a detailed description of the daily life of a slave hunter.
However, it documents a historical figure and explains why Valentín
Páez became a slave hunter. Páez tells the narrator the tragic and
heartbreaking story of how, while he was tending cattle, a group of
runaway slaves attacked his home and killed and burned his wife,
three children, and brother-in-law. The massacre turned a good and
noble man into one of the most ruthless slave hunters in Cuban history. Unlike other slave hunters, Páez did not hunt slaves for money
but for revenge.

Like the antislavery narrative, both the diary and the short story
force readers to understand, and even side with, their protagonists.
In the *Diario*, slaves steal, kidnap other slaves, destroy property, and
kill whites. The information provided clearly shows that the slaves'
actions fall outside the law that governed Cuban society. As a member and enforcer of colonial society, the reader understands that the
slaves must be punished for breaking the law. Similarly, in the short
story, we are led to experience the unjust sufferings of a man who
lost his entire family to a fugitive slave attack. Revenge, in this case,
is a justifiable and necessary act. The narration of both works explains the capture and even death of runaway slaves.

An atmosphere of terror, uprisings, and massacres of whites may
not have allowed a nineteenth-century reader to understand why
slaves escaped from their masters and committed the brutal acts of
which they were so often accused. The slavery laws were designed to
protect and promote the slavery system; that is, the production of
sugar, coffee, tobacco, cattle, and the rights of whites. Slaves caught
outside the law were severely punished. In an attempt to provide a
different and perhaps more contemporary perspective, both Villaverde and Friol have added an introduction to the diary, thus offering
a broader understanding of Estévez's account. Without Villaverde's
narration in 1884 (or Friol's in 1973), few readers of the diary before
the abolition of slavery in Cuba were privileged to more than one
interpretation of Estévez's and Morilla's texts, interpretations already seen in the antislavery novels and made in part possible by a
shift in historical perspective which the end of slavery provided. But
a second reading of Estévez's diary and Morilla's short story allows
an underlying discourse to surface and question the dominant intention of the work, a discourse present during the time of writing and
contained in the antislavery literature. The most interesting of the

two is the *Diario*. Like Hernán Cortez's carefully written letters or
Lazarillo de Tormes's picaresque story, Estévez's narration does more
than report periodic trips to hunt runaway slaves. The *Diario* is a
preconceived scheme made to justify the slave hunter's acts, hide
certain information, and influence the reader. The *Diario* contains a
number of events that are mentioned but not explained and dates
that contradict information provided. The lack of consistency undermines the even tone and statistical nature of the *Diario*.

The first disruption in the diary's chronology occurs on April 16,
1837, the date Estévez says he returned home. The entry is followed
by a note indicating the death of five men thought to be runaway
slaves. The next entry is dated April 30 and makes reference to the
previous one when Estévez returned home; it refers to the date not
as April 16 but as April 19. Then it states that Estévez rested on the
20th and 21st of the month in question. In the same entry he mentions an operation that lasted ten days; that is, from the 19th to the
28th. The dates of the expedition contradict the information in the
same entry, which included the days he returned home and rested. It
is possible to accept the inconsistencies at face value. But in his introduction to the diary, Friol compares the "original" diary with Villaverde's copy and observes that Villaverde made some modifica-
tions.[114] In his own introduction, Villaverde mentions the stylistic
changes made: "As the attentive reader can observe, we have been
able to preserve the colorful style and even the at times vulgar language of the narrator, changing for the sake of clarity, shortening
some paragraphs, as demanded by the change in events, and beginning the official parts, which were in essence in the month in which
the originals were given to the inspectors of the band."[115] When
copying Estévez's diary, Villaverde's stylistic changes recall Suárez y
Romero's copying of Manzano's autobiography; they both are texts
based on earlier works and have been given a literary quality not
present in the originals.

However, if some of the substantive changes we have cited above
were produced not by Estévez but by Villaverde, then his intervention
in the text resembles more closely not Suárez y Romero's but Richard
Madden's translation of "Life of the Negro Poet." Madden's changes
were not only stylistic to conform to the English language but substantive, making Manzano's antislavery case stronger.[116] Because of
his conscious or unconscious intervention in the text, Villaverde's
"rewriting" may have produced the contradictions that have allowed
us to see another side of the *Diario*. But it is also possible to postu-
late that not all of the inconsistencies we have encountered are due
to Villaverde's transcription "errors," and some may be attributed to

Estévez himself. If that is the case, then the contradictions we are alluding to point to a fragmentation in time and suggest a need to correct the past; that is, to manipulate the text, and therefore the reader, and rewrite history. The April 16 and April 19 dates of his return home read together indicate that Estévez rested not two but five days. Writing, as permanence, attempts to legitimize and substitute itself for the past. The April 19 entry by itself seems to be consistent with other dates provided in the same entry.

The chronology of the *Diario* is further complicated by a July 1 entry in which Estévez admits suppressing information, specifically the names of places searched, and by a July 25 entry in which the slave hunter states that his superiors requested an account of his campaigns since he had not turned anything in after July 1. Although Estévez gives a detailed account of what he and his men did from July 2 to July 15, the record from the 15th to his July 25 entry is sketchy and general and claims he was in the mountains capturing fugitive slaves. Moreover, in an unspecified entry, Estévez records that on August 27 he returned to his town, on the 28th he and his men went to the coast, on the 29th they searched the hills, finding many ranches and capturing four slaves, and on the 30th they left for the Candelaria Mill. The next date recorded is August 27, indicating that he did not return home as mentioned but went back into the hills, finding another ranch and capturing one of two slaves. In a follow-up note to the entry, Estévez contradicts himself again by recalling that on August 27, a Sunday, he and his men hid in Pedro Mantilla's coffee plantation but were later discovered by a dog. Estévez offered the unconvincing story that they were looking for runaway slaves. A scuffle between master and slave hunters followed. The note ends by calling for more government support for his actions and reveals that this type of opposition to his work is not new, especially among owners of small holdings. In a subsequent entry, Estévez continues his complaints, adding to them the lack of money paid by the patrons of the expedition and the resignation of four of his men because of a reduction in salary. The entry, however, does not explain the basis for the complaints; that is, why the salaries were reduced. On July 5, 1838, Estévez continues to lament about not receiving the needed cooperation from plantation owners to exterminate runaway slaves. In the same entry, Estévez tells of a letter he had to write regarding the death of three slaves. He also mentions that two slaves were captured unharmed, implying that others may have been harmed.

Other entries continue to show tension between hunters and masters, tension created by Estévez's inability or unwillingness to differentiate between fugitive and plantation slaves. (Estévez reports that his dogs had mistaken plantation workers for runaway slaves.) And on November 17, 1839, he states that charges were brought against him by his mortal enemy, D. J. B. Torres, for the death of a slave by one of Estévez's dogs. Moreover, on March 17, 1840, Estévez received a superior order to return to San Diego, whereupon he was arrested and remained in jail until March 31.

What follows are more complaints regarding restrictions placed on Estévez, limiting his effectiveness on the job. In a note he suggests the idea of corraling free blacks as a means of combating runaway slaves. This method was effective and supported by slave masters in the north, where no one cared if a free black was injured. However, the situation in the south suggested precaution, and Estévez was seeking advice from the junta. (In the north, sugar was grown and treatment of slaves was more ruthless; in the south, coffee and tobacco were cultivated and masters adhered more closely to slavery laws.)[117] In November 1841, Estévez received an order from the captain general to return to the city and face charges for the death of a slave captured by his men. Finally, in April 1842, he mentions his resignation, which was accepted May 18, one day before the final entry.

The above information disrupts the statistical and monotonous nature of the diary to reveal a different discourse from the one intended. The contradictions, repetitions, and clarifications contained in the work are not isolated instances but are present throughout. When the events are reread as a separate subtext, they reveal a different Estévez, not the one hired to uphold the cruel slavery system, but one who distorted it even further, often killing indiscriminately. This was done to such a degree that he even encountered opposition from some of the plantation owners he was to have served. They objected to his behavior and indeed to his mistreatment of plantation and fugitive slaves, as the charges brought against him indicated. Although not specified, Estévez's behavior must have gone beyond permissive slavery laws. Estévez even wanted to exterminate free blacks to stop the communication between them and fugitive slaves. This and other activities caused alarm among inspectors, who restricted his activities and forced his resignation.

In contrast to the *Diario*, the short story takes an unexpected turn at the end. In spite of the narrator's sympathy for Páez's tragic life and admiration for his bravery, the short story does not continue in this direction and therefore makes the ending ambiguous. While relating his deplorable story, Páez, with his ruthless companion Bayamés and their dogs, sees and chases a group of fugitive slaves. The curious narrator follows and arrives in time to witness the killing of a runaway slave by two of the dogs. The slave pleads for help and the narrator attempts unsuccessfully to get the dogs to heel. Lamenting at not having his pistols with him, the narrator goes to his horse to get them. Unfortunately for the fugitive slave and rather fortunately for the narrator, the victim was dead by the time the narrator returned. The story is ambiguous insofar as it does not make clear whom the narrator was going to kill; that is, whether he was going to shoot the slave and put him out of his misery or shoot the dogs and save the slave. Killing the slave to "save" him from the dogs would have been consistent with the narrator's good nature. We should recall that when listening to Páez's tragedy, the narrator was so moved that he even implored Páez not to continue. However, killing the dogs to save the victim, as the story strongly suggests, is still in agreement with the narrator's character but not with the logic of the short story. Killing the dogs would imply a merciful act on the part of the narrator, but also a confrontation with Páez, leading to a possible questioning of his sympathy for the man he admired. Upon Páez's return, the narrator would be forced to explain why he killed the dogs to save a slave, a fugitive slave who might have been responsible for the death of the slave hunter's family. Would the narrator have then been willing to fight Páez and Bayamés to save the fugitive slave? We do not think so, since there does not appear to be any ideological difference between them.

The inquisitive reader does not have to go any further in his investigation. The narrator never gets the opportunity to prove what he meant when he decided to "help" the fugitive slave. The conflict was avoided when the narrator was "conveniently" delayed while getting his pistols. His horse had broken loose from where he had been tied and was pasturing in the valley. This delay, contrived by the short story writer, avoids a confrontation between the narrator and Páez, or between the narrator and the slavery system. However, the intention of wanting to help the fugitive slave begins to undermine the slavery system. It also offers a point of view on slavery not present intentionally in the *Diario*.

Both the diary and the short story provide a valuable picture of the life and activities of Cuban slave hunters in general and Valentín Páez and Francisco Estévez in particular. The texts also offer an insight into their protagonists' psyches. The *Diario*'s even tone serves to mask important information regarding Estévez's savage activities. The listing format of this narration does not allow for a contextual explanation of what actually occurred on some campaigns. Estévez's account and point of view are the only information available to the reader. Although we are not told who proposed the idea of a diary, it does serve as a way for the inspectors to monitor and therefore control Estévez's activities: toward the middle and end of the *Diario*, Estévez repeatedly acknowledged that he must submit monthly reports to combat allegations against him. But Estévez also uses the *Diario* to hide his cruel acts. The plantation owners' objections to Estévez's methods may have been common knowledge, and he felt obligated to record his activities to combat possible allegations against him. The *Diario* masks dates and events and attempts to provide official readers of the diary with his point of view. We should keep in mind that toward the beginning moments of the diary, Estévez includes letters which show that Francisco Pacheco and Lucas Villaverde asked him to hunt fugitive slaves. In another letter, don Juan Herreros y Campos grants him permission to request the necessary help for the success of his mission. This last one also asks Estévez to report those who refuse to help him. Although we are not told when the letters were reproduced in the diary, whether it was during the moment in which the entries were made or after Estévez encountered difficulties with slave owners, the letters, read with the rest of the text, show that Estévez had the support to carry out his task without impediments from others. The latter part of the diary reveals that he did not receive the support promised and what little was given was withdrawn when Estévez carried his actions to the extreme. From Estévez's point of view, his numerous complaints about the hard work, low pay, difficult assignments, and lack of support were not taken seriously. The statistical format of the diary does not allow for a narrative of how runaway slaves were treated when caught or of the cause of death. And if it did, the reader would have to question the information, since the only credible witnesses were the slave hunters themselves. After all, as a first-person narrator, Estévez was the only one who gave accounts of his expedition.

Like the *Diario*, "El ranchador" contains two controlled discourses. On the one hand, we have an explanation of and a justification for the atrocities Páez committed. On the other hand, the perspective changes when the narrator sees for himself the brutal killings. He, as a witness to the killing of runaway slaves, is important to an overall understanding of the story. At first, the narrator, as a representative of those who uphold slavery, is drawn to the slave hunters and the stories told regarding fugitive slave attacks on white dwellings. Later, his perspective shifts when he experiences for himself the brutal battle. If he once believed that the fugitive slave was the victimizer, he now understands that in reality the slave is the victim. At the end of the story, standing on top of a mountain in the middle of the night, the narrator sees a fire in the distance, smells burning human flesh, and curses the destiny of his country. Although his reaction is more personal than ideological, it nevertheless questions the slavery system. The narrator's frustration recalls the reaction of slave owners like Miguel de Aldama, who opposed the slave trade and blamed slavers for the horrible condition of the country.[118] The slavery issue, which included the fear of an increasing number of slaves as well as their mistreatment, had divided the colony. The division worked to the advantage of colonial administrators since it shifted the focus away from the issue of Cuba's independence from Spain to a possible slave takeover of the island. The slavery debate became more important than independence. For Morilla, the act of writing the short story serves as a way of coming to terms with his own ambivalence regarding slavery; that is, the suffering of Páez and other slave hunters and his concern for the mistreatment of runaway slaves. Both the diary and the short story capture a cruel moment in Cuban history, but it is the fictional narrative mode which dares, however mildly, to question it and produce with the *Diario* a dialogue on slavery.

The proslavery and antislavery narratives reflect the different positions regarding slavery in the society from which they emerge. As a whole, the literature reveals the two sides of the slavery issue. When read together, there is no doubt about the daring discourse of the antislavery works regarding the slave. There is also no question about the proslavery narrative's view regarding the slave hunter. In spite of what may appear to be two different perspectives, the underlying discourse of the proslavery literature puts its own intent into question and begins to echo concerns already expressed by the antislavery works. Even though the diary and the short story narrate the life of a slave hunter, they reveal different factions within the proslavery discourse.

The historical events justify to a proslavery reader Estévez's and Páez's brutal and savage treatment of runaway slaves and free blacks in Cuba. By the time Estévez completed his *Diario de un rancheador* (1842), the Del Monte literary salon was entering its final stage; Del Monte left the island the following year. The transition from one perspective to another is consistent with the repressive mode which led to the events of the Ladder Conspiracy of 1844. All slave masters, even the "kind" ones, would be put on the alert. Many would not hesitate to take action against their own slaves in light of a possible slave uprising that threatened to turn Cuba into another Haiti. However, a small but increasing number felt that the only way to alleviate Cuba's slavery problems was to stop the slave traffic and import white and Chinese wage laborers.

The threat of a slave revolution in Cuba may have forced Morilla not to publish his "El ranchador" until 1856, many years after the events of the Ladder Conspiracy. We should note that after the mid-nineteenth century, a reduced number of African captured slaves were entering Cuba and the annexationist movement was gaining momentum. These two factors may help to explain the inherent dialogue in Morilla's story. A questioning of slavery was already present as early as the time of the writing, allowing for a more coherent understanding of the antislavery narratives. Regardless of the conscious or unconscious positions taken by the proslavery and antislavery writers, the act of writing captures and records a moment of transition in a historical continuum that would inevitably lead to the emancipation of Cuban slaves. The proslavery and antislavery narratives were both written in and belong to the Cuban historical process and underscore the direction in which the slavery issue would unfold. Estévez's diary and Morilla's short story point to the abolition of slavery but also to Lino Novás Calvo's *El negrero,* a novel about the famous Spanish slave trader Pedro Blanco. Although the time of the writing and the narrative perspective are different, just as with Estévez and Páez, a recounting of his life will condemn Blanco and his actions. However, it will not be until the Cuban Revolution, specifically with Barnet's *The Autobiography of a Runaway Slave* and Leante's *Los guerrilleros negros,* that a more radical point of view will be revealed. The proslavery works described the life of the slave hunter from his perspective. Barnet and Leante will reinterpret history and uncover the life of this same slaver and of his counterpart, the fugitive slave, but this time from the runaway slave's point of view.

# TWO

# Textual Multiplications
## Juan Francisco Manzano's Autobiografía and Cirilo Villaverde's Cecilia Valdés

*Thirty Years*

*When I think on the course I have run,*
*from my childhood itself to this day*
*I tremble, and fain would I shun,*
*The remembrance its terrors array.*

*I marvel at struggles endured,*
*With a destiny frightful as mine,*
*At strength for such efforts: —assured*
*Tho' I am, 'tis in vain to repine.*
*I have known this sad life thirty years,*
*and to me, thirty years it has been*
*of suff'ring, of sorrow and tears,*
*Ev'ry day of its bondage I've seen.*

*But 'tis nothing the past—or the pains,*
*Hitherto I have struggled to bear,*
*When I think, oh, my God! on the chains,*
*that I know I'm yet destined to wear!*
    —JUAN FRANCISCO MANZANO (TRANS. RICHARD MADDEN)

*The value of the transcendental arche (archie) must make*
*its necessity felt before letting itself be erased. The concept*
*of arche-trace must comply with both that necessity and*
*that erasure. It is in fact contradictory and not acceptable*
*within the logic of identity. The trace is not only the disap-*
*pearance of origin—within the discourse that we sustain*
*and according to the path that we follow it means that the*
*origin did not even disappear, that it was never consti-*
*tuted except reciprocally by a nonorigin, the trace, which*
*thus becomes the origin of the origin. From then on, to*

*wrench the concept of the trace from the classical scheme,*
*which would derive it from a presence or from an originary*
*nontrace and which would make of it an empirical mark,*
*one must indeed speak of an originary trace or arche-trace.*
*Yet we know that the concept destroys its name and that,*
*if all begins with the trace, there is above all no originary*
*trace.*                                    —DERRIDA, OF GRAMMATOLOGY

I    When he read his poem "Thirty Years" in Domingo del
     Monte's literary salon in 1836, the slave Juan Francisco
     Manzano was a published poet. Under the protection of Del
Monte, Manzano edited the *Poesías líricas* (1821) and *Flores pasa-*
*geras* [sic] (1830). Fina García Marruz conjectures that don Nicolás
de Cárdenas y Manzano, the second son of the marquesa de Prado
Ameno, introduced Manzano to Del Monte;[1] don Nicolás had been
one of Manzano's masters and was a member of Del Monte's literary
circle. The same year Manzano read his poem, members of the Del
Monte salon, including don Nicolás, purchased his freedom.[2]

In 1835 Del Monte requested that Manzano write his autobiography.[3] However, to make it presentable to an interested public, Manzano's story was altered before it reached its readers. Anselmo Suárez y Romero corrected the slave's grammar and syntax. I believe
that it was this version which Del Monte circulated in his literary
salon and gave to the abolitionist Richard Madden to include in an
antislavery portfolio. Madden translated the autobiography and entitled it "Life of the Negro Poet." Along with some of the slave's
poems and interviews with Del Monte, as well as some of his own
poems on slavery, Madden published it as *Poems by a Slave in the*
*Island of Cuba* in England in 1840. Thus Manzano's autobiography
was available in print to the English-speaking reader shortly after it
was written. Manzano's original was lost and did not appear until
José Luciano Franco published it a century later, in 1937.[4] Recently,
Manzano's autobiography has undergone a renaissance of sorts. Since
Franco's edition, Manzano's autobiography, with his poems and the
play *Zafira*, was reedited by the Instituto Cubano del Libro in 1972.[5]
Like Suárez y Romero a century before, Ivan Schulman corrected
Manzano's grammatical mistakes contained in the Franco version
and published the slave's life under the title *Autobiografía de un es-*
*clavo* in 1975.[6] Most recently, Edward Mullen published a reedition
of Madden's English translations in 1981 which he entitled *The Life*
*and Poems of a Cuban Slave*.[7] Manzano's *Autobiografía* has also
been translated into other languages.[8] The many editions of Manzano's work are not a reproduction of the "original" but contain

enough significant changes, omissions, and distortions to be considered different texts. Together they represent multiple dimensions of Juan Francisco Manzano the slave.

From the moment Manzano wrote his autobiography, he passed from slave to author, from the black world into the white, from obscurity into history. Slave rebellions and the killing of whites represent a rejection of white values, but the process of writing is an acceptance of and a communion with Western culture and history. As author, Manzano has distanced himself from African and slave traditions and has erased his past as origin. But the act of writing has given his autobiography a degree of permanence and "veracity." What we may have considered to be an original moment in Manzano's life, a time before the act of writing, has already been mediated by Manzano's willingness to embrace Western values. Most importantly, by setting his ideas down in writing, Manzano has allowed for multiple (mis)interpretations of his text(s).

The many editions of Manzano's life can be traced to two earlier texts, the Spanish original, which the slave wrote, and the English translation. In a textual analysis of Manzano's "original," I will focus on a tension in Manzano's writings which reveals two aspects of his life which trap him between his past and his present; that is, between his common slave status and his privileged position among the members of the Del Monte group. And in a comparative reading between the "original" as published by Franco and the English as edited by Madden, I will further show that one is not a translation of the other but a rewriting of Manzano's autobiography. Just as *El negro Francisco* is a rewriting of *Francisco,* there are sufficient differences between the English and the Spanish to read them as two distinct works.

Manzano's *Autobiografía* is the only slave account written in nineteenth-century Spanish America. It represents a broad picture of slavery, from Manzano's childhood to his final escape to Havana. Unlike the other antislavery works written by members of Del Monte's literary circle, Manzano's autobiography offers an insider's perspective into slavery insofar as he describes slavery from his own slave condition. Because of his slave status, Manzano's *Autobiografía* is written with great pains. Cintio Vitier says that the grammatical "errors are not really mistakes but appear in the text like the scars on his body."[9] Manzano's attempt to write his autobiography and the impossibility of doing so in standard Spanish uncover an internal struggle between the slave he was and the educated writer he became.

Writing, as Manzano knew it, was not a common practice among slaves. Neither was it legal for slaves to publish. Manzano learned to read and write on his own. According to his autobiography, the slave stayed up late at night and copied the writings his master discarded. Manzano's painful attempt to express his thoughts on paper implied that by imitating his master and other whites he could better himself. Accepting a white value-structure represented a conflict for Manzano. For him slave status implied an inferiority he could not accept; poetry and writing became ways of transgressing the boundaries of slavery. Manzano's transition from slavery to freedom, from one culture to another, places him in the "middest," between history and disappearance, between writing and silence, that is, between Genesis and the Apocalypse.[10]

Manzano's daring task of bridging through writing the cultural and historical gap between the life of whites and of blacks allows him to reveal the sufferings of an urban slave who was threatened with being sent to the Molino, a sugar mill in the province of Camagüey, to modify, control, and punish his behavior. Some accounts are shocking and vividly describe this human drama. Like the other antislavery narratives, Manzano's life is a testament of the cruelties of the slavery system. In one incident, Manzano was mistakenly accused of stealing a capon. To avoid further punishment, he had to admit to an act he did not commit. As Manzano was forced to run, two dogs attacked him, injuring him seriously:

> One taking hold of the left side of my face pierced it through, and the other lacerated my left thigh and leg in a shocking manner, which wounds are open yet, notwithstanding it happened twenty-four years ago. The mayoral alighted on the moment, and separated me from their grasps, but my blood flowed profusely, particularly from my leg—he then pulled me by the rope, making use at the same time, of the most disgusting language; this pull partly dislocated my right arm, which at times pains me yet. . . . the mayoral and six negroes surrounded me, and at the word "upon him," they threw me down; two of them held my hands, two my legs, and the other sat upon my back. They then asked me about the missing capon, and I did not know what to say. Twenty-five lashes were laid on me, they then asked me again to tell the truth. I was perplexed; at last, thinking to escape further punishment, I said, "I stole it."[11]

In practice, the slave had no rights. Manzano narrates other accounts which were in complete violation of slavery laws and in-

tended to persuade the reader into assuming an antislavery position.
In an effort to free her son from the yoke of slavery, Manzano's
mother paid to buy his freedom. The marquesa de Prado Ameno,
Manzano's worst mistress, kept both the slave and the money. Madden recreates Manzano's words in the following manner:

> I met my mother one day, who said to me, "Juan, I have got the money
> to purchase your liberty; as your father is dead, you must act as a fa-
> ther to your brothers; they shall not chastise you any more." My only
> answer was a flood of tears; she went away and I to my business; but
> the result of my mother's visit was disappointment; the money was
> not paid [the original states: "My mother's money was taken from
> her"], and I daily expected the time of my liberty, but that time was
> not destined for many a long year to come. (89)[12]

Madden, in a note, explains to his British readers that "the slaves,
(namely those in the Spanish colonies) are generally appraised at
four hundred dollars; that a slave paying down the fourth part of his
value, or one hundred dollars, immediately acquires a right to be a
coartado—that is, that he can work out, paying his master three rea-
les de vellon or bits a-day, until he can make a further deposit" (206).

Scenes such as the ones described, although present throughout
the autobiography and informing the reader of the evils of slavery,
are offset by others which contradict the indictment of slavery. Contrary to Del Monte's determination to have Manzano denounce slavery, the autobiography also reveals a strong urge to narrate happy
moments under the same oppressive system. From the outset we are
told that while in the custody of his first mistress, sra. Beatriz de
Justis, Manzano and his family were privileged slaves. Manzano, who
was more in the arms of his mistress than in those of his mother, became "'the child of her old age'" (80). Manzano tells us that "after
some time I was taken to the house of Donna Joaquina, who treated
me like a white child, saw that I was properly clothed, and even
combed my hair herself; and as in the time of the Marquesa de J., she
allowed me not to play with the other negro children at church" (83).
Manzano continues to distance himself from other blacks when he
informs us that, being a mulatto, he was forbidden by his father to
play with the darker slaves (68).

From Manzano's dual or middle perspective, the autobiography
gives us a complete picture of slavery; just as there were bad masters,
there were also good ones. For example, sra. Beatriz treated her female
slaves as if they were her own daughters the day they were married

and, in some cases, she set them free. Her benevolence was also shown when she granted Manzano's soon-to-be-born twin brother and sister their freedom.

Narrating both the good and bad moments under slavery confirms Manzano's honesty and illustrates the conflict in the autobiography. Manzano is psychologically torn between the privileges he received under one master and the punishment of the other. The ex-slave's life can be divided into three parts, which his good and bad masters represented: As a child Manzano was raised by sra. Beatriz, who treated him like any ordinary (white) child. After her death, he passed on to sra. de Prado Ameno, who often punished him like a slave. Then he was transferred to don Nicolás and his wife, who treated him like his first master. Finally, he returned to the sra. de Prado Ameno, from whom he later escaped. Going back and forth between good and evil masters illustrates the psychological trauma of the writer, who lived both sides of the slavery issue and could never come to terms with his slave status. Under the kind masters, Manzano experienced a freedom of sorts; under the marquesa de Prado Ameno, he lived the cruelty of slavery.

The contradictions between good and bad masters in the autobiography may be due to Manzano's awareness of the act of writing. When he wrote his autobiography, Manzano was a well-known figure. By 1837, he had published widely in magazines such as *El Album*, *El Aguinaldo Habanero*, and *La Moda o Recreo de las Damas*.[13] Roberto Friol states that Madden's attempt to conceal Manzano's identity was useless. The authorities knew that at the time Manzano was the only ex-slave poet in Cuba.[14] Moreover, Manzano was known to members of the Del Monte group. Although Manzano's autobiography would not be published in Cuba until the twentieth century, Suárez y Romero's version of the manuscript circulated among the members of the group. Other antislavery works, such as Suárez y Romero's *Francisco*, were read by Del Monte, Félix Tanco y Bosmeniel, José Zacarías González del Valle, Richard Madden, and Ramón de Palma, among others.[15]

Manzano was indeed aware of the past of the narration and the present time of the writing. Throughout the autobiography, Manzano points to the current status of whites and identifies them to the reader. For example, the srta. doña Beatriz de Cárdenas is Sister Purita in the convent of the Ursulin nuns (467); sr. don Manuel Oreylli (*sic*) is count of Buena Vista (34); and Master Pancho is sr. don Francisco de Cárdenas y Manzano (55).

The slave author was concerned about reader response. He wanted to give an accurate portrayal of his life and slavery. However, he also wanted to protect himself from whites antagonistic to his cause. Manzano may have feared that his masters would learn about the manuscript and take some form of action against him. The second part of the autobiography was lost by Ramón de Palma and fell into the hands of the slave's ex-master. The fear of reprisal explains why Manzano, in spite of his punishment under the marquesa de Prado Ameno, chose to talk favorably about her, saying that he loved her as a mother (66). It may also explain the silent moments in the text in which the slave wants to tell the reader about the horrors of slavery but skips them and limits himself to what he calls most "essential" accounts. Manzano is cautious about revealing his painful past; he is well aware of his slave condition and that the marquesa de Prado Ameno is still alive. In a letter to Del Monte dated June 25, 1835, Manzano writes: "Remember, Sir, when you read this letter, that I am a slave, and that a slave is nothing in the eyes of his master. Don't lose sight of what I have achieved. Consider me a martyr and you will find that the numerous whippings which mutilated my still undeveloped body will never make me think badly of you and trusting in you, I dare to speak about what has happened to me even though the person responsible for my suffering is still alive." [16]

In some respects, Manzano's autobiography is a justification of his innocence before the marquesa de Prado Ameno and the reader. She is the only mistress who punishes him. As her slave, Manzano is accused of wrongdoing, which he denies. But Manzano's autobiography vindicates him. In spite of the accusations, Manzano, on two separate occasions, convinces the administrator, Saturnino, of his innocence. According to Manzano, he was going to be punished for defending his mother's name (60) and selling a bracelet and paying for masses for his mother without his mistress's permission (64). In a separate incident, Manzano persuades another *mayoral* not to punish him because he was unaware of not having permission to visit his mother (47–48). In all cases, Manzano's story was so convincing that the two *mayorales* disobeyed the marquesa de Prado Ameno's orders to punish him. As Manzano narrates his story to the overseers, he also successfully reaches his audience. At the time of Manzano's writing, María de la Concepción Manzano, marquesa de Prado Ameno, was alive. She died on February 26, 1853, and was buried in Havana. [17]

In spite of his trust in Del Monte, Manzano nevertheless expressed difficulty in narrating the cruelties of slavery. Fear may not have been the only reason. Manzano, aware of the permanence of writing, used the opportunity to describe his importance as a slave writer. In a letter dated December 11, 1834, Manzano thanks Del Monte for making an effort to publish his poems in Europe.[18] In another letter dated September 29, 1835, Manzano knows that his work is on exhibition: "By accident I saw Dr. don Dionisio. I spoke to him about the matter and he told me not to worry, that he would not forget me because he was interested in proving to some in Europe that he was correct, that a house servant, a poet, recited poems by heart. Some doubted that it was done by someone without an education."[19] Aware that he was on display, Manzano used the occasion to write about slavery and also about his privileged position as a slave who, unlike many others, learned to read and write on his own and had many literary accomplishments.

From this other perspective, the silent moments to which we alluded acquire a different interpretation. Let us consider more closely Manzano's hesitation to narrate the evils of slavery. On two separate occasions, Manzano states that he will limit his descriptions of painful acts to important events. In the original, Manzano says: "Skipping many periods, I leave behind a multitude of painful events. I will limit myself to the most essential as examples of many other sad vicissitudes" (Franco, 49; Madden, 95).[20] A few pages later, Manzano repeats the same idea: "But let us skip from 1810, 1811 and 1812 up to 1835, the present, leaving in the interim, a vast field of vicissitudes, choosing from it the gravest blow with which fortune forced me from the paternal or native house to experience the many pits which awaited me to devour my inexpert and weak body" (Franco, 51; Madden, 96). A reading of Manzano's autobiography and his correspondence with Del Monte provides answers to our concerns. There is a close relationship between the text and the slave poet's letters to Del Monte; the text narrates events mentioned in them. In the September 29 letter to Del Monte, Manzano clarifies the silent moments in the text:

> At once I saw in it [your letter] what you ask, I have prepared myself to tell a part of the history of my life, reserving the most interesting events in the event some day I find myself sitting in a corner of my country, calm, my luck and subsistence secured, to write a novel typically Cuban: For the moment, it is not convenient to give this matter all of the marvelous development of diverse events and scenes, because it would require a volume; in spite of this, you would not lack material. Tomorrow I will start to set aside at night some hours for this result.[21]

Although Manzano describes cruelties under slavery, he is not comfortable about revealing some acts which he feels will put him, as a slave, in some form of danger. He is only willing to do so after he gains his freedom.[22]

But if we continue to read Manzano's autobiography and letters together, more information about the act of writing is revealed. Although some critics claim that Del Monte controlled the autobiography from above,[23] perhaps the opposite should be considered. A comparative reading between the autobiography and other letters suggests that the patrician may have been responsible for encouraging Manzano to stress the unhappy moments under slavery. In the already mentioned June 25 letter, Manzano responds to what may have been an inquiry by Del Monte to write his autobiography: "I expect to finish soon, limiting myself only to the most interesting accounts."[24] The same sentence in the letter is repeated twice in the text when Manzano recalls a need to stress the most painful parts of his life. In essence, Manzano, as narrator of his autobiography, is responding to Del Monte's request that the slave write about his condition under slavery. Moreover, in the same letter, Manzano underscores his trust in Del Monte, putting the burden of the slave's safety on his patron. And only after these textual inquiries does Manzano highlight his slave condition.

Manzano writes the *Autobiografía* to satisfy Del Monte's request and narrates his sufferings under slavery. But the slave also uses the manuscript to influence his readers and prove his innocence against all accusations by his masters. Anyone reading the manuscript, whether a member of the Del Monte group or a government official, could understand how a good slave who loved and was loved by his masters had no other alternative but to escape from the cruel marquesa de Prado Ameno. As I have mentioned, it was she who kept the money Manzano's mother had gathered to buy her son's freedom, thus, in effect, violating the law. She not only denied him a freedom which was paid for but punished him severely. In the previously mentioned June 25 letter, Manzano tells Del Monte that his mistress forced him to flee in order to end his sufferings.[25] This information is also present in the words of the free servant who encouraged Manzano to escape: " 'My friend, if you suffer it is your fault; you are treated worse than the meanest slave; make your escape, and present yourself before the Captain-General at Havana, state your ill treatment to him, and he will do you justice'" (105). We can assume that Manzano followed the advice of the free servant and fled to Havana. As daring as it may have appeared, Manzano's escape was not illegal but in accordance with slavery laws. The words of the friend recall still another text. The royal decree of December 23, 1789, imposed fines on masters who abused their slaves. Section 10 of the decree states that excessive punishment would result in the confiscation of the slave.[26] In certain cases, it was permissible for the slave to escape and seek protection from an authority figure. Fiction parallels history. In the ending of *El negro Francisco*, both Francisco and Camila were going to flee from their present master and seek the help of Delmonte. Although the fictional Francisco did not carry out the plan, Manzano did and was helped not by the captain general, as the autobiography suggests, but by Del Monte and members of the literary circle. Manzano intentionally manipulates his autobiography to justify his escape from the marquesa de Prado Ameno to her, the reader, and colonial authorities and absolve him from any wrongdoing and punishment.

Further research into Manzano's life reveals information not included in his *Autobiografía* but which may have been incorporated into Part Two. Calcagno refers to the second part in a note at the end of the first manuscript. "At the bottom of the manuscript there is a note which states as follows: 'The second part was never written.' Nevertheless, we know that it was written and that Suárez y Romero gave it to the poet Ramón de Palma to copy and correct the grammar and was lost in his possession."[27] After his escape, sometime between 1814 and 1817, Manzano was employed by different masters, including don Tello de Mantilla, who was kind to him. He was given permission to earn a living as a carpenter and confectioner and was married twice. His first wife was Marcelina Campos, who died while married to the slave poet. Friol suspects that she was Lesbia in some poems.[28] In 1835 Manzano married again. His second wife was the free mulatto María del Rosario, whom he referred to as Delia in other poems. In 1835 he became doña María de la Luz de Zayas's slave. That same year he joined the Del Monte group. Finally, he received his liberty in 1836. Although Del Monte was instrumental in the effort to free the slave, many contributed to the price of Manzano's freedom.[29] In a letter dated July 23, 1836, to Del Monte, José Miguel Angulo y Heredia explains Manzano's freedom:

> With regard to Manzano, finally we gathered the 800 pesos and Pepe de la Luz and I went in person to give the ransom money to doña María de Zayas. She flew off the handle for the outrageous ingratitude of that slave *dog* and considered it an insolence that she be deprived of a servant of such quality after he had cost her so much trouble to acquire and train. He immediately left the house, has opened a sweet shop, and everything is going perfectly well for him since his candy is in

style. I communicate this to you because I know it will bring you
great satisfaction for the good deed of liberating him to which you so
generously contributed.[30]

In 1837 Richard Madden arrived in Cuba. The following year he
met Manzano and a few years later translated and published the free
slave's poems and life story in England. In 1842, Manzano published
his first and only play, *Zafira*, a five-act tragedy. Four years after
Madden translated and published Manzano's works, José de la Concepción Valdés, Plácido, who was identified as the leader of the Ladder Conspiracy of 1844, falsely accused Manzano and Del Monte of
participating in the uprising.[31] According to García Marruz, Manzano had been mistaken for a Manuel Manzano who was also a black
poet and carpenter from Matanzas.[32] The conspiracy was also an attempt to do away with the growing and prosperous free black population and groups antagonistic to the slavery cause. Events leading to
the conspiracy also forced Del Monte to disband his literary circle
and flee the island. Manzano was acquitted—he served a one-year
jail term and was released in 1845. Plácido confessed to the alleged
conspiracy and was put to death. After this dramatic event, which
sent shock waves through the free black and slave communities,
Manzano never wrote again and retired from public life. Manzano
died in 1853.[33]

Let us look at the different versions of Manzano's autobiography.
We know that there is an original manuscript, which is full of grammatical errors, and another which circulated among the members of
the Del Monte group. In a letter to his friend Vidal Morales y Morales dated April 7, 1859, which accompanied the Manzano manuscript, Suárez y Romero confesses to correcting grammatical mistakes: "I declare solemnly that when I corrected Manzano's originals,
I hardly did anything else but to amend grammatical mistakes, without altering words and constructions used by the author. And I now
confess that if this copy was more polished, it would result in pages
more worthy of the image, without losing the candor and truth with
which they were written."[34]

Comments and corrections by members of the Del Monte circle
were not uncommon and occurred in the works of other writers of
the time. In fact, these early works were written by more than one
individual. For example, Suárez y Romero, who corrected Manzano's
manuscript, had his own novel edited by his friend González del
Valle, who made suggestions regarding style and even suppressed
parts of it.[35]

There are at least two Manzano manuscripts in Spanish, the one Franco published in 1937, containing numerous grammatical mistakes, and the one corrected by Suárez y Romero. However, it is now possible to verify which copy of the autobiography Del Monte gave to Madden; that is, the one corrected by Suárez y Romero or the one written by Manzano himself. I support Schulman's contention that it is the Suárez y Romero version. But if the various editions are copies of the original, a simultaneous reading of the Spanish and English manuscripts reveals serious discrepancies between the two. Although Madden's "Life of the Negro Poet" is a translation of Manzano's autobiography, there are significant differences between the two which shed light on the translation and the time of its publication.

In comparing the Spanish version with the English edition, one notices that grammatical mistakes present in the original are absent in the translation. The translation is written in standard, not broken, English. This change may be attributed to Suárez y Romero's version or to Madden, who copied and perhaps corrected the autobiography. The Manzano scars which Cintio Vitier observed when reading the original have been healed in Madden's version. Other changes in the translation conform to the logic of the English language; for example, sentences are not continuous but shorter. Still other changes cannot be totally explained by the nature of English and can be considered errors in the translation.

A comparison between the original and the translation will uncover the following minor discrepancies. "Famosa asienda" (*sic*; famous or well-known hacienda) is translated as "beautiful estate"; "don Jaime Florid" appears as "don Jaime Florido"; the "conde de Jibacoa" appears as both the "count of J." and as the "count of G."; and "*décima*" (an eight-syllable, ten-line metric) in some cases is translated as "sonnet." These minor discrepancies point to others which are more serious in nature. Continuing this comparison, we notice omissions in the translation; some are stylistic, but others are not. Other sections have been transposed and do not follow the sequence found in the original.

As I have noted, the translation contains omissions. For example, at the outset of Manzano's life, Madden writes: ". . . [She] carried them to town, where she gave them instruction conformable to their new condition. Her house was always filled with these young slaves instructed in everything necessary" (Madden, 80). The original reads as follows: ". . . no asiendose de este modo notable *la falta de tres o cuatro qe. no estubiesen aptas pr. sus años dolensias o livertad y.* . . ." (Franco, 33, my emphasis). The English omits the phrase "three or four were absent because of their age or freedom." The absence of certain words and the transposition of the sentence structure in the translation have altered the meaning of the original. A significant omission is made when, after punishing Manzano, his mistress, the marquesa de Prado Ameno, decides to treat him better. The English omits Manzano's defense of his mistress, whom, in spite of her punishment, he loved very much (103). In the original, he states: "And I loved her like a mother. I didn't like to hear the servants ridiculing her if it wasn't evident to me that the one who told her the story was the one who offended her. One told a story where she couldn't hear it and the one who told it used this method to bother her. This was a maxim I heard her repeat many times" (Franco, 66; Madden, 103). Manzano's kindness toward his mistress has been deleted from Madden's translation.

In another incident towards the end of the autobiography, Manzano is threatened with the Molino for dropping a water barrel. The English edition stops and the Spanish continues: "I saw myself without parents in the Molino, not even a relative. In other words, mulatto among blacks. My father was proud and never allowed gossipers in his house, nor for his children to play with the darkies of the estate. My mother lived with him and his children, for this reason we were not very much loved" (Franco, 68; Madden, 106). Manzano's dissociation from other black slaves has been suppressed in the English edition.

Moreover, the original reveals the identity of the servant who advised Manzano to flee. He was not an ordinary servant, as the translation suggests, but a friend of the Manzano family. The Spanish reads: "He was always like that, good friends with my father and treated my mother with respect, even after she was widowed" (Franco, 69; Madden, 105).

These and other omissions change, however slightly, the character of the autobiography. They eliminate many of the contradictions in the original manuscript which Manzano experienced while trapped between the slave and white worlds. The translation, therefore, heightens the drama of the slave's sufferings. These changes may be explained as editorial to bring consistency to the writing. However, they are consistent with Madden's abolitionist ideology. Madden, who had joined the British abolitionist movement, was a member of the Anti-Slavery Society.[36] The transposition and omission of important sections in "Life of the Negro Poet" can be attributed to Madden's attempt to make the slave narration stronger than the original and more appealing to its militant British public. The shift of sentences and paragraphs is a conscious effort to (re)organize Manzano's writing with the intention of controlling and reshaping his life; that is, changing Manzano's perception of his life or the perception he wanted others to have of himself. A comparative reading between Manzano's original and Madden's translation confirms our observations and uncovers other changes in the translation.

With some omissions, stylistic changes and errors in the English, both original and translation, narrate the same events, including a late return to the Molino. When hanging on the back of the carriage, the sleepy Manzano dropped a lantern. For this carelessness, Manzano is punished by the overseer. After this unfortunate mishap, the Spanish and the English versions differ: The original narrates a lost coin which the marquesa de Prado Ameno accuses Manzano of stealing. Manzano claims that the coin was given to him by his master, don Nicolás, who is unable to recognize it as his. If this unfortunate event can be misconstrued as a possible Manzano lie, the translation clearly heightens the unjust punishment of a slave. It narrates not the coin incident but the more brutal punishment Manzano receives for having taken a geranium plant leaf.

Toward the end of the original *Autobiografía*, Manzano informs his readers that he is going to select the most serious events. He then proceeds to describe the following incidents: the geranium plant (Franco, 51; Madden, 88), the alleged stealing of the capon (Franco, 53–54; Madden, 89–90), and the falling roof, which misses Manzano but kills his fellow slave Andrés (Franco, 55; Madden, 91). However, in the English translation, these events are taken out of place, transposed, and made to follow an earlier incident when the sleepy Manzano is punished for dropping the lantern while riding on the back of the *quitrín* (Franco, 44; Madden, 87).

Following the three above-mentioned incidents, the English and the Spanish continue with the transfer of Manzano into the service of his master Pancho. In the original, Manzano informs us that he was treated like a son and he loved his master very dearly, an important detail absent in the English. But before the English version narrates Manzano's good fortune under this master, it continues to describe another sequence of unfortunate events which, in the original, followed the lantern occurrence. They are the possession of a coin which master Nicolás denies ever giving Manzano (Franco, 45; Madden, 92); a visit to see his mother without permission (Franco, 47; Madden, 93); and the alleged stealing of a peseta which had gotten stuck between the crack of a table (Franco, 48; Madden, 94). The English version continues in the order in which it appears in the original, narrating the mistress's accusations that Manzano was worse than Voltaire and Rousseau (Franco, 48; Madden, 95) and Manzano's transfer to Estorino's house, where he assisted him as a painter.

The omissions and transposition of events eliminate for the English reader the many conflicts in Manzano's life present in the original, thus providing a clearer understanding of Manzano's sufferings. The Spanish version also presents moments of distress, but they are offset by intercalating positive incidents, thus diminishing the intensity of the slave's pain and punishment. This is particularly evident when Manzano is transferred to Estorino's house, an event in the Spanish which appears between the two sets of events previously described; that is, between the lost peseta and the taking of the geranium leaf. However, in the English, the transfer to help Estorino is placed strategically toward the end of "Life of the Negro Poet," which is followed by his stay with don Nicolás; in the original it follows the capon incident. By the time the English reader arrives at the Estorino and don Nicolás passages, he is so disturbed by Manzano's ill fortune that he may even view the slave's stay with him as a welcome relief. In the translation, not until these last events does Manzano contemplate his escape. Manzano's life elicits a strong reaction from the Spanish reader. For example, Calcagno views Manzano's transfer to the service of don Nicolás as a relief of sorts: "These few days of happiness are no more than an oasis in the extensive desert of his existence."[37] As a reader of the Spanish, Calcagno was deeply moved by Manzano's fate and would have reacted in a similar manner to his stay with Estorino and don Nicolás. For a reader of the translation, the intensity of Manzano's sufferings and the Estorino event at the end make his experience more dramatic, Manzano's pain more intense, and his salvation more urgent.

Madden suppressed the temporal dimension of "Life of the Negro Poet," allowing him to reorganize the autobiography without being accountable to history. Although Manzano does his best to document events by providing dates, the translation omits many of them and time, as a concept, becomes more general and less significant. For example, toward the end of the autobiography we find the following temporal discrepancies. In the original, Manzano is sent to the Molino for the third time. After eight or ten days, his mistress comes for him (Franco, 64). In the English edition, she arrives after ten days (Madden, 102). This discrepancy is followed by a section missing in the English which mentions that don Saturnino was about twenty-five to twenty-eight years old (Franco, 64). Shortly after, Manzano informs us that his mistress could not be without him for more than ten days and, for this reason, his stay at the Molino was never more than eleven to twelve days (Franco, 65). The translation cites the same events, but instead of ten days it mentions "a length of time" and the eleven to twelve days become "nine or ten days." Moreover, the marquesa de Prado Ameno comes for him on Monday at eleven o'clock (Franco, 68); the translation does not cite the day of the week but just the time (Madden, 105). Finally, it was at five P.M. when the servant told him to take out the horse from the stable (Franco, 69); the translation records no time (Madden, 105). In other examples, the translation leaves out dates, making it difficult to recreate the slave's historical background which is made possible in the original. Exclusion of some elements of time in the English eliminates contradictions present in the chronology of the original. It also allows the reader to focus exclusively on Manzano's punishments.

What may have been minor stylistic corrections or honest transcription and translation mistakes become significant when comparing the two autobiographies. If read alone, the English edition is a convincing denunciation which, unlike the original, does not convey the uncertainty in Manzano's thoughts when, for example, he forgets specific dates. This may appear to be contradictory when we learn that Manzano had an excellent memory for poetry but apparently not for dates. The generality of time gives the reader a less specific understanding of Manzano's ideas and contradictions. In so doing, the English version acquires a literary quality at the expense of revealing the psychological dimension present in the Spanish. But when comparing the two, it is not the Spanish original but the English translation which makes the strongest denunciation against the Cuban slavery system.

Madden, considered by the captain general to be a dangerous abolitionist,[38] may himself have been responsible for changes in the translation. During his stay in Havana, Madden even clashed with Cuban authorities.[39] Madden had plans to denounce slavery on the island. He intended to present Manzano's *Autobiografía* and Suárez y Romero's *Francisco* to the London Anti-Slavery Society. After his return to England, Madden read his findings before the General Anti-Slavery Convention. The paper was to have been published in the conference proceedings, translated into Spanish, and disseminated throughout the Spanish colonies.[40] Perhaps Madden decided not to translate and publish Suárez y Romero's romantic novel, which was less suitable for his antislavery cause. Nevertheless, literature was an abolitionist weapon. The convention adopted the following resolution: "That while the literature of Great Britain exercises so vast an influence over the public opinion of America, we deem it the duty of British abolitionists . . . through . . . leading religious, political, and literary periodicals . . . to spread before the American public evidence of the deep indignation of the civilized world against a slave-holding republic."[41]

By translating and publishing Manzano's work, Madden aided the antislavery cause and made a statement about his position. He also united his voice with the voices of Manzano and many others who shared his position. In his preface to *Poems by a Slave in the Island of Cuba*, Madden makes his intent clear: "I am sensible I have not done justice to these Poems, but I trust I have done enough to vindicate in some degree the character of negro intellect, at least the attempt affords me an opportunity of recording my conviction, that the blessings of education and good government are only wanting to make the natives of Africa, intellectually and morally, equal to the people of any nation on the surface of the globe."[42] As we have seen, Madden was directly involved in the rewriting of Manzano's autobiography. He also interjected his ideas by including in *Poems by a Slave in the Island of Cuba* his own poems, entitled "The Slave-Trade Merchant" and "The Sugar Estate," which, according to Madden, "give a short but faithful sketch of the Cuban slave-trade merchant and planter in verse."[43]

Madden's participation as editor, translator, and poet already prefigures the changes he would make in Manzano's life. Many abolitionists like Madden had a long-standing interest in stopping the slave trade and abolishing slavery in Cuba. A staunch supporter of the abolitionist movement, Madden eliminated contradictions in the manuscript and rearranged events to make Manzano's case clearer to coincide not with Manzano's reality but with his own abolitionist ideas. Madden misplaced Manzano the person and created Manzano the character to make the translation the strongest antislavery document possible.

Suárez y Romero's grammatical corrections of Manzano's *Autobiografía* and Madden's translation of "Life of the Negro Poet" can now be better understood as supplements of Manzano's life. However, these traces have taken on a significance of their own and for each reader, whether British or Cuban, they have come to represent Manzano himself. This affirmation is valid, especially since both Madden and Suárez y Romero have also participated in writing Manzano's autobiography. However, they are not the only ones; there are others who have also intervened in Manzano's text. For example, in his preface Madden complicates things further when he states that his literal translations had been revised by a Spaniard.[44] In a recent edition of Manzano's autobiography, Schulman also participates in the act of writing. Like Suárez y Romero, Schulman corrects the original manuscript of all the misspellings and run-on sentences and divides it into paragraphs, thus giving coherence to Manzano's ideas. A comparative reading between Schulman's and Franco's editions will show that the contemporary editor of Manzano's autobiography also made substantive changes in the manuscript.

The various interventions in Manzano's autobiography do not allow us to read the "original" manuscript but one which other readers of the autobiography have rewritten. As we have seen, Manzano's autobiography is not one but many texts, depending on which version we read. This is even true of the "original" Franco found, which many believe to be the one Manzano wrote. In his *Suite para Juan Francisco Manzano*, Friol reveals that Manzano's *Autobiografía*, as published by Franco, is not the same as the one contained in the Biblioteca Nacional José Martí. Franco himself made certain changes and omissions when transcribing the original and, like the other editors, in an attempt to make the autobiography more legible, he altered the manuscript and thereby Manzano's life as reproduced in the autobiography. Friol, who consulted the original manuscript at the Biblioteca Nacional José Martí, found some discrepancies which include deliberate changes in the 1937 "original" and in the 1972 copy.[45]

Suárez y Romero, Madden, Schulman, and Franco in their own way have attempted to rewrite Manzano's autobiography and turn Manzano into not the person he was but the person each editor thought he should have been. To a certain extent, there is a spiritual transference from Manzano to Suárez y Romero, to Madden, to Franco, and, most recently, to Schulman, who writes the autobiography Manzano himself would like to have written. The editors, as surely as slave masters, continue to mold and control Manzano's life.

The tensions felt by Manzano, who was caught between two worlds, and their transference into the writing of the *Autobiografía* have been increased by the number of texts produced, each distinct from the other. Like Del Monte, who wanted to help Manzano gain his freedom, Franco, Suárez y Romero, Schulman, Calcagno, and Madden in their own way assisted Manzano with his manuscript. But in so doing they have also altered it. Each has written (or rewritten) Manzano's life to respond to a different time and a different reader. For just as Manzano had many masters while in slavery, in his passage into history the multiple editions continue to dominate and subjugate Manzano's writing. Just as there is no original unsupplemented nature for Derrida, Manzano the slave has disappeared and has been transformed into the different versions of his autobiography.[46] Manzano, a slave once subject to the powers of his masters, is now the victim of the strategies of writing and reading.

| II | Juan Francisco Manzano the person disappeared, but the act of writing generated other editions of his autobiography with significant variations, enough to consider them different texts. These other versions have obtained a reality of their own as Manzano's "original" text. Each editor has joined Manzano in writing the autobiography to offer another version of the slave's life. Therefore, as text, Manzano's life has taken on many forms.

Cirilo Villaverde's *Cecilia Valdés* is also a product of multiple texts. Villaverde, who was a member of Del Monte's literary circle and had met Manzano, also wrote an antislavery novel. If Manzano's autobiography was written in Cuba and published in England, Villaverde's novel was also started in Cuba in Del Monte's literary salon and concluded in New York many years later. Like Manzano's "multiple" texts, Villaverde's *Cecilia Valdés* was published three times; first as a two-part short story in *La Siempreviva*[47] and a first version of the novel in 1839.[48] But the definitive work, as we know it, was not completed until 1879 in New York.[49] Unlike Manzano's work, the early versions of *Cecilia Valdés* were preparations in a writing process which would culminate in the final edition of the novel. Villaverde wrote his most important work in stages and only in its final form does it take on antislavery characteristics: The short story and the first volume of *Cecilia Valdés* describe aspects of nineteenth-century Cuban society, but the definitive version of *Cecilia Valdés* offers a complete picture of Cuban slave society.

*Cecilia Valdés* is the most important novel written in nineteenth-century Cuba and perhaps one of the most significant works published in Latin America during the same period. Elías Entralgo states: "*Cecilia Valdés* is our most representative literary myth. For Cuban literature, it is the equivalent of what the *Quijote* is for the Spanish, *Hamlet* for the English or *Faust* for the German literatures."[50]

In a comparative reading, I will analyze the three versions of Villaverde's *Cecilia Valdés* and show that even though the short story and the first volume have the same title, the first two publications differ from the last one. In spite of the similarity in characters and theme, only the 1882 version contains antislavery sentiments. Some critics believe that the definitive version of the novel was a continuation of the first volume, which they also considered antislavery.[51] If this were the case, Villaverde's short story and novel would have been the only antislavery narratives published in Cuba during the time of the writing, a highly unlikely case, since all works had to be cleared by three censors.[52] All the early antislavery works were published abroad: Manzano's "Life of the Negro Poet" in England in 1840; Gertrudis Gómez de Avellaneda's *Sab* in Madrid in 1841; Antonio Zambrana's *El negro Francisco* in Santiago de Chile in 1873; and Villaverde's *Cecilia Valdés* in New York.

Villaverde's life and literary production can be divided into two stages: the first, his formative years in Cuba, during which he published the short story and the novel; the second, his political involvement in Cuba and exile to the United States, where he completed the definitive version of *Cecilia Valdés*. By writing his early works, Villaverde was already researching his *Cecilia Valdés*. A review of his life and works provides an understanding of the concerns present in his last and most important work.

Like many Cuban writers of the nineteenth century, Villaverde was an intellectual who pursued many interests; he was a novelist, a journalist, and a political activist. Born on October 28, 1812, in the jurisdiction of San Diego de Núñez, in the region of Vuelta Abajo, Pinar del Río, Villaverde was the sixth of ten children of don Lucas Villaverde y Morejón and doña Dolores de la Paz y Tagle. Of modest economic means, the Villaverde family lived on a sugar plantation, where the father worked as a doctor. The plantation contained more than three hundred slaves, exposing the young Villaverde to the evils of the slavery system; he would recall his early experiences on the sugar plantation in writing the definitive version of *Cecilia Valdés*. Of these early years, Julio C. Sánchez writes:

> His mischief and trips allowed him to see the wicked atrocities of the overseer, the inhuman, cruel, and endless work of blacks, and distrust between naiveté and malice which developed in the slave's soul. He freely penetrated the superstitions, beliefs, atavism, fantasies, and legends which were the vital strength in the recently imported African primitivism, in the mysterious background, devotions, and miracles so pleasing to the uneducated taste and feared by the white farmer. He possessed a source of information which revealed the popular Cuban soul and much of the slave's resentment. He had direct dealings with events and fraud so varied and surprising like the ones that can be reproduced and are produced within the context of the human and primitive residents of the countryside and the blacks of the barracoons. These experiences will always be present in his novels.[53]

At the age of seven, Villaverde began his education, attending the classes offered by a priest of the church of San Diego; however, they

were soon interrupted when the teacher died. At eleven he traveled
to Havana, where he stayed with his father's widowed aunt and attended Antonio Vázquez's school. Villaverde later studied Latin with
his maternal grandfather, a storyteller of sorts who influenced Villaverde's later writings. In the introduction to *El penitente* (published in serial form in 1844 and in book form in 1889), Villaverde
highlights the importance of this colorful figure; the grandfather
converses with the author and even has the last word in the closing
moments of the novel.[54]

Villaverde returned to formal education by attending Father Morales's school and later studying philosophy at the Seminario de San
Carlos, where he obtained a law degree in 1834. The Seminario was
the center of cultural progress, breaking with scholasticism and instructing its students in art, science, research, and politics.[55] Drawing from his experiences, Villaverde mentions the Seminario in
*Cecilia Valdés*, and the character Leonardo Gamboa attends the
Seminario in the same year Villaverde did. At the Seminario, Villaverde befriended José Antonio Saco and other future Cuban no-
tables. Simultaneously he studied drawing at the Convento de San
Agustín. After briefly practicing law, Villaverde abandoned the profession because of corrupt lawyers and judges.[56]

Villaverde's disenchantment with the law profession and his
change of fields were important for his livelihood and his development as a writer. He taught at the Colegio Real Cubano and the Colegio Buenavista in Havana and then at La Empresa in Matanzas. He
pursued his interest in literature and published his first four short
novels, *El ave muerta*, *La peña blanca*, *El perjurio*, and *La cueva de
Taganana*, in the newspaper *Miscelanea de Util y Agradable Recreo* in 1837. *El ave muerta* narrates an incestuous relationship
between the protagonists, who do not know that they are brother and
sister,[57] a theme repeated in *La peña blanca* but, more importantly,
in the definitive version of *Cecilia Valdés*.

These early works are not without flaws. The novelist Ramón de
Palma has suggested that Villaverde's characters are not realistic and
some of their behaviors are never explained. For example, in *La
cueva de Taganana*, Fernando enters and leaves Paulina's room for
no apparent reason and his crimes and evil character remain a mystery to the reader.[58] However, Palma also recognized in those early
works the excellent qualities seen later in *Dos amores*, published in
serial form in 1843 and in book form in 1858, and *Cecilia Valdés*.
Following Palma's romantic style, Villaverde wrote *El espetón de
oro*, which contained Palma's introduction and was published in *El*

*Album* in 1838. *El espetón de oro,* reprinted in book form the same year, is considered the first book published in Cuba.[59]

Villaverde had other critics. In an essay entitled "Martín Morúa Delgado: Impresiones literarias. Las novelas del sr. Villaverde," Morúa pointed out numerous faults contained in *Cecilia Valdés.*[60] Morúa is perhaps the first Cuban writer to experience an anxiety of influence with regard to Villaverde's work. Morúa himself went on to write his version of *Cecilia Valdés,* which he entitled *Sofía.* Contemporary Cuban writers have also been inspired by Villaverde's masterpiece; their works include such novels as Alejo Carpentier's *Manhunt* (1954), Guillermo Cabrera Infante's *Three Trapped Tigers* (1967), César Leante's *Muelle de Caballería* (1973), Cintio Vitier's *De peña pobre* (1980), and Reinaldo Arenas's *Graveyard of the Angels* (1987).

Domingo del Monte was Villaverde's most influential teacher and, like other young writers, Villaverde profited from his direction. Although Del Monte had not commissioned Villaverde to write an antislavery novel, he advised him and other writers to abandon the romantic tradition and accept Realism, which would allow them to depict accurately Cuban society. For Del Monte, the change in literary focus also represented a possible means of combating slavery and altering Cuban colonial society. Villaverde was influenced by Del Monte and the early antislavery works, and his *Cecilia Valdés* was the last antislavery novel to be published before the emancipation of Cuban slaves in 1886.

A leader among young Cuban-born writers, Del Monte shared books in his vast library with Villaverde and other friends and instructed them on important writers and trends.[61] Villaverde's *Cecilia Valdés* represents a rejection of the Romanticism and *costumbrismo* (literature of manners) of his early works in favor of a more realistic expression of Cuban problems. Villaverde wrote his novel in the tradition of Walter Scott and Manzoni and did so many years before Zola and Galdós became established figures.

*Cecilia Valdés* is a realistic novel. In his prologue, Villaverde explains:

> Far from inventing or pretending imaginary and unrealistic characters and scenes, I have carried realism, as I understand it, to the point of presenting the principal characters of the novel with all their "hairs and ear-marks," as they vulgarly express it; clothed in the dress that they wore in their lifetime, the majority under their true Christian surnames; speaking the same language they spoke in the historical

scenes in which they appear, copying as far as possible, d'après nature, their physical and moral features, in order that those who knew
them in the flesh or by tradition should recognize them without difficulty and should at least say: "The resemblance is undeniable."[62]

Many of the characters in Cecilia Valdés are real. In a letter dated
November 21, 1883, the author confirms what he stated in the prologue and confesses to Julio Rosa, a pseudonym for Francisco Puig de
la Puente, the nature of his characters:

> In your letter of the 6th you ask me if the characters in my novel were
> real and true, and immediately you would like to know what hap-
> pened to some of them. Although I have taken all those who figure in
> it from among my friends, schoolmates, acquaintances, parents, etc. it
> cannot be said that they are portraits. They have all served me to out-
> line the scenes of real life of my country during a particular period;
> but with some exceptions, I did not describe any of them d'après na-
> ture. Doctor Mateu, Cocco, Cándido Valdés, Fernando O'Reilly, Cán-
> dido Rubio, father and son, or Gamboa, don Joaquín Gómez, Me-
> drago . . . Uribe, the tailor, and others such as these are portraits. . . .
> But Cecilia, Isabel, Adela, Rosa Ilincheta, Pimienta, María de Regla,
> Dionisio, the cook, Catalapiedra, etc. are copies of imaginary char-
> acters which existed by mere transference and composition in my
> mind . . . for Cecilia, a very beautiful mulatto with whom my school-
> mate and friend in Havana, Cándido Rubio, had a love affair.[63]

By 1841, Villaverde's literary career was under way. In his early
works, Villaverde wavered between documenting history and customs and writing about frustrated love, two literary interests which
would be combined in Cecilia Valdés. Of the other works published
in this first stage, his best known include El guajiro (published in
serial form in 1842 and in book form in 1890), in which he documents the life of a Cuban peasant in the region of Vuelta Abajo. The
story is a pretext for describing the customs of an important rural
sector of Cuban society. El penitente (1844), which pertains to Bernardo de Gálvez's conquest of Florida, narrates primitive Cuban society and the people and customs of the time. Mainly a historical
novel, it also describes the frustrated love between Rosalinda and Alfonso. In Alfonso's absence, Rosalinda marries Eguiluz. Alfonso returns and, attempting to stab Rosalinda's child, by accident kills her
instead. The shift of one murder to another is reproduced in the closing moments of Cecilia Valdés. Cecilia, who seeks revenge, asks her
admirer, Pimienta, to kill Isabel Ilincheta, Leonardo's wife-to-be.

However, and not by accident, Pimienta seeks his own revenge and does not kill Isabel as instructed but Leonardo Gamboa. *Dos amores* (1843) describes Celeste's love for her lover, Teodoro, and her hatred for don Camilo; when the latter is not able to win Celeste's affection, he forces her father into bankruptcy. *La joven de la flecha de oro* (published in serial form in 1840 and in book form in 1841) narrates a prearranged marriage between Paulina and a contemporary friend of her father's, Simón Alegrías, in which she is forced to give up her love for the younger Jacobo. Under the guise of a better life, Paulina becomes a prisoner of her own husband. The 1839 volume of *Cecilia Valdés* is also a part of Villaverde's most representative works.

Of his other works during this first stage, *Excursión a Vuelta Abajo*, published in two parts, in *El Album* in 1838 and in *Faro Industrial de La Habana* in 1842, gathered in one volume in 1891, is of notable importance. Like some of the other narrations, the two travel stories describe the countryside and the customs of the region, a journey which covered the limits of Guanajay to the Cabo de San Antonio. However, Villaverde's picturesque narration recalls the nature scenes the author describes in his introduction to Francisco Estévez's *Diario de un rancheador,*[64] which he heard about as a child and later possessed. Villaverde published only the introduction under the "Palenques de negros cimarrones" in 1890.[65] More importantly, Villaverde included the historical figure of Estévez in the definitive version of his *Cecilia Valdés*. To do so, Villaverde broke with the chronology of the novel and the diary and fused both narrative times to bring this cruel figure into his novel, continuing to rewrite his *Cecilia Valdés*. Villaverde also broke with its chronology to include other important characters, as we shall later see.

*Cecilia Valdés* is Villaverde's most important work. The short story, which serves as the nucleus of the first volume, narrates the life of Cecilia, a ten-year-old orphan mulatto girl whose beauty is admired by the Gamboa family and who resembles members of the family, especially the father. The second part of the story is a conversation between Cecilia and her grandmother Josefa in which Cecilia relates her experience with the Gamboas. The grandmother is alarmed and pleads with Cecilia not to visit the Gamboas again, telling her a story about a girl like Cecilia who is kidnapped by a student, like the young Leocadio Gamboa, and literally swallowed by the earth. The short story ends with a vicious description of Leocadio, Cecilia's disappearance and downfall, and the grandmother's death.

There are only minor differences between the short story and the first two chapters of the 1839 version of the novel. In a comparison between the two, we notice, for example, that Leocadio's name is changed to Leonardo and Susanita, Cecilia's mother, becomes Rosario Alarcón. In the 1882 edition, the name Leocadio is given to a coach driver. The story and the first volume of *Cecilia Valdés* coincide word for word and paragraph for paragraph. We must note that, although both the short story and the first volume narrate the love relationship between Leonardo and Cecilia, the theme of incest, important in the final edition, is never mentioned explicitly. Josefa's advice can be interpreted as a maternal concern for her granddaughter, and the resemblance between Cecilia and the Gamboas can be coincidental. Blacks and the theme of slavery, so important in the definitive version of *Cecilia Valdés*, are not present in the short story and appear as only a marginal element in the novel. The only nonwhites mentioned in the versions of 1839 are urban mulattos.

The change in focus between the early works and the definitive version of *Cecilia Valdés* is evident in Villaverde's life. In his mid-thirties Villaverde abandoned novelistic concerns for political activities in the separatist movement but later completed *Cecilia Valdés.* As he became more committed to Cuba's separation from Spain, Villaverde favored a more politically oriented writing, which included journalism, and an antislavery position in the definitive version of his novel. In terms of adventures, some aspects of Villaverde's life rival his own fiction.

By 1847 Villaverde was a conspirator in the Club de la Habana, a group of well-to-do Cubans who desired separation of Cuba from Spain and annexation to the United States.[66] Many of its members promoted annexation to preserve slavery in Cuba, but others like Villaverde admired the democratic life of the northern states. Some simply preferred annexation to Spain's domination over the island. Pablo, a character in *La joven de la flecha de oro,* who lived in the United States for eight years, best represents Villaverde's position. When referring to the United States, Pablo speaks highly of a civilization that respects the rights and liberties of both men and women. María Paulina, Villaverde's protagonist, recalls her counterparts in the North. Like his future wife, Emilia Casanova, María Paulina is an individual who consistently asserts her rights and can even be considered a precursor of the feminist movement.

While in Cuba, Villaverde had joined Gen. Narciso López in a failed uprising against the colonial government. López escaped to the United States, and Villaverde was captured and jailed on October 20, 1848. After a few months of detention, Villaverde escaped with the aid of a guard, García Rey, and a prisoner, Vicente Fernández Blanco, reaching Florida in April 1849.[67] He traveled to New York and became López's secretary. With the help of Villaverde and others, General López conducted three expeditions to Cuba, in 1848, 1849, and, the most successful one, 1850. López invaded the island for the last time in August 1851. He was betrayed, captured, and executed in September.[68] As a posthumous homage to General López, Villaverde began (but never completed) the story of his life; the incomplete version was published under the title *To the Public (General Lopez, the Cuban Patriot)* in New York, dated 1851.[69]

Villaverde's annexationist ideas received another blow in a debate with José Antonio Saco. Unlike Villaverde, Saco favored independence, not annexation: he believed that U.S. citizens would take over the island; Cuba would not be annexed but absorbed into the Union. Villaverde answered Saco with his *El señor Saco con respecto a la revolución de Cuba*, published in New York in 1851.[70]

Shortly after he arrived in New York, Villaverde collaborated in the separatist magazine *La Verdad* and, in 1853, became its editor. That same year he founded and published the weekly *El Independiente* in New Orleans. Villaverde returned to New York in 1860 and published *La América, Frank Leslie's Magazine,* and *El Avisador Hispano Americano.* He was also editor of *El Espejo Masónico* and *La Ilustración Americana* from 1865 to 1873, *El Espejo* from 1874 to 1894, and *El Tribunal Cubano* in 1878.

At the outset of the Ten Years' War, which lasted from 1868 to 1878 and marked the first of two stages of insurrection against Spain (the second was from 1895 to 1898), Villaverde renewed his interest in politics, with a slightly different but significant change. Rather than annexationist, he now favored Saco's position and total independence of the island. In a document addressed to Carlos Manuel de Céspedes, entitled *La revolución de Cuba vista desde Nueva York* (1869), Villaverde warns the Cuban patriot of the intent of the United States not to help the rebel forces.[71] By supporting Céspedes and other rebels, Villaverde explicitly embraced the antislavery cause. The Constituent Convention of the Guáimaro Assembly, in which Antonio Zambrana, author of *El negro Francisco,* participated, made provision for the emancipation of slaves in Cuba.[72]

While living in the United States, in 1855 Villaverde married Emilia Casanova, a Cuban whose family fled the island because of their support for Cuban independence. Villaverde returned to teaching and even opened and directed a school in 1864. This aspect of his life and his ideas regarding the Civil War in the United States and its implications for Cuban history are documented in *Apuntes biográficos de Emilia Casanova de Villaverde,* published in New York in 1874.[73]

Villaverde made two brief trips to Cuba, the first from 1858 to 1860 and the second for two weeks in 1888. During the first trip he acquired La Antilla publishing company, which published Suárez y Romero's *Artículos*. With the close collaboration of Francisco Calcagno, he also founded the magazine *La Habana*. Villaverde also planned to edit his own complete works. With the omission of his first four stories, Villaverde would have printed the works in six volumes. Meanwhile, Villaverde attempted unsuccessfully to rewrite his *Cecilia Valdés:* "I undertook the venture of revising, of recasting the other novel, *Cecilia Valdés* (an intermediate version, very incomplete) of which only the first volume existed in print and a small part of the second in manuscript form. I had outlined the new plan to its most minute details, when once again I had to abandon my country."[74] Fearful of Captain General Concha's powers, Villaverde returned to New York. There he completed his last and most important work, *Cecilia Valdés*. Villaverde died fifteen years later on October 20, 1894; his body was shipped to Cuba and was buried in the Havana Cemeterio de Colón on December 12 of the same year.[75]

The first and last versions of *Cecilia Valdés* span Villaverde's literary career. A concern for certain themes in his early works, Del Monte's influence, and Villaverde's political involvement were important factors which contributed to the rewriting of *Cecilia Valdés*. A comparison between the first two versions and the last one will show the political and antislavery motives of this important work.

By rewriting his novel, Villaverde altered the previous versions; changes in the work were not only necessary but inevitable. In his 1879 prologue to the final version, Villaverde confesses that when he escaped from Cuba in 1849 he left behind all his manuscripts and books; once he received them he no longer had any use for them.[76] We also know that Villaverde made extensive revisions in his final draft. In a letter to the journalist and writer Julio Rojas dated May 18, 1884, Villaverde reveals that he reduced his eleven hundred–page manuscript to one-third the original size.[77] The changes made from the first to the final versions of *Cecilia Valdés* are evident in a close reading of the texts.

The forty-three-year interval that elapsed between the first two versions of *Cecilia Valdés* and the final one proves revealing regarding the theme of slavery. Except for stylistic and name changes, the short story and the first two chapters of the 1839 version coincide, not with the first, but with the second and third chapters of the 1882 edition. Beyond these similarities, the versions of 1839 and 1882 are different. For example, the 1839 version ends with Leonardo's practical joke on Solfa, followed by Leonardo's conversation with Diego Meneses regarding Cecilia, Isabel, and Antonia. Unlike the 1839 version, volume 1 of the 1882 edition ends with the formal dance in which Cecilia encounters the Gamboa cook Dionisio. Some events appear out of sequence and do not take place in the definitive version until volume 2. For example, Leonardo's and Meneses' conversation regarding the young Gamboa's love affair of the 1839 version does not appear until the second volume of the 1882 edition. In spite of what Villaverde states in his prologue, I wonder if he really consulted the 1839 edition in writing the definitive one. Although there is a coincidence in characters, the two works develop in completely different directions. I propose, on the other hand, that Villaverde did make use of his short story, because it is reproduced almost verbatim in chapters 2 and 3 of the 1882 edition and narrates Josefa's death, an account absent from the first volume of the 1839 version. The first volume of the 1882 edition narrates Leonardo's and Cecilia's incestuous relationship, a central theme absent from the previous editions. Practically everyone but Cecilia and Leonardo know that Cándido Gamboa is Cecilia's father.

The three versions of *Cecilia Valdés* were written with different purposes. The short story narrates the demise of Cecilia's romance. The 1839 version takes up this theme but also documents the once-popular Ferias del Angel. This is made explicit in Villaverde's dedication to Manuel del Portillo, a friend who inspired the author to write about the celebration. Villaverde included it in the novel and it is made explicit throughout the text: More than three-quarters of the novel narrates October 23, 1831, the Eve of San Rafael.[78] The last version of *Cecilia Valdés*, an antislavery novel, is a political denunciation against the colonial government. The 1882 edition rewrites the two earlier versions and places the action of the novel within the historical context of the administration of Gen. Francisco Vives. This is evident in the second chapter:

> A few years after the events just recorded, martial law was put into effect in Cuba, following the fall of the second and short period of constitutional government, and Don Francisco Dionisio Vives was appointed Captain-General. In those days, if one frequented the district of Havana known as *El Barrio del Angel*, he could not fail to notice a little girl, about 12 or 13 years of age [the original states eleven to twelve years old], playing or wandering about alone in the streets. This fact, and other circumstances about to be related, made her a conspicuous figure in the neighborhood. (28)[79]

Although Cecilia's approximate age is the same as in the other versions, the dates have been changed to situate the 1882 edition at the time of the corrupt Vives government. Let us compare: The first two versions mention that around 1826 or 1827 Cecilia was ten years old. This means that Cecilia was born either in 1816 or 1817. However, in the final version, Cecilia was born in 1812, and in the second chapter she was eleven or twelve years old. This slight change in time places the present narrative time around 1823 and frames the Vives government, which lasted from 1823 to 1832.

> The complete freedom with which *el monte* [a card game] was openly played everywhere in the island, especially during the governorship of Captain-General Don Francisco Dionisio Vives, proved beyond peradventure that his policy or that of his government was based upon the Machiavellian principle of "corrupt in order to rule," copied from the celebrated method of the Roman statesman, *divide et imperia*, because the corruption of the people served to divide their minds in order that they themselves should not be aware of their own misery and decline. (47)[80]

If we take into consideration the time of the conclusion, the novel ends not in 1831, the year of the Ferias del Angel of the first version, but in 1832. (In the definitive version of *Cecilia Valdés* Villaverde tells us that the Ferias del Angel ended in 1832.) In his prologue Villaverde informs his readers that the novel develops between 1812 and 1831 (51). I contend otherwise. Although Cecilia's one-year detention in the Paula hospital could have been imposed at the time of her sentence, that is, in 1831, Isabel Ilincheta's one-year stay in the convent, which she entered also in 1831, could only have been determined after the end of her stay there. This is evident in the following passage: "Isabel Ilincheta, having given up hope of ever finding happiness or peace of soul in the social sphere into which it had been her lot to be born, sought seclusion in the convent of the nuns of Santa Teresa, the Carmelites, and after a year's novitiate took the veil" (546). Therefore, from the point of view of the narrator, the time of the conclusion is 1832, the end of the Vives government.[81]

The date on which Cecilia was born is also important, not only because it was the same year in which Villaverde was born (interestingly, they also have the same initials),[82] but more significantly because 1812 is the year of the Aponte Conspiracy, in which free blacks, with the help of Haitians, attempted to liberate Cuban slaves; the conspiracy was suppressed in its early stages.[83] However, by pointing to the Aponte Conspiracy, the novel alludes to another uprising, the

Ladder Conspiracy of 1844, as we shall later see. The time span of the novel was a period in which blacks outnumbered whites in Cuba. The fear of a Haitian-type revolution in Cuba and the availability of African slaves caused whites to fear blacks and oppress slaves even more. While the 1839 version is limited to describing the relationship between Cecilia, Leonardo, and Isabel, the first volume of the 1882 edition provides important information regarding blacks and slavery.

Unlike the earlier antislavery narratives, Villaverde's protagonists are not all slaves. Villaverde's realistic narration allows him to describe in detail the slave society of the nineteenth century with all its complexities. His characters are victims of the forces in society. On the one hand, Cecilia is a free mulatto who falls in love with Leonardo Gamboa and, to improve her social, racial, and economic position, desires to marry him. On the other, for Leonardo it was socially acceptable for him to have sexual relationships with black and mulatto women but not to marry them. In this sense, the "love" theme explored in Suárez y Romero's *Francisco* and Tanco's "Petrona y Rosalía" is present in Villaverde's work. After all, Leonardo was following in his father's footsteps. Both father and son love their mulatto mistresses more than the white women they married or intended to marry, doña Rosa and Isabel Ilincheta, respectively. But Leonardo's attraction for Cecilia is also based on his love for his full sister, Adela, who looks exactly like Cecilia. This is most evident when María de Regla, Cecilia's and Adela's wet nurse, who had not seen Cecilia since she nursed her, is astonished by the resemblance between the half sisters: "The Negress crossed her arms and looked at Cecilia face to face. Every now and then she would murmur softly: 'See! the same forehead! the same nose! the same mouth! the same eyes! even the little dimple in the chin! *sí*, her hair, her body, her manner, the little angel herself! why, her living image!'" (539). Here Villaverde alludes to a more direct incestuous desire Leonardo had for Adela which would culminate in his relationship with his half sister, Cecilia. But by concentrating on describing the early part of the nineteenth century, Villaverde exposes the many facets of a society which is based on the separation and exploitation of the races.

The definitive edition of *Cecilia Valdés* is indeed an antislavery novel. The first volume conveys aspects of the history of the slave trade which are absent in the first volume of the 1839 version. The history of the slave trade will be developed in detail by Lino Novás Calvo in *El negrero* (1933). The 1882 edition shows how Cándido Gamboa enriches himself by trafficking in slaves, how slaves were thrown overboard so slavers could outrun British ships, and how, piled one on top of the other, they suffocated in the bowels of ships. These revelations even horrified slave owner doña Rosa Gamboa. The second volume conforms more closely to the earlier antislavery works insofar as it sets the stage for a description of slavery in the sugar mill. The lives of slaves and free blacks are an important component of this society. We are told the story of the former slave Dolores Santa Cruz, whose hard work brought her freedom and enough money to buy a house and slaves. She lost everything, however, including her sanity, to the legal system that disputed her ownership of the house.

We are also told of a well-known tailor, Francisco Uribe, who practiced a profession limited mainly to *pardos* and *morenos* (both terms refer to shades of blackness; a *pardo* is lighter than a *moreno*). According to Villaverde, Uribe was one of the preferred tailors of well-to-do whites. But Uribe achieved his prominence after the narrative ended; that is, between 1833 and 1844. Uribe established his shop on 57 Ricla Street in October 1833.[84] As with the slave hunter Estévez, to include Uribe Villaverde broke with the chronology of the novel and inserted a posterior moment into the time of the narration. There were other prominent tailors whose chronology would have been consistent with Villaverde's time span. For example, Villaverde could have included Leandro Varona, a tailor and captain of the Batallón de Pardos Leales de La Habana (Uribe was only a sergeant); his shop was located on Obrapia Street. Varona practiced his trade during the time of the novel, and his net worth was more than 4,718 pesos. His death on September 28, 1832, which marks the end of the Vives government, would have conformed more closely to the structure of the novel.[85] Other notable tailors during the time of the narration were Joaquín López, Montes de Oca, and Ramón Rodríguez.[86] Perhaps Villaverde included Uribe for personal reasons; since Uribe worked for whites, Villaverde or his friends may have known him. Thus Villaverde brought a familiar figure into his narration.

There were also political reasons for including Uribe in the novel. To those who knew him, his presence in the novel recalls his death. In 1844 Uribe was accused of participating in the Ladder Conspiracy and was sentenced to die. The prosperous Uribe had amassed considerable wealth, which included twelve slaves, two houses, and a small fortune of more than 7,398 pesos.[87] Villaverde included Uribe and other successful mulattoes who were victims of the conspiracy to refer to the events of 1844. This is also the case with mulatto musicians mentioned in the novel. For example, Brindis de Salas, lieutenant of the Batallón de Morenos Leales de La Habana, was a musician and a highly respected individual. Bachiller y Morales considers him to have been "a gentleman of pleasant and ceremonious manners, formal in his social relation; he was the cream of the crop of the *politicians* of this species, and his aristocratic tendencies made him become friends with gentlemen and professors of the other race."[88] Brindis de Salas was implicated in the Ladder Conspiracy and forced into exile. He returned to the island in a clandestine manner and was caught and imprisoned. Although he received amnesty in 1852, he never regained the popularity he had before 1844.[89] Other notable mulattoes included by Villaverde in his novel suffered the consequences of the Ladder Conspiracy: the violinist Ulpiano Estrada, known in the novel as "el maestro Ulpiano," and Sgt. Tomás Buelta y Flores, composer, director, and distinguished musician of the Real Casa de Beneficencia.[90]

Villaverde and his readers may have known and had some dealings with Uribe, Brindis de Salas, Buelta y Flores, and others. Familiar with their situations, Villaverde's readers were certainly aware that these and other well-to-do mulattoes were either put to death or punished during the Ladder Conspiracy for no apparent political reason. Morúa Delgado remembered Uribe within the context of the conspiracy, as

> that mulatto was subjected to imprisonment and suffering by the obstinate government, which did not have any other origin than in the systematic persecution declared by all the representative classes of the colony against the black and mixed class for the crime of possessing large sums of money, accumulated by the strength of their own personal labor. . . . By the way, I have under oath of the people of that period, that tailor Francisco de Paula Uribe did not do anything else in his life other than to make lots of clothes which the rich Havana *dandy* paid generously for those who worked, and often spent their money in the most extravagant and loud manner, which is typical of the lower classes and without honorable reason scorned by all disorganized society. His crime, with those of the majority of the colored families which at that time experienced the wickedness of a bastard regime, was to distinguish himself by his vain competition with the privileged colonists.[91]

Perhaps the most important mulatto mentioned in *Cecilia Valdés* is the poet Plácido, Gabriel de la Concepción Valdés, whose own life, in some respects, parallels that of Cecilia but who, like Uribe, suffered the consequences of the conspiracy. Son of a clandestine relationship between a white dancer, Concepción Vázquez, and a mulatto hairdresser, Diego Ferrer Matoso, Plácido was born in the Casa de Beneficencia y Maternidad, the same place where Cecilia was born and where they both, as was customary, received the founder's surname, Valdés. Like Cecilia, he fell in love with a white, but unlike her he married the woman he called Celia in his poems, although he sustained only a brief relationship with her.[92]

Although a poet, Plácido earned a living by making ornamental hair combs, some of tortoiseshell, and by working as a typesetter. A gifted poet, he composed his first poem at the age of twelve. At the age of twenty-five, in homage to the Spanish poet Francisco Martínez de la Rosa, Plácido wrote his "La siempreviva," a composition which brought him fame not only in Havana but in Spain and Mexico. Plácido was not liked by everyone. While in charge of the poetry section of the newspaper *La Aurora de Matanzas*, he was criticized for writing laudatory verses to distinguished people and receiving payment in gold. Also, as a mulatto, he was hated by many whites.[93]

During the time of the narration, between 1826 and 1832, Plácido lived in Matanzas. While there, the characters in *Cecilia Valdés* had already heard of his reputation. However, not until the end of the narration, in 1832, did Plácido gain recognition. He wrote "La siempreviva" in 1834 and by 1836 he was considered the most popular poet of the times. That same year the poet José María Heredia visited Plácido and offered to pay his expenses to live in Mexico, but the mulatto poet declined. Plácido's first collection of poems, *Poesías de Plácido*, was published after the narration in 1838.[94]

Like Uribe, Plácido is another figure who was taken out of his historical setting and included in the time of the narration. And like the tailor, he was accused by Leopoldo O'Donnell of being one of the leaders of the Ladder Conspiracy; on June 22, 1844, he and ten others were shot in the back by a firing squad. Villaverde, indeed, had the Ladder Conspiracy in mind when selecting his characters and he altered historical time to bring them into his narration. This is evident in the last chapter of the first volume of the 1882 edition, which is different from the last chapter of the 1839 version. While at a dance, black and mulatto characters go and pay their respects to Cecilia. In this section, Villaverde records the victims of the Ladder Conspiracy:

> Among them we may mention Brindis, the musician, a man of distinguished bearing and excellent manners; Tondá, the protégé of Captain-General Vives, a young Negro, intelligent and brave as a lion; Vargas and Dodge of Matanzas, a barber and a carpenter respectively, both of whom took part in the alleged conspiracy of the Negroes in 1844 and were shot in an execution held in the Paseo de Versailles in that city;

José de la Concepción Valdés, whose pen-name was Plácido, the most inspired of Cuban poets, who had the misfortune to follow in the footsteps of the two just mentioned; Tomás Vuelta y Flores, celebrated violinist and composer of well-known country dances, who that same year died on the rack, a torture decreed by the judges to force him to confess complicity in a crime, the existence of which had never been legally proved; Francisco de Paula Uribe, a skillful tailor, who took his own life with a barber's razor rather than lose it at the hands of the authorities, at the very moment when he was being locked up in one of the cells of the Cabaña Fortress; Juan Francisco Manzano, sentimental poet, who just recently had been granted his liberty, thanks to the benevolence of certain literary men of Havana; and of course José Dolores Pimienta, tailor and skilful clarinetist, and handsome as he was modest and correct in his personal conduct. (316–317)

We have noted elsewhere that Juan Francisco Manzano received his freedom in 1836. Of the nine characters mentioned, all but two were accused of participating in the conspiracy.

The final edition of *Cecilia Valdés*, both within and outside the time of the narration, suggests that the oppressive conditions of blacks and slaves form a hermetic system from which there is no escape, at least not through legal means. Furthermore, slavelike conditions existed even outside the slavery system and included the systematic massacre of many prominent blacks whose reputation and wealth rivaled those of some whites. The cruelties of slavery are clearly visible in the second volume of the novel, when the Gamboas return to their sugar mill. Going one step beyond the other antislavery novels written under Del Monte's supervision, *Cecilia Valdés* gives us a vivid description of runaway slaves both in the city and in the country and the reasons for their daring actions. For example, the life of the slave Pedro provides a disturbing account of a Maroon who, after being bitten and captured by dogs, is placed in the *cepo* (shackle). He is later taken to the infirmary, where he commits suicide by swallowing his tongue. If Suárez y Romero's Francisco hanged himself because of Dorotea's rejection, Pedro prefers to die a slow and painful death than return to slavery. María de Regla narrates the story:

"As I was looking out of the window at the dance, I heard Pedro move, turned my head and noticed he had his fingers in his mouth. I thought nothing about it, but he made a movement as if nauseated. I ran to his side. He took his fingers out of his mouth, ground his teeth and succeeded in grasping the cot with both hands. He began to get convul-

sions. I was horrified. I sent for the doctor, and at that moment he lay
dead in my arms. He lay just as he was when don José, the doctor,
found him. I have seen many die here but never such a horrible death."
(415)

Contrary to María de Regla, Cocco and don Cándido are unaffected
by the story and return to the house to drink coffee.

Perhaps the most significant addition to the 1882 novel is the increased presence of doña Rosa, Leonardo's mother. A peripheral
character in the first two versions, she has a more visible and important role and can even be considered one of the most powerful characters, not only because of her material wealth, for it is her sugar
mill, but because of the strength of her personality. She is the reason
don Cándido does not send Leonardo abroad to prevent his relationship with Cecilia, and although doña Rosa has a weakness for her
only son, it is she who controls him. She consents to, and pays for,
the support of his mistress, Cecilia, and even tells him when it is
time to end the relationship and marry Isabel, a white woman of his
own class.

As in the early antislavery stories, *Cecilia Valdés* calls into question the concept of family and motherhood in nineteenth-century
white Cuban society. The black slave María de Regla, the maternal
counterpart of doña Rosa, is the "real" mother of all the children in
the novel. Doña Rosa was unable to nurse her children and had her
slave, María de Regla, feed Adela, an act doña Rosa always resented
and regretted. María de Regla nursed Adela, her own daughter, Dolores, and also Cecilia; she was, therefore, their symbolic mother.
Among the mothers in the novel, neither doña Rosa, Adela's mother,
nor Rosario Alarcón, Cecilia's mother, nurses her own child. Only
the black wet nurse, María de Regla, is described as performing the
motherly act of nursing. María de Regla, whose name suggests both
the Virgen María (Virgin Mary) and the Cuban black Virgen de Regla,
known in Afro-Cuban culture as Yemayá, is not only the mother of
Adela, Cecilia, and Dolores but the mother of the white, mulatto,
and black races her daughters represent. Symbolically, María de Regla is the mother of the Cuban people. Her presence in the novel is
well timed. She is present at the opening and closing of the novel:
She is in the first chapter of the 1882 edition, when she is called
upon to nourish the newly born Cecilia, and in the last one, when
she is asked by Leonardo to visit Cecilia in jail. (The first chapter of
the last edition is not contained in the first two versions.) María de
Regla's presence is felt throughout the novel; it is she and not doña
Rosa who knows the secrets of don Cándido's life.

In Villaverde's novel, Pimienta, Cecilia's frustrated mulatto lover, kills Leonardo Gamboa. Pimienta, at the end of volume I, protects Cecilia with a knife from the black slave Dionisio. At the end of volume 2, Pimienta continues to protect Cecilia; however, he becomes an independent character, this time acting on his own and, instead of killing Isabel as Cecilia asks, he stabs Leonardo. This act is a radical departure from other antislavery novels, even though the murder is committed by a free mulatto rather than a slave. Leonardo's death has broader implications; it suggests the end of the Gamboa family, of a mother who lived for her son and of a father who saw in his son a means of carrying on his recently received title of nobility. In addition, the death of Leonardo signals an end to historical exploitation of black and mulatto women by white men. This pattern of exploitation, which was present in other antislavery novels, had existed in Cecilia's family for generations. It began with Magdalena Morales, Cecilia's great-grandmother, and will end with Cecilia's daughter: both 1839 versions state that the exploitation will end in the fifth generation. This locates the beginning of the historical exploitation during the early part of the eighteenth century, possibly when Cecilia's family were slaves, and forecasts radical changes in the Spanish government by the middle of the nineteenth century. Villaverde omitted this information from the 1882 edition because neither the emancipation of slaves in 1886 nor the liberation of Cuba from Spain in 1898 had occurred during the proposed fifth generation.

The incest between Leonardo and Cecilia is at the core of the novel and has fundamental implications for a developing Cuban culture within a slave society. César Leante has already stated that Cecilia and Leonardo had to be brother and sister because so are the races which they represent.[95] From this perspective, I propose that the theme of incest is the foundation of Cuban slave culture and complements the novel's antislavery discourse. In his *Totem and Taboo*, Freud tells us that incest is one of the two most ancient taboos.[96] Although the laws of avoidance may have prevented marriage between whites and blacks or mulattoes, the power relation in nineteenth-century slave society encouraged their sexual relations. Freud associates incest with an infantile trait and, in contemporary society, with neurosis. Both Cecilia and Leonardo, as symbolic representation of the emerging Cuban slave culture, are trapped in an earlier stage from which they cannot escape. The colonial and slave society and the characters subjected to that system in one way or another contribute to the incest. On the one hand, Leonardo is a child and doña Rosa treats him as such. On the other, doña Rosa is also responsible for Leonardo's infantile behavior. In any event, he and Cecilia are "neurotics" and so is the slave society which allowed them to come together.

If both Leonardo and Cecilia represent the young Cuban culture, the novel proposes that the island's culture is based on the violation of a taboo; that is, on a neurosis. In the nineteenth century, slave culture was destined to destroy itself. The slavery system was responsible for the incest between brother and sister. The sexual violation has an immediate effect and causes Leonardo's death and the destruction of his family; symbolically, it also causes the decay of the Cuban family, which had its origin in slave society. Citing Frazer, Freud tells us that among Australian aborigines and in the Ta-ta-thi tribe of New South Wales the penalty for having sex with a member of a forbidden clan is death. In this sense, Leonardo's death is justified, for he broke the sacred taboo and committed incest. With this in mind, Pimienta, his executioner, does not represent the individual act of a jealous lover. On the contrary, he is the conscience of a Cuban society which punishes Leonardo for the crime he committed. Pimienta is the savior of a contemporary Cuban culture opposed to slavery and the slave trade.

The ending of Villaverde's novel has a lasting effect on the reader and is, therefore, more striking than other antislavery works because of the daring killing of a white by a mulatto. Of those who wrote under Del Monte's tutelage, only Villaverde proposes this new solution to the slavery issue. Although Manzano reacts emotionally to the whipping of his mother, his feelings are never translated into action.[97] Similarly, in Zambrana's *El negro Francisco*, the protagonist contemplates killing his master but is later dissuaded by his lover, Camila.[98] Only in *Cecilia Valdés* do we have a daring killing of a white by a mulatto. Villaverde's political activism, his freedom from persecution while in the United States, and the emancipation of slaves in the northern country were important factors which contributed to his description of Leonardo's death. This ending may be offensive to some, but it is indeed suggestive to others. The novel never makes clear whether Pimienta was caught, leaving the possibility of his escape. Moreover, the killing has other positive implications. For example, when Cecilia is detained in the Paula hospital, she is reunited with her mother.

The 1882 version of *Cecilia Valdés* ends an important phase in Cuban literature in general and in the development of the antislavery narrative in particular: *Cecilia Valdés* is the last antislavery novel to be published before the emancipation of Cuban slaves in 1886. The last novel in this literary trend, it is also the most daring in its symbolic treatment of the death of a white man who exploited black women, thus rewriting the ending of Manzano's, Suárez y Romero's, Tanco's, and Zambrana's works. The killer, a mulatto, escapes and is never convicted for his crime. For Villaverde there is a higher form of justice with its own regulations which also conspires against the slavery system.

The multiple versions of Manzano's autobiography and Villaverde's *Cecilia Valdés* reveal that the transference of their characters from one text to another offers a dynamic dimension to their development. In Madden's translation, Manzano's sufferings are more heightened than in the original autobiography. In Villaverde's final edition of *Cecilia Valdés*, the antislavery narrative has acquired a more aggressive meaning, as the ending of the novel suggests. Crossing the space from one version to the other has allowed for a clearer definition of the characters and the works in their antislavery stance. Crossing another space, a geographical one, from Cuba to England or the United States, where the works were published, explains the shift in focus.

In spite of the suggestive ending of Manzano's escape, as described in his autobiography, or Leonardo's death and Pimienta's flight from justice, the emancipation of Cuban slaves has not significantly improved the lives of blacks and mulattoes. What appears to be the circularity of history anticipates the emergence of another type of antislavery narrative in the postemancipation period and into the twentieth century that will narrate slavery from a more condemnatory point of view and denounce the slavelike conditions that will exist in Cuba during the time of their writing.

# THREE

# Time in Fiction

## Francisco Calcagno's *Romualdo, uno de tantos* and *Aponte* and Martín Morúa Delgado's *Sofía* and *La familia Unzúazu*

> *Every writer knows that the choice of a beginning for what he will write is crucial not only because it determines much of what follows but also because a work's beginning is, practically speaking, the main entrance to what it offers. Moreover, in retrospect we can regard a beginning as the point at which, in a given work, the writer departs from all other works; a beginning immediately establishes relationships with works already existing, relationships of either continuity or antagonism or some mixture of both.*
>
> —SAID, *BEGINNINGS*

I   Juan Francisco Manzano's *Autobiografía* served as an Urtext for the early antislavery writers, but it was not readily available to other writers in print until 1937. Nevertheless, critic and novelist Francisco Calcagno, writing in the second half of the nineteenth century, consulted Anselmo Suárez y Romero's version of Manzano's autobiography and reproduced sections of it in his *Poetas de color*, which he published in 1878. While preparing his *Diccionario biográfico cubano* (1878), Calcagno also had access to Anselmo Suárez y Romero's *Francisco*, even though his novel was published in New York in 1880 but not in Cuba until 1947. Calcagno was a close friend of Suárez y Romero's and dedicated a chapter of his novel *Los crímenes de Concha* to him. In "El buen amo," Calcagno highlights their concerns about slavery. Calcagno recalls that on June 23, 1845, Suárez y Romero and he witnessed the garroting of Teodoro, a black accused of murder, whom Suárez y Romero believed to be innocent. Answering his absent friend, Calcagno informs him that after investigating the case, he concluded that Teodoro was guilty. Teodoro's mother, resisting separation from her son, was beaten by the overseer whom the slave later kills. It appears that Suárez y Romero was right but for the wrong reasons. Calcagno concludes his dictionary entry on Suárez y Romero in the following manner: "Such was Suárez y Romero, whose real value up to now has been known by only a few friends, because his unpublished treasure is worth more than the published."[1] Calcagno included himself in the intimate group of friends, since Suárez y Romero's *Francisco*, like Manzano's autobiography, was a source of inspiration to Calcagno when he wrote *Los crímenes de Concha* and *Romualdo, uno de tantos*.

Similarly, if Suárez y Romero's and Manzano's works became important points of departure for Calcagno, other writers such as Martín Morúa Delgado, publishing his *Sofía* and *La familia Unzúazu* in the same period as Calcagno, would find their inspiration and rebellion not only in the early works but, more importantly, in Cirilo Villaverde's *Cecilia Valdés*; Morúa's *Sofía* is a rewriting of *Cecilia Valdés*. Thus, although the slave Manzano provided a theme for early antislavery writers, it was not just his autobiography but mainly the works of fiction which became sources of inspiration for Calcagno and Morúa, the first two writers who published antislavery novels in Cuba immediately after the postslavery period.

Best known for his important *Diccionario biográfico cubano*, Francisco Calcagno wrote at least two novels whose themes pertain to slavery: *Romualdo, uno de tantos* and *Aponte*. Although *Romualdo, uno de tantos* was first published in 1881, I have decided to include it in the postslavery period, not only because it was not known in its present form until after the emancipation of slaves, but because it uses a narrative strategy similar to *Aponte*'s.[2] Like the earlier antislavery writers, Calcagno mixes fact with fiction. His novels contain historical figures which also appear in his *Diccionario biográfico cubano*, a work Calcagno was completing while writing his fiction. In many cases, the biographical information in one text is reproduced in the other. Calcagno published the first part of *Diccionario biográfico cubano* in 1878, three years before the publication of *Romualdo, uno de tantos* and twenty-three years before *Aponte*. But the time in which he wrote his works is different from the time of publication: he finished writing the first in 1869 and the second in 1885.

The works written during the second half of the nineteenth century expand upon the theme of the first antislavery works with the intention of understanding slavery from another point of view; that is, not only as a past event but within the context of the present time of the authors' writing. The relationship between the past of the narration and the present time of the writing poses a problematic in writing the postantislavery novel. The two periods, though different, are fused in the text and create multiple levels of readings. Calcagno's slavery themes are part of a continuum in literary history. By narrating the past, Calcagno is also describing the sociopolitical environment, not only during the time of the narration but, most importantly, in the society in which he lived. The passage of time allowed Calcagno to describe a view of slavery different from the first works.

The narrative strategies contained in *Romualdo, uno de tantos* and *Aponte* are already present in *Los crímenes de Concha*, which Calcagno wrote in 1863 and, due to censorship, published in 1887.[3] The novel, subtitled *Escenas cubanas,* contains commonplaces which will be repeated in the others: the evils of slavery, the separation of the family, the privileged treatment of slaves and the resulting consequences, and the malevolence of whites opposed to the manumission of slaves. Teodoro's case is one among many, a theme repeated with Romualdo. Abolition is seen as a way of helping blacks and restoring honor to whites.

Like Villaverde's novel, *Romualdo, uno de tantos* offers a complete picture of the slavery period. Time has afforded both writers a more coherent understanding of slavery. Calcagno's descriptions are all-encompassing and provide detailed information about slavery: from the slave master and overseer who punish their slaves to those who hunt, buy, and sell slaves for profit. Calcagno's novel, like others before it, narrates a tragic and unjust situation in which the reader is forced to identify with the slave's misfortunes.

As with Antonio Zambrana, who rewrote Suárez y Romero's novel in his, *Francisco* influenced Calcagno's work. Calcagno repeats the impossible love between the black Francisco and the mulatto Dorotea and has his Romualdo fall in love with a slave by the same name, Dorotea. A jealous white like Ricardo punishes Romualdo because he, too, desires the female slave. In the same manner as Suárez y Romero's novel, Romualdo and Dorotea have a child, who symbolizes the pessimistic future of the island.

Although there are similarities between *Francisco* and *Romualdo, uno de tantos*, Calcagno introduces differences as well. If Francisco is a black and Dorotea a mulatto, Calcagno, like Zambrana, inverts the racial composition of the slaves and describes his Romualdo as a mulatto and Dorotea as a black. In Suárez y Romero's novel, the master falls in love with a mulatto slave; in Calcagno's story the overseer desires a black slave. These slight changes are significant and can be attributed to the difference in the time of writing and the

history of the works' publications. By the time Calcagno wrote his
novel the Ten Years' War was under way, and by the time he published it slaves had entered into a gradual system of emancipation
which would liberate them by 1886. Writers like Calcagno began to
express themselves more freely and provided a more realistic description of the racial composition of the characters. Rewriting the
ending of *Francisco,* Romualdo does not commit suicide; he chooses
a more aggressive alternative and, like Manzano, escapes. But, unlike the slave poet who flees to the city to seek the captain general's
or Del Monte's help, the contemporary Romualdo joins the runaway
slave communities in the mountains.

The family is a central theme in Calcagno's novel, a theme made
popular in *Cecilia Valdés.*[4] The family tension in Calcagno's novel
is not without serious consequences. Romualdo, a six-year-old free
mulatto, is stolen from his mother, sold into slavery to his father,
and remains on a sugar plantation for thirty years. Unknowingly, the
father punishes his son without compassion. The family drama is
further intensified by Romualdo's own family situation. The separation of the natural marriage between Romualdo and Dorotea and her
subsequent death are complicated by his daughter Felicia's death by
hunger. As with the early antislavery works, the reader is drawn into
the protagonist's life and is forced to identify if not with the injustices committed against the mulatto then with the father's own
trauma; that is, the reader's trauma. Toward the end of the novel, the
father discovers the true identity of the only heir to his fortune. Unfortunately, it is too late. The intent of the plot is clear: The father
was an accomplice to his son's death.[5] Within a broader context,
slave owners are destroying the Cuban family and murdering their
own children.

The condemnation of slavery is strongest when the village priest
discovers that Castaneiro is Romualdo's father. Suspecting that
Romualdo, an intelligent mulatto, is the son of a free man, the priest
of Magarabomba searches for the father. However, when talking to
the mother, the priest appears to be speaking directly both to the absent father and to an accomplice reader:

> You miserable; without knowing it, you have spent half of your life
> tormenting your own son. O! What horror, what horror! We live in
> an atmosphere of crime, the air which surrounds us is filled with
> crime. We breathe the crime to which we are so accustomed, like
> worms who are born into their filthy mud. And we will remain like
> that as long as that sacrilegious institution endures which contami-
> nates and degrades everything and in which we all have a part: the

buyer and the seller, the owner and the nonowner, and also the seer
and the nonspeaker, because silence is also a crime.[6]

The reader is drawn into the narration and is implicated, like another character, in the slavery drama.

The time of narration is important in the postantislavery narrative. Calcagno's novel continues the narrative time of *Cecilia Valdés* and *Los crímenes de Concha*. The first encompasses the corrupt Vives administration, from 1823 to 1832, and the second the Ricaforte, from 1832 to 1834. *Romualdo, uno de tantos* describes the less corrupt but nevertheless ruthless Tacón government, from 1834 to 1838. By placing the novel within a specific historical context, Calcagno highlights the evils of slavery and, at the same time, makes a commentary about an administration which promoted that institution. A contextual understanding of the novel adds a different dimension to its antislavery position. The relation between the text, as an antislavery work, the context, the Tacón administration, and the time in which the work was written, the Lersundi and Dulce governments, allows for a multiple and problematic reading of Calcagno's novel, which shows the difficulty of those who tried to situate themselves within a counter-discourse on slavery. For example, from a contemporary perspective, we may question whether there is a strong antislavery sentiment since the protagonist is not a black but a mulatto. The denouncement of the slavery system is proclaimed not by the slave but by the priest. The question of race is important. Like Manzano, a mulatto who did not want to associate with other blacks, there is a significant difference between Romualdo and other slaves. The protagonist suffers more because he is mulatto and therefore closer to whites. Like the prayer Romualdo (mis)-learned, the slave's skin color warns the priest of the possibility of Romualdo's free status.

There are two possible interpretations. First, Calcagno may have revealed his own racial bias when choosing a mulatto protagonist over a black one. Second, as with other antislavery works, he wanted to write a novel that would be persuasive but the least offensive to his readers. Although this latter presupposition may not be valid during the time of publication in which slaves were emancipated gradually, it is relevant if we situate the novel not in 1881 but within the time of its writing, during the second Lersundi government and the Dulce administration in 1869, twelve years before emancipation.[7]

The political context of the novel is historically accurate, as an investigation into the Tacón administration will show. On more than one occasion we are reminded that the story takes place in

1836, the year Manzano received his freedom and violence and corruption, prevalent in the Vives government, had been eradicated by Captain General Tacón. Tacón did do away with corruption, but he was also known for carrying out an oppressive campaign against Cubans.[8]

Let us explore the time of the narration. In 1836, the regent Cristina, who was in power in Spain for the young Isabel, ordered the publication of the Constitution of 1812, thus returning to power liberals and constitutionalists. As governor of his province, Santiago de Cuba, General Lorenzo took immediate steps to implement the constitution. Tacón objected. He waited for instructions from Spain which affirmed his authority on the island, instructing him not to implement the constitution. Tacón then took measures to contain General Lorenzo's rebellion and forced him into exile, first to Jamaica and later to Spain.[9]

Situating the novel during the time of the Tacón government undermines the antislavery nature of Calcagno's work. Whether Calcagno sympathized with Tacón and his strong hand against Cuban constitutionalists and liberals may not be as important as his admiration for the captain general's strict discipline. From this broader perspective, the novel continues to narrate the evils of colonial society. The only difference is that Romualdo now represents not the tragic slave discussed in the early antislavery narratives but any individual stolen and sold into slavery. As the title of the novel suggests, Romualdo is one example among many. This was not an uncommon act during the time of the narration, nor was it limited to mulattoes, blacks, and slaves; at times it included whites as well. Calcagno, in fact, entitled chapter 8 "Plagio," which, in nineteenth-century Cuba, referred to kidnapping, an unforgivable crime which, we are told, everyone seemed to forget. Calcagno uses Romualdo to recreate memory, denounce a common crime, and support Tacón's efforts to fight corruption and unlawful acts: "And they [the robberies] became so frequent that it was necessary to draft a special law for the kidnapping cases: On one occasion, in 1834, three brothers were successively snatched from their mother, and the act was attributed to the famous bandit about whom we will talk more" (84). The quotation refers to the infamous Juan Rivero. This same problem, we are told, continues during the present time of the writing, in 1869. Calcagno admired Tacón's strict discipline and sense of order, even though he suppressed liberties on the island. In his *Diccionario biográfico cubano*, Calcagno, at the expense of being redundant, reveals his feelings about the same Tacón administration he writes about in his fiction:

It should be understood the sad state of social disorder in which the country was: Total lack of personal security, robberies and murders took place with frightening impunity. . . . Such had been the ineptitude of the previous governments and such lamentable state of things demanded the energy of a Tacón . . . He prevented [crime] by punishing the robbers and murderers, put an end to the caseless lawyer, incurable cancer of our social body, hunted the lazy, reformed the police, prohibited the carrying of arms, established military patrols, cleaned and paved the streets, got rid of the dogs which roamed about, constructed sewers, parks, public buildings, and, finally, he raised, according to R. Madden's expression, "a type of civilization on a rock foundation." We are not trying to undertake his defense nor his disgrace, but consider what would be the carelessness and venality of his predecessors in a city which was turned into refuge for bandits. During his administration 190 were deported and the number of detainees rose to 1,015, in a jail that was no longer "an infernal of immortality" as Mr. Tacón used to say in his letters.[10]

In spite of the accomplishments, not everyone agrees with Calcagno's assessment of the Tacón government, which he considered reformist. A more recent historian, Fernando Portuondo, for example, states that, regardless of all the good Tacón did, it does not compensate for the lack of political and civil liberty.[11]

The information regarding Tacón's administration contained in the *Diccionario biográfico cubano* and in the novel is similar and appears to have been written around the same time. Let us explore further Calcagno's motivation for situating the novelistic time during the Tacón government. First, Calcagno sympathized with Tacón and, therefore, supported law and order and perhaps Spanish rule over Cuba. Second, he believed that, in spite of Tacón's strict discipline, Cuba still had crime, including the stealing of free blacks. Third, he broadened the fight against crime in Cuba to include the capture of runaway slaves. It is during the same Tacón government that slave hunters, under the leadership of Armona, capture or kill runaway slaves.

Calcagno's obsession with law and order allows us to recall another event in 1836. That same year Armona captured and killed the well-known bandit and slave stealer Juan Rivero. In fact and in fiction, the outlaw Rivero is important. The fictional biography in chapter 11, entitled "Juan Rivero," resembles his life; that is, as Calcagno wrote it in his *Diccionario biográfico cubano*. In both fact and fiction, Armona captures Juan Rivero and also entraps runaway slaves. Within the context of the antislavery novel, it is ironic that in the *Diccionario biográfico cubano* Calcagno speaks favorably of Armona's law and order accomplishments:

> Although censure can be unjust when accused of being violent and despotic, one cannot ignore the services that it rendered: Perhaps it went too far in its attributions, but governors Vives, Ricaforte, and Tacón admired more than once the heroic deeds of the *partida de Armona* which had become a guarantee of order and a base of security of the roads. After its sad function during *El Aguila Negra* conspiracy, in 1829, we should also mention the case of the many bandits from which it freed the island, among them the so called *El Rubio* (see Fernz.), Caniquí (see Ciru), Miguel Padrón, Juan Rivero and others.[12]

Armona captured Juan Rivero and also hunted fugitive slaves. There is a similarity between Caniquí and Romualdo insofar as both were runaway slaves. Caniquí is the subject of Antonio Ramos's novel; Ramos, unlike Calcagno (but within a different context from his), would praise the slave fifty years later for his rebellious spirit.

We may wonder if Calcagno's intent to situate his narrative time in 1836 was meant to recall specifically individuals like Captain General Tacón, General Lorenzo, Armona, and Juan Rivero. Calcagno's insistence on law and order and his favorable comments about Tacón and Armona establish a parallel between Tacón's suppression of the rebel General Lorenzo and Armona's successful expeditions against Juan Rivero and runaway slaves, which, in fiction, included the capture and death of Romualdo. Furthermore, the year 1836 also brings together Armona and Lorenzo. That year, Armona was sent to Puerto Príncipe for precautionary measures concerning Lorenzo's rebellion and the escalation of the revolution in Oriente (142).

Although *Romualdo, uno de tantos* describes the injustices committed against one of many free mulattoes sold into slavery, the novel is also a tribute to the Tacón government and its efforts to eradicate crime. From this perspective, Romualdo is incidental to slavery but central to the theme of kidnapping. But Calcagno's comments on law and order during Tacón's government can be viewed as an opportunity the author seizes to develop the theme of slavery. We should also recall that Romualdo was sold to work as a slave in his father's sugar mill. Whichever position we take, antislavery sentiments are perceived in subtle ways throughout the narration. Toward the end of the novel, the overseer who punished Romualdo and the slave seller who sold him are justifiably killed by slaves, but in turn the slaves are also killed. (Nowhere in the novel does a slave kill a white without also being killed.) Within the context of the date of publication, this represented an antiblack statement. However, within the time of the writing it was considered daring and serves to dramatize the destruction of the family. Whites deserved to die and blacks were involved in their tragic deaths. Like Zambrana's Carlos, a white comes to the defense of the slaves, perhaps to put the burden of emancipation not on the slaves but the whites. The priest sees that slaves do not have an alternative and goes so far as to justify the death of whites. As before, Calcagno speaks to the reader: "Do you believe blameworthy those unfortunate souls who look for their liberty and rights in the mountains? No! Even if they kill me to defend themselves. They would not have gone to that extreme if all the legal doors were not closed to them. Let us go and save them from the rage of the other slave hunters!" (136). And as in the early novels, the denouncement of slavery was made by whites for white readers.

The fugitive slaves' murder of whites, no matter how evil they were, is a radical departure from previous antislavery works. There are other events which highlight the antislavery commentary of this work. The priest of Magarabomba converted a rich plantation owner, Romualdo's father, against slavery. The priest acquired a certificate from Tacón himself for the protagonist's freedom, reaffirming Tacón's good nature and an official interest in seeing Romualdo rescued from slavery. Toward the end of the novel the antislavery sentiment is underscored. Before dying, Romualdo measures his legal status against the freedom gained while fighting the slave hunters. In other words, not the paper but his fighting gave him freedom from whites. As with Francisco, death is his ultimate escape.

Let us explore the context of Calcagno's writing. The subtleties in the narration may establish a relationship between the time of the narration and the time in which the novel was completed. In essence, the novel offers two historical periods fused into one. Just as General Lorenzo rebelled against the Tacón government in 1836, a major rebellion in Cuba against the Lersundi government took place in 1868, one year before Calcagno finished his novel. For Ramiro Guerra, Lersundi's attempt to establish order in Oriente paralleled Tacón's action in 1837.[13] Also in 1868, Carlos Manuel de Céspedes rose against the Spanish authorities in Bayamo. One month later, Ignacio Agramonte, with Gen. Manuel de Quesada, did the same in the region of Puerto Príncipe. Puerto Príncipe unites the past with the present time of the writing. This is the same area in which Armona waited for orders to attack General Lorenzo's forces and the same place where runaway slaves chose to live and fight for their freedom. Furthermore, Puerto Príncipe is the region in which Armona captured Romualdo and other fugitive slaves. Although Carlos Manuel de Céspedes and other rebels later became heroes, in 1869 they were considered outlaws.[14]

In Spain, General Serrano's government, which favored a constitutional monarchy, replaced Lersundi with the abolitionist Domingo Dulce. Dulce proposed to eliminate censorship and restore freedom of the press, freedom of assembly, and representation to the Spanish courts. He soon met with opposition from well-to-do Cubans who opposed rebel forces and were loyal to Spain. The Serrano government recalled a previous constitutional monarchy, that of María Cristina in 1836. Dulce's implementation of liberal reforms in Cuba resembled the actions taken by Lorenzo to implement the 1812 constitution in Oriente.[15] As with Del Monte and the early antislavery writers who found encouragement in Lorenzo, perhaps Calcagno found the same support under the Dulce government to write about slavery. But, within a month of his arrival, Dulce had given in to conservative groups and, like his predecessor Lersundi, suspended political freedom. At the time of Calcagno's writing, the press again was censored, and, as in previous times, Calcagno encountered difficulty in writing and publishing his work. In his *Cuba: Economía y sociedad*, Levi Marrero reproduces a document Serrano wrote in 1862 which underscores the problems of writing about slavery. Writings from abroad circulated in Cuba and disturbed peace and tranquility on the island. Serrano believed that the subject of slavery was not ready to be written about and advises the governors not to touch such a volatile issue which could affect the prosperity of the country. Serrano concludes:

> Therefore, I entrust you to watch over with the greatest scruples, so that newspapers which are published in your jurisdiction do not consent to insert articles, start polemics, nor even publish foreign news which refers to slavery. The same precaution you take with newspapers, you should have with pamphlets and books, regardless of their origin. Gather them as soon as you receive notice of their whereabouts and try to adopt these dispositions with prudence and convenient reservation so that the same measures do not produce alarm and excite curiosity of those who have not yet read the works or writings which we intend collecting.[16]

The document helps to explain why Calcagno waited twelve years to publish *Romualdo, uno de tantos* and twenty-four years to publish *Los crímenes de Concha*. In spite of Dulce's shift in political position, a group of conservative militant volunteers forced him to resign on June 5, 1869. The new captain general, General Caballero de Rodas, a conservative, sided with the volunteers and enjoyed the support of Cuba's two most powerful sugar planters, Manuel Calvo and Julián de Zulueta. The rapid change in government, the growing rebel group seeking independence, and the volunteers who supported Spanish rule created disorder on the island.[17]

Calcagno may have looked to the Tacón era with some nostalgia for law and order lacking during the time he was writing his novel. With censorship and conservative elements in power, Calcagno, if he indeed had antislavery sentiments (and I believe he did), used 1836 as a way to refer to the lawlessness of 1869, the year he wrote his novel. Unable to express stronger antislavery opinions, he focused on the theme of corruption, evident during the time of the writing and the time of the narration, to expound upon a racial condition. As with previous antislavery works, a suggestive narration was less threatening to a wider public, allowing the reader to identify with and accept the plight of the black and mulatto characters. Although the date of publication demands a stronger denouncement of the slavery system, the time of the writing suggests that even though some thirty years had elapsed since the past of the narration, little had changed for blacks, mulattoes, and slaves and for authors who condemned their unjust condition. Calcagno attempted to situate his counter-discourse on slavery between the extremes of criminals like Juan Rubio, on the one hand, and fugitive slaves who were killing whites, on the other. This in part explains why *Romualdo, uno de tantos*, written in 1869, was not published until 1881 but was confiscated by the government and not published in its final version until 1891,[18] twenty-two years after it was written, five years after the emancipation of slaves in 1886, and seven years before Cuba's independence from Spain in 1898.

The complexity of Calcagno's novel is also present in his *Aponte*, published twenty years after *Romualdo, uno de tantos*. The difference between the time he wrote and published his novel allows us to explore similar levels of interpretation in his *Aponte*. As with *Romualdo, uno de tantos* and *Los crímenes de Concha*, Calcagno chose to narrate the past; Calcagno wrote his *Aponte* in 1885, but it pertains to the Aponte Conspiracy of 1812.

Although the title of the novel alludes to the historical figure Aponte and his well-known efforts to overthrow the Spanish government, emancipate all slaves, and establish in Cuba a republic similar to that of Haiti, *Aponte* has very little to do with the black leader. According to the narration, the plot refers to a "real" incident that developed independently of the Aponte Conspiracy but, in the end, coincided with it.[19] As in *Romualdo, uno de tantos, Aponte* continues the theme of slavery and runaway slaves, but, more than the other work and like *Los crímenes de Concha,* it centers on a critique of aristocratic life and refers to the Aponte Conspiracy of 1812.

As a historical and novelistic character, Aponte is mainly present in the prologue, already prefiguring the relationship between fact (the prologue) and fiction (the text). According to the narrator, Aponte and eight of his men were sentenced to death by hanging. They were hanged on April 8, 1812, and on the following day their bodies were seen by many, a sight described as "repugnante y salvador" (disgusting and saving). The narrator also describes the location of two of the decapitated heads displayed in cages: One head belonged to Aponte, the other to an unknown, almost white mulatto, underscoring the problem of color and race in nineteenth-century Cuba. The narration proceeds to explore the identity of the unknown mulatto.

As with *Romualdo, uno de tantos,* in writing *Aponte* Calcagno used historical data obtained while researching his *Diccionario biográfico cubano.* Under the entry of Aponte, Calcagno summarizes the rebel's actions as described in the novel. In fiction, Calcagno writes: "When a prisoner in the fight in Peñas-Altas, grave of so many ignored heros whose names unjust history has forgotten, except for those of Orihuela and Quintero, he was some forty years old. Aponte and eight of his henchmen were locked up in the Cabaña where *licenciado Rendón,* prosecutor of the cause, stayed for two months, substantiating the case with mastery worthy of royal gratitude, later manifested by conferring upon his widow the title of vice-countess of Peñas-Altas."[20] In fact, Calcagno documents the same incident as follows:

> Almost all of the leaders of the uprising were captured in their initial movements by a group of countrymen led by the mentioned Orihuela. Aponte and eight of his cohorts were taken to Havana, locked up in the Cabaña, and condemned to hang; the sentence was executed in May of the mentioned year. Apodaca entrusted the substantiation of that sensational event to Ldo. Rendón (q.v.) who was transferred immediately to the Cabaña, from which he did not emerge until concluding all of the indictment. From here, the title of marquis of Rendón and vice-countess of Peñas-Altas was conferred upon his widow doña María de las Nieves de Suazo in 1839.[21]

In describing this "devilish" figure, the narrator blames Aponte less
for his conspiracy against whites to help blacks than (as whites believed at the beginning of the century) for his plan to establish in
Cuba a black republic. The information present in the prologue and
recalled at the end of the novel serves as the background and historical context for the narration.

The words "repugnante y salvador" used in the prologue provide
an insight into a certain reading of the novel. Although the adjec-
tives appear to be in opposition to each other, they are held together
by a conjunction which allows both words to interrelate with the
noun they modify. Structurally speaking, the novel develops in a
similar relationship of opposites, between the prologue, which describes the aftermath of the sentencing of Aponte and his men, and
the body of the novel, which pertains mainly to the activities of the
marqués de Represalia; that is, between fact and fiction. A similar
relationship between opposites exists regarding the theme suggested
by the title of the novel and what is actually narrated in the content
of the work, or even between the protagonist's dual personality, between the slave Hipólito and his transformation into nobility as the
marqués de Represalia.

The novel's introduction and the entries in the dictionary describe events from the dominant view of the times. But within the
context of the fiction and other antislavery narratives, it serves to
entice the reader into reading about a story different from what the
title and the prologue would suggest. The title is used as a means of
calling the reader's attention to Aponte, not to reveal the history of
his story but to explain the life and death of an unknown and almost
white mulatto who was hanged along with Aponte. After capturing
the reader with the prologue, Calcagno abandons the official history
of Aponte and seizes the opportunity to describe aristocratic and
slave life during the early part of the nineteenth century. The two
diametrically opposed societies and cultures come together in another plan, this one devised not by the narrator but by the slave
owner Juan Pérez. As the initiator of one set of events in the novel,
Pérez uses his slave Hipólito to seek revenge against a woman he
loved. Pérez's plan is worthy of its own novel. His scheme includes
sending his slave Hipólito to Spain and educating him in a manner
befitting nobility. After a two-year period, the slave returns, transformed into the marqués de Represalia (reprisal). His task is simple,
to court the countess Ana Luisa and embarrass her and her husband,
the count of San Marcos. Pérez, who was rich and attempted to court
the countess but held no noble title, had not been given the satisfaction of a duel with the count. Pérez's slave will avenge his master's

pride. Calcagno's novel raises a fundamental question implicit in the time of the narration but also certainly an issue during the time of the writing: the ongoing debate as to whether a black or mulatto, through education, can escape his slave condition. In Cuba, this points to the slave poet Juan Francisco Manzano. The debate suggests a more general question, which addresses the problematics between heredity and environment.

Calcagno's antislavery ideas are in direct contrast to others present during the time he wrote and published his novel. Many supporters of slavery who after emancipation became the champions of racial discrimination believed in the inherent inferiority of blacks, subscribed to the ideas of Gobineau, Nietzsche, and even Hegel, and, in America, to those of Sarmiento. These influential thinkers praised the advancement of European civilization and looked down on Africa and people of color as inferior to whites. In Cuba, Gustavo Enríquez Mustelier's *La extinción del negro,* reflects the ideas of European and American intellectuals by accepting the inferiority of blacks. He and others relied on Darwin's *Origin of Species* and appropriated science and biology to justify their own superiority over people of African descent. For him, man should not change nature but merely interpret it: "Slavery would be the political and legal sanction of an objective reality, purely biological. . . . Laws cannot modify the biological and social phenomena; they should only limit themselves to interpreting them, adopting to them."[22] He continues: "Human solidarity results here in a lyrical and irrational preoccupation. The rights of man could be just for those who have reached the same stage of biological evolution; but, strictly speaking, it is not enough to belong to the human species to understand those rights and use them. Can the votes of these blacks equal that of Spencer? Men of the white race, even in inferior ethnic groups, are an abyss apart from these beings which appear to be closer to the anthropoid monkeys than to civilized whites."[23]

In some ways, Mustelier's position resembles Calcagno's when the former predicts the disappearance of pure blacks as biologically natural. Like Romualdo, Hipólito, the son of a white man and a slave, is considered to be intelligent and may even represent the new fusion of the races. For Mustelier, the assimilation of blacks may produce a superior race. "Slowly he will be assimilated into the white race and the quadroon will result, as an ethnic type, physically superior and could even result, in the future, in the intellectual, superior to the pure members of any of the two races."[24] With his character, Calcagno is combatting the notion of the superiority of one race over the other. If Calcagno's portrayal of Hipólito does represent the type of individual Mustelier is describing, then Calcagno's character is not of the future but is a person already present in the early part of the nineteenth century. Fusion and assimilation have been in progress for some time.

Hipólito is a superior being. When he arrived from Spain, he had been transformed into a marquis with all the social graces and responsibilities associated with the title. His title was convincing, and he was accepted immediately by members of the aristocracy. The argument put forth by Calcagno is twofold: On the one hand, he criticizes the aristocratic emphasis on titles; on the other, he suggests that slaves like Hipólito can, in fact, escape their own condition and be educated. After proper training, there is little if any difference between a slave and a white. (Hipólito's only flaw is that, on occasion, his Cuban accent surfaces.) However, we may argue that not all slaves can transcend their servitude since the protagonist is not a black but a light mulatto, allowing Hipólito to transcend his blackness. This may be a valid point, but we must take into account that, if Calcagno was not referring to all black and mulatto slaves, he would have been more effective in portraying a free mulatto as a protagonist, as he did in *Romualdo, uno de tantos*. Calcagno's convictions are also expressed in the prologue of *Los crímenes de Concha* when he foresees that slaves, during the time of writing the novel in 1865 and the prologue in 1883, needed to be prepared for freedom. Within the context of *Aponte*, slaves indeed can be prepared for freedom. Moreover, by using a slave as a protagonist, Calcagno increases the humiliation of the count and countess. Since the novel was conceived before the emancipation of slaves, a mulatto protagonist may have been more credible to a white audience, especially a mulatto courting a white woman.

To some extent, the narration recalls Manzano's autobiography, which Calcagno had read. Manzano's life is reproduced in the *Diccionario biográfico cubano* and in greater detail in Calcagno's *Poetas de color*, published the same year. Yet it is with Manzano that we detect a certain affinity between Calcagno and blacks. In his *Poetas de color*, Calcagno considered himself not only nonwhite but a slave when he included himself among the "colored" poets; he published some of his own poems under the pseudonym "Moreno esclavo Narciso Blanco" (Colored Slave Narciso Blanco).[25]

Calcagno's ideas regarding race are better developed in an obscure book neglected by critics. Published in 1888, three years after he completed *Aponte, En busca del eslabón* is an anthropological novel whose characters travel to Africa seeking an answer to the question of the missing link. Calcagno uses Darwin's ideas and those of other critics and philosophers when considering blacks as human but inferior to whites. Refuting the ideas of conservatives such as Schoemering, who proved that the digestive system of blacks is closer to that of the monkey than that of whites,[26] the character Stanley defends blacks against slavery. In a manner which recalled the abolitionist priest of Magarabomba, Stanley takes issue with the scientific discourse of the time and exclaims: "Never! The black is not yet a man, but neither is he the monkey; and nothing can give us the right to be masters and least to mistreat them; the mistreatment is not justified not even when it oppresses oxens and horses. And to be born a slave! What sophism can excuse the crime of preparing chains for the innocent? Black slavery will always be a black stain on the white conscience."[27] Although Stanley's statement was considered radical in the nineteenth century, arguing against the natural rights of whites to enslave blacks, he makes an important distinction between blacks in Africa and their counterparts in America. He considers the former closer to beasts,[28] thus giving some validity to the European civilization process. After all, he contends, it is in the best interest of the social development of whites that blacks should be emancipated. Thus Calcagno places the responsibility on whites, as he had done in *Romualdo, uno de tantos.* From this perspective, with the educated Hipólito Calcagno seeks a position acceptable to whites from which to refute the inferiority of blacks.[29]

The relationship between the title, as the thematic indicator of the novel, and the content, as the work itself (that is, the relationship between what should be and what actually is), is developed in the novel as a relationship between reality and appearance, between essence and representation. According to the content, in Western society perception is more important than one's actual self. The collective unconscious is a determining force, insofar as it captures a (mis)perception and transforms it into reality. Hipólito, the slave, is accepted as the marqués de Represalia, his Platonic relationship with the countess is interpreted as an affair, and for others rumors about them have become reality.

Within the context of slavery, blacks and slaves are believed to be closer to animals. Moreover, Hipólito, who had been suspected of escaping slavery to join Aponte, was, in reality, in Spain. The rumor becomes a self-fulfilling prophecy. Toward the end of the novel, Hipólito, to take revenge against his master, does seek Aponte's help. The structure of reversals continues and is applicable to rebel blacks. Aponte questions Hipólito's fugitive actions, since he considered Pérez a good slave master. But through Hipólito, the reader discovers that enslavement of morality and dignity is as bad as enslavement of the body, foreshadowing an issue that is important in the postslavery period; that is, during the time in which the author wrote the novel.

The displacement of theme suggested by the novel's title and evident in the narration also affects Juan Pérez, who conceives of the plan to avenge himself against the count and countess. But, like a contemporary author or narrator of fiction, Pérez loses control of the action when his slave internalizes his acquired role. Believing himself to be a white, a marquis, and his master's equal, Hipólito receives the news of his freedom with indifference. The freedom granted for a job well done meant nothing to him. Most importantly, as his master had done before him, Hipólito sought retribution, for his dignity had been offended.

In analyzing the system of reversals, the opposite of what I have explained may also be true. In accordance with the ideas of social determinism, the novel serves as a warning to whites about the danger of educating slaves and blacks. With nobility titles available to anyone, slaves, at least with the help of benevolent masters, but also on their own, may become equal to whites. This point of view is further substantiated by Calcagno's comments in the introduction, when he succumbs to an idea of the past; that is, a fear that if Aponte succeeded in establishing a black republic, white women would be at his disposal. Calcagno reflects the same concern in his *Diccionario biográfico cubano*. In his entry under Aponte, the historiographer writes: "In 1812 and under the government of Someruelos, he fabricated a conspiracy among those of his color, whose objective was to assassinate all whites, keep the white women and establish here an empire similar to that of Soulouquen."[30] The same fear is also present in the prologue and in Hipólito's relationship with the countess. The narrator continues: "It is true, he would not return to being a slave; but would he return to being a mulatto, and what did it mean being a mulatto and free, for someone who had been a marquis and passed as the preferred lover of one of the prominent ladies of Havana high society?" (222). Calcagno expresses a collective fear, not only regarding Aponte's armed rebellion but also about violating the "sanctity" of white women. If noble titles can hide the essence of slaves or blacks, a black man can become the lover of a white woman. However suggestive, the novel does not support this contention: Many, including Juan Pérez, desired the countess; only Hipólito establishes an intimate relationship with her, and that is nonsexual.

There is another reversal that must be explored. The power of the master balances the lack of power of the slave or, in other words, the power of whites refers to the lack of power of blacks. But at the same time, the power of blacks points to the helplessness of whites. In a similar manner, the initiator of the plot, Pérez, is diametrically opposed to Aponte, the initiator of another event. But if Pérez may represent good, then Aponte, his opposite, is evil. In a religious sense, one appears to be the creator, God, and the other the destroyer, the devil. In a binary relationship betwen black and white, good and evil, the terms may be inverted, as the early antislavery novels have shown. For example, the oxymoron "repugnante y salvador" may be changed to "salvador y repugnante" without losing its semantic value. However, in substituting one term for the other, the second term becomes contaminated by the traces of the presence of the first. In other words, what was *repugnante* is tainted by *salvador* and vice versa. Another example can be seen with "good and evil." In the reversal, what appeared to be good is now evil, and what was evil is now good. Regarding the narration, the binary opposition may allow us to consider the marqués de Represalia, that is, Hipólito, and others in a positive light when comparing them to men like Pérez, who used his power or, more correctly, lack of power to seek reprisal against others. Contrary to Pérez, Aponte was viewed as a madman who wanted to make Cuba another Haiti. Unlike the image whites had of him, Aponte believed Pérez to be benevolent to his slaves. For those who were not able to obtain justice, Aponte and Maroons in the mountains became not destroyers but saviors of sorts.

The narration is ironic insofar as Hipólito's transformation or metamorphosis was so complete that his search for a system of justice comparable to his acquired status is unattainable to him: The justice available to him as a white is now denied him as a slave. Justice is not based on innocence or guilt but on race. Yet, it is not Hipólito the white but Hipólito the slave who has dignity. Unable or unwilling to rid himself of his acquired mask, the slave seeks retribution from his master for offending his sense of dignity, a dignity not inherited but acquired. Hipólito's nobility name is also important. In his transformation, the slave was named the marqués de Represalia, representing Pérez's reprisal against the count and countess. But Hipólito's title attains a more personal meaning when he, the marqués de Represalia, seeks reprisal not only against the count but against his master.

The system of inversion and reversal, of binary opposition, brings us back to the relationship between the title and the novel, between the prologue and the content. In the title and the prologue Aponte is described as the initiator of events that would lead to the destruction of Cuba. The content of the novel reveals Juan Pérez, another initiator of events, who in a society guided by perceptions and representations devises a plot as intriguing and as complicated as that of Aponte. Within a certain perspective, both Aponte and Pérez are, like Hipólito, seeking justice in what they perceive to be an unjust society. If the reader can understand the injustices committed against Hipólito and Pérez, then he may in retrospect understand the inequities committed against Aponte. The ending of the novel does not justify Aponte's death, but it does allow us to understand why slaves like Hipólito joined the Aponte Conspiracy; they did so seeking retribution for the inequities of whites. The ending of *Aponte* resembles that of *Romualdo, uno de tantos*. Let us recall that the priest of Magarabomba interpreted Romualdo's actions as his only defense against a legal system denied to him. In this sense, Aponte's actions can be justified; the white legal system had also been denied to him.

If Juan Pérez and Aponte are opposites and initiators of events within the context of slavery, the novel also points to the reader as a possible narrator of his environment in the nineteenth century. That is, if we consider the scientific discourse of the time as expressed by *En busca del eslabón* and *Aponte*, not only are blacks superior to animals but, as shocking as it was both during the time of the narration and the time of writing, they are members of the human race. Moreover, if the reader takes an active role in the transformation of Cuban reality, which includes the abolition of slavery, he can, as the initiator of events, bring blacks into the legal system and avoid a violent response from them, such as the Aponte Conspiracy of 1812.

In the novel, Aponte represented a threat to many, but for others he stood for justice. The connection between Hipólito and Aponte is made when the slave has no other recourse but to demand justice from another black, Aponte. To some extent, the ending is another rewriting of Manzano's autobiography, insofar as the slave escapes and seeks the help of whites. But like Romualdo, Hipólito also dies, thus continuing to reflect the time of writing. From the perspective of Hipólito and other oppressed blacks, Aponte did not represent the subversive individual whites wanted to see but a black savior. For blacks, European justice is only for whites and is devised to perpetuate those in power. Slaves and other blacks in the early part of the nineteenth century sought the help of Aponte.

Calcagno attempted to situate his counter-discourse within changing times, that is, before and after the emancipation of slaves, but also during a period in which current theories justified the inferiority of blacks. His project was successful insofar as given the conditions present during the time of the narration and the time in which the novel was written, he shows that blacks will always be instruments of whites and can only be helped by other blacks. Calcagno foresaw that for blacks to better themselves whites must educate whites, as demonstrated in *Romualdo, uno de tantos,* and blacks should only rely on other blacks, as seen in *Aponte.* Only then can the racial attitudes toward blacks really change.

| II | Ten years before Calcagno's *Aponte,* Martín Morúa Delgado published his *Sofía.* In his novel, Morúa, like Calcagno, offered a detailed description of the slavery system. But unlike him, Morúa was a black with first-hand experience with Cuban slave society.[31] Morúa wrote a series of works entitled "Things of My Land" that narrate life in Cuba. The purpose of his project, which consisted of two novels, is made explicit in the introduction to his first novel, *Sofía.* Like members of the Del Monte literary circle, Morúa wanted to document aspects of Cuban life, which inevitably included the theme of slavery.[32]

Morúa wrote *Sofía* after the abolition of slavery, between 1888 and 1890, while living abroad. After a ten-year absence, he returned to Cuba in 1890. With the help of his writer friend Raimundo Cabrera (to whom he dedicates the novel), Morúa published his first novel in 1891.[33] Shortly after the publication of *Sofía,* Morúa started his second and final novel, *La familia Unzúazu.* This second novel continues the themes and characters of the first, but Morúa warns us that one is independent of the other.[34] Morúa did not complete *La familia Unzúazu* until 1896, and it was not published until 1901.[35]

Again, the time of writing and the time of narration reflect two distinct historical periods. By the time Morúa completed his novels, slaves had been emancipated in Cuba and, with his second novel, the Spanish-Cuban-American War was under way. However, even though slavery had ended, as in Calcagno's novels the inferiority of blacks and their integration into Cuban society continued to concern many. Slavery and the subjugation of free blacks in the slavery and postslavery period, in fact, represented a historical development which confirmed the presumed inferiority of the black race. *Sofía* and *La familia Unzúazu,* like the other novels of this postslavery period, denounced different aspects of the slavery system and the corrupt colonial society. Morúa's novels continued to narrate the chronology begun by Calcagno and included the consequences of the Ten Years' War and the Guerra Chiquita of 1879–80. This was an important period in Cuban history, setting the stage for events that culminated in the emancipation of slaves. Slaves who fought in the Ten Years' War were granted their freedom immediately afterward, while others participated in a patronage system devised for gradual emancipation, starting in 1880 and ending in 1886.

After the start of the Ten Years' War, the Guáimaro assembly in Camagüey was instrumental in setting the stage for independence from Spain and the manumission of slaves in Cuba. On April 12, 1869, rebel leaders gathered in the town of Guáimaro to bring unity to the revolutionary cause, define its goals, and select the leaders of the independence movement. From the start of the rebellion on October 10, 1868, the rebel Carlos Manuel de Céspedes became a controversial figure. His leadership created differences between the rebels of Oriente and Camagüey provinces. Céspedes, who was from Oriente, named himself captain general of the republic. Other insurrectionist leaders in Camagüey such as Ignacio Agramonte objected. In the interest of unity, the two parties arrived at a compromise at the Guáimaro assembly. Céspedes was named president of the republic and the more experienced military leader, Manuel de Quesada, chief of the liberation army. Among other resolutions to secure Cuba's independence from Spain, the assembly voted to abolish slavery.[36] Unlike the period in which Calcagno wrote *Romualdo, uno de tantos*, by the time Morúa finished his novels, Céspedes and others were no longer considered outlaws by many but patriots fighting against slavery and Cuba's colonial status.

After the end of the Ten Years' War, the rebels negotiated a general amnesty for those who participated in the insurrection. The amnesty included freedom for slaves and Chinese who fought in the war and for leaders who agreed to leave Cuba. Not all were satisfied with the outcome of the Zanjón Peace Treaty. The mulatto Antonio Maceo and Calixto García vowed to continue the fight; they felt that the treaty neither abolished slavery totally nor made Cuba independent. After a March 16, 1878, meeting between Maceo and the Spanish representative, Martínez Campos, the Cuban rebels issued the "Protesta de Baragúa," a denunciation of the Zanjón Peace Treaty and a commitment to continue fighting. The Guerra Chiquita soon followed.

The Guerra Chiquita was initiated by Antonio Aguilera and had its major impact in Oriente and Las Villas. Most of the rebels who joined this war had participated in the Ten Years' War and did not emigrate with their officers. In spite of the patriotic commitment of the rebels, many considered the Guerra Chiquita a racial uprising. Black rebel leaders Quintín Banderas, Guillermón Moncada, and Belizario Grave de Peralta joined the rebellion in Holguín on August 25, 1879.[37] Calixto García, who had sought political asylum abroad when the Guerra Chiquita started, became the leader of the rebellion.

The war was short-lived: by the time García and his men landed on the island on May 7, 1880, the war was over. Juan Gualberto Gómez believed that the Guerra Chiquita failed because of García's late arrival. Troops waiting for him were disorganized and scattered throughout the territory. Many were even unaware of his landing. Even after García finally arrived, the troops lacked unity and coordination.[38] Betrayals, lack of organization, and decisive measures taken by Captain General Blanco and General Polavieja in Oriente also contributed to the rebels' defeat. Gen. Calixto García surrendered on August 4, 1880. He and others were sent to prison in Spain.[39]

Both *Sofía* and *La familia Unzúazu* take place between 1878 and 1880 and describe in detail the Cuban society of those years. In fact, the mulatto character Fidelio in *La familia Unzúazu* is imprisoned because, as a black, he is suspected of aiding the rebels. However, while Morúa's second novel reflects the historical events of the period, *Sofía* is mainly a commentary on, and a rewriting of, Cirilo Villaverde's *Cecilia Valdés*.

Published nine years after Villaverde's masterpiece, *Sofía* contains textual indications that Morúa had already read *Cecilia Valdés* and was influenced by Villaverde's work. More importantly, Morúa sought to correct in his own novel what he considered to be mistakes in Villaverde's masterpiece. Morúa found inherent weaknesses in what he referred to as "a long story." Morúa's ideas about writing in general and Villaverde's works in particular are highlighted in his *Impresiones literarias. Las novelas del sr. Villaverde*, published one year after *Sofía*. In his four-part essay, Morúa outlines what a work of literature should be: aesthetically pleasing and utilitarian, that is, it should be well written and have a moral ending. Responding to a different group of writers than Villaverde, Morúa agreed with modernist thinkers who believed that art and science should be combined in a work of fiction. This approach allowed him to accept the works of Daudet, Chatrian, Erckmann, Flaubert, and Balzac over those of Goncourt, Ohnet, and Maupassant and to admire only the Zola of *La Curée*. Morúa saw Erckmann and Chatrian as writers who were interested in describing the different social levels of their own society.[40] Like his French counterparts, Morúa uses his *Sofía* and *La familia Unzúazu* to narrate the life of the wealthy Unzúazu family, thus revealing their problems, tragedies, expectations, and political ideas and giving the reader a panoramic view of life in nineteenth-century Cuba.

Morúa believed that Cuba had talented writers; he was not surprised by Galdós's reference to Villaverde's *Cecilia Valdés*. According to Morúa, Galdós "never thought that a Cuban could write such a good thing."[41] But Morúa preferred the better written works of Gertrudis Gómez de Avellaneda. If we consider the opinion of other critics, Morúa overreacted to Villaverde's work. In his *Tema negro,* José A. Fernández de Castro chose Villaverde's novel over Gómez de Avellaneda's when comparing their respective *Cecilia Valdés* and *Sab.* Fernández de Castro notices defects in *Sab* which he attributes to Gómez de Avellaneda's residency away from the Cuban environment, forcing her to rely on recollections. Moreover, Fernández de Castro cites Mitjanes, who criticizes as unrealistic Sab's sacrifice to unite his mistress and a man who did not deserve her. Fernández de Castro suggests that Avellaneda did not include *Sab* in her *Obras completas* because she realized that her novel was not very good.[42] (I should also stress that it was omitted because of its abolitionist theme.)

Morúa recognized the popularity of Villaverde's novel but also criticized its lack of a moral ending, which is necessary to improve society and alter history. He attacked the "aberration of the historical novel genre," which, according to him, did not allow art to be perfected. He considered it neither history nor a novel: "And at the most, in its excessive subtlety, it serves only as a transparent screen which partially hides the insufficient imagination of the person who composes it."[43]

Morúa's exposé precedes a commentary about major and minor characters in *Cecilia Valdés* of which none, for him, seem to stand out. Morúa points to other mistakes. For example, Villaverde erred in the historical accuracy of Tonda's death, the reproduction of María de Regla's speech, and the historical description of the well-known tailor Francisco Uribe. He lacked familiarity with popular language, made grammatical mistakes, and did not include among his characters the essential *personaje simpático,* a requirement for every work of art. Thus, in *Sofía,* whose title implies a certain wisdom not found in the title of Villaverde's work, Morúa corrects inaccuracies in *Cecilia Valdés.*

Although Morúa is accurate in some of his assessments of Villaverde's work, other observations are not well founded. For example, Morúa cannot accept Leonardo's marriage to Isabel Ilincheta, whom Villaverde describes as ugly. Outraged by what Villaverde did, Morúa states: "Nor do I want her to be a goddess, no; not a conventional heroine; but I will not forgive Mr. Villaverde who just like that, in a slapdash way, sacrifices her. What is that? Let her remain an old maid, taking care of her farm, in the middle of her refinery, cooed at by her pigeons, worshiped by members of her family, venerated by her slaves, blessed by God."[44] Morúa omits the necessary comparison between Cecilia and Isabel to establish Leonardo's overwhelming desire for the mulatto, someone darker than he. Regardless of how each felt toward the other, both Leonardo and Isabel responded to their parents' desire that they marry each other.

Morúa's criticism goes to the heart of Villaverde's novel when he questions the unlikelihood that everyone except Cecilia and Leonardo knew that they were brother and sister. Even though we are tempted to agree with Morúa, his criticism may not be a surprise to a contemporary reader, especially when considering Gabriel García Márquez's *Chronicle of a Death Foretold,* in which everyone in the town except Santiago Nasar knew that he was going to be killed by the Vicario brothers.[45] The overt and implied criticism of Villaverde's novel is continued in Morúa's *Sofía* insofar as it proceeds to correct or rewrite *Cecilia Valdés.* Like Villaverde, Morúa narrates an incestuous relationship between brother and sister, between Sofía and Federico, between a white and a "mulatto." But unlike Cecilia and Leonardo, Morúa makes sure that the incest between Federico and Sofía is a surprise not only to the readers but to the characters themselves. Morúa allows Magdalena to inform her younger sister of her true identity. Sofía then realizes that her half brother is the father of her child. The news disconcerts the sick Sofía and leads to her death. As with the earlier antislavery works, Morúa shows that morality, dignity, and taboos are stronger than economic factors in society.

We may wonder if Morúa would have written his *Sofía* if Villaverde's novel had not existed. Cecilia Valdés and Sofía resemble one another. Cecilia sought to improve her social position and the racial composition of her child by marrying Leonardo Gamboa; the slave Sofía thought of the same possibilities with Federico. For both slaves and free blacks, relationships with whites represented one way women of color could escape their slavelike condition and move up the social ladder. But, in Sofía's case, it appears less likely that a white would have married a slave than a free black. Morúa may have resorted to his own personal situation regarding his slave mother and white father to narrate fictional discourse. However, Leonardo and Federico were aware of their strengths and used their wealth and social position to conquer Cecilia and Sofía, respectively.

*Sofía* and *Cecilia Valdés* have similar endings. The mulatto Pimienta sought revenge by killing not Isabel, as Cecilia wanted, but Leonardo Gamboa; the slave Liberato, in Morúa's novel, seeks similar retribution. However, Liberato's motivations are different from those of Pimienta. There is no evidence of any admiration for, or love between, Liberato and Sofía, nor is it ever made clear if Liberato killed his master because he had slapped the slave or because he wanted to protect Sofía. In spite of these differences, both novels highlight the killer's escape from justice. In Villaverde's novel, Pimienta kills Leonardo, flees, and is never caught. In Morúa's novel, Liberato does not kill Sofía's lover but, more daringly, stabs their master, Nudoso del Tronco. And even though Liberato is caught, his mistress, Ana María, seeking to embarrass Nudoso's lover, influences the corrupt judicial system, which this time works in favor of a black. Liberato goes free.

There is no question that Morúa's *Sofía* profitted from his reading of *Cecilia Valdés*. Although there is a remote possibility that Morúa portrayed the problems of the society in which he lived independently of Villaverde's novel, I have noticed more than a mere coincidence between the two writers' works. The characters of one work appear to be present in the other. For instance, the beautiful slave Sofía, who in reality is not a slave, recalls Cecilia Valdés; Leonardo, Cecilia's half brother, is Federico, Sofía's half brother; Cándido Gamboa, who made his money in the slave trade, is Unzúazu; both Gamboa and Unzúazu take their respective daughters away from their mothers.[46] Moreover, Ana María resembles doña Rosa: both marry Spaniards but are financially better off than their husbands; both women marry at their fathers' insistence.

There are also obvious differences between the two works. For example, as we have stated, Liberato does not appear to be in love with Sofía and does not kill Federico but the brother-in-law Nudoso. Moreover, Villaverde describes Pimienta as a free black, while Morúa characterizes Liberato as a *ñáñigo*, a member of an African religious group and mutual aid society. Morúa interjects his knowledge of Afro-Cuban culture by having Liberato kill Nudoso in the manner known to the *ñáñigo* secret society. Liberato's action is not a single, isolated incident as is Pimienta's. It represents a collective action on the part of a member of a society which, some believed, rivaled the power of whites. The *ñáñigos* were a marginal element in Cuban society. Enrique Fernández Carrillo provides some information regarding this group. According to him, very little is known about the *ñáñigo* mutual aid society. It originated in central Africa and was brought to Cuba by the Carabalí people, the largest group of slaves from this African region. The secret society had been significantly transformed from its inception in Cuba and had no written laws. The members were divided into groups in which the oldest commands. Many considered the *ñáñigos* to be violent and accused them of being fanatics. Reflecting a white dominant point of view, Carrillo summarizes this group's actions in a biased manner: "But the *ñáñigo* is ignorant and the association allows anyone to enter; the acts of the associates are purely personal and not imposed by ritual. It is satiated with fanaticism, with idolatry to which it gives cult, with the blindness that distinguishes it, to be condemned by all truths.''[47] Regardless of what whites may have believed about this secret society, they were not exempt from similar conspiracies. Just as Juan Pérez's actions reflected Aponte's conspiracy in Calcagno's novel, at Ana María's request her lawyer contrived a plot to free the jailed Liberato which included killing a policeman in the same manner Nudoso had been murdered. This created uncertainty as to the identity of Nudoso's and the policeman's killer and led to Liberato's release from jail. More importantly, unlike Villaverde's novel, *Sofía* contains the *simpático* Gonzaga, a good-natured character who believes in and fights for justice.

In some respects, symbols of *Cecilia Valdés* appear to be inverted in *Sofía*. As I have indicated, Morúa uses the same theme found in Villaverde's novel. Unlike the antislavery writers and according to the changing times, Morúa subjects not a mulatto but a white to suffering the cruelties of the slavery system. This causes the situation to be even more dramatic, since the reader will discover that Sofía, like Romualdo, was punished without cause; in fact, she was not a slave but a white. Like Villaverde and Calcagno, Morúa reveals the unfairness and arbitrariness of the slavery system, which, in his work, punishes a white and wealthy woman who is mistakenly identified as a slave.

The themes of incest and illegitimacy are taken one step further to directly affect the upper class. A relationship between Morúa's two novels is created when Sofía's desire for a child and a lover or a husband is materialized in *La familia Unzúazu* with her half sister Magdalena, who has an illegitimate child with Gonzaga. But unlike Sofía, who miscarries, Magdalena's child will be a healthy girl, the author's vision of Cuba's future. The theme takes its final turn with the eldest sister, Ana María: Cecilia Valdés and the slave Sofía are taken advantage of by a white. In *La familia Unzúazu*, the symbols of sexual oppression against black women are inverted and applied to whites; the black slave Liberato seeks sexual revenge and rapes his mistress. Morúa looked to equal the score: If Villaverde wrote about white men raping mulatto women, Morúa, who himself was a black, would write about a black man raping a white woman. After the rape, there is a coincidence and therefore an identity of sorts between the oldest and youngest sisters. Like Sofía, Ana María is pregnant but has an abortion.

If we continue to seek a relationship between *Sofía* and *La fa-*

*milia Unzúazu*, Morúa rewrites the ending of Villaverde's novel. Morúa also breaks the cycle of oppression of women portrayed, for example, in *Cecilia Valdés*. Gonzaga's union with Magdalena will provide a stable home for their female child. Cecilia was raised not by her mother and father but by her grandmother. Gonzaga's and Magdalena's child, as a symbol of the next generation, will be reared by both her parents. For Morúa, this society is no longer made up of the mixing of the races and pertains only to whites.

A comparative reading of Morúa's *Sofía*, his *Impresiones literarias*, and *Cecilia Valdés* reveals that Morúa indeed modeled his novel after Villaverde's. However, there are aspects of slavery included in *Sofía* but not in *Cecilia Valdés* that are essential for understanding slavery during the second third of the nineteenth century. Like Calcagno, Morúa was also concerned with *plagio*, the stealing of slaves, and made this illegal act the center of the plot. Although Sofía is not physically taken from her family and sold to a slave owner, as Romualdo was, she is nevertheless robbed of her freedom and forced to be a slave. She as a white is made to experience the life of a slave.

In documenting other aspects of slavery not present in *Cecilia Valdés*, Morúa criticizes Nudoso del Tronco's attempt to "comply" with the law before selling or sending Sofía to the mill. In so doing, he explains the importance of *el papel*, a license given to a slave to find another master. Some licensed slaves never returned to their masters and sought refuge in the black barrio of San Lázaro or at the home of a free black, thus in many cases consolidating tribal unity. The slave Liberato often escaped and met with other free blacks in their communities. It was there that he learned about and joined the *ñáñigos*.[48]

In some instances, the licenses were forged, a practice that was in place during the narrative time of *Romualdo, uno de tantos*. To counter the common practice of forgery, Captain General Tacón on March 17, 1835, issued the following order: "I have determined, to avoid doubts, that the masters of the referred day laborers whom they allow to live on their own or sleep outside their homes, give said licenses endorsed by the police inspector of the district and captains of the outer regions, free, which will avoid the fleeing of many which perhaps lived under this refuge."[49] He added that the missing slaves be advertised in the *Diario* during three consecutive days; on the eighth day, after the ad ended, the slave would be considered a fugitive.

Our investigation into runaway slavery in the city is relevant to Morúa's novel because Nudoso, who had issued Sofía a three-day license, on the last day accused her of attempting to escape. As punishment, she would be sent back to the sugar mill. It was Nudoso's effort to force her into a carriage that caused Sofía to hemorrhage. This was the first of a sequence of events that would lead to her premature death. Morúa's inclusion of the license episode not only describes how slave owners were able to get around the law to continue punishing their slaves but also reveals the tragedy in Sofía's life, especially since she had found a buyer, even at the very high price Nudoso had set. Nudoso's action to send her to the sugar mill was a way of denying her true identity and increasing his financial power.

Sofía's tragedy is directly related to a white attitude toward slavery prevalent in the colonial society in which she lived. Her innocence is juxtaposed to the selfish interests of her white owners; the contrast underscores her moral superiority over those considered to be more powerful than she. Moreover, through Sofía and her interaction with different environments, that is, the city and the country, Morúa questions the racial nature of slavery. The concept of destiny as a consequence of race becomes an important issue when Sofía, as a white, is subjected to the same conditions as blacks.

There is another reversal which takes into account Calcagno's *Aponte*. As we have seen, Calcagno narrated the story of a slave who learned to read and write and was able to pass for a marquis and win the admiration of whites. Morúa inverts that situation and shows how a white person, through mistaken identity, was forced to believe she was a slave. Environment over heredity is an issue here. As a child, Sofía accepted her slave condition and had no inherent feelings about her true race. On the contrary, she internalized the slave behavior and even had the same aspirations as blacks and slaves, including the desire to marry a white to escape from her servitude. Morúa, like Calcagno, is arguing against certain dominant ideas prevalent in his society, as expressed by *La extinción del negro*, and supports environment over race as a determiner of human behavior. For him, slavery is not a racial but a social and economic condition. To those who did not know her, Sofía was white. To those around her, she was a slave. Her slave status determined her appearance and the outcome of her life. More accurately, the social environment conditioned the makeup of her being. While in the sugar plantation, she acquired the habits of rural slaves. Given these unfortunate conditions, anyone could be forced to act like a black slave. However, some of the changes were not permanent and the situation in part was reversed, as was the case in the company of Magdalena, who corrected the slave's speech and taught her the proper behaviors associated with high Western culture. Therefore, we may argue that slaves can be taught European values. The opposite is also true. Because Sofía was white, she inherently had the capacity to recover her natural status. In spite of her improved articulation, Sofía still believed she was a slave and continued to share slave aspirations, hoping that Federico would buy her freedom and marry her. For Morúa, Sofía's social and economic environments determine her destiny and race.

Believing Sofía to be a slave, all the members of the Nudoso-Unzúazu family conspire consciously or unconsciously in her death. Each person, including the kind Magdalena, reflects the stereotypical attitudes toward slavery and also discredits him/herself by revealing selfish greed. The depth of Morúa's characters allows us to understand the psychological drama behind each act. And although the novel does criticize the behavior of whites, the narration cannot be considered sympathetic toward blacks, for they are also included in Morúa's criticism, one which will be evident in *La familia Unzúazu*. The experienced midwife, Maló, misdiagnoses Sofía and through the use of medicinal herbs endangers her life. Morúa prefers Dr. Alvarado, a man of Western science, who scolds Maló for her practice and operates to save Sofía's life.[50]

*Sofía* is a commentary about the slave society of the mid to late nineteenth century and about colonial life in Cuba. As in the early antislavery works, all live in a morally decaying and promiscuous society. Although the struggle for power between whites, blacks, and mulattoes who desire freedom and economic mobility is an important theme, we should remember that it is Unzúazu's extramarital relationship with Sofía's mother which gives rise to the present drama. Unlike *Cecilia Valdés* or any of the other antislavery novels, Unzúazu's lover is not the traditional *mulata* but a white Canary Islander, thus reflecting a more contemporary period in which whites were brought to Cuba to counterbalance the majority black population. Nevertheless, promiscuity is widespread. This is not only the case with Unzúazu, who fathered Sofía, but also with Nudoso del Tronco, who had a mulatto lover. However, we wonder if promiscuity is more a documentation of "cosas de mi tierra" (things of my country) than an actual criticism. The friendship that Gonzaga and Magdalena develop in *Sofía* will culminate in an affair in *La familia Unzúazu* and repeat a well-known pattern seen in other characters. Ultimately, the composition and treatment of the Cuban family is the issue.

If *Sofía* is a rewriting of *Cecilia Valdés* and reflects aspects of colonial society, Morúa's *La familia Unzúazu* is deeply rooted in nineteenth-century Cuban history and the author's own life. In some respects, it is a rewriting or recasting of his own past. Morúa's second novel continues to describe the historical problems of the period in which it was written. Many Cubans were tired of the fighting that erupted during the Ten Years' War. As the war came to an end, the anticolonial rebels were considered outlaws. For blacks, very little had changed from the first to the second half of the century. The *plagio* present in the Tacón administration was still rampant during the time in which Morúa lived. A conversation between the characters of *La familia Unzúazu* recalls the theme of *Romualdo, uno de tantos* in which during the first decades of the century children were stolen and sold as slaves. In the present, the problem is even more evident. The slave trade was officially terminated in 1869 and slavery was on its way out, but slave masters resorted to any means possible to acquire new slaves, including the purchase of stolen ones.

The present continues to resemble the past, but with some differences. A fear of blacks prevailed during the Ten Years' War and the Guerra Chiquita. In their own interest, those who wanted to perpetuate slavery were quick to identify rebel uprisings against Spain as a means of creating a racial confrontation between the black and white races. This was a useful tactic which discouraged support of the black rebels who also sought independence from Spain. An old but effective method was used to hinder the separatist movement. Spanish officials continued their fear tactics by recalling the events of the Haitian rebellion and the Aponte and Ladder conspiracies. In defense of blacks, a witness of the time saw the black threat as a lie created by jealous whites who questioned black loyalty and played on the fear of others. He contradicted assertions that during the Ten Years' War and the rebellions resulting from the Zanjón Treaty that blacks intended to rebel against whites. Those who feared blacks also feared that Cuba would become a Haitian colony. The accusations caused laughter among blacks.[51]

In its most recent stage, the fear of blacks was present during and after the 1868 and 1879 uprisings; many blacks were watched and some were even persecuted. In a response entitled "Contestación a dos desdichados autonomistas," a group of blacks living in New York specifically blamed the Autonomist party for creating "el fantasma negro" (the black bogeyman). Members of the group cited persecution of blacks during the Guerra Chiquita as one of the many reasons why they would not join the rank and file of the party.[52] Some fifty years later, Nicolás Guillén would summarize the times in which Morúa lived: "The 'black fear,' which many wanted to see in the Guerra Chiquita (which had already been used as a govern-

mental recourse in 1868 and would be again in 1895), made it so men
of dark skin, aside from that of their Cubanness, were watched and
followed for only one reason. Among them was Morúa who, after
suffering imprisonment in the San Severino Castle in Matanzas, obtained permission to leave the country, with destination the United
States."[53]

During the approximate time of the narration, Morúa himself experienced the fear of rebels and blacks. As a young man, Morúa supported the separatist movement and participated actively in the
events associated with the Guerra Chiquita. Morúa even conspired
in the Club Revolucionario of Mantanzas, which helped gather arms
and munitions for the rebel leader Cecilio González. Morúa served
as a messenger between the rebel leader and his followers in Pueblo
Nuevo; he was detained and searched when he returned from a visit
to the rebel camp on April 14, 1880. Government officials did not
find the papers Morúa was carrying; nevertheless, he remained in
jail for eight days and was interrogated. He soon found out that his
co-conspirators who transported arms to the rebels had also been
captured. The military representative read Morúa a list of names
known to him as members of the club, a list on which he probably
appeared. Morúa served for forty-five days at the Castillo de San Severino and discovered that Cecilio González's emissary to Matanzas,
Pablo González, had revealed to the authorities the plot in which
Morúa was identified as carrying documents to Cecilio González.[54]
With some important changes, Morúa reproduces his detainment
and imprisonment in *La familia Unzúazu*. As we might suspect,
Morúa's second novel contains autobiographical information.[55] At
the outset of the novel, the mulatto Fidelio is jailed for sharing his
patriotic beliefs with a rebel. Even though his encounter did not go
beyond a brief conversation, the rebel's confession was sufficient to
have Fidelio sent to prison.

If there are some common characteristics between the mulatto
Fidelio and Morúa, there are other events that do not coincide with a
reading of Morúa's life. In light of Morúa's participation in the Club
Revolucionario, his character, Fidelio, is innocent. But Fidelio's reaction to the accusations is surprisingly mild. He does not protest
the mistake or injustice perpetrated against him. The difference in
reactions between Morúa and Fidelio to past events underscores
both the fictional nature of *La familia Unzúazu* and the time in
which Morúa wrote his novel. The novel was completed in 1896,
sixteen years after Morúa's involvement in the Club Revolucionario.
The change in tone may suggest the need to reproduce not what ac-

tually occurred to Morúa in the past but his perspective during the time of the writing. The latter point of view takes into consideration a different understanding of history which includes the historical outcome of the Guerra Chiquita, the emancipation of Cuban slaves in 1886, and the start of the War of Independence in 1895.

The failure of the Guerra Chiquita and Morúa's own betrayal were translated into narrative plot as the imprisonment of an innocent man who was confined for expressing his opinion, the failure of armed insurrection, and the betrayal of the rebels. In the novel, the rebels were accused of unlawful acts, including acts against the government, and they were lucky if they were deported. In history, Morúa left for New York; in fiction, Fidelio was rescued by Gonzaga.

Although the novel does not deviate totally from autobiographical information, the events surrounding Fidelio's and Morúa's imprisonments allow us to understand the shift from events in the author's life to narrative discourse. The shift is made not only to utilize some experiences which complement the plot and document aspects of his life but, most important, to rewrite some events which conform to a contemporary understanding of the past. In writing about a previous time, Morúa no longer saw the need to insist on a militant past which resulted in his betrayal by someone who believed in the same cause he did. In changing some events, Morúa wanted to alter the direction of his past to conform to what his biography should have been rather than what it was.

There are similarities between Morúa and his fictional character. For example, both Morúa and Fidelio were mulattoes and both were barrel makers; Morúa later became secretary of his guild. Both author and character wanted to found a newspaper. Morúa realized his desire in November 1879 when he founded *El Pueblo,* a weekly paper which he used to express a concern for the common people and which bore the name of his town, Pueblo Nuevo, in Matanzas. Affected by the course of events that would result in his imprisonment, Morúa allowed his character to follow in his footsteps. Morúa did so by inverting the events in his own life. Morúa first founded the paper and later was jailed. Fidelio, who had first been jailed, now desired a newspaper in which he would defend not only blacks but whites as well: "A newspaper in which he would express his ideas; a newspaper in which he could defend above all reason the law, justice, according to his personal criterion, and combat, without truce and hate, injustice, and evil wherever it appeared."[56] But in his *El Pueblo,* Morúa had proposed to defend blacks from discrimination and the popular belief that blacks were inferior. Morúa also supported the integration of Cubans, regardless of race or color. The paper's motto was "There is no life without liberty; but there is no liberty without learning."[57]

As a viable alternative for blacks, the paper had been discussed by Gonzaga in *Sofía*. The ideas of Gonzaga in the first novel are transferred to Fidelio in the second, as Morúa inserts himself as character in both novels. The inclusion becomes evident when Olvera mentions that he had heard of a young black who had published a well-written newspaper for the benefit of blacks in Cuba. Given the date in the narration, the reference may be to Juan Gualberto Gómez's *La Fraternidad* or to Manual García Albuquerque's *El Ciudadano*, two black-oriented newspapers founded in 1879. Morúa had attempted to work for Gómez and actually did work for García but objected to the direction taken by the other editors, which he perceived to be detrimental to blacks.[58] Most likely, however, the reference is to Morúa's own *El Pueblo*, which was also founded in 1879.

To the objection of many, Gonzaga, who backed rebel forces with his money during the Ten Years' War, supported the idea that blacks should have their own paper. However, he did so not for the benefit of blacks, as we would suspect, but for the good of whites, an argument more acceptable to Morúa's readers. His position included, perhaps, the stereotypical vision of the times: The newspaper was in reality useless to whites but would serve as a means for whites to control and help guide blacks in their thinking.

Gonzaga's ideas recall Manzano's *Autobiografía* and Calcagno's *Hipólito* insofar as both slaves through education transcend their slave condition. But Gonzaga's exposé does not make clear whether he is expressing his own feelings regarding blacks or whether he has modified his ideas in order to appeal to a more conservative audience; that is, to reassure whites that a black newspaper would not be a threat to them. Gonzaga's words appear to contradict his image as an understanding and benevolent man. In *Sofía*, Gonzaga had been described as a radical. As a separatist, he fled the country and, with his inheritance, supported numerous rebel uprisings. Although he did not have the money, Morúa mirrors his character and aided rebels while abroad, between 1880 and 1890. In exile, Morúa met Máximo Gómez and worked with José Martí and his Partido Revolucionario. *Sofía* describes Gonzaga, who returned to Cuba after the war, as a good friend of the onetime trafficker in slaves Nudoso del Tronco. If we accept Gonzaga's word as mentioned above, then he too believed in the inferiority of blacks.

In many respects, Gonzaga is a complex character. Julián González notices a discrepancy between the protagonist's actions and the way

he is portrayed to the reader.[59] In spite of the ambiguity of his position, like Domingo del Monte and members of his literary circle
Gonzaga represented one side of the slavery issue. Gonzaga's position can best be explained as being not so much in favor of blacks as
for a revolutionary ideal which included the emancipation of blacks.
But the novel also responds to more contemporary issues, the equality of rights which went beyond concern for blacks to include rights
for women. This broader position is best expressed by Ana Betancourt, who petitioned the revolutionary legislators in 1869, proposing that once the republic was established and slavery abolished,
women be granted the rights they merited.[60]

Although Gonzaga supported emancipation of blacks, he, like
Morúa, recognized that for blacks to better themselves they had to
abandon their African heritage and follow the path established by
whites, a path Juan Francisco Manzano had already envisioned. Continual enslavement of blacks would in the long run be more harmful
to whites. Having a profound understanding of the concept of writing, Gonzaga is aware that the act of writing, as a system with its
own sets of constraints, would force blacks into accepting Western
values as their own. To educate blacks and teach them how to write
implies, during this stage of Cuban history, their participation in the
colonial system, creating the illusion that blacks on their own can
institutionalize some form of change.

Fidelio, having internalized Gonzaga's own ideas about the newspaper, is destined to disillusionment and frustration. His enthusiasm for founding a newspaper and helping blacks in Cuba will be in
vain since, according to the Gonzaga of the first novel, whites would
not read newspapers published by blacks and, in the interest of
whites, blacks should be guided in the "right" direction.

It is also possible that the Gonzaga of the first novel is not the
same character of the second novel. The five years that elapsed between the writing of *Sofía* and *La familia Unzúazu* allowed Morúa
to reassess his ideas regarding the actual function of a black press
during the years of the narration and certainly during the years when
he wrote his two novels: Morúa wrote *Sofía* while living abroad; *La
familia Unzúazu* was conceived of and written while in Cuba. When
Morúa returned in 1890, he was no longer the youngster who published *El Pueblo* but a well-educated man who spoke a number of
foreign languages and recognized the importance of his ideas.[61] After
his return, Morúa saw that the situation of blacks had changed suffi-
ciently to justify Fidelio's enthusiasm. In coming to terms with this
analysis, we must keep in mind that Morúa published his paper
from 1870 to 1880, twelve years before the publication of *Sofía*; per-

haps, based on a broader experience, he wanted to communicate through his novel the impact a newspaper can have in reaching a wider audience.

The debates reproduced in *La familia Unzúazu* regarding blacks and slavery are important for understanding Morúa's novels and his perceptions on the subject. As one would expect, some ideas present in *Sofía* are continued in *La familia Unzúazu*. In the second novel, the question of race is openly debated among Gonzaga, Dr. Alvarado, and Fidelio. Their main concern pertains to the transition of blacks from slavery to freedom. The groundwork set after the Ten Years' War for the emancipation of slaves would be completed in 1886, six years before the end of the narration and fifteen years before the publication of the novel. By the time the novel was completed in 1896, it was evident that the situation of blacks in Cuba had not changed significantly. But Morúa, among others, believed that blacks had made considerable gains. Morúa imposed onto the time of the narration an understanding of the race situation during the time of the writing. The characters already anticipate the problems that will be facing Cubans in the near future; that is, during the time in which the author writes his work. In reproducing the ideas on race, Morúa attributes to Gonzaga thoughts that appear to be out of character for him but coincide with his opinion in the first novel regarding blacks and the newspaper. If his actions in the first novel indicate benevolence toward the slave Sofía, in *La familia Unzúazu* Gonzaga opts for the supremacy of whites over emancipated blacks.[62]

In his important speech, Gonzaga reassures whites that the emancipation of slaves will not, in any way, be a danger to them. Although free in body, they will remain slaves in spirit. And the democratic system which will replace the colonial government will continue to guarantee the superiority of whites. In a strange way, *La familia Unzúazu* not only looks back into history in order to understand the past but outlines the events yet to unfold in the years after its publication in 1901. Within the context of the novel, we wonder if Morúa, in expressing the complexity of Gonzaga's character, failed to be consistent regarding his actions and his comments on slavery. Perhaps Gonzaga's kind attitude toward blacks is restricted to isolated situations and to blacks he knew who would not pose a threat to him, a threat more prevalent after emancipation. It is, however, also possible that Gonzaga, like many other liberals at the outset of the Ten Years' War, was idealistic about a harmonious society in which blacks could be equal to whites. His position in later years changed and now reveals a more realistic situation in which whites appear to be protecting their privileges in view of the need to integrate ex-slaves into Cuban society and the social and economic advances made by blacks. The narrator explains the ideological and historical transition: "The freedman was a citizen in the same manner as the colonist, and both remained tied to identical metropolitan coloniz-ing forces. The slave, as an inescapable consequence of circum-stances, had won everything" (165 – 166).

After the Ten Years' War, Gonzaga's position reflected not the radical ideas which desire the abolition of the colonial structure but the more moderate yet still dangerous ideas that allowed him to seek solutions working from within. For Gonzaga, Fidelio, and Morúa, publishing a newspaper represented an alternative to armed insurrection. Morúa continued to pursue his interests by expressing them in fiction. However, perhaps the limitations Gonzaga foresaw regarding writing and the publication of a newspaper can be applied to novels in general and to Morúa's work in particular.

The ideas implicit in the novels regarding the race questions are made more explicit in Morúa's "Factores sociales" in *La Nueva Era*, a magazine he published to promote "the doctrines of progress, so-cial advancement, popular liberation, civil equality, and human uni-versal harmony." A discussion of *La Nueva Era* should not be over-looked; published in 1892, one year after the publication of *Sofía*, four years before the completion of *La familia Unzúazu* and nine years before its publication, "Factores sociales" outlines Morúa's ideas regarding race which he shared during the time he wrote his novel. In the three separate essays,[63] Morúa offers his views about the black race in which he rightfully objects to the injustices com-mitted against this group of Cubans. Although his intentions appear to be genuine, Morúa demeans blacks in order to compare them to whites. He argues for the equality of blacks but accepts their inferi-ority and savagery to affirm that whites had undergone similar condi-tions. Moreover, he opposed classifying blacks and mulattoes as one group, a practice, according to him, proslavers initiated. The mulatto children who did not have their white fathers to take care of them erroneously identified themselves with their mothers' black race.

What Gonzaga foresaw in fiction has come true in history. The "color class" became accustomed to receiving all their necessities from the government, which, in some respects, made them vulner-able. Postemancipation blacks were ignorant. Consequently, Dr. Al-varado's assertion coincided with Morúa's ideas that in the six years that blacks had been free they had not advanced and their condition had not changed.

In the essay, Morúa, as Manzano had done in his *Autobiografía*, establishes a distance between blacks and mulattoes; that is, between himself and other blacks and between recently emancipated blacks and those who were already free. After emancipation, there was no significant change in the attitudes of ex-slaves. However, the newly emancipated blacks wanted to imitate and compete with whites for luxury goods. Continuing the division between one group and the other, Morúa observed that free blacks were different; they worked, cultivated the land, had their own commerce, industries, property, and moderate wealth. Once emancipated, the newly freed blacks were interested only in having fun and participating in activities enjoyed by established free blacks.

Morúa's tone at times is condescending and patronizing toward other blacks. In substance, parts of the essay recall the opinions of Gonzaga, who felt blacks needed to be guided, and of Dr. Alvarado, who was pessimistic regarding the future of blacks. Morúa writes that blacks are of age and should work to improve their conditions and stop being moral slaves.[64] For Morúa, blacks continued to depend on whites. In *La familia Unzúazu*, even the mulatto Fidelio had to depend on Gonzaga's assistance to be released from jail; in history, Morúa also depended on his white friends. Moreover, Fidelio participates in social and race discussions with Gonzaga and Dr. Alvarado only at their invitation; and if there is a continuity between the first and second novel, Fidelio of *La familia Unzúazu*, as we have already noted, internalizes the ideas of the newspaper which Gonzaga had expressed in *Sofía*.

Although Morúa fought for separatism, freedom, and justice for blacks, his ideas changed after the emancipation of slaves in 1886. After that historic moment, he believed that blacks had obtained equal status to whites and began to press for unity among the Cuban people. His position led him into confrontation with other black leaders, including Juan Gualberto Gómez, who felt that even though blacks were free they still lagged behind whites, who, in many cases, continued to discriminate against them. Among other differences, Gómez favored the formation of a party of color and Morúa opposed it, noting that blacks and whites were citizens with equal rights.[65]

While supporting integration, Morúa opposed the ideas of the Directorio Central de las Sociedades de la Raza de Color de Cuba, an organization calling for the unity of blacks to obtain rights promised to them. Morúa rejected any proposition to form groups on the basis of race because they would be divisive and perpetuate the differences among the races. He favored common rights for all and the self-uplifting of blacks. In "Factores sociales," Morúa underscores this same message:

> Reunited blacks will never get from the government anything but benefits for blacks. And that is not what they should strive for. As long as "concessions are made to the colored class," they will remain inferior, to which the previous regime has condemned them and which ties them to the present routine practices. Everything has to be obtained as a member of the Cuban society and not as an individual of one race or another, and it is easier to obtain everything in this way than not to obtain it by projecting a pompous manner. You only have to start by practicing precisely the opposite of what the *petty-leaders-* of the absurd Negrophilism, already decaying, still dominant, suggest.[66]

Gonzaga's and Dr. Alvarado's pessimism regarding blacks is not limited to the lack of advancement of this group but includes the misguidance black leaders offer their followers.

Morúa ends "Factores sociales" by proposing that black membership in the Autonomist party is the only solution to the race problem. After working some ten years with the separatist movement abroad, Morúa became disillusioned with failed attempts to rid Cuba of the colonial government. Upon his return to Cuba in 1891, Morúa joined the Autonomists; this was the same year he published the essay and one year after *Sofía* reached the Cuban public. Morúa believed that his political party opened its doors to all classes. From its first proclamation in 1878, the Central Committee asked for the immediate emancipation of slaves.[67] But, as we have noted, many blacks opposed membership in a party whose policies sought co-existence with Spain rather than independence. For Morúa, sufficient progress had been made, and some progress was better than none. It was also better than the idealism of the separatists, who had not achieved their goals. Under the Autonomist banner, blacks would continue to sacrifice themselves for the betterment of Cuba:

> Each one of the individuals who enrolls will practice, of course, the right which can be enjoyed today, working in associations to obtain partial suffrage, which is the only one which can be obtained; suffrage for those who know how to read and write, the educated vote, certain that what they do not obtain in unity with the Autonomist party, it will not be obtained for them by any commission or body of procurators, which will do nothing more than constitute a laughable

bureaucracy which will waste time and spend uselessly the money of the conceited grantors of power.[68]

Morúa's membership in the Autonomist party was not long-lived. When it became evident that the revolution of 1895 would triumph, Morúa's position changed again. He abandoned the party and joined the rebels. Although his former party supported armed insurrection in 1868, it felt that the promises of 1878 were being kept and on that basis opposed the rebellion.[69]

But Morúa would change his ideas one more time. After the Spanish-Cuban-American War, Morúa became more conservative. With the creation of the young republic, he abandoned his antiannexationist views of the past and supported close relations with the United States and application of the Monroe Doctrine to Cuba. Contrary to the opinions of Juan Gualberto Gómez and others, Morúa voted for the Platt Amendment, which allowed for a U.S. invasion of the island. It was approved by the Constituent Assembly by a vote of 15 to 14 and added to the Cuban constitution by a vote of 16 to 11. Not only did the United States pressure its acceptance, but those who voted for it believed that if they did not include the amendment Cuban independence would be jeopardized. Others, like Juan Gualberto Gómez, opposed the amendment and refused to compromise the freedom of the country.[70] Morúa and Gómez were indeed on opposite sides when it came to the needs of blacks. Julián González reconstructs Morúa's and Gómez's positions during the meetings to adopt the amendment. González recalls that Gómez did not accept the amendment because it would be detrimental to the "color class" and he considered himself a descendant of Africans. While every black supported Gómez's declaration, Morúa found himself in a difficult position.[71]

When he published *La familia Unzúazu*, Morúa was an influential politician. Morúa, who had once claimed not to be politically ambitious, went from expressing his opinions in newspaper and magazine articles to translating them into law. After supporting black membership in the Autonomist party, Morúa denied his interest in politics and political positions and that he intended to supplant others.[72] Unfortunately, Morúa's adversaries were right. After the Spanish-Cuban-American War, Morúa became involved in the political process and was elected to the Cuban House in 1901 and to the Senate in 1902. In 1904–05, Morúa campaigned vigorously for the election of President Gen. José Miguel Gómez and Vice-President Alfredo Zayas, who were elected in 1909. Morúa achieved his highest recognition when he became, under the administration of his friend José Miguel Gómez, president of the Senate in 1909. Although Morúa's ideas continued to favor integration and equality for all, his policies were harmful to many blacks. Once in a position of power, Morúa sought to implement ideas that were already present in his "Factores sociales." He fought to end black political groups, such as the Directorio, and forced blacks to join existing parties. As a member of the Constituent Assembly, Morúa wrote the electoral law for the elections of 1902. Morúa is best known for the amendment to the electoral law popularly known as the Morúa Amendment. It outlawed parties based on race and set the stage for a calamity which was to affect the lives of many blacks in the years to come. The law favored unity among Cubans of all races and excluded blacks from establishing their own party. Morúa's original motion read as follows: "No association, under any circumstance, constituted exclusively by individuals of a race or color, or by birth of a particular class, wealth, or professional title will be considered a political or independent group."[73] In its final version, the amendment was changed in appearance, but not in substance.

Most importantly, the Morúa law was used in 1912 against the Partido Independiente de Color, under the leadership of Evaristo Estenoz. In the uprising, blacks fought for promises made to them during the Spanish-Cuban-American War and for a repeal of the Morúa Amendment. After the uprising, stronger measures against blacks were passed; the Congress approved a law prohibiting any black from becoming president of the republic.[74] Morúa's ideas supported and promoted mainstream politics. In comparison to other blacks of his time such as Gómez,[75] Morúa's ideas were moderate at best. Unlike Morúa, Gómez was a recognized leader among members of the Cuban black community.

As I have proposed, Morúa's ideas regarding blacks during the time of writing and publication of his novel are reflected in fiction. Although Fidelio is unjustly jailed, we can better understand why he is not bitter about what occurred and why he looks for no other solution but to work within the colonial system. The other black character, Liberato, a slave more daring but less educated than Fidelio, becomes an outlaw. However, in light of Morúa's differentiation between historically free blacks and slaves (or recently freed blacks), Liberato and Fidelio do not propose two solutions for blacks in Cuba; each represents a separate solution, one for slaves and one for free blacks. There are multiple ways of interpreting the actions of these two men. On the one hand, free blacks and mulattoes like Fidelio should use the tools provided by the colonial society to express their ideas. On the other hand, slaves like Liberato have no

other alternative but to fight for their own sense of justice and freedom. Fidelio's name suggests loyalty and passivity and Liberato's
embodies the essence of his freedom. Regardless of their social and
economic conditions, Fidelio symbolizes solutions for mulattoes
and Liberato for blacks. Morúa tempts us to speculate that for him,
mulattoes are passive and blacks are violent. Liberato's unlawful solution cannot be a long-term alternative. Liberato rapes his mistress,
Ana María, and after his escape she places a bounty on his head. Violence is not necessary, especially when there are benevolent people
like Gonzaga who are willing to aid blacks. In the first novel, when
no one was willing to help Sofía, Gonzaga offered her food and a temporary home. Moreover, if we continue to read "Factores sociales"
and *Sofía* together, we come to a different understanding about Liberato's action in murdering Nudoso del Tronco. If the act appeared to
be a temporary salvation for Sofía, who was going to be sent to the
sugar mill, this nevertheless violent and illegal act was placed in the
hands not of Fidelio, as Villaverde might have done, but of the slave
Liberato. Morúa does everything possible to insulate Fidelio from a
disturbed Unzúazu family. His marginal contact is through Gonzaga
and Dr. Alvarado.

Morúa's feelings toward Liberato are evident at the end of section 6
of "Factores sociales" when he writes about the distasteful culture
of blacks which has not contributed to the black man's development. The cultural decay reached its lowest point with the *ñañi-
guismo político*, "which appears to want to take us back to savage
times of detestable hatred in the streets and public plazas."[76] Morúa's
ideas about the *ñáñigos* is reflected in more detail when he narrates
their history in *La familia Unzúazu*. Morúa criticizes the African
associations, supported by free blacks, as immoral centers which, in
the interest of their territory or association, took advantage of public
events to carry out their "savage" acts. These organizations, according to him, infested all levels of society, even the colonial administration (177–181). Within the context of the essay and the times,
as a *ñáñigo* Liberato committed a savage act, and if not apprehended
he would be forced to live as a fugitive for the rest of his life. In the
long run, by killing Nudoso del Tronco, Liberato did not help Sofía.
Liberato may have been instrumental in stalling Sofía's premature
death by preventing Nudoso del Tronco from sending her to the
sugar mill. But within the context of slavery, Nudoso's death provided a certain type of justice not available to slaves.[77]

Finally, the expected union between Gonzaga and Magdalena is
significant insofar as they represent the most benevolent characters
in the novel and therefore reflect an optimistic outcome of historical

events. Gonzaga not only got the mulatto Fidelio out of jail but re-warded the loyal slave María de Jesús with her freedom. He also helped the former doorman of the Unzúazu family move up the eco-nomic ladder; he acquired his own business of three coaches and five horses. Unlike Cándido Gamboa in *Cecilia Valdés* and others before him, Gonzaga has assumed with Magdalena the responsibility of raising their bastard child. After his sick wife's death, more than likely he will marry Magdalena. In comparison to other works of fic-tion, Gonzaga has taken one step forward, especially if we take into account his personal relationship with Magdalena, which continues to rewrite Villaverde's novel. But as a political character he has re-sisted the idealism shown in Morúa's first novel, perhaps responding more to a reconstruction of narrative time than to the author's own development during the time of writing. As a privileged character, Gonzaga's prophecy regarding the need to discriminate against blacks in order to control them would be felt in spite of Cuba's indepen-dence from Spain in 1898 and the establishment of the republic in 1902. It would be evident throughout the unfolding of Cuban his-tory. The task assigned to Fidelio will not be enough to prevent the calamity Dr. Alvarado predicted would occur, one that Morúa as a politician created and that took place after Morúa's death, with the massacre of blacks and the destruction of the Partido Independiente de Color.

# FOUR

# Historical Fictions
## Displacement and Change—Lino Novás Calvo's El *negrero* and Alejo Carpentier's The *Kingdom of This World*

A ia bombai, bombe,
Lamma ramana quana,
E van vanta,
Vana docki.

(We swear to destroy the whites
and all that they possess;
let us die rather than give up.)

—DROUIN DE BERCY

I Fiction served as a model of sorts for writers publishing after the start of the gradual emancipation of slaves, which lasted from 1880 to 1886. As I have noted, Francisco Calcagno and Martín Morúa Delgado relied on Anselmo Suárez y Romero's *Francisco* and Cirilo Villaverde's *Cecilia Valdés*, although they also resorted to some biographical and autobiographical information for their novelistic productions. Lino Novás Calvo and Alejo Carpentier, also writing in the postslavery period but during another moment of historical transition well after the Cuban republic was established in 1902, mixed history and fiction and based their novels on documentable historical figures and events. Both Carpentier and Novás Calvo responded to the interest of blacks in Europe and on the island and their works reflect the time in which they were written. They base their works on authorial figures which in Cuba recall the ruthless Machado dictatorship. Novás Calvo and Carpentier began their literary careers during the Machado years and both published in the *Revista de Avance*, of which Carpentier was a founding member. Carpentier also joined the Protesta de los Trece and participated in the Grupo Minorista. He was jailed under the Machado government, and it was in prison that he wrote a draft of his first novel, ¡Ecue Yamba-O! (1933).

By mixing history with fiction, Novás Calvo's *El negrero* concentrates on the life of the slaver Pedro Blanco and Carpentier's *The Kingdom of This World* on that of Henri Christophe and others, but, most importantly, on the transition of Saint Domingue from slavery to emancipation, from colony to republic. And if Calcagno's and Morúa's novels coincided with thematics already seen in the early antislavery narratives, Novás Calvo's *El negrero* also recalls the early proslavery literature; that is, Francisco Estévez's *Diario de un rancheador* and José Morilla's "El ranchador." As we saw in chapter 2, section IV, the proslavery narrative is based on the lives of historical figures who gained fame hunting slaves in the first half of the nineteenth century. Novás Calvo narrates the biography of the most successful slave trader during the period in which Estévez and Valentín Páez lived. As one witness of the nineteenth century put it, "Anybody engaged in the Spanish trade would be aware that Pedro Blanco was the largest slave trader in the world."[1]

Published in 1933, Novás Calvo's *Bildungsroman* follows closely Blanco's biography, from his mischievous childhood to his life as a slave trader and pirate. Blanco's apprenticeship on board slave ships culminates with him turning Gallinas into one of the most important factories supplying slaves to the New World. But the novel also offers another side of slavery seen briefly in *Cecilia Valdés:* it focuses on the slave trade, from the time slaves were captured in the interior of Africa to their sale to slave traders, their journey through the Middle Passage, their arrival on Cuban shores, and, finally, their sale to the plantation owners.

An overview of the slave trade will provide a context to better understand Novás Calvo's usage of history, and an intertextual reading between it and other slaver biographies will show that *El negrero* borrows from them in order to create the historical yet fictitious Pedro Blanco Fernández de Trava. However, a comparison between the novel and history also reveals that some of the works Novás Calvo consulted were not free of fictional elements and conform to the same writing strategies employed by him. These "misrepresentations" suggest that Novás Calvo's novel can be situated in the same interpretative space as that of other biographies and works of history. And like the works in the postslavery period, Novás Calvo profited from events which were unfolding during the time in which he was writing his novel. To some degree, the events of the present time of writing resemble those of the past of the narration, thus providing him with a clearer understanding of the historical period and allowing him to fuse two moments into one which the text represents. By writing *El negrero,* Novás Calvo has attempted to rewrite history in order for the past to correspond with a contemporary interpretation of the life of Blanco, one of the most ruthless and successful slavers of the nineteenth century.

The African slave trade began in 1442, when the Portuguese explorer Antam Gonsalvez transported ten black Moors to Lisbon to "save their souls."[2] African slaves were soon brought to the New World: The first black slaves to arrive were Spanish-born domestic servants of the conquerors and colonizers. The need for slave labor increased as the Amerindian population was decimated by ill treatment and disease. Slaves were brought with such frequency that to control the numbers the decree of July 22, 1513 imposed a two-ducat charge per slave arriving in America. Las Casas records the incipient slave trade in the following manner:

> The council of the Indies determined, on the recommendation of the
> Sevillian officials . . . to send 4,000 of them to the four Islands of
> Hispaniola, San Juan, Cuba and Jamaica. A Spaniard on leave from
> the Indies asked for such license from Governor Bresa [Laurent de
> Gouvenot], a Flemish gentleman of the King's most private circles.
> The license was granted and sold for 25,000 ducats to Genoese mer-
> chants on the condition—among many others—that no license for
> black trade would be issued within a period of eight years. The Ge-
> noese sold it at a rate of 8 ducats minimum for each Negro.[3]

Since the demand for black slaves was greater than the number available in Spain, Emperor Carlos V allowed non-Christian slaves to be taken from the Guinea Islands and transported directly to the Antilles.[4]

Most African slaves were brought to replace the almost extinct Amerindian slaves in the mines and in agriculture. Black slaves were used in limited numbers with Amerindians in Mexican and Peruvian mines. The numbers, however, increased with the discovery of gold, diamonds, and copper in Venezuela, Colombia, and Brazil. From 1694 to 1762 there were more than eighty to one hundred thousand black slaves working in mines and in mine-related tasks.[5] Mass enslavement also fulfilled the needs of the emerging agricultural industry, particularly the sugar industry, first in the British, French, Dutch, and Danish Antilles and northern Brazil and later in Cuba and the other Spanish-speaking islands.

Spain joined directly in the slave trade when it realized that Portuguese, British, and French shippers were smuggling slaves into the Spanish colonies. In 1777, Spain traded a small area of Spanish coast and an island off the southern coast of Brazil to Portugal for the island of Fernando Poo in the Gulf of Guinea, the islet of Anno Bom, and the right to establish a post on Corsico Island north of the Gabon River. British intervention in Fernando Poo and later French occupation of Corsico Island forced slave traders to turn toward the coastal areas of the River Pongo and Gallinas for slaves.[6]

Slaves were sold in Gallinas only after 1813. Soon after his arrival in 1822, Blanco made Gallinas one of the most important slave centers of the nineteenth century. Mannix and Cowley describe this slave center and Blanco's operation there in a manner which recalls the narration:

> Don Pedro had chosen an admirable site for illegal trading, because of the dangerous bar at the mouth of the river and because of the single winding channel, known only to native pilots. Slaves were provided in large numbers by—but not from—the Vai, a powerful Mohammedan nation that had once held aloof from slave trading. Seduced by Don Pedro's rum and gunpowder, the Vai moved into the coastal region and began attacking their weaker neighbors. Don Pedro kept a stock of more than a thousand slaves in ten or a dozen barracoons on a series of marshy islands. On the other island, near the mouth of the Gallinas, he had his business headquarters, run by a general manager with the assistance of two cashiers, five bookkeepers and ten clerks, all Europeans.[7]

In history and in the novel, Blanco remained in Gallinas from 1822 to 1839.[8]

The horror stories narrated in *El negrero*, in which millions of African slaves died in the Middle Passage, were commonplace in history and documented in many works. What may have been acceptable events to a nineteenth-century reader solicit a strong reaction from opponents of the slave trade but also from readers in the postslavery period. Malcolm Cowley, for example, writes:

> In order to make the venture pay, the slaves were packed as tightly as cases of Scotch whiskey. The *Volador* . . . was the size of a small coasting schooner; she carried 747 negroes, of whom 136 died in the middle passage. The degree of mortality was not unusual; neither was the overcrowding. The slaves were laid on their sides, spoon-fashion, the bent knees of one fitting into the hamstrings of his neighbor. On some vessels, they could not even lie down; they spent the voyage sitting in each other's laps. The stench was terrific. A British officer testified that one could smell a slaver "five miles down wind."[9]

Overcrowding and deception were common practices among slave factors and traders. In his autobiography, slaver Richard Drake reveals that the schooner *Ponchecta*, which weighed eighty tons, was able to cram in 25 percent more slaves than provided by law. The law allowed five slaves for every two tons. In the deception, the *Ponchecta* was rated by the imperial license for one hundred tons. After loading at various slave factories, the *Ponchecta* was overloaded with seven hundred slaves. About one week later, during a severe storm, the ship was run down and sank with all the slaves aboard.[10]

During Pedro Blanco's life, many of the slaves bought, captured, or stolen from the West Coast of Africa were transported to Cuba, which emerged as the leading sugar-producing country in the world. By 1807, the British had abolished the slave trade from its possessions and pressured other countries to do the same. In 1817, Great Britain forced Spain to sign a treaty eliminating the trafficking of slaves north of the African equator by 1818 and south of the equator by 1820. For this act, Spain received 400,000 pounds sterling from the British.[11] However, the British initiative did not put an end to the slave trade. The demand for slaves continued and the clandestine slave trade, which soon followed, became more ruthless and oppressive.

Pedro Blanco's Gallinas was located about one hundred miles northwest of Monrovia. Blanco's slaves were widely sought-after. In many respects, slaves bought north of the equator were more desirable than those south of it. The length of the journey was an important factor. José Antonio Saco explains that slaves marketed south of the equator were less expensive than those to the north. The difficult coastal line, the lack of large quantities of slaves, the long journey, in which many died on board, and the necessary stop at the Príncipe or Saint Thomas islands contributed to the reduced price.[12] After the suppression of the slave trade, John Ormond's operation on the River Pongo, north of Sierra Leone, and Pedro Blanco's Gallinas on the Liberian coast (presently the Kerefe River area of Sierra Leone) became two of the most important slave centers of their time. In history, Blanco shipped over five thousand slaves annually to the New World;[13] in the novel, the same number of slaves were packed into slaver vessels in a matter of months.

By 1827, Blanco was one of the most powerful men in the slave trade. A slave trader for fifteen years, Blanco outsmarted both the British navy and his competitors. Blanco was known as "el Mago-Espejo-Sol" (the magician of the sun-mirror) because of the vigilant system he set up to protect his trade; he erected lookout posts on the beaches and islands of the lagoon and his men were trained with telescopes and mirrors to watch for British men-of-war. Blanco was also known as "el señor Gallinas" to the other slave factory own-ers.[14] According to Ward, Blanco had surpassed Captain Kearney's reputation and had improved on his methods and, with the help of King Siacca, always kept his barracoon filled with slaves. Even with the increased surveillance of the British navy, Blanco was able to load a ship under cover of darkness in a matter of hours. Spanish ves-sels before 1835 could not be captured if slaves were found on board.[15]

In a comparison between the two, both history and Novás Calvo's novel provide similar insights into Blanco's life. He became rich and powerful, surrounding himself with European luxury. His bills were accepted as bank notes in West African coastal countries and in major capitals such as Havana, Paris, and London.[16] To consolidate his power and assure himself a constant supply of slaves, Blanco set up depots throughout what is now the western part of Sierra Leone and Liberia, such as the one run by Theodore Canot in New Sestros (New Cess). Canot transported slaves on board Spanish, Portuguese, American, and Russian ships to Blanco.[17] However, Novás Calvo de-viates from history to stress Blanco's power and importance. In writ-ing his novel, Novás Calvo appropriates aspects of Blanco's life, as we would expect, but also attributes to him characteristics of other slavers. In so doing, he creates an interplay between biography and history but also fiction insofar as he creates a historical fiction. Novás Calvo's project is to narrate Blanco's biography and to offer an interpretation which corresponds more closely to the outcome of historical events; that is, the suppression of the slave trade and the emancipation of slaves in Cuba. We notice a displacement from his-tory to fiction when, for example, Blanco does not marry African King Siacca's daughter, as was customary for slave factors to do, but Elvira, the daughter of another important slave trader, Da Souza, thus consolidating two powerful slave factories.

The fictionalization or misrepresentation of history regarding Blanco's marriage is substantiated by Martín Morúa Delgado's "Dos langostas." When denouncing two men acting against the interests of the black race, one of whom was Rodolfo Fernández Trava, Pedro Blanco's grandchild, Morúa provides some information about the slaver's life.[18] In an attempt to discredit Fernández Trava, Morúa gives the following account of Pedro Blanco's experiences which in part coincides with Novás Calvo's novel, except for the paragraph on Blanco's marriage: "This king had a large family and, among them, a daughter with whom don Pedro fell in love. With the interest of being a relative of King Manhas's family, as he was called, he could have greater liberty to execute his plans. He convinced the old king, who finally gave in so that his daughter could belong to the good don

Pedro Blanco. With that union, the heavens opened to don Pedro, as it is commonly said, since the unhappy young woman would serve as a wife and instrument for his *finis coronat opus*." [19]

I suspect that Novás Calvo was not familiar with Morúa's article, since a comparative reading between *El negrero* and "Dos langostas" reveals significant differences between the two works. After a successful slave-trading business, Blanco, in Novás Calvo's work, wanted to retire from the trade to spend more time with his sister, whom he loved very much, while Blanco, in Morúa's article, wanted to leave the slave trade not to be with his sister but with his daughter Rosa. Morúa continues:

> His daughter was of age, to whom he wanted to give the best education, when he received notice from Havana that his relative gave signs of bankruptcy; he had not been seen for some time in that city.
>
> It was to be seen, and we can imagine the expression on don Pedro's face, having been tricked by his disciple. He left immediately on one of his three ships, and arrived in Havana, first visiting O'Donnell, then the governor of the island. O'Donnell received him in a bad mood, lamenting the dirty tricks of Blanco's relative. And no matter how long and hard they looked for him, they could not find the crafty disciple who knew how to take advantage marvelously of the master's lessons. This setback made don Pedro Blanco retire to private life and decide to stay on the island and have his daughter brought to him, the only person who had inspired love in his life. [20]

Although we are aware that Morúa's article was an attempt to discredit Fernández Trava, we have not found any evidence to believe that the events reported by Morúa are less than factual.

Even if Morúa did change some events to discredit Fernández Trava and his grandfather, Pedro Blanco, other discrepancies show that when he arrived in Gallinas Blanco was not a mate but captain of a slave ship. Little information is available regarding Blanco and, in some instances, it is not clear and often contradictory. One source explains the complexity of Blanco's life:

> Biographers do not agree on the circumstances which led him to establish himself in that area: some say that in 1821 he embarked as a sailor or helmsman of the slaver brigantine *Segundo Campeador*, of which soon after he was a boatswain. With the proceeds he obtained from that trip, he chartered a ship with which he captured a Portu-

guese brigantine which carried more than four hundred blacks, putting the crew to the sword. Other writers say that he belonged to a distinguished family and that he studied navigation. After obtaining the title of pilot, he left for Havana, where, because of the difficult situation in which he found himself, he accepted the position of second in command in a ship preparing to go to Africa in search of slaves. Having anchored in Gallinas, he went inland to negotiate with the indigenous chiefs. At the time, a British cruiser forced the slaver vessel to escape under full sail, leaving him abandoned on land in a compromising situation, except for befriending those kinglets and marrying the daughter of one of the most powerful of them called Siaca (1829).[21]

I have found no evidence to support some contentions, but the fact that Blanco was indeed a mate on a sailing vessel is supported by other sources such as Johnston's *The Negro in the New World.*[22] Moreover, the quotation coincides with Morúa Delgado's information regarding Blanco's marriage to the daughter of a powerful African king. However, for Morúa, Blanco did not marry King Siacca's daughter, as stated in the above quotation, but the daughter of King Manhas.

A further review of the literature available on Blanco continues to question how he arrived in Gallinas and on which ship he traveled. Levi Marrero, basing his information on the accounts of Canot, Ward, and Mannix and Cowley, suggests that Blanco was commissioned in Havana to carry out a clandestine operation to Africa. This was not carried out until many years later, in 1824, with the shipment of one hundred slaves, which he sent back on board *El Conquistador* while he remained to trade merchandise. According to Marrero, Blanco initiated his career as a slaver not in Gallinas but in Lomboko. An "honest" man, Blanco paid the sponsors of the expedition four years later.[23]

There are other irreconcilable differences between the various interpretations offered by Blanco's biographers and that presented in the novel. For the purpose of exploring the relationship between fact and Novás Calvo's novel, I have done a close reading of the information provided by the works of history and how that information is represented in *El negrero.* Although the novel contains information offered by Blanco's biographers, it shows further that the *Segundo Campeador* did not dock in Gallinas but in São Paolo de Loanda, a Portuguese slave station, and that Blanco was not a boatswain but remained the helmsman of the ship, which after loading a slave cargo returned safely to Regla. The novel does not record that Blanco traveled to Lomboko. It states that Blanco arrived in Gallinas after his escape from Ormond's factory as the captain of a lugger rather than the *Segundo Campeador*, from Bangalang rather than from Havana.

Novás Calvo does narrate an event similar to the one mentioned by Blanco's biographers and Marrero but, again, with some differences. Some time after his initial contact with Gallinas and while in Havana, Blanco was commissioned to go to Africa and buy slaves. As the captain of the *Tomasa*, he attacked a Portuguese vessel, the *María Grande*, overloaded with eight hundred slaves. After a brief stay in Puerto Rico to revive the slaves and make them appear as if they were traveling from that island, he reached Cuban shores aboard the Portuguese vessel. Also, according to the novel, in 1821, a few months after Napoleon's death, Blanco returned to Gallinas, where he lived for many years. In this second journey he was captain of the *Conquistador* and his men were good sailors, but neither fighters nor ambitious. For this reason he was not able to pirate other ships. As in the histories, Blanco does run into a ship, but, unlike those descriptions, it is an empty vessel with a dead crew which he is not able to loot. But similar to Marrero's account, when Blanco arrives in Gallinas he seizes the one hundred slaves in his friends' factories, and, after leaving an IOU, sends them on board the *Conquistador* to Cuba. Referring to Canot's narration, Novás Calvo also states that Blanco paid his debt four years later (183).[24] When analyzing fiction, we can presume that Novás Calvo rewrote Blanco's life to underscore the protagonist's importance. But, then, how do we explain the differences among the interpretations of the biographers, Marrero, Johnston, and Morúa Delgado?

Novás Calvo subtitled his work *Vida novelada de Pedro Blanco Fernández de Trava*, which already suggests a mixture of fact and fiction. What is fact and what is fiction may be determined by comparing Novás Calvo's narration with the lives of those slavers who interacted with Pedro Blanco. Of these, Theodore Canot's biography is of notable importance. According to history and *El negrero*, in 1836 Canot became one of Blanco's most trusted employees and was empowered to set up a depot in New Sestros in Liberia. Canot's biography was written in 1854, the same year in which Blanco died; Blanco's was not written until 1932. The fact that Canot's biography was written before Blanco's allowed for the writing of Blanco's life to be patterned after his younger counterpart. In this project, Novás Calvo's novel was influenced by Brantz Mayer's *Adventures of an African Slaver*, specifically the Cowley edition.[25] Thus Theodore Canot's life became a model for the fictionalization of *El negrero*.

The presence of *Adventures of an African Slaver* is particularly noticeable in book 3, which follows closely Blanco's activities in Gallinas and his encounter with Theodore Canot. In this section, Novás Calvo includes the only epigraph in the novel, a fragment extracted from Canot's recollection. Novás Calvo had an excellent command of English and translated many works from English to Spanish. We can assume that Novás Calvo stressed the importance of the slaver's sister rather than his daughter because of the same emphasis in Canot's narration.[26] In Mayer's book, Canot recalls his experiences with Blanco: "On another island, more remote, was his residence, where the only white person was a sister, who, for a while, shared with Don Pedro his solitary and penitential domain."[27] Novás Calvo translates and includes the same passage in his epigraph: "En un islote más alejado tenía su residencia, donde no entraba jamás otro blanco que una hermana suya, que compartió algún tiempo con don Pedro aquel dominio solitario y siniestro" (187).

Moreover, Novás Calvo's novel contains a side and overhead sketch of a slave ship with the caption "Cargamento de un negrero dispuesto a levar anclas" (cargo of a slave ship ready to set sail). This is an exact reproduction of the one found in Mayer's book opposite the title page with the caption "A black cargo ready for an ocean voyage."[28] Having pointed out the presence of one book in the other, we find other similarities between Blanco and Canot.[29] For example, both men's fathers traveled abroad. Canot's father was a soldier and Blanco's a sailor; both of their fathers died and both Canot and Blanco were raised by their mothers, who were poor (Mayer, 1; Novás Calvo, 9). Blanco's economic condition, as expressed by Novás Calvo and Canot, challenges the above biographical investigation, suggesting that the slaver was from a distinguished family. As a child, Blanco had a vivid imagination, while Canot was an avid reader of travel books; both even began to live their accounts (Novás Calvo, 10–11; Mayer, 2). Both studied navigation and, at one time or another, were protected and helped by an uncle who provided an important link for the nephew's initiation into the slave trade. In Blanco's case, his maternal uncle paid for the young Pedro to study navigation (14) and later helped him find a job in Havana by giving Pedro two letters of recommendation, one to a friend, Cosmé Martinón, and the other for a relative, Marchena (95–97). It was Marchena who encouraged Blanco not to leave the slave trade (97). Similarly, Canot's life was saved by Rafael, a man who claimed to be his uncle. In reality, Rafael was a schoolmate and professional companion of the deceased uncle. Rafael became Canot's surrogate uncle

(37–39) and recommended Canot to Carlo, an Italian grocery store owner who engaged in the slave trade (59). Blanco also had an Italian friend by the name of Carlo who, like the other Carlo, lived in Regla and was engaged in the slave trade (92). Both appear to be the same Carlo. Toward the end of *El negrero*, Novás Calvo establishes a link between his work and Canot's. We are told that Carlo wrote a letter recommending Canot to Blanco: "Carlo wrote him a long letter announcing his retirement . . . In passing, Carlo told him about Captain Teodoro Canot, an Italian of French origin who had left from Matanzas with a ship consigned to Cha-Cha. Carlo recommended him to Pedro as the bravest and most experienced of the slave trader captains, of course, after him" (245). But neither the letter nor Carlo's mention of Blanco's name is present in Canot's account. There is, however, a difference in time: Blanco met his friend Carlo in 1818 (245) and Canot his in 1826 (62).

If we continue to explore the lives of the two slavers, we notice that both men joined the slave trade at an early age and both knew and met two of the most important slavers of the times, Da Souza (Cha-Cha) of Whydah on the Slave Coast, and John Ormond (Mongo John) of Bangalang. Blanco had worked for both Da Souza and Mongo John, while Canot consigned a ship to Da Souza and also worked for Mongo John. As Mongo John's bookkeepers, both met Unga-Golah and described their experiences with Ormond's harem keeper and thief of the warehouse, which both Canot and Blanco guarded. After a brief apprenticeship, both fled from Ormond and founded their own factories in western Africa: Blanco in Gallinas and Canot in Kambia. There is more than a coincidence in paths here; one description appears to be a copy of the other.[30]

It is also possible to assume that the coincidence in both Canot's and Blanco's lives is not a fictional recreation of biography but of history; that is, both conform to a general profile of a slaver. These men were usually from broken homes, were looked after by a relative, usually an uncle, and, like the first explorers of the New World, were in search of riches. Richard Drake's autobiography, for example, recalls and in many ways summarizes Canot's and Blanco's initiation into the slave trade:

> I never saw my father. He was a seafaring man, sailing as mate of a
> coaster and was lost in a gale four months after his marriage with
> my mother, the daughter of a spinner in one of the cotton mills at
> Stockford, England. I can just remember her and also a room full of
> strange people, a red box and a man standing beside it, talking in a
> loud voice; then a dismal walk through the rain, to a field where

some men had just finished digging a hole in the ground. My home after that was in the Stockford workhouse until one day the work-master came in company with a swarthy-featured stranger and said: "Look sharp, my lad, and you'll see your uncle!" I did "look sharp" and saw a man about thirty years old, dressed in a jaunty suit of sailor's store clothes, with a broad palmleaf hat on his head, round gold rings in his ears and heavy gold watch seals hanging from his fob. This grand-looking personage spoke kindly to me, gave me a few half-pence, told me to cheer up and try to be a man and then walked away with Mr. Crump, the master. He never came to the workhouse again but I was told that he had left some money for me with the parish overseers and promised to look after me as I grew older.[31]

It is evident that these prominent slave traders came from broken homes in which the father figure was absent and the uncle was the only male figure which they could follow. However, if Blanco did come from a distinguished family, Novás Calvo's rewriting of the character's past suggests a complicity with the biography of other slavers. For Blanco, Canot, Drake, and others, the slave trade became a means of escaping their immediate conditions and a way to earn large sums of money within a relatively short period of time.

If we continue to read both Mayer's and Novás Calvo's works side by side, we notice certain discrepancies in the ordering of events. For example, we are told that in 1820 Blanco leaves Havana and goes to Africa, where he meets and works for Mongo John. On September 2, 1826, Canot leaves Havana on the *Aerostático* and also meets and works for Mongo John. Although both worked as accountants for Mongo John and gained valuable experience under his tutelage, neither one stayed longer than one year. The discrepancy between the lives of the two men arises with Mongo John's previous helper, the Englishman Edward Joseph. According to Novás Calvo, Joseph was aware that Ormond wanted to replace him with someone else. He became disenchanted and decided to leave Ormond and work in a factory that belonged to a Spaniard in Sierra Leone. In Canot's version, Joseph is sent for because of Canot's ill health. Toward the end of the two narrations, both Canot and Blanco meet in Gallinas, where Blanco becomes Canot's employer, and Canot is instructed to set up a branch factory in New Sestros. What is unusual about the accounts is that although Blanco, Canot, and Joseph were clerks for Ormond, neither Novás Calvo's nor Mayer's narrations mention that either Blanco or Canot knew that the other had met Joseph and that each had worked for Ormond. This is inconsistent with other informa-tion available, since traders, according to both works, often spoke of their experiences and adventures. It appears that Novás Calvo borrows from Canot's description; only the names of the characters have been changed.

By following Canot's story, Novás Calvo privileges this slaver's narration and omits other details about Blanco's biography. For example, he excludes other slavers who worked for Blanco. In another biography, African slaver Capt. Richard Drake had met Blanco at his uncle Diego Ramos's house and went to work for him many years later. Drake narrates his reunion with Blanco and a request that Drake work for him: "I was glad to accept his offer of a situation at Gallinas and settled down as half-clerk, half doctor for Don Pedro Blanco. I formerly knew him on the Kambia, I had been in possession of influence and wealth and he was an adventurer seeking a location. Since that time I had squandered a fortune and he had accumulated one. . . . I kept my place with him for six years and during that time made one voyage as clerk and one as captain of a slaver."[32] There is no mention in *El negrero* of Drake or of his Uncle Ramos during the time Drake was to have worked for Blanco, from 1830 to 1836. As one might suspect, neither is there any mention of Drake in Canot's narration.

If Novás Calvo's narration of Pedro Blanco is in fact a *vida novelada* (novelized life), Drake's absence in Gallinas may be due to his absence in Canot's recollection and indeed responds to the fictionalized part of the biography. Similarly, the novel does not mention either Mr. Kidd or Mr. Zulueta of the prestigious house of Zulueta and Company of London, identified by Henry William Macaulay before the House of Commons as having brought slave ships for Pedro Blanco and therefore being accomplices in the slave trade. Mr. Macaulay's testimony is as follows: "Zulueta was known at Sierra Leone as the correspondent of the largest slave dealer on the coast, Pedro Blanco; all the bills which Pedro Blanco drew upon England were drawn upon Zulueta, and passed current in the colony with Pedro Blanco's name upon them, and Zulueta's as the drawee. Zulueta was also subsequently found to be engaged in connexion with a slave-vessel called the Gollupchik."[33]

*El negrero* contains further omissions and misinformation regarding Blanco's life. For example, other slavers have reported Blanco's correct name as Pedro Blanco, not Pedro Blanco Fernández de Trava, as recorded in the title of the novel. According to Morúa Delgado, the second last name attributed to Pedro Blanco was acquired many years later when Blanco returned to Barcelona, where his daughter Rosa married a Fernández-Trava. Rosa's son, Blanco's grandson, was named Rodolfo Fernández-Trava y Blanco. Novás Calvo appropriates

Rodolfo's last name and attributes it to the historical Pedro Blanco, thus imposing a contemporary misunderstanding onto the past and making him the fictitious Pedro Blanco Fernández de Trava.[34]

In his "El negrero y el abolicionismo en América," Antonio Benítez Rojo uncovers more historical information about Pedro Blanco's activities not included in the novel. An 1839 incident pertains to a slave Blanco sold, his rebellion on board the ship *Amistad,* which was on its way from Havana to Guanajá, and the ship's capture near Long Island. The seriousness of this case involved both the Spanish and U.S. governments and required the intervention of President Van Buren and the defense of John Quincy Adams. The slaves were eventually freed and returned to Africa.[35] The absence of this information allows Novás Calvo to focus his narration on the slave trade between Europe, Africa, and the Caribbean; its inclusion would have added another and more complete dimension to the slave trade.

A final comparison of Novás Calvo's and Mayer's accounts allows us to explore further the events surrounding King Siacca, who supplied Blanco with slaves and who, after Blanco's departure, acquired Blanco's title and was also known as the king of Gallinas.[36] The king's name has been spelled or misspelled in different ways. For example, Novás Calvo writes it as Shiakar; a Spanish encyclopedia spells it as Siaca; Marrero reproduces it as Siaka; in English it is written similar to Spanish but with two *c*s as in Siacca. However, this misunderstanding is clarified by Canot's biography, which, like Novás Calvo, spells it Shiakar.

Because of the use of historical information, Novás Calvo's novel is also a biography and therefore pertains to the life of a man in history. Yet it is difficult to determine what is fiction and what is history both in Novás Calvo's work and in the works he consulted. For example, while Novás Calvo extracted from Canot's narration what he considered to be historical data, Sir Harry Johnston questions the historical accuracy of Canot's story. In one instance, Johnston reproduces Canot's words about a savage cannibalistic ritual but includes the following note: "The whole of this episode may be mere sensational fiction. The Vai people at Digbi have never been cannibals."[37] In another instance, Johnston states: "Whether his story is all true or whether Canot was an earlier De Rougemont, is impossible to determine. There seems, as already shown, to be some discrepancy between Canot's account of Ormond, the mulatto slave trader on the River Pongo (if one compares dates) and the information given of Ormond's Liverpool father in Wadstrom's compilation."[38] In spite of some revelations, we must point out that Johnston himself does not faithfully reproduce Canot's narration. A close reading of Canot's biography allows us to notice discrepancies in Johnston's writings. For example, Johnston states: "Unlike most of his colleagues (if one may believe his asseverations), he led a clean, gentlemanly life, even though he was a slave trader. Of course, when he willingly permitted inspection of his depots on the Liberian coast, there were no slaves *en evidence*, and everything was arranged to convey the impression of lawful trading in the ordinary products of the country."[39]

Contrary to Johnston's reading, in chapter 44, "Blockaded by a British Cruiser," Canot describes how he invited the British captain of the *Bonito* to inspect his barracoons, which, at that moment, contained 250 slaves.[40] When taking into consideration the mixing of factual and fictional accounts present in Novás Calvo's *El negrero*, we must underscore the same mixture present in Canot's and Johnston's books. Marrero himself makes a similar mistake by attributing to Blanco the name Fernández de la Trava, a name he borrowed from Novás Calvo's novel, as the historian's footnote indicates.[41] But whereas Novás Calvo creates the fictional Fernández de Trava, Marrero displaces history (or is it fiction?) even further by adding the article *la* to Blanco's name and creating the character "Fernández de la Trava." It should be also clear that Marrero, like Johnston, relies on Canot's recollections for his information, which, like Novás Calvo's work, suggests that the memoirs are more than biography. The coming together of fact and fiction allows us to read *El negrero* alongside texts of biography and history, such as Johnston's and Canot's works, and its information be given the same weight as the other texts, thus displacing fiction from narrative discourse back into history.

It is not my intention to prove or disprove the recollections of Canot, Johnston, or Wadstrom. I am mainly interested in displacement and changes between history and fiction in narration and similarities in description between *Adventures of an African Slaver* and *El negrero*. The section with Ormond suggests the presence of Canot's book in Novás Calvo's. The lives of both Pedro Blanco and Canot may have been similar and, as both works pointed out, coincided. A reading of these and other texts shows that Canot's narration is an important source for Novás Calvo's description of Pedro Blanco and a reconstruction of his life, especially during the time both men met. Equally important, the same reading allows us to understand that texts are independent of history and historical events. History is not a linear process that occurs in a particular time and space but a written account subject to all writing and reading strategies, such as Johnston's misreadings suggest. In this case, texts provide their own history by relying on other works rather than historical events; history can only exist in writing and, therefore, in other texts.

Approximately one hundred years after Blanco's dominion over Gallinas, Novás Calvo would write the *Vida novelada de Pedro Blanco Fernández de Trava.*[42] Although Novás Calvo stated in an interview that he "wrote the book at the suggestion of the publishers who were interested in a book of adventures,"[43] a century later Blanco's omnipotent powers recall the ruthless Machado dictatorship, which governed Cuba from 1924 to 1933. Novás Calvo was in Spain during the latter part of the Machado reign but remained informed of the political situation in Cuba through journals and letters from his friends. His sentiments resulted in the writing of "La noche de Ramón Yendía," a story about the last day of the Machado dictatorship, which he is said to have written in 1933, the year Machado fled Cuba and the year *El negrero* was published.[44] There is, to some extent, a relationship between Yendía and Blanco: the neurosis of one character recalls it in the other and both meet unfortunate and tragic deaths. During the same period Novás Calvo wrote "Aquella noche salieron los muertos," published in 1932.[45] This story recalls the theme of *El negrero* and describes the following events: Captain Amiana's control over a slave colony, a betrayal by one of his men, the death of the captain, and the freeing of the slaves. However, the description of Captain Amiana and his control over the island alludes to the Machado dictatorship. The method used to kill Captain Amiana resembles the assassination attempt on Machado. Members of the opposition planned to use the burial of Clemente Vázquez Bello, the president of the Senate and a close friend of Machado, to kill the dictator and his staff. At the last possible moment, Vázquez Bello's widow changed the burial site to her husband's native city of Santa Clara, thus averting Machado's death. In fiction, Novás Calvo carries the execution to its conclusion.

During the historical setting of the narration, Novás Calvo resorted to current dictatorial images available during the time of writing to aid in describing a protagonist who lived within a different historical setting.[46] The few factual works available that describe Blanco's character all do so favorably. Canot describes him as a "well-educated mariner from Malaga" and Johnston as "a man of cultivated mind 'not naturally cruel' (as is always said about the Robespierres and Neros of this world)."[47] Yet Novás Calvo deviates from those descriptions and depicts him as ruthless and merciless. By the time Nóvas Calvo wrote *El negrero*, history had shifted. Although Pedro Blanco's profession and behavior were sanctioned during the early part of his involvement in the slave trade (even though the British navy attempted to bring the Spanish slave trade to an end), by the time he retired and certainly by the time Novás Calvo completed his novel, slavery and the slave trade in the nineteenth century were looked upon from a different point of view. Ultimately, Novás Calvo's narration condemns Blanco as a man and a slaver.

As with the antislavery narratives written in the postslavery period, the time in which Novás Calvo wrote his novel is indeed imposed on the time of the narration. Novás Calvo's desire to write *El negrero* reflects the increased interest in blacks in both Cuba and Europe. A few years before Novás Calvo left Cuba for Spain, José Zacarías Tallet and Ramón Guirao initiated the Afro-Cuban poetry movement, which in Cuba had its roots in the antislavery narrative and in Fernando Ortiz's books on blacks in Cuba. Black poetry in Cuba and Puerto Rico culminated in *negrismo,* as expressed in the works of Luis Palés Matos and Nicolás Guillén and much later in the Dominican Republic with Manuel del Cabral. Similar to *negrismo* in the Spanish Caribbean, Francophone students living in Paris also took pride in their own situation. Their concern led to Etienne Léro, Jules Monnerot, and René Ménil and their publication of *Légitime Défense* (1932) and, most important, to Aimé Césaire, Léon Damas, and Léopold Senghor and their *L'Etudiant Noir* (1934).[48] Cuban novelists would soon follow this trend. In 1936 Antonio Ramos wrote his *Caniquí,* a novel in which slavery in broader terms included the slavelike conditions that existed in Cuba during the Machado and post-Machado years. Alejo Carpentier wrote his *¡Ecue Yamba-O!* in 1927 while a prisoner during the Machado administration and it, like *El negrero,* was published in 1933. However, these works also incorporated popular European ideas of the period, reflecting the time in which the works were written. For example, Carpentier's first novel, which is divided into "Infancia," "Adolescencia," and "La ciudad," conforms to Spengler's cycles of death and rebirth of culture. Both Novás Calvo and Carpentier were associated with the avant-guarde *Revista de Avance* and were familiar with current literary trends.[49]

While in Spain, Novás Calvo met important literary figures and participated in many cultural activities. In 1933, Novás Calvo had already been appointed secretary of the literary section of the Ateneo of Madrid. Spanish writers of the time had a profound influence on Novás Calvo's work. Pío Baroja's *Paradox, Rey,* in particular is represented in *El negrero.* Baroja's novel, like many other works with a black theme, reflected a European obsession with Africa and a search for the origins of civilization. At the outset of the novel, Diz, a Sancho

Panza type, expresses European concern for an idealized continent: "Africa! Admirable country! The real cradle of civilization! . . . It is the only place where one can live with dignity." He continues: "Africa! Sublime land untouched by civilization!"[50]

Like other slave narratives, Baroja's novel takes place in an area off the coast of Guinea, one of the main centers of the slave trade. As in the slave trade, those who go off to search for the beginning of civilization are buffoon types who not only represent the makeup of European civilization but also prefigure the destiny of Africa. The intent of Baroja's novel is further highlighted by Miss Pich, an early feminist who, viewing Western civilization from a nonmale perspective, concluded that men are inferior because they falsify history. The falsification of European and African history is precisely what is at stake; that is, a single interpretation of history. Westerners who write history, in particular the history of foreign cultures such as Africa, do so from their own cultural referent.[51] The concept of power is measured not only in physical conquest of a people but also in writing their history from another point of view, a theme that is evident in Carpentier's *The Kingdom of This World*, as we shall later see.

In his novel, Baroja attempts to address the issue of the decaying Western society and its impact on other continents and cultures. Decay in this sense does not mean a downfall of Western society, as Spengler had proposed in his *Decline of the West*, but a continual representation that alienates it from any "natural" or "original" state. In the early stages of the novel, the misfits of Western civilization are immediately separated from the opportunists. Only the former group, led by Paradox, attempts to integrate itself into the African environment. We are reminded throughout the novel that members of this group prefer to cope with the difficulties of their situation than return to Europe.[52] But their use of Western ideas and technology to help Bu-Tata in general and to assist it to rediscover the environment through European language and to use European common sense as a type of law in specific does not equal the French civilization process, which amounts to nothing less than a total destruction of the African village. As in *El negrero*, Western culture prospers from Africa and, in return, destroys Africa and African culture. As a form of advanced society, French civilization proves to be more "savage" than that of the natives of Guinea. Above all, it is Baroja's pessimism which is found in Novás Calvo's work.

Within the Western context of *Paradox, Rey, El negrero* is an important contribution to understanding the "paradox" of Western culture; Novás Calvo's novel demystifies a European vision of Africa as expressed by the surrealists, the poets of negritude, and others, wherein the mythological African past was a symbol of origin. The historical reality of Africa was much different. Although the slave trade provided a triangular relationship among Europe, Africa, and America and a link in the formation of Caribbean people, Africa is not presented as a place of origin and harmony but of discord caused mainly by the European presence. In Viconian terms, the European presence in Africa, which is directly associated with the slave trade, as in America, destroyed any natural or normal development of indigenous cultures and institutions. Some form of slavery had existed in Africa, but it was the Europeans who made slavery and the slave trade a wide-scale, dehumanizing, commercial enterprise. Many accounts point to the enormous profits in selling human beings where slaves were separated from their families and considered no more than a commodity. In his autobiography, Capt. Richard Drake describes how, working for Pedro Blanco in 1835, he filled a ship with 250 men and 100 boys and girls destined for Cuba. The $16 per head cost would bring in $350 each, yielding a profit of $120,400. Of this sum, $20,000 was used to cover expenses. The total earnings for the voyage was over $100,000.[53]

According to the novel, the European presence on the African continent altered society and was directly responsible for its corruption.

The natives were not as of yet corrupted by the Europeans (that is, they had not become crafty, they had not acquired malice), nor were they tied to any great king. Those two things were left to be done, and they would be done. The existence of many rival clans would prevent them from uniting. The lack of any one religion made them more susceptible to corruption. Pedro had studied all that and had consulted with Martínez. . . . The most important thing was to corrupt the chiefs and then give them weapons, because the weapons would cause war. (204)

In his *The Royal Navy and the Slavers*, Ward suggests that navy men recognized that the Europeans were responsible for corrupting the Africans and destroying native institutions by promoting the slave trade. They even made a distinction between slavers like Pedro Blanco and African leaders:

Without being sentimental towards the chiefs, they felt that they were more sinned against than sinning. Denman said that the Gallinas was a good country, and it had formerly had a good trade before the Spaniards came and spoilt it all. It produced camwood and ivory, and there was some gold further inland. There was cotton, indigo, pepper, oil palm, sugar and tobacco; all of these might be commercially developed, and there were chances of a cattle industry. But the Spaniards had ruined all this by concentrating on the slave trade.[54]

In both fact and Novás Calvo's novel, Blanco, like many other slavers, sold rum, gunpowder, and arms to the African tribes, instigated and promoted war among them, and encouraged the tribal kings to sell him their prisoners.

The slave trade was a complex network which entailed more than shipping Africans to the New World. The slave trade corrupted everyone, from the British navy and authorities in Sierra Leone to the captain general, who received a percentage of smuggled slaves. The slave trade transcended race and sex and included the sale of whites as well as blacks and male and female slave traffickers. Stedman describes a woman who, after her husband's death, kept a harem of men.[55] The morally corrupt European civilization which sanctioned the slave trade also forgave those who were at the center of corruption and allowed them to become respectable members of society. In his own self-interest, Blanco kept a watch over Fernando Poo and reported to the Ministry of Ultramar British encroachment on the island. Spanish authorities welcomed his help; the British presence was more dangerous than the activities of the slave trader. Blanco was named commander of the Armada in 1843 in recognition of his brief service to the Spanish government, thus overlooking his fifteen years as a slave trader, but his title was retracted toward the end of the same year. Others like John Newton were more successful. Newton underwent a conversion from freethinker to Christianity and from slave dealer to an outspoken opponent of slavery as his "Thoughts upon the African Slave Trade" in 1788, his testimony to the Privy Council in 1789, and his answers to a committee of the House of Commons in 1790 suggest.[56] Similarly, toward the latter part of his life, Canot married Elisa McKinley, who claimed to be President McKinley's sister, and, through the influence of his brother, was appointed collector of the port of Noumea in New Caledonia. When he died of a heart attack in 1860, he was aspiring to be named civil governor of New Caledonia.[57] Blanco's moral corruption is not an isolated case but is repeated in the slaver journals of Theodore Canot, Nicholas Owen, and John Newton, for example, and their attitudes must be considered a part of Western civilization.[58]

By mixing history and fiction, Novás Calvo's novel, unlike what actually occurred in the nineteenth century, does not forgive Blanco; on the contrary, it condemns him. For this the author resorts to a

thematic already present in the antislavery novel. Novás Calvo opens
and closes his novel with references to Blanco's family in gcneral and
his sister in particular. His fragmented family tied him to the slave
trade and contributed to his formation as a slaver. Conversely, slavery and the slave trade contributed to the decay of the family and
certainly complemented the moral decline of the West. We must
keep in mind that Canot, Blanco, Drake, and other slavers were each
raised in a household in which the father was absent and in which a
relative involved in the slave trade played a fundamental role in the
youth's life. In each case the unbalanced family life was an important factor in the child's upbringing.

From the opening chapter of El negrero, which narrates Blanco's
childhood, Novás Calvo offers a framework from which to understand the life of a slave trader. Given the factual accounts of Blanco's
life, it becomes apparent why Novás Calvo chose to substitute the
slaver's concern for his sister over his daughter, as a comparative
reading between the novel and texts of history has shown. By following closely Canot's narration, Novás Calvo used Blanco's relationship with his sister to underscore the further disintegration of the
slaver's character and family. Blanco's attraction for his sister leads
to incest, a theme made popular in Cecilia Valdés, and causes his
fall from innocence and his initiation into the slave trade. When
away from his native Spain, Blanco receives news about and from his
sister Rosa which guides his motives and marks the different stages
in his life.

In 1836, Blanco made arrangements to retire from Gallinas to
take better care of his sister. Toward the end of the novel, the filial
relationship recalls the past when Blanco projects and imposes his
situation onto his children by naming them Pedro and Rosa after
himself and his sister. Moreover, the sibling relationship is transcended when Blanco tells his children that Rosa is their lost mother,
implying that he and Rosa are more than just brother and sister but
husband and wife. Taboo and incest present in Cecilia Valdés and
other antislavery works are continued by Novás Calvo and become
the crux of the novel.

From a psychoanalytic standpoint, Blanco became fixated in an
infantile stage and his behavior is neurotic. Freud explains that the
"horror of incest displayed by savages"

> is essentially an *infantile* feature and that it reveals a striking agree-
> ment with the mental life of neurotic patients. Psycho-analysis has
> taught us that a boy's earliest choice of objects for his love is inces-
> tuous and that those objects are forbidden ones—his mother and his

sister. We have learnt, too, the manner in which, as he grows up, he liberates himself from this incestuous attraction. A neurotic, on the other hand, invariably exhibits some degree of psychical infantilism. He has either failed to get free from the psycho-sexual conditions that prevailed in his childhood or he has returned to them—two possibilities which may be summed up as developmental inhibitions and regression. Thus incestuous fixations of libido continue to play (or begin once more to play) the principal part in his unconscious mental life. We have arrived at the point of regarding a child's relationship to his parents, dominated as it is by incestuous longings, as the nuclear complex of neurosis.[59]

Blanco, trapped in infancy, could not repress his incestuous wishes and acted them out. If we follow Freud's ideas to their logical conclusion, Blanco's savagery as a slave trader was a result of his inability to transcend an earlier stage in his development which resulted in his neurosis. Within a broader context, all slave traders, though perhaps not for the same reasons, may have been neurotic. In addition, as a promoter and profiter of slavery and the slave trade, he suffers from the same psychological symptom which reflects upon Western society and culture. During the nineteenth century and the slave trade, Western culture was stagnant and did not develop.

Blanco's incest with his sister and the violation of his own sacred family in broader terms become an analogy for the European violation of the African people and their families through rape, murder, and enslavement. Within the context of the antislavery works, incest and slavery go together. The taboo also suggests that the human family, in which Europeans and Africans are brothers and sisters, has also been violated.

In the novel, the events in Pedro Blanco's life are a combination of Blanco's biography and those of Canot and other slavers. As the only extensive account of this famous Spanish slaver, Novás Calvo's story has become a source for those investigating Blanco's life. But unlike the nineteenth-century accounts of his life, Novás Calvo offers a different interpretation of history; that is, of a barbaric man who supported slavery, became a slaverunner and seller, and, like Ormond, Drake, and other slave traders, went crazy. After his sister's death, Blanco had her embalmed in order to keep her with him. Toward the last two years of his life, Blanco was confined to his residence by two keepers. The only thing that calmed him was the box which enclosed his sister's body, a personified image of death. Blanco could not escape from his past. His delirium made him relive his life as a slaver. Thinking that the box contained a treasure, the keepers attempted to steal it. In a rage, Blanco broke out of his straitjacket and almost killed one of the keepers. After Blanco's death, his daughter found the box open, and the two corpses appeared to be staring at each other.

From the perspective of the time of the writing, Novás Calvo's novel takes issue with contemporary works which base the decline of Western Europe on events that unfolded during the early part of the twentieth century; that is, during World War I and the Vanguard Movements. By writing his novel, Novás Calvo situates himself within the ideas of the times and dialogues with other works, such as Spengler's *Decline of the West*. Within this context, *El negrero* suggests that the demise of European culture occurred much earlier, in the nineteenth century (and perhaps earlier), during the time of the narration and Pedro Blanco's life. The slave trade was widespread and affected practically all major Western powers. It was the selling of Africans and their labor which was at the center of European civilization and prosperity. At the same time, slavery and the slave trade severely altered African culture and also caused Europe's own moral downfall. In spite of the emancipation of slaves in the nineteenth century in Latin America and the Caribbean, the corruption present during the historical time of Novás Calvo's *El negrero* continues into the present time of the writing.

II  Novás Calvo's *El negrero* traces the decline of Europe to European corruption of Africa and the slave trade. Carpentier's *The Kingdom of This World* complements Novás Calvo's historical development of slavery and describes the same European presence and corruption not in West Coast Africa but in Haiti and the Caribbean. Just as the European civilization destroyed the native institutions in Africa, the same historical process did not allow them to develop in the New World. While researching Haitian history and culture Carpentier explores the rebellion in Saint Domingue, an event publicized in nineteenth-century Cuba to create a fear of blacks and suppress any attempt to emancipate slaves in the slavery period or to organize blacks in the postslavery period, as represented, for example, by the Aponte Conspiracy and the Partido Independiente de Color, respectively. By writing *The Kingdom of This World*, Carpentier accepts an interpretation which conforms to the white fear prevalent during the time the Del Monte literary circle met, a fear which undermined movements of emancipation and independence. However, he also shows that the rebellion which whites feared was caused, as Francisco Calcagno discloses in *Romualdo, uno de tantos*, by Europeans attempting to enslave Africans. Whereas

Novás Calvo documents the life of a neurotic man who became a slaver, Carpentier narrates the European corruption of America and the creation of institutions based on oppression and rebellion which set into motion unique patterns in Caribbean history still present during the time Carpentier and Novás Calvo were writing their works.

Carpentier's concern for history reflects a fundamental component of Western culture. By writing about the lives of an important but marginal segment of Western society, he brings the history of blacks to the foreground of contemporary Spanish American literature. In his prologue to the novel, Carpentier confirms the historicity of the narration:

> A succession of extraordinary events is narrated there, which occurred in Saint-Domingue in a specific period that does not reach the span of a lifetime, allowing the marvelous to flow freely from a reality which has been followed in every detail. For it must be kept in mind that the story about to be read is based on extremely rigorous documentation. A documentation that not only respects the true history of the events, the names of characters—including secondary ones, of places and events, but that it also conceals, beneath its apparent atemporality, a detailed correspondence of dates and chronology.[60]

The structures of history are present in Carpentier's *The Kingdom of This World*, a work which touches upon the very core of Haitian and Caribbean society. After reading William Seabrook's *The Magic Island* in 1939 and a subsequent trip to the island in 1943 with the French actor Louis Jouvet, Carpentier became attracted to Haitian history and culture.[61] Carpentier was impressed by what he learned and sought to research *The Kingdom of This World* not from a dominant white but from a marginal black point of view, therefore avoiding a European interpretation of history. While in Haiti, Carpentier learned about the myths of the Haitian people and incorporated them into his novel. However, Carpentier's concern for the theme of blacks and slavery is not an isolated phenomenon. It is related to the nineteenth-century Cuban antislavery novel and to his participation in surrealism.[62] Carpentier's *¡Ecue Yamba-O!* (1933), for example, is a novel which fuses these two literary currents.

From our comparative standpoint, we are interested in the presence of whites and blacks in history and the role their respective cultures played in the formation of Haitian society. Although Carpentier was not as preoccupied with the incipient conflicts between Africans and Europeans as Novás Calvo, he addresses an important concern Vico develops in *The New Science* regarding the genesis of nations;[63] in the New World, Carpentier refers to the events surrounding the founding of the Haitian Republic. The tensions described in the novel were indeed present from the moment Africans were brought to the New World. However, they became more intense during the time of the narration, toward the end of the eighteenth century, mainly due to the development of the sugar industry. The Haitian revolution brought the black struggle to a climax, though not to an end.

*The Kingdom of This World* is perhaps Carpentier's most important work for a broad understanding of Caribbean history. As recently as 1979, while reading on Cuban television "La cultura de los pueblos que habitan en las tierras del mar Caribe," Carpentier continued to emphasize themes already present in *The Kingdom of This World*, including Mackandal's power to overthrow the white colonialists in Saint Domingue and the historical pact at Bois Caiman. In his speech, Carpentier described the pact in a manner which recalls his fiction: "It is curious that the Oath of Bois Caiman gives birth to the real concept of independence. That is, on the same land coexist the concept of colonization brought by the Spaniards to Saint Domingue and the concept of decolonization or the beginning of the wars of independence, of decolonization, the anticolonial wars which will be prolonged until the present."[64] Carpentier reinterprets events to adhere to his concept of history. He recognizes that the first war for independence was fought not in Saint Domingue but in the United States. Nevertheless, he believes that it was the second revolution, not the first, which produced the most radical change in society.

It is clear from his talk on the Caribbean that Carpentier noticed the repetition of historical events, the cycles of history.[65] For him, the cycles of oppression and rebellion already present in *The Kingdom of This World* influenced his overall vision of Spanish American history, from the conquest to the Cuban Revolution:

> The colonizer became the aristocracy, the oligarchy fighting against
> the creole as defined by Bolívar in the paragraph which I just read.
> Finally, with the wars of independence, it was the uprising of the
> creole, of the native of America, against the Spaniard who, according
> to latitudes, was called the *Godo*, the *Mantuano*, the *Chapetón*, etc.
> But the creole victor creates a new oligarchy with which the slave,
> the dispossessed, and an emerging middle class, which includes
> almost all of the intelligentsia, will have to fight: intellectuals, writ-

ers, professors, teachers, finally, that admirable middle class which is growing during all of the nineteenth century until it meets the present.[66]

The revolutionary Carpentier continued the chronology of American history to include present-day Cuba. But if the earlier Carpentier proposed a hermetic structure, the contemporary one suggests that present-day Cuba has broken out of the cycle, thus reading current Cuban history as a final chapter of his novel.[67]

According to *The Kingdom of This World*, the coming together of Africans and Europeans set into motion cycles in Caribbean literature and history. The two cultures also serve as a point of departure for Carpentier's concept of the marvelous in American reality. The theme of blacks and whites is a dominant aspect in *The Kingdom of This World*, but an origin of their conflicts, as represented by the slave trade, is absent from the narration. Nevertheless, in the prologue of the novel Carpentier provides a discussion of the emergence of European and American realities.[68] For Carpentier, marvelous realism is a fundamental component for understanding American history in general and *The Kingdom of This World* in particular. According to him, the marvelous is a European concept which dates from the beginning of Western literature and continues into the present with surrealism.[69] Carpentier defines the marvelous as follows:

> The marvelous comes about in an unmistakable manner when an unexpected alternation of reality (a miracle) appears, of a privileged revelation of reality, of an unusual illumination or a uniquely flattering of the unnoticed richness of reality, of a widening of the scales and categories of reality, perceived with great particular intensity in virtue of an exaltation of the spirit which guides it to a sort of "limited state."
> To begin, the marvelous sensation presupposes a faith. Those who do not believe in saints cannot be cured by miracles of saints, or those who are not Quijotes can enter, in body, soul, and possessions in the world of *Amadís de Gaula* or *Tirante el blanco.*[70]

Carpentier distinguishes between the marvelous and marvelous realism insofar as the first pertains to Europe and European literature and the second to Haiti and all of America.[71] Carpentier recalls that André Masson was not able to capture the magic of the Martiniquan jungle, but the Cuban painter Wifredo Lam effectively depicted the magic of American vegetation.

However, the terms *lo maravilloso* and *lo real maravilloso* are unclear and ambiguous in their application in Carpentier's novel and prologue. The ambiguity occurs in Carpentier's examples of marvelous realism as manifested in the New World. Mackandal's metamorphosis took place in Haiti. Yet the idea of a search for the eternal fountain of youth originated not in America but in Europe. While suggesting in his prologue that marvelous realism is a European phenomenon in America, Carpentier neglects to explain the origin of other magical elements of Caribbean history and literature as represented, for example, by African culture. Carpentier subscribes to the importance Vico attributes to *naissance,* or origin, by including in the prologue a description of European ideas; however, he omits a similar discussion about African religions and culture, even though they are present in the novel. Opposing fact and fiction, the prologue and the novel, as two modes of narration, are the source of different origins: The first provides an explanation of magic in European society; the second does the same, but for Africa.

African culture and religion are dominant components of *The Kingdom of This World.*[72] Should Carpentier have included in his prologue an explanation of the origin of voodoo or African traditions when discussing the presence of marvelous reality in America? The absence of any discussion of African culture and religion reveals a contradiction between the prologue and the novel. In the novel, Carpentier narrates the importance voodoo played in the development of the plot. But within the context of the prologue, all extraordinary realities, such as Mackandal's and Ti Noel's transformations, cannot be a part of the marvelous, since this term is associated with European culture, but of marvelous realism present in American reality. By not considering other magical elements in the prologue, African metamorphoses in the novel appear as isolated events without any substantiation. Within the context of the fiction, European civilization is not magical but real. Therefore, the marvelous realism which Carpentier discusses in his prologue typifies the *marvelous* of African religion and the *realism* of European culture. Together, they provide a different understanding of Carpentier's prologue by proposing that marvelous realism (as the coming together of European and African cultures) is indeed part of America.

The only indication of the marvelous in America, as explained in the prologue, is the apparition of Corneille Breille. Breille, who had been immured by Christophe, suddenly appears during the Mass of the Assumption in the church of Limonade. His presence is not a manifestation of Christophe's subconscious, since others, such as the celebrant Juan de Dios González, not only saw but were affected by it. Within the context of the prologue, this unique development is in accordance with marvelous realism as a European manifestation in America. But it does not agree with the definition offered by the novel, which suggests that marvelous realism is a consequence of African religion and culture. In another reading of "Chronicle of August 15," Breille's apparition and its impact on Christophe conform not to the definition provided in the prologue but to that of the novel. His presence in the church of Limonade occurs within the context of African, rather than European, tradition.

> Against the advice of all, he had ordered the Mass of the Assumption in the church of Limonade. . . . Yet the King felt himself surrounded by a hostile atmosphere. The populace that had hailed him on his arrival was sullen with evil intentions, recalling all too well, there in that fertile land, the crops lost because the men were working on the Citadel. In some remote house—he suspected—there was probably an image of him stuck full of pins or hung head down with a knife plunged in the region of the heart. From far off there came from time to time the beat of drums which he felt sure were not imploring a long life for him. (135–136)

Breille's presence is a direct result not of European magic but African voodoo performed against Christophe. Christophe's paralysis and suicide were caused by his enemies, who used African religion to overthrow him. The descriptions that follow substantiate this interpretation. As Christophe lay on the floor, voodoo continues to be omnipresent. "A rhythm was growing in the King's ears which might have been that of his own veins or that of the drums being beaten in the hills" (138).[73] The drums were beating and lightning struck the church tower; the drums are gods or contain gods; the thunderbolt is a representation of Ogoun, the god of iron and fire and Shangó, the god of thunder and lightning.[74] Christophe's state of shock and paralysis was indeed a consequence of voodoo. Basing his studies on the importance of voodoo, Alfred Metraux helps to clarify Christophe's suicide: "Suicide is not regarded as a truly voluntary act, but as the consequence of a state of mental alienation brought about by a sorcerer."[75]

The displacement from prologue to novel, from fact to fiction, from the presence of the marvelous as a European idea to the marvelous realism as a manifestation of African traditions represents the difference between Europe and Africa, white and black cultures.

In Haitian history, the coming together of different races and cultures can be divided into three ages: Carpentier describes the first age as a series of binary oppositions between Europe and Africa, history and nature, Christianity and voodoo, master and slave, Monsieur Lenormand de Mezy and Ti Noel, writing and oral tradition. But the founding of the republic in the second age and the unification of Haiti in the third bring the opposing forces together.

Compared to Africa, European culture is false, as Carpentier suggests by the waxed heads, the pig's head, and the faces on the prints. While Carpentier lived in Paris during the 1920s and 1930s, the downfall of Europe was a popular idea, dramatized by Spengler's *Decline of the West* and surrealism.[76] As with Novás Calvo's *El negrero*, according to Carpentier's *The Kingdom of This World* the decadence of Europe and European culture is not a twentieth-century phenomenon but was present centuries before during slavery and certainly during the time of the narration. The heads appear to have been cut off by the guillotine, an instrument made popular by the French Revolution, which had triumphed during the time of the narration.

Moreover, although the prologue omitted any explanation of the magical as a manifestation of African tradition, in this first section of the novel Carpentier provides an origin of African traditions important for understanding the action. The first section serves as a prologue of sorts in which Carpentier provides information about Africa absent in his prologue; he explains marvelous realism in America and its manifestation within the context of the novel. In the African world there is no disparity between man and civilization; on the contrary, there is harmony between man and nature.

The Mandingue Negro would tell of things that had happened in the great kingdoms of Popo, of Arada, of the Nagos, or the Fulah. He spoke of the great migration of tribes, of age-long wars, of epic battles in which the animals had been allies of men. He knew of the story of Adonhueso, of the King of Angola, of King Da, the incarnation of the Serpent, which is the eternal beginning, never ending, who took his pleasure mystically with a queen who was the Rainbow, patroness of the Waters and of all Bringing Forth. But, above all, it was with the tale of Kankan Muza that he achieved the gift of tongues, the fierce Muza, founder of the invincible empire of the Mandingues. . . . Moreover, those kings rode with lances in hand at the head of their hordes, and they were made invulnerable by the science of the Preparers, and fell wounded only if in some way they had offended the gods of Lightning or of the Forge. They were kings, true kings, and

not those sovereigns wigged in false hair who played at cup and ball
and were gods only when they strutted the stage of their court the-
atres, effeminately pointing a leg in the measures of a rigadoon.
(13–14)

If the faces of European rulers are reproductions of the original, that
is, a mimetic representation, and are engraved on a paper like writing, for Ti Noel the stories of Africa and African kings are part of
Mackandal's memory and are transmitted through oral tradition.
The king's metamorphosis recalls those of Mackandal and Ti Noel,
which take place within the context of African culture and religion.
We can divide Carpentier's narration into three historical ages:
Slavery, emancipation and independence, and the reunification of
the republic; each one has important cultural ramifications. In the
first age, the polarity between African and European traditions, present in the first chapter, continues throughout the narration. The
presence of the two cultures allows for a double interpretation of the
novel, one pertaining to the real and the other to the magical. This is
most evident in an all too well known passage in which blacks and
whites interpret Mackandal's burning at the stake differently.

Macandal was now lashed to the post. The executioner had picked
up an ember with the tongs. With a gesture rehearsed the evening
before in front of a mirror, the Governor unsheathed his dress sword
and gave the order for the sentence to be carried out. The fire began to rise toward the Mandingue, licking his legs. At that moment
Macandal moved the stump of his arm, which they had been unable
to tie up, in a threatening gesture which was none the less terrible
for being partial, howling unknown spells and violently thrusting his
torso forward. The bonds fell off and the body of the Negro rose in
the air, flying overhead, until it plunged into the black waves of the
sea of slaves. A single cry filled the square:
    "Macandal saved!"
Pandemonium followed. The guards fell with rifle butts on the
howling blacks, who now seemed to overflow the streets, climbing
toward the windows. And the noise and screaming and uproar were
such that very few saw that Macandal, held by ten soldiers, had been
thrust head first into the fire, and that a flame fed by his burning
hair had drowned his last cry. When the slaves were restored to order,
the fire was burning normally like any fire of good wood, and the
breeze blowing from the sea was lifting the smoke toward the windows where more than one lady who had fainted had recovered
consciousness. There was no longer anything to see. (51–52)

The difference between the two interpretations is directly related to the cultural and religious backgrounds of those viewing Mackandal's execution: the whites witnessed Mackandal's death, the blacks his salvation. Both cultures and interpretations are diametrically opposed and irreconcilable. The polarity in this part of the novel is expressed in the reproduction of the events, in two paragraphs separated by "Mackandal sauvé," the first containing the black version and the second the white one. Where one group saw life, the other saw death.

In a second age, the synthesis between Africa and Europe takes place when African religion and Western history come together. If Mackandal represented a close link with Africa, Bouckman embodies a shift from the past. Bois Caiman is a first indication of a union, if slight, between Europe and Africa. Like Mackandal before him, Bouckman summons the African gods to combat the slave masters. But Bouckman also had knowledge of the French Revolution and the declaration of French deputies to emancipate slaves. Bouckman's knowledge of history and voodoo is associated with a more general and political act to liberate blacks in Saint Domingue. In comparison to Bouckman's rebellion, Mackandal's use of voodoo against the slave owners in the first age represents an isolated act. The union between history and African religion in the novel led to the emancipation of slaves and the formation of the first independent black republic.

The fusion of Africa and Europe also occurs with Pauline Bonaparte and Solimán, two characters who accept each other's culture; but it is best depicted by Henri Christophe, a descendant of slaves who abandons his African traditions and rules the northern part of Haiti, not as an African but as a European monarch. In keeping with Vico's emphasis on the origins and births of nations, Christophe represents a political shift in history, from slavery to emancipation, from colony to republic. Once the republic was established, the white rulers were forced to leave and blacks took their place. However, the past structures evident during white control of the island continued. With Christophe, the oppression of blacks is no longer racially but politically and economically motivated.

Solimán and Christophe are the antitheses of Mackandal and also of Ti Noel.[77] Unlike them, Ti Noel remains loyal to African tradition and culture. Both Christophe and Solimán are punished for abandoning African religion. As with Mackandal's death or salvation, Solimán's final days in Rome have a dual interpretation. On the one hand, Solimán contracted malaria. On the other, he was being punished by the Loas. "It seemed to him that he had fallen into a trance upon the stones of a grave, as happened Back There to certain of the possessed, whom the peasants both feared and revered because they were on better terms than anyone else with the Masters of the Graveyards" (167). Solimán's possession, and therefore spiritual sickness, explains why Dr. Antommarchi, Napoleon's doctor on St. Helena, could not save him. The possessed Solimán recognized his estrangement from African culture and religion and wanted to return to Saint Domingue. Speaking to the god of the road, he repeated: "Papa Legba, l'ouvri barrié-a pou moin, ago, agó yé, Papa Legba, ouvri barrié-a pou moin, pou moin passé" (Father Legba, open the barrier [the door] so that I can pass through it [in essence, he is asking to be carried back to Saint Domingue]) (168).[78]

Similarly, Christophe's denial of his heritage allows him to view blacks as if they were other. As with Solimán, his separation from them and embracement of white culture and values cause Christophe's downfall. The Citadel, which represents Christophe's defense against a French invasion, does not save him from voodoo and his people. Like Solimán, Christophe renounced African religion, and the Loas, but also the Catholic saints, in turn betrayed and punished him. For Christophe everything was lost; there was no chance of turning back. "All the mirrors of Sans Souci were simultaneously ablaze."[79]

The third age is marked by the presence of the Surveyors during Jean Pierre Boyer's government, the political unification of the northern and southern parts of Haiti, and the annexation of the eastern part of Hispaniola. This age also has a racial designation and is noted, not for blacks like Christophe, but for a new mulatto aristocracy. The power and might which ruled the previous ages would, during the third age, be disguised as law and order. Slavery, replaced by Christophe's forced labor, would continue under a prison system. In history, faced with economic decline and political unrest, Boyer abandoned a moderate position and used tactics known to Christophe, forcing Haitians to plant and harvest under armed guard. However, Boyer was overthrown by a conspiracy of mulattoes in 1843. Soon after, the mulattoes lost power to black leaders, who ruled the country for seventy-two years. The coming together of European and African cultures illustrates historical shifts which are represented by the acquisition of power first by whites and later by blacks and mulattoes.

As we have seen, Carpentier's novel proposes multiple readings based on the interaction of the white and black races. In another reading, the second and third ages, symbolized by Christophe and the Mulatto Republicans, respectively, may represent a continuation of the age in which whites and blacks first came together. What appeared to be structures based on white, black, and mulatto rules are now independent of race. The change in historical time is only one continuation of a deeper structure of rebellion and oppression present from the time the two cultures first interacted. The novel proposes the following diachronic development, which is consistent with the two interpretations of the novel: In colonial Saint Domingue, Monsieur Lenormand de Mezy's enslavement of Ti Noel and Mackandal is replaced by Monsieur Blancheland's systematic extermination of all slaves as well as free blacks and mulattoes. This is later repeated by Leclerc, whose rule is represented by Pauline Bonaparte's decadence and sensual nature and by Rochambeau, whose authority was marked by orgies and a decline in law and order. In the republic, the French dominion was followed by Henri Christophe's reign, which, according to Ti Noel, was worse than the period of slavery. Finally, after the reunification of the island, Christophe's ruthless dominion will be continued by the Mulatto Republicans, who are the new masters of the Plaine du Nord.

Just as there is a structure of oppression associated in one form or another with Western culture, there is another structure of rebellion linked to African religion. Mackandal's fight against slave masters is continued by Bouckman's struggle to emancipate slaves, by Dessaline's rebellion against colonial forces to establish an independent republic, and, finally, by Ti Noel's uprisings, first against Henri Christophe and later against the Mulatto Republicans. Blacks who remain loyal to their African origins are destined to continue to fight for a lost freedom.

As a totality, the historical continuity from eighteenth to nineteenth century, from slavery to emancipation, from colony to republic is not lineal but cyclical. What may have been perceived as two independent structures with African and European origins in Haiti and the Caribbean fuse into one grand design, starting with Mackandal's fight against slave owners and ending, in the novel, with Ti Noel's rebellion against the Mulatto Republicans. Like the events in the novel, this grand design is open to two interpretations with important cultural referents. If there are movements of oppression, there will be others of liberation. However, the converse is true—if there are movements of liberation, there will be others of oppression. In history and in fiction, the rebellion of slaves was met with the white suppression of blacks and the white suppression caused the rebellion of slaves. In other words, Mackandal's rebellion led to his capture and death (or salvation), but, also, the enslavement of blacks led to Mackandal's actions. What appears to be inevitable

is the displacement of one by the other, and this proposes to continue into the present time in which Carpentier pronounced his
television speech. Neither fiction nor history provides a sign of any
historical relief. The presence of whites in the Caribbean did not
allow indigenous institutions to flourish in the manner Vico prescribed; with the massacre of Amerindians, those that did develop
were foreign.[80] Thus, the foundation of Caribbean culture and history is based on a foreign rather than indigenous culture. In the Caribbean, the presence of Africans and Europeans led to the creation
of another development in human history than the one explained in
The New Science. The one that did develop in the Caribbean is
based on liberation and oppression and perhaps is destined to repeat
itself.

History appears to narrate the ending of The Kingdom of This
World. When Carpentier arrived in Haiti in 1943, Elie Lescot was
the Haitian president. Taking advantage of the events of World War II,
he utilized his power to enrich himself and his friends. However,
strong dissatisfaction with the Lescot administration led to the election of Dumarsais Estimé in 1946. Unlike Lescot, Estimé was considered a leader of the Haitian people and fought for their rights. But
his government was soon followed by the father and son Duvalier
dictatorships, which were among the most oppressive in Caribbean
history. Given the structure proposed by Carpentier, we could have
foreseen the defeat of Jean Claude Duvalier in favor of a coalition
government which would be more responsive to the masses, and
also a shift away from that government and the imposition of another more ruthless one which Lt. Gen. Henri Namphy represents.

By ending the narration in the manner in which it began, the
novel proposes still another interpretation, perhaps of one cycle.[81]
The final chapter, entitled "Agnus Dei," represents a realization
that nothing has changed. After the ransacking of Sans Souci, Ti
Noel, like the geese fleeing from turmoil, escapes to join the animal
and insect world. He soon discovers that, like human society, they
too have laws and regulations. Even the geese, with their egalitarian
form of government, which "denied all superiority of individual over
individual of the same species" (182), objected to Ti Noel's metamorphosis. In the body of a goose, he notices that human society is
not significantly different from that of animals. For him, "the clan
now seemed a community of aristocrats, tightly closed against anyone of a different caste," resembling the system of government he
had come to know so well. "It had been made crystal clear to him
that being a goose did not imply that all geese were equal" (183).

The similarities between the human and animal worlds reveal, for

Carpentier, structures found in Africa, Haiti, and other parts of the Caribbean. If certain people and cultures seek power to control, others must fight for their freedom from domination. Ti Noel's profound understanding of the animal and human worlds implies his acceptance to continue an endless struggle for liberation. In spite of their historical unity, African and Western societies will always be separate. The cycle is clearly visible in the four chapters in the novel. As we have noted, in the first there is a distinction between master and slave, black and white, oppressor and oppressed. In the second, with Pauline and Solimán, there is a fusion of sorts between the two cultures. In the third, the mixing of the cultures culminates with Henri Christophe, the "European" monarch. But Christophe's death in the third and Solimán's in the fourth are directly associated with their abandonment of African culture. For this they are punished by the gods. Ti Noel also in the fourth chapter, unlike Christophe and Solimán, lives on and remains loyal to his culture and religion. Therefore, he follows in a tradition of African kings and of Mackandal in the New World. Both at the outset of the novel and at the end he reaffirms the separation of African and Western cultures.

The polarity of European and African cultures evident in this last interpretation allows for a different reading of *The Kingdom of This World*, this one suggesting that the cycles are not historical but religious. An emphasis on the black/religious/"natural" aspect of the novel undermines the historical structures we have been describing. If some have already referred to the importance of Moreau de Saint-Mery's work for writing *The Kingdom of This World*, Jean Price-Mars's *So Spoke the Uncle* (1928) offers an important dimension to Carpentier's work. Price-Mars, whose work was well known when Carpentier visited Haiti, wrote during the U.S. occupation and gave new hope with his cultural interpretation of Haitian customs. He wrote at a time before *negrismo* and negritude became popular forms of expressing black pride and identity in the Caribbean. During this time, blacks were considered biologically, culturally, and historically inferior to whites. *So Spoke the Uncle* was the first book to explain Haitian religion and customs through African origins, an interpretation which would be included later in *The Kingdom of This World*. Price-Mars considered oral tradition and legends part of Haitian folklore. Most important, he also studied voodoo as the culture of the rural masses and, unlike others, he did not look upon it as a cult but as a religion.

Price-Mars's studies of Vodoun, from which voodoo is derived,[82] revealed that man has no free will; voodoo controls the individual, who is no more than an instrument of Makou, the supreme being.

Makou expresses his will through voodoo. Unlike Vico's study of human society, Vodoun is a creation of God; nothing happens without the participation of the Spirits, the Vodoun.[83] "The Vodoun are embodied in human beings whom they use to make known their wishes as well as in natural phenomena which represent manifestations of their anger, vengeance, and power."[84] Voodoo or African religion and culture is, by the will of the gods, antagonistic to white culture. Therefore, Mackandal, Bouckman, Ti Noel, and others are only servants of the religion. Price-Mars has Bouckman, within the context of voodoo, reveal the true meaning of the rebellion:

> Good Lord who made the sun
> Which shines on us from on high,
> Who raises the sea,
> Who makes the tempest roar,
> Hear you, people, the Good Lord
> Is hidden in his cloud.
> From there he looks down on us
> And sees all that the white men do.
> The God of the white men commands crime,
> Ours solicits good deeds,
> But this God who is so good [ours]
> Orders us to vengeance.
> He will guide our hand.
> And give us assistance.
> Break the image of the god of the white men
> Who has thirst for our tears
> Hear in our hearts the call of liberty![85]

In a manner which recalls Price-Mars and with minor differences, Carpentier reproduces Bouckman's sacramental words: "The white men's God orders the crime. Our gods demand vengeance from us. They will guide our arms and give us help. Destroy the image of the white man's God who thirsts for our tears; let us listen to the cry of freedom within ourselves" (67).

From a religious perspective, throughout the novel there has been no historical development of cultures. On the contrary, everything remains the same; only time has changed. The only difference is the reader's point of view or interpretation. What Western culture considers to be historical, African culture considers religious. Both Carpentier and Price-Mars see that the long struggle has been transferred from one individual to another and man is but an instrument. Moreover, Price-Mars describes the struggle in a manner which agrees with a religious interpretation of *The Kingdom of This World* when he observes that despite the passage of time and changing events he believes that the changes are more apparent than real and there has been "only a substitution of masters."[86]

By observing Haitian society, both Carpentier and Price-Mars reflect upon the importance of the past in the formation of American culture, religion, and history. From a black perspective, both recognize the role voodoo played in the foundation of Haitian culture and the fight for independence. Reading both works together, Price-Mars is a contemporary Ti Noel. As with his other transformations, Ti Noel now becomes an intellectual fighting for freedom from the occupation.

In conclusion, let us come back to Vico. If we accept the importance of the genesis of nations insofar as it pertains to the founding of Haitian culture, two competing interpretations based on African and European cultures will always exist. However, in spite of what Carpentier suggested in his "La cultura de los pueblos que habitan en las tierras del mar Caribe," in Haiti and the Caribbean there will be no return to a just and simple life but instead a struggle to recover what has always existed in African religion since the arrival of foreigners to the New World. The cycle will be self-repeating *ad infinitum.*

# FIVE

# The Politics of Memory
## Miguel Barnet's The Autobiography of a Runaway Slave and César Leante's Los guerrilleros negros

> *Los recuerdos, de niño*
> *sombras de mochas ásperas,*
> *piel curtida*
> *por el viento y el sol. Mirada*
> *de lejanía y de venganza.*
> *Eran los macheteros.*
>
> *Centrales: Jatibonico, Jaronú,*
> *Steward, Vertientes, Lugareño,*
> *O el Chaparra, con Menocal*
> *sonando el cuero.*
>
> *De niño, en el recuerdo,*
> *los macheteros.*
> —NICOLÁS GUILLÉN, *SOL DE DOMINGO*

I — Written and published during the Cuban revolutionary period, Miguel Barnet's *Autobiography of a Runaway Slave* (1966) and César Leante's *Los guerrilleros negros* (1976), like Carpentier's *The Kingdom of This World*, recount historical events. Carpentier's writings were important for younger Cuban writers such as Barnet and Leante, who published their works after the success of the revolution, but also for many Spanish American narrators such as Gabriel García Márquez and Mario Vargas Llosa. Carpentier's essay on marvelous realism also became important for younger writers.

The Cuban Revolution provided both young and established writers with the opportunity of publishing their works. Among these, Barnet and Leante attempted to rewrite literary history by introducing images present in Cuban history that had remained unexplored in the literature of the past century. One of these is the rebel slave. For example, Leante's interpretation of slavery challenges the one offered by the early works, including the proslavery literature. Unlike Francisco Estévez's *Diario de un rancheador* and José Morilla's "El ranchador," which describe the life of the slave hunter in the eastern region of Vuelta Abajo, Leante takes his narration to Oriente, the opposite side of the island, and reveals the life of the slave hunter's counterpart, the runaway slave. Whereas Morilla and Estévez showed the runaway slave as a merciless black who killed indiscriminately, Leante's novel is an important intertext for understanding the slave's action. From his perspective, the slave attacks are not casual but rather political and strategic, meant to protect the slave's regained freedom.

These and other events were known in the Caribbean islands of the nineteenth century; nevertheless, they remained absent from the pages of the incipient narrative. The early Cuban antislavery writers concentrated on revealing a different aspect of slavery, that of the domestic house slave. There is no question that the antislavery works uncovered the cruelties of the slavery system and represented a threat to the Spanish authorities. However, they portrayed an incomplete picture of slavery insofar as the early works described the life of a passive slave. In *Francisco*, freedom was not equated with emancipation, but with the desire to choose one's lover and love freely. For Manzano, freedom meant having not a cruel but a just and kind master. Manzano complained about his treatment under the marquesa de Prado Ameno, but he was also happy under doña Beatriz de Justis and under don Nicolás. Only after the marquesa's mistreatment does Manzano escape, and then only to find another master.

Montejo's testimony recalls Manzano's autobiography, and with Manzano's *Autobiografía, The Autobiography of a Runaway Slave* closes a narrative cycle of sorts. However, the passage of time from the nineteenth to the twentieth century, from slavery to revolution accounts for significant differences between the slaves. Manzano's autobiography narrates the life of a privileged slave who learned to read and write, had good and bad masters, happy and sad moments under slavery. Montejo's life is not of a privileged but of a common slave who accepted his African heritage and traditions; it is the first personal and detailed account of a Maroon slave in Cuban and Spanish American literature and a valuable document to historians and students of slavery.[1] Although both were runaway slaves, unlike Manzano Montejo rejected the white slavery system in all its manifestations. He did not learn to read and write, and he did not escape to the city to seek the captain general's help or that of any other white but to the mountains and away from any semblance of Western culture and society.

With the evolution of the antislavery narrative, time allowed for more daring yet realistic images to be described and provide a comprehensive vision of slavery in Cuba. In the late nineteenth century, writers such as Francisco Calcagno did narrate aspects of the fugitive slave, but their historical circumstances would impose limits on their writings. Their characters only reacted in a manner which was acceptable to the society in which the works were written. Like writers in other periods, Barnet's and Leante's writings would respond to the demands placed on them by events of the Cuban Revolution.

Like *The Kingdom of This World*, *The Autobiography of a Runaway Slave* covers a broad period of time and, in keeping with Vico's concern for origins, it narrates an important transition in Cuban history, from slavery to emancipation; that is, from the Ten Years' War to the founding of the Cuban Republic. Equally important, there is a historical link between the two works. Both delineate the history of abolition in the Caribbean from the first to the last countries to abolish slavery: Saint Domingue in 1791 and Cuba in 1886.[2] (Haiti and Cuba also represent the first and last countries to become independent republics, Haiti in 1804 and Cuba one century later in 1902.) Carpentier's and Barnet's narratives, as representative of Haitian and Cuban histories, respectively, offer a historical continuum of blacks and slaves from the seventeenth to the twentieth century. As a unity, they open and close a Caribbean cycle.[3]

Barnet's text suggests a similar thematic structure to that of *The Kingdom of This World*. But unlike Carpentier's recreation of Haitian history, *The Autobiography of a Runaway Slave* describes the life of Esteban Montejo, a 105-year-old Cuban who remembers his past with exceptional clarity. Montejo's recollections are illuminating and demystifying, often challenging accepted notions of Cuban history. Barnet, a Cuban ethnologist, wrote the "autobiography" from interviews with Montejo which he transcribed and edited. The autobiography highlights Montejo's life during three distinct moments in Cuban history. As a child, Montejo was a slave in a sugar mill and escaped to the mountains. After slavery, Montejo returned to civilization and worked at the Purio and Ariosa plantations. Later, he joined the *mambises* and fought against Spanish domination during the War of Independence.

By documenting the history of blacks and slaves in Cuba, Barnet reproduces a cyclical structure already seen in Carpentier's novel. Carpentier proposes cycles in slavery present up to the arrival of the Mulatto Republicans. Barnet's narration is part of a contiguous structure which chronologically and thematically parallels Carpentier's novel and Cuban history from slavery and colony to the founding of the Cuban Republic, the time of the narration, and perhaps to the Cuban Revolution, the time in which Barnet conducted the interviews and wrote Montejo's life. Like the different ages in *The Kingdom of This World*, Barnet divides *The Autobiography of a Runaway Slave* into three historical periods: slavery, abolition, and the War of Independence. As in Carpentier's novel, each successive age may be a manifestation of a previous one: In Viconian terms, abolition and the War of Independence can be the *ricorsos* of the age of slavery. The historical transformations in Cuban and Haitian societies were supposed to bring change to the lives of their citizens. But, similar to *The Kingdom of This World*, in Cuba there is no historical relief or salvation for slaves or blacks. In spite of the chronological progression of history, life for blacks in general and Montejo in particular has changed very little and appears to be repeated throughout the three periods. In all of them, blacks work in sugarcane fields and mills, live in barracoons, earn little money, and endure constant discrimination. Montejo himself is aware of the cycles of history. He is conscious that after the radical transformations in Cuban society, as represented by abolition and the War of Independence, the present continues to resemble the past. After emancipation, Montejo recalls certain moments under slavery:

> The first plantation I worked on was called Purio. I turned up there one day in the rags I stood in and a hat I had collected on the way. I went in and asked the overseer if there was work for me. He said yes. I remember he was Spanish, with moustaches, and his name was Pepe. There were overseers in these parts until quite recently, the difference being that they didn't lay about them as they used to do under slavery. But they were men of the same breed, harsh, overbearing. There were still barracoons after Abolition, the same as before. Many of them were newly built of masonry, the old ones having collapsed under the rain and storms. The barracoon at Purio was strong and looked as if it had been recently completed. They told me to go and live there. I soon made myself at home, for it wasn't too bad. They had taken the bolts off the doors and the workers themselves had cut holes in the walls for ventilation. They no longer had to worry about escapes or anything like that, for the Negroes were free now, or so they said. But I could not help noticing that bad things still went on. There were bosses who still believed that the blacks were created for locks and bolts and whips, and treated them as before. It struck me that many Negroes did not know that things had changed, because they went on saying, "Give me your blessing, my master."[4]

Like the transition from slavery to abolition, the stage from abolition to independence and republic offered little hope for Montejo and other blacks. For them, life in the republic in some ways resembled their existence under slavery. Montejo's narration ends on a pessimistic note. In history, after the Spanish-Cuban-American War, the United States substituted for Spanish dominion over the island. Montejo unmasks the sinking of the *Maine* as a U.S. pretext for invading Cuba and undermining the victory of Cuban forces. But some Cuban officials collaborated with the new invaders and divided the country's wealth. Disenchanted with the outcome of the war, Montejo returned to his native province of Las Villas and, as before, worked in a sugar mill, where only time had changed. When he reached the San Agustín Maguaraya plantation, Montejo remembered: "It seemed as though everything had gone back in time" (222).[5]

The repetitions in *The Autobiography of a Runaway Slave* are part of the resurgence of history, but also of African oral tradition and of Montejo's own recollections. Montejo's conversations with Barnet commemorate the past and follow the structure of oral performance.[6] Like Mackandal, Ti Noel, and the gatekeepers of the antislavery novel, Montejo is the recipient and transmitter of stories and conversations about African myth and religion and of popular beliefs. In this sense, *The Autobiography of a Runaway Slave* resembles other contemporary works such as García Márquez's *Chronicle of a Death Foretold* and Carlos Fuentes's *Distant Relations*.[7] In these novels, with Victor Heredia's story, in Fuentes's work, or the death of Santiago Nasar in García Márquez's novel, memory is preserved by oral communication (and ultimately by writing). The protagonist-narrator is the recipient of events transmitted to him in conversations. As with any chronicle, the narrator-protagonist reproduces events and, along with his own testimony, passes them on to an anxious listener and hopes that he will continue in the tradition. Similarly, in Montejo's case he is a witness of history but also a receiver and transmitter of stories. In the interview, he tells them to Barnet, who, in turn, writes them down and conveys them to the reader.

*The Autobiography of a Runaway Slave* is a historical document but also a personal narration subject to the strategies of memory. Montejo's recollections fuse past narratives with those of his own experience, often justifying and clarifying them. A man of African descent, Montejo privileges myth and religion over written literature and history. Contrary to the tragic ending of Suárez y Romero's *Francisco*, Montejo did not believe that blacks committed suicide. He, as a witness of history, "never saw such a thing." Although he does admit that the Amerindians hung themselves to escape religious conversion, blacks, consistent with African traditions, by flying returned to their own land: "The Musundi Congolese were the ones that flew the most; they disappeared by means of witch-craft. They did the same as the Canary Island witches, but without making a sound. There are those who say the Negroes threw themselves into rivers. This is untrue. The truth is they fastened a chain to their waists which was full of magic. That was where their power came from. I know all this intimately, and it is true beyond a doubt" (43–44).[8]

When juxtaposing Montejo's narration with works of history, we discover that Montejo's ideas are based on folk myths and also on some misconceptions.[9] While in a cave, Montejo believed that the *majá*, the largest of Caribbean snakes, was deadly. Although it is not difficult to understand Montejo's apprehension, the *majá* is not dangerous to man but only to chickens and other fowl. Hiding his fear of snakes, Montejo comments on the magical aspects of the *majá*; a Congolese told him that the snakes lived over one thousand years and then turned into "marine creatures" (*serpientes* in the original) and lived among the fish. However, we come back to the concept of memory. What is in question is not whether the story is true or false but the time in which Montejo spoke to the Congolese about the *majases*. Was it in slavery, as the chronology appears to indicate, or did the conversations take place after slavery, when sharing his experiences with others? In other words, we may assume that Montejo had knowledge of snakes before fleeing slavery, but was he at this early stage aware of their religious metamorphosis?

While in the same cave(?) Montejo also lived with bats. Still in the slavery period, Montejo breaks with the chronology of the narration and now refers to a time after abolition, when he told a Congolese that he had lived among bats. The Congolese responded: "'A Creole like you doesn't know a thing. In my country what you call a bat is as big as a pigeon.' I know this was untrue. They fooled half the world with their tales. But I just listened and was inwardly amused" (48). The bat description follows that of the snake and appears on the same page. Although Montejo does not say so, the thematic unity of the paragraphs suggests that the Congolese who spoke to him about the snakes is the same one who spoke to him about the bats or, perhaps, even the one who recounted the story about the flying Congolese. Moreover, given the manner in which Montejo has narrated his life, for the chronology to be accurate Montejo should have been exposed as a child to African myths and traditions, which he then reconstructed in the appropriate sections. We should emphasize that

Montejo fled slavery at an early age and for many years remained isolated in the mountains. More likely than not, Montejo acquired a more profound religious knowledge after emancipation. If this is true, then the narration cannot be conceived as a chronicle with a historical development but as a fictional discourse which breaks with history and is subject to the stategies of memory.

The concept of memory questions the historical interpretation of *The Autobiography of a Runaway Slave;* the narration is no longer a reproduction of the past but represents a collapse of historical time in which the present and the past are fused. The repetitions present in the narration, which include the thematic coincidences during slavery, abolition, and the War of Independence, are not caused necessarily by historical cycles but by Montejo's ability to recollect certain events which are of personal interest to him. For example, his descriptions of games, religion, women, and work on sugar plantations during slavery, abolition, and the republic are not a reconstruction of the historical past but a repetition of recurrent themes that acquire their own identity and that, in the present, continue to be of importance to Montejo. Some events even use similar syntax and grammatical constructions. Montejo's reference to the infirmary serves as a case in point. He offers the following information regarding his place of birth: "Like all children born into slavery, *criollitos* as they called them, I was born in an infirmary where they took the pregnant Negresses to give birth" (18). Some pages later, when describing the sugar mill, Montejo explains the infirmary in a manner which recalls the first description: "All the plantations had an infirmary near the barracoon, a big wooden hut where they took the pregnant women. You were born there and stayed there till you were six or seven, when you went to live in the barracoons and began work, like the rest" (38).[10] Montejo himself is aware that he is defying chronology and imposing onto the past certain ideas gathered after slavery. In the same slavery section, Montejo talks about the names of musical instruments played by the *guajiros,* or Cuban peasants, but goes on to confess that although he uses the names he did not learn them until "after I left the forest because, as a runaway, I was ignorant of everything" (50). These and other incidents are a part of the informant's memory, but in the narration they appear to reconstruct history.

For Montejo, memory operates in two different ways with similar results. The first interpretation coincides with the importance Vico places on origin and suggests that memory is formulated and guided by the early events as described in the section entitled "Slavery." Like Vico, Freud emphasizes origin. According to a Freudian study of the individual, Montejo's experiences during his formative years would be crucial. As a youth Montejo's personality and interests were formed, setting the stage for the retention of similar structures that would be narrated as history in the following periods. From the information provided, his desire for independence, which includes his skepticism and rebellion, is part of a conditioning process which took place during his early years and is now a part of his adult personality. The act of remembering would be an acceptance of, and a communion with, the past.

However, an anti-Freudian structure, in which the present acquires a privileged position, is also valid. According to this interpretation, the most recent events portrayed in the last section, War of Independence, but also during the time in which the interviews took place in the Cuban Revolution, have preconditioned and even altered Montejo's past. That is, a contemporary understanding of history, culture, and religion are imposed on an earlier moment. Montejo becomes a reader and intepreter of his own life and attributes current ideas to the period when he was a child or a young man. With narrative time in mind, the events in the text conform to and coincide with present values in which revolution, independence, and hostility toward the United States are dominant factors of present-day Cuban society. Therefore, the present becomes a way of (re)shaping memory; a present concern indeed affects the past. For Eugene Vance the present is implicit in his definition of memory:

> By "commemoration" I mean any gesture, ritualized or not, whose end is to recover, in the name of a collectivity, some being or event either anterior in time or outside of time in order to fecundate, animate, or make meaningful a moment in the present. Commemoration is the conquest of whatever in society or in the self is perceived as habitual, factual, static, mechanical, corporeal, inert, worldly, vacant, and so forth.[11]

For some students of Cuban history, the revolutionary government has been exemplary in integrating blacks into the mainstream of society. In its attempt to overturn capitalism, the government identified with and promoted the concerns of marginal groups which included blacks. Like many people during the initial years of the revolution, Montejo appears to agree with the defiant policies of the government. Thus, a contemporary moment allowed him to reshape the past. Montejo's narration is a commemoration of past events.

The political and economic realities of the republic and the Cuban Revolution conditioned Montejo's recollection, but the ex-slave may have included ideas of his own. As Vance points out, Roland knew his battles would immortalize him. For Vance, the "truth is in the uttering, not in the utterance."[12] Similarly, Montejo was aware of Barnet's interests in African religion and myths. Perhaps Montejo knew that he was the only living runaway slave in Cuba and that his activities were going to be recorded. Montejo was conscious of his own grandeur and literary destiny. Like Manzano, who used his narration to underscore his privileged status as a slave, Montejo, under different circumstances, recognizes his own importance and sets the stage for controlling the narration. Montejo kept track of Barnet's notebook and insisted that he write many things down. As in the chansons de geste, Montejo is a hero of sorts who explains to Barnet what the ethnologist, due to his own social and historic circumstances, wants to hear. In spite of Barnet's diligence in verifying historical events, Montejo seized the opportunity to glorify himself and others. Montejo recreates his own life by choosing subjects which would be of interest to his listener.

From a different point of view, Barnet also controls the narration. As the motivator, transcriber, and editor Barnet is also an agent of memory. Barnet recognizes his role as mediator, not only in seeking aesthetic qualities but in facilitating the past in forming a collective memory. For Vance, the voice of the poet preserves memory in history and gives rebirth to the hero. In this sense, Barnet's ideas on the documentary novel are useful.[13] In his essay on the genre, "La novela testimonio: Socio-literatura," Barnet explains his own performance:

Without meaning to I was searching for an identity, for a sincere confession. In this relationship between author and protagonist or researcher-informant one has to look for an unfolding [*desdoblamiento*], becoming the other by prying apart one's self. In other words, one must try to live one's life in order also to live another life, that of one's character. The *gestor* of the documentary novel lives a second life that is real, that transforms him in an essential way. . . . I said that there was a distancing. There is also a de-personalization. One is the other already and only by being so can one think like him, speak like him, feel deeply life's blows, communicated to one by the informant and feel them like one's own. There is the poetry, the mystery of this kind of work. And, clearly, that wide open door that allows one to penetrate into the collective conscience, into the we. The dream of the *gestor* of the documentary novel, that thirst for expansion, for knowledge and identity, was also Malinowsky's, Ortiz', Nina Rodriguez', and that of the French novelists of the nineteenth century.[14]

Like Charlemagne or the transcriber of the *Chanson de Roland*, Barnet was instrumental in documenting a fragment of history previously unknown to the Western world. More importantly, Barnet is the creator of memory. He not only transcribed and edited the interviews with Montejo but also provided questions to guide and shape his recollections and the text, often motivated by his own interests.

In the introduction to the Spanish original, Barnet tells us that he was inspired by a newspaper article which appeared in 1963 honoring citizens over one hundred years old. Of the male and female slaves, Barnet chose Esteban Montejo, a runaway slave. For Barnet, Montejo represented a unique opportunity for research. Barnet himself confesses that although Montejo was willing to be a good informant, the ethnologist's concerns were different from those of the ex-slave, who spoke of themes which were of interest to him in no particular chronological order. Nevertheless, the interview developed into two sessions: After the initial interviews, in which religion was a main topic, the idea of a book emerged for which another set of questions was formulated. Even though Montejo chose many of the themes for the second session, Barnet was interested in others and therefore became a catalyst of Montejo's memory. Now Barnet had a specific project, which he describes in the Spanish introduction:

> We were concerned about specific problems such as the social environment of the barracoons and the celibate life of runaway slaves. In Cuba, documents which reconstruct these aspects of life under slavery are scarce. From these, no more than a detailed description of the architecture of the barracoons could be found, which called our attention to the social life inside these jails. Also, we wanted to describe the resources employed by the informant to subsist in the most absolute solitude of the thicket, the techniques to obtain fire, to hunt, etc.; as well as his psychic relationship with elements of nature, plants and animals, especially birds.[15]

Barnet's memory fuses with Montejo's. As the ethnologist, aware of the lack of historical information on the subject of slavery, Barnet was guided by a concern to fill a void in literature and history. Writing or rewriting history was indeed an important component of the project, which Barnet completed successfully. Many years later, he admitted that his work with Montejo filled gaps in Cuban historiography and the novel.[16]

Barnet recognizes the loyalty he must maintain to history and to his protagonist. Although he does not intend to create a literary document or a novel, as he states in the Spanish introduction, *The Autobiography of a Runaway Slave* dialogues with other works and historical moments. Roberto González Echevarría insists on the literariness of Barnet's work and suggests that Esteban Montejo's given name recalls that of two important literary figures, Joyce's Stephen Dedalus and Carpentier's Esteban in *Explosion in a Cathedral*; his last name is a corruption of *mont haut*, high mountain, a symbol of his freedom.[17]

However contradictory, many years after writing the introduction Barnet is aware that in his documentary genre no matter how loyal he is to history he is also creating fiction. The recreation becomes explicit when discussing his text on Rita Montaner, which is written in a similar style to his other testimonial works. Barnet describes his portrayal of Rita Montaner in the following manner: "Then, I did a lyrical recreation of her life, with the *entourage*, with the ambiance of the period. Moreover, Rita is the synthesis of many things: The fusion of two races, a versatile artist. . . . If you wish, I took all that to a different dimension, to a poetic dimension. Perhaps, it is a bit exaggerated, but in literature one has to exaggerate, one has to beautify."[18]

As the creator of memory and fiction, Barnet intervenes most noticeably as he reconstructs Montejo's language and paraphrases much of his story, though he is careful to maintain the informant's syntax. When transforming him into a literary figure, Barnet could no longer be loyal to Montejo the person. In a manner which recalls Richard Madden's translation and also his and Anselmo Suárez y Romero's rewritings of Manzano's autobiography, Barnet set out to create not only what Montejo was but also, and even more important, the person he should have been. For example, the variations present in Montejo's speech were corrected to give it a uniformity consistent with Montejo's character; as a writer, Barnet is in command of Montejo's speech. The English introduction, which is significantly different from the Spanish, reveals Barnet's intention: "I wanted his story to sound spontaneous and as if it came from the heart, and so I inserted words and expressions characteristic of Esteban wherever they seemed appropriate." In his essay on the documentary novel, Barnet further explains the use of language:

> In a documentary novel spoken discourse is the fundamental trait of the language, the only way it takes on life. But it must be a recreated spoken language, not a mere reproduction of what was on tape. From the recording I take the tone, the anecdotes, the inflections; the rest,

the style and fine points, I add myself. A book like Oscar Lewis' *La Vida* is a great contribution to the psychology and sociology of marginalized masses. It is, simply and plainly: *I write what you tell me and in the way you tell me.* Lewis' approach has little to do with the documentary novels I write. To my way of thinking, literary imagination should go hand in hand with sociological imagination. A documentary novelist should give free rein to his or her imagination, so long as it does not distort the protagonist's character or betray his or her language. Imagination, invention within a realistic essence, is the only way a writer can get the most out of a given phenomenon. In *Rachel*, for example, I say: "This is her story, her life as she told it to me and as I later told it back to her." Many things are implicit in that statement.[19]

Written memory is not a spontaneous recollection but a careful recreation of the past, a well-ordered scheme subject to editorial intervention and manipulation. Like oral memory, written memory is not the production of any individual but a communal activity in which others participate. Within any given publication, communal writing includes the editor, copy editor, and typesetter. Barnet's editorial task was motivated by dominant aspects of Montejo's narration, the ethnologist's own thematic interests, and the constraints imposed upon him by language. It appears that the editing was done with precision, but we have little information regarding the actual process. For example, did the present work come from the second set of questions, that is, when Barnet envisioned the "autobiography," or did he use some of the answers provided in the first interview when seeking information mainly on religion? Certainly, substantial information was excluded from the final version of the autobiography.

Perhaps Barnet's editing had another purpose. Barnet was not only interested in filling a literary void but, like Montejo, was also reflecting a certain political reality imposed upon him by the Cuban Revolution. Barnet was aware of the importance of his task. In the English introduction, he reveals his own interest as well as information about Montejo's life not included in the text. Barnet wanted to highlight the Ten Years' War, which, in revolutionary Cuba, has been interpreted as the start of the struggle for independence which culminated in Castro's triumph. In so doing, Barnet forces the issue and writes that Montejo was a fugitive between 1868 and 1878. But if we reconstruct the chronology provided, the parenthetical reference to the war is somewhat misleading, since Montejo must have escaped toward the end of the war. Born around 1860, Montejo was only eight at the start of the war. More importantly, in the same paragraph and referring to the same war, Barnet provides information not contained in the text: "It was bewildering to see horses charging and men cutting each other's heads off with machetes and not knowing what it was all about. Esteban told me once that the experience was like standing drunk in front of the sea" (9). In a subsequent essay on the documentary novel, Barnet reveals a little more about the tapes' contents. Referring to the counterpoint technique he used in *La canción de Rachel* and the protagonist's support of the government's position against the Partido Independiente de Color, Barnet cites the following: "Then there are characters with different perspectives on the same event, such as Esteban Montejo, among others, who defend the Guerrita del Doce [upheaval of blacks in the Independent Party of Colored People] to the hilt."[20] Any description of the Ten Years' War or the Race War of 1912 is conspicuously absent from the autobiography.

*The Autobiography of a Runaway Slave* is not without political motivation. In the Spanish introduction and throughout the text, Barnet highlights the relationship between Montejo and the Cuban Revolution: "The revolutionary spirit is illustrated not only in the account itself but in his actual attitude. Esteban Montejo, at the age of 105 years, constitutes a good example of a revolutionary conduct and quality. His revolutionary tradition, first a runaway slave, later a liberator, still later a member of the Partido Socialista Popular, is presently vivified in his identification with the Cuban Revolution."[21] This information is absent from the English translation, and we can assume that it was included only in the Spanish edition for the Cuban reading public.

Indeed, Montejo's independent nature, his rejection of slavery, and his opposition—first to Spanish occupation and later to U.S. intervention—recall the position of the Cuban revolutionary government. But, unlike other Maroon slaves and the Castro revolutionary forces, Montejo was only a partial rebel. During slavery, he did not join other Maroons who fought and gave up their lives to end slavery, as Leante's character did in *Los guerrilleros negros*, but preferred to live in isolation until emancipation.

The allusion to Cuban politics may be a personal statement reflecting not Montejo's but Barnet's standing within the revolution. Born in 1940, Barnet belongs to the second generation of writers of the Cuban Revolution, publishing his first collection of poems, *La piedra fina y el pavorreal*, in 1963. Barnet, like many during the initial years of the revolution, identified with and profited from the transformation of Cuban society. The revolutionary government's interest in promoting culture allowed Barnet and other writers of the first and second generations to publish their works. The revolution made Barnet aware of his country's history and culture; but before this radical change in government, Barnet had been a stranger to Cuban culture. He had studied in U.S. schools and lived and spent most of his time in activities closely related to North America, and only after 1959 did he become aware of his national culture.[22] Before the revolution, there were few avenues open to writers. In order to make a living, many were forced to accept jobs that were at best marginal to their literary interests. For example, Leante and Carpentier made a living writing for the radio.

In spite of his enthusiasm for the revolution, Barnet and others encountered problems with the government. Barnet was associated with a second generation group of poets known as El Puente after a private publishing house of the same name which operated between 1960 and 1965. In 1964, El Puente published his second book of poetry, *Isla de Güijes*. But the El Puente group fell from grace and was accused of stressing the aesthetic over the political.[23] Regardless of their revolutionary commitment, group members were considered antisocial and homosexual and some were sent to rehabilitation camps, known as Unidades Militares de Ayuda a la Producción (Military Units of Aid to Production). Those under detention and others were excluded from cultural and literary activities.[24]

During these years Barnet had gone unpublished in Cuba. Perhaps Barnet seized upon the story of Montejo as an opportunity to break with the recent past. Although a committed ethnologist, Barnet was aware of the importance of blacks for the revolution and the historical and cultural significance of his subject matter. He may have stressed the independent and revolutionary aspects of Montejo's life as a way of overcoming bureaucratic censorship. Contrary to the slavery period, Barnet, Leante, and others seized the theme of slavery as a way of avoiding writing about more problematical themes which pertained to the present and required them to glorify the revolution. Whatever the causes, the results were clear. After the publication of *The Autobiography of a Runaway Slave*, Barnet was not only reintegrated into the literary establishment but he became an important writer. (More likely than not, it was because he became an international figure that Barnet was allowed to rejoin the literary establishment.) His subject matter was appropriate, one which the literary and political establishments were commited to support. From the moment of publication, *The Autobiography of a Runaway*

*Slave* has met with unprecedented success. *Cimarrón* and *Hombres de mal tiempo* are two documentaries based on events narrated by Montejo. The novel was also transformed into a radio serial which lasted over a year, as well as a theatrical pantomime production directed by Olga and Ramón Flores.[25] The opera version of Barnet's work with music by Hans Werner Henze and script by Hans Magnus Enzensberger had tremendous success in Cuba and received much deserved attention as it toured England, France, and Italy in 1970.[26]

Barnet's reintegration into the Cuban Revolution may help us to understand the emphasis the autobiography places on the Spanish-Cuban-American War. Barnet's emphasis in his introduction and his comments on the Ten Years' War point directly to the Spanish-Cuban-American War, but, even more important, to the Cuban Revolution. It also may reveal Barnet's acquired revolutionary perspective. For him and government officials, the Cuban Revolution accomplished what the Ten Years' War and Spanish-Cuban-American War set out to do; that is, liberate Cuba from Western domination.

The fact that the novel ends with the Spanish-Cuban-American War raises other questions about Montejo's views of blacks and Barnet's reasons for not pursuing such an important subject after the founding of the republic. We must stress that the autobiography ends with the founding of the republic and Máximo Gómez's death in 1905, and there is no attempt to continue the narration into the present, even though in the Spanish introduction Barnet had established a nexus between the past and the present time in which the work was written.

Since Montejo lived more than a century, would it not have been of historical importance to document his views during the republic and still another transformation, the Cuban Revolution? In this regard, Barnet's project appears to be incomplete; he could have taken advantage of his informant to narrate other important but sensitive moments in Cuban history. For example, he could have explored Montejo's opinions regarding the Race War of 1912, in which thousands of blacks who organized under the Partido Independiente de Color were killed. Many blacks demanded rights promised to them during the War of Independence and protested the Morúa Law, which forbade political parties to organize on the basis of race. As with the other historical periods, Montejo's insights would have been helpful in understanding this tragic period in Cuban history.

As readers of the autobiography, we do have some clues regarding Montejo's opinions. If the present is contained in the past, then words as signs reflect this and perhaps other events fused into the narration; that is, if memory is not the reconstruction of chronology but a compression of historical time transferred into a time outside any given chronology, Montejo's frustration at the end of the novel may have been directly related to the disenfranchisement of blacks during the Race War. As we have suggested, Montejo interjected emotions onto his past which may have been formed in subsequent years. Montejo was, in this sense, already aware of future events in the republic which include the Race War of 1912.

Barnet was indeed aware of the uprising because this is one of the themes explored by his protagonist in *La canción de Rachel*, a novel about a Cuban *vedette* (theatrical star) who lived at the turn of the century; Barnet's second novel was published in 1969, three years after *The Autobiography of a Runaway Slave*.[27] Barnet used the information provided by Montejo's interviews to explore this theme in his other work. In his second novel, Barnet fused both Rachel's and Montejo's narrations. Montejo appears as a character in *La canción de Rachel*, and, consistent with *The Autobiography of a Runaway Slave*, he expresses a candid view which shows all indications of belonging to Barnet's first interviews. In the second documentary novel, Montejo contradicts Rachel, who is a symbol of life during the Cuban Republic and affirms his solidarity with Estenoz and Ivonet, the leaders of the Partido Independiente de Color:

> And what the hell did they think, that we were going to surrender peacefully, that we were going to hand in our weapons and pull down our pants? Nothing of the sort. And we demonstrated it to them.
> They called us savages, black as a boot, and a thousand other insults. But when was it that in this country the people were offered a program more democratic than that of the Independientes de Color, when we fought hand to hand to gain benefits for blacks, when we left the war shoeless and in rags, hungry, like Quintín Banderas himself, and later they killed him while he was getting water from his well? Don't let them spread rumors. The moment of truth has finally arrived. And none of us who risked his life in that war is going to keep his mouth shut.
>     At least, anyone who comes to me to tell me that if racism, that if blacks were bloodthirsty, I am going to give him a punch that they will never forget Esteban Montejo.
>     I don't know what journalists, writers, and politicians think about that. But as a man, a citizen, and a revolutionary, I think that that fight was just. With all its selfishness and faults, but necessary. Blacks did not have anything to hold onto, they could not breathe, and they had been generals and educated men, like Juan Gualberto

Gómez. I am not interested in what that woman says; I see things from a different point of view.[28]

The events of 1912 raise other questions. If Barnet and Montejo discussed the racial war, why did Barnet edit it from the final version of the autobiography?

The period surrounding the Partido Independiente de Color may have proven to be problematical for an overall understanding of blacks in Cuba and Barnet's reintegration into literary production in the revolution. It may have been politically expedient to finish the testimonial novel at the end of the Spanish-Cuban-American War, thus alluding to the triumph of the Cuban Revolution. Under slavery, during the Ten Years' War, and at the time of the Spanish-Cuban-American War, the enemy was a foreign power. Even Cuban-born slave owners like Leonardo Gamboa in Cirilo Villaverde's *Cecilia Valdés* were overcome by a sense of nationalism and thus objected to Spanish dominion over the island. But the Race War of 1912 was a national problem. Though Rachel claims that the war came to an end because of the threat of a U.S. invasion,[29] only Cuban nationals were directly involved in the massacre of 1912. It was a campaign of Cubans against other Cubans sufficient to discourage any black movement for many decades. By ending the narration after the Spanish-Cuban-American War, Barnet leaves us with the impression that, at least from Montejo's point of view, Cuban problems were foreign-related.

Given our concept of memory or, for that matter, the cycles of history, Montejo's pessimism regarding blacks was present during the time of the narration; that is, in the republic and before the triumph of the revolution. If this is so, then what about Montejo's impression of blacks during the time in which the interviews took place; that is, during the Castro government? If the narration were to continue into the present time of the writing, would Montejo's pessimism have been repeated in Castro's Cuba? Did the revolution for blacks present a moment of relief, in which history would be not repeated but, rather, extricated from past structures, as Carpentier outlined in his "La cultura de los pueblos que habitan en las tierras del mar Caribe"?[30] If this were the case, Barnet would have been politically prudent to have taken into account such an important testimony about the revolution. The testimony would have highlighted Montejo's contemporary revolutionary spirit, one which would have included his participation in the Partido Socialista Popular during the republic, as pointed out in the Spanish introduction, and also his

activities in the revolution. This version of Montejo's autobiography
would have conformed to the demands of critics such as Roberto Fernández Retamar and Antonio Portuondo when inspiring Cuban writers to produce works which glorify the revolution. Barnet himself
would have been proclaimed as a true revolutionary writer.

Or did Montejo, as in other parts of the narration, demystify and
problematize the present conditions of blacks because, as he believed, "the truth cannot be silenced" (223)? Did life for blacks during the revolution represent a continuation of previous cycles? If we
accept the fusion between the beginning and the end of the narration
and the time in which the interviews took place, did Montejo's frustration at the end of the War of Independence reflect a contemporary
feeling in the revolution? That is, was Montejo imposing a present
pessimism onto the past? [31] Although these are hypothetical questions which may never be answered, they do suggest that the end of
the narration is not conclusive but open-ended. Nevertheless, there
are some textual signals which point to a possible solution to our
problematic quest.

From this perspective, the novel's pessimism continues to be felt.
Montejo, in fact, reveals a contemporary moment in the narration;
that is, in the revolution. In the final paragraph, Montejo recalls a
time, perhaps during the Ten Years' War, when he was forced to be
silent. Consistent with his past (or is it the present?), Montejo rejects
any type of conformity and continues to assert his independence. His
autobiography ends with the following statement: "That's why I say
I don't want to die, so I can fight in all the battles to come. And I'm
not going into the trenches or using any of those modern weapons. A
machete will do for me" (223). The modern weapon can be a reference to rifles used during the Spanish-Cuban-American War, as the
time of the narration indicates, but, more likely than not, they refer
to machine guns used by soldiers and the militia in defense of the
revolution, as the time in which the interviews were conducted
suggests.

Although *The Autobiography of a Runaway Slave* ends on a revolutionary note, the reader cannot be certain if Montejo's battle cry
refers to events which followed in history; that is, to his support of
the Partido Independiente de Color in 1912, and, perhaps, to the uprisings against Machado in 1933. Or does the narration defy chronology, as we have suspected, and refer to activities in the revolution? The suggested ambiguity is never clarified, for what follows is
a silence; that is, the blank page. Yet the absence of any other signs
or symbols on the page takes us back to another sentence in the final

paragraph. If the present here is mixed with the past, then how do we come to terms with another type of silence? In spite of the extensive conversations between Montejo and Barnet, the informant has not revealed the entire story: "If I could, I would come right out and tell the whole story now." Did Montejo tell the whole story? Was he aware that no matter what he said, Barnet would write his recollection, that is, his own version of the story? Has Barnet controlled and therefore silenced parts of the ex-slave's life and voice? In a different manner, does the end recall the early years of Montejo's life, years before the time of the narration, in which he felt he needed to be silent? If history repeats itself in the "present," does Montejo again feel he has to be silent? Is Montejo a silent witness of the Cuban Revolution? And does Montejo's willingness to reject modern weapons and take up his *machete*, a symbol of past struggles, imply that for blacks nothing has really changed? Or is the silence a reference to Barnet's own signature; that is, to one of the changes he inserted in the narration, as he indicated in the English introduction? If this is so, the silence is a reference not to Montejo but to Barnet's own condition as a writer. Then, is it Barnet who really wants to come out and tell the whole story but knows that it will not be possible to do so after experiencing censorship during the early years of the Revolution? Does Barnet's writing point to a form of self-censorship in revolutionary Cuba?

The tension to which I have alluded in the autobiography's ending and the questions raised are implicit in a reading of both the English and Spanish titles: The vernacular uses the term *biografía* and the translation "autobiography," one pointing to Barnet's presence and the other to that of Montejo. Foucault deduced that the author limits signification and regulates fiction but also perceives that as society changes so will the "author-function." With the Cuban Revolution and the documentary novel, the proliferation of "author-function" is expressed, though with other types of constraints. Although the documentary novel has not reached the point of anonymity where it is no longer essential to ask who really spoke, it does suggest a multiplicity of voices, recollections, and interpretations.[32] It is Montejo's story but it is Barnet's writing. It is indeed both.[33] Montejo's narration is a nostalgic account of the past in which the past compares favorably with the present. Barnet's narration is a mechanism for controlling the past and present. His concern is to make Montejo a revolutionary hero, and in so doing Barnet has also become a hero of sorts. Both are agents of memory and therefore participate in the creation of memory. Memory, which is present in a collective oral tradition, is passed onto a collective writing.

**II**     *The Autobiography of a Runaway Slave* recalls Manzano's autobiography by providing a contemporary reader with the testimony of a slave who flees slavery not to the city but to the mountains. Leante's *Los guerrilleros negros,* perhaps inspired by Barnet's work, takes the slave figure one step farther; by closely following the life of his protagonist, Ventura Sánchez, Leante novelizes the biography of this historical figure and reveals that there were other slaves who fled into the mountains not to live in isolation, as Montejo did, but to join other runaway slaves in the fight for freedom. Leante shows the political and economic profitability of runaway slaves who came together. Very much different from Francisco Estévez's *Diario de un rancheador,* Leante uncovers information about life in the *palenques* but narrates it from the point of view not of the slave hunter but of the fugitive slave.

Like the literature, works of history published in the revolution offer a different interpretation of the Cuban past. Contemporary historians are documenting another side of history which complements the events of the revolution. Among them, José Luciano Franco has been a leader in bringing to light the history of Cuban slaves. In this sense, both historians and writers have allowed for a certain memory or recollection of history to surface.[34]

Franco's texts provide a context from which to understand Leante's novel and show that rebellions were not isolated events but accompanied the European presence in the Caribbean from the start. In Cuba, the Amerindians began their resistance under chieftains like Hatuey, Caguax, and Guamá. Black African slaves soon replaced the extinct natives and, like them, sought freedom in the mountains. As early as 1677 the black workers of the copper mines of Santiago del Prado rebelled against the authorities and for generations resisted in the mountains. The copper miners' rebellion constituted the first successful insurrection in Cuba, winning their freedom in 1800.[35] Rebellion of runaway and rebellious slaves was not limited to Cuba, nor was this the first. Insurrections were recorded as early as 1522 and appeared all over the American continent.[36]

During the sixteenth and seventeenth centuries, not all runaway slaves escaped to the mountains; some went to the coast and joined pirates, corsairs, and smugglers. For them, the sea offered both a relief from slavery and an opportunity to fight against the Spanish enemy. The Cuban runaway slave Diego Grillo, better known as

Captain Dieguillo, was a distinguished figure during this period throughout the Caribbean.[37]

Those who did escape to the mountains joined other fugitive slaves and formed communities which were well protected against slave hunters. Franco describes the communities in a manner which recalls Leante's novel:

> During the eighteenth and nineteenth centuries, they organized camps and protected areas in which they sought refuge in almost unvarying style throughout the entire extension of the island of Cuba. For their defense, they surrounded them with traps armed with sharpened stakes which hampered the hunters' movements. They were placed in some cases in pits dug along the paths and covered with straw which were easily jumped over by blacks in their escape; aside from their extreme agility, they knew their exact location. This was something which did not take place with their hunters, who should have moved with supreme care, fearing with each step of falling into one of those pits and being badly wounded by their sharp points, riders or horses alike, and even the dogs used to hunt runaway slaves.[38]

According to Franco, the slave community consisted of fifteen or twenty scattered huts hidden in thick vegetation. The communities were a commercial unit in which cultivated agricultural products and food, wax, and honey were sold to nearby towns and plantations in exchange for sugar, clothing, and weapons. The slaves traded with whites, free blacks, and pirates and smugglers off Cuba's coast.[39]

Only after the culmination of a series of cycles and events in both history and literature could a revolutionary or rebellious image be narrated. As with *The Autobiography of a Runaway Slave, Los guerrilleros negros* responds to the sociopolitical reality of the Cuban Revolution. Literature with increasing frequency expressed Afro-Cuban images and culture. Lourdes Casal's sociological study comparing pre- and postrevolutionary novelistic characters shows an increase in the number of blacks in literature and a betterment in the positions they occupy.[40]

Like other recent works, Leante's novel partakes of a tradition directly associated with the revolution; revolution and revolutionary activity are no longer considered marginal and incidental but are factors essential for change. Leante, like the present Cuban government, will analyze the past from a specific, revolutionary present. Just as the political leaders and historians have reevaluated history and now view the 1959 takeover as part of a process that began with Carlos Manuel de Céspedes' uprising in 1868, a theme reiterated in Barnet's documentary novel, Leante rewrites that origin by introducing the slave rebellion into literature as the beginning of modern Cuban history.

But, writing about the distant past became an escape of sorts for authors living in Cuba. With the pressures from Cuban political leaders and critics to write about the accomplishments of the Cuban Revolution, some authors felt they could not accurately portray the present without describing the complex Cuban phenomenon. Those like Guillermo Cabrera Infante, who wrote about a recent past, were accused of nostalgia for a prerevolutionary society. Others who described the present, like Heberto Padilla in his well-known *Outside the Game*, received jail sentences for plotting against the government.[41] As a possible way of avoiding censorship, for Leante and other writers the remote past became a less problematic subject to include in novelistic discourse, one acceptable to the Cuban establishment.[42]

The dominant structures in Cuban history have shifted, allowing Leante to make central what was once a marginal topic. Cuban official interest in reinterpreting history has provided Leante, among other writers, with the incentive to do the same. Leante has to look for accounts of the Cuban experience in the past. When doing so, he interpolates on past accounts a contemporary understanding of history.

The term *guerrilla*, used in Leante's title, is not of recent usage. But there is no doubt that Leante's application of this term also corresponds to a contemporary meaning. Esteban Montejo uses the term in its historical and derogatory context. Although Montejo limits his use to those who fought during the War for Independence, we can nevertheless assume that his remarks pertain to supporters of slavery.

> The real guerrillas were stupid countrymen. Don't anyone try to tell me a man of letters would become a guerrilla. There were white guerrillas as well as black ones: Spanish ones, Canary Islanders, Cubans. I never saw a Chinese one.
>
> The guerrilla tactics were different from those of the liberating army. Fire blazed from their eyes, they were men full of poison, rotten to the core. When they saw a group of *Mambises* they used to fall on them, and if they captured them they killed them all outright. When you fought face-to-face with Spaniards they never killed like that, in cold blood. They did things differently. I wouldn't say we

fought on equal terms, though. They all had proper equipment, good mounts, reins, spurs, all the kit; we had almost nothing. Having all these things, the guerrillas thought they were superior.[43]

Montejo's *guerrilleros* were Cuban peasants who were employed as infantry and cavalrymen by the Spaniards to fight against other Cubans. These men were an important addition to the Spanish forces. Fernando Portuondo's *guerrilleros* concur with Montejo's. According to Portuondo, at the start of the Ten Years' War the term referred to paid Canary Islanders, many of whom were farmers, who backed the Spanish regulars.[44] But after the Spanish victory in the Ten Years' War, the same *guerrilleros*, no longer needed by Spanish authorities, joined the Cuban insurrection.[45]

If Montejo's description of the guerrilla of the nineteenth century is accurate, Leante collapses or fuses history: The *guerrillero* tactics recall more closely the strategy used not by slaves or islanders but by Castro's forces to defeat the Batista dictatorship, subsequently made popular by Ché Guevara in *Guerrilla Warfare* (1960). Guevara's methods are those used by Leante's fugitive slaves. Regarding guerrilla tactics, Guevara states: "The fundamental characteristic of a guerrilla band is mobility. This permits it in a few minutes to move far from a specific theatre and in a few hours far even from the region, if that becomes necessary; permits it constantly to change front and avoid any type of encirclement. As the circumstances of the war require, the guerrilla band can dedicate itself exclusively to fleeing from an encirclement which is the enemy's only way of forcing the band into a decisive fight that could be unfavourable."[46] Like the slaves, guerrillas travel in small bands. Guevara continues: "The numerical inferiority of the guerrilla makes it necessary that attacks always be carried out by surprise; this great advantage is what permits the guerrilla fighter to inflict losses on the enemy without suffering losses."

Leante thus appropriates the nineteenth-century term and gives it a contemporary meaning. He ascribes the term *guerrillero* to those runaway slaves who not only escaped from their masters but reunited in the mountains and fought against them. In so doing, Leante forms a historical chain, linking the runaway slaves and Castro's forces in the struggle for freedom against their masters, Batista, and the U.S. influence in Cuba evident since the Spanish-Cuban-American War. According to Leante, the battles which culminated in the triumph of the Castro forces did not start with the Ten Years' War nor with the Spanish-Cuban-American War but with the first slave uprisings.

The *guerrilleros*, as Montejo points out, were not only blacks but, to the amazement of the black characters in the novel, included whites as well. Leante's *guerrilleros*, contrary to Montejo's personalized and demystifying narrative, resemble more closely those former slaves described by Franco in *Los palenques de los negros cimarrones*, though, like Leante, Franco's observation is not totally free of a contemporary referent and even recalls Guevara's work: "During past centuries in Cuba, the *palenques* were the only signs of nonconformity against the colonial regime, a virile protest against the infamies of slavery. The ability and dexterity of the *cimarrones* in guerrilla warfare and in knowing how to utilize correctly the topography of the mountainous zones, jungles, and swamps allowed them to evade the persecution of the *rancheadores* and, at times, defeat the same regular troops and militia which hunted them."[47] Montejo's and Portuondo's guerrillas were men who lived "inside the law." They attempted through armed struggle to support the existing Spanish order. Leante's guerrillas were fugitive slaves who lived outside the law and were hunted for their crime of seeking freedom.

That Leante is rewriting becomes evident from the start. By following history, *Los guerrilleros negros* contains scenes that have become familiar sights in other works. Like Barnet's testimonial novel, Leante's narration is a conglomeration of voices, images, and texts and there is an intertextual connection between it and other works. Leante incorporates information contained in the texts of history and, more importantly, in antislavery narratives. Ventura Sánchez, a Cuban slave, was born in an infirmary, the same place where Suárez y Romero's Francisco recovered from the lashes he received at Ricardo's request. The infirmary is also the place where Tanco y Bosmeniel's Petrona gave birth to Rosalía and where Montejo was born. Old taita Quiala represented for Ventura what taita Pedro in Suárez y Romero did for Francisco and possibly what Mackandal did in Carpentier's novel for Ti Noel: a cultural and spiritual link between the protagonist and the Africa they had heard of but never seen.

Leante appropriates scenes and images from past works in order to rewrite them from a privileged point in history. In essence, Leante's novel is the physical recipient of the slavery theme explored in previous works; his novel commemorates the earlier ones. The descriptions of taita Quiala and his immediate surroundings are strikingly similar to those of taita Pedro. In fact, one is a copy of the other. Suárez y Romero describes his character in the following manner:

Un negro anciano, de setenta años era el guardiero de aquel punto;
inútil, más bien por las llagas innumerables y envejecidas de sus pier-
nas que por lo avanzado de la edad, vivía solitario, a semejanza de un
desterrado, en el pequeño bohío o rancho que él mismo se había fabricado casi sobre la ribera. ¿Quiénes le acompañaban en su retiro?
Un perrillo sato, flaco, de hocico largo y aguzado, y diez gallinas . . .

[A seventy-year-old black man was the guardian of that area; he
was useless, more on account of his numerous old leg sores than
because of his advanced age. He lived alone, similar to an outcast, in
the small hut or ranch that he himself had built near the riverbank.
Who accompanied him in his retirement? A skinny mutt, with a
long and pointed snout, and ten chickens . . .]

Suárez y Romero continues:

Rara vez aparacía este viejo en el batey, algún domingo, algún día de
fiesta, a punto que le ladraban los perros al extrañarle vestido de un
chaquetón de paño, la camisa por fuera y un gorro blanco y encar-
nado en la cabeza; y habíais de ver entonces su apuro en espantarlos
con el bastón y a voces . . .

[This old man appeared on the grounds surrounding the sugar mill
so very rarely, some Sundays, some holidays, to the point where dogs
barked at him when they noticed him dressed strangely in a cloth
jacket, his shirt untucked and a white and red cap on his head; and
you should have noticed then his hurry to frighten them with his
cane, shouting . . .][48]

Leante describes his keeper in an almost identical manner:

Taita Quiala era un negro tan viejo que ignoraba su edad; pero debía
rebasar los ochenta años . . . Se cubría la cabeza, totalmente blanca
y coposa, con un gorro de lana, y para caminar se apoyaba en un alto
bastón de caña brava. . . . Habitaba un bohío vara en tierra que él
mismo se había fabricado al pie de un frondoso jaguey, donde criaba
algunas gallinas y se hacía acompañar por un perro sucio y esque-
lético, de pelambre carmelita, que lo seguía dócilmente a todas
partes y les ladraba a los extraños. . . . Rara veces se le veía en el
batey, excepto cuando se presentaba ante el mayoral en busca de sus
provisiones.

[Taita Quiala was a black so old that he did not know his age; but
he must have been well over eighty years old. . . . He covered his
head, completely white and bushy, with a woolen cap, and to walk
he supported himself on a tall bamboo cane. . . . He lived in a hut
that he had built at the foot of a leafy matador liana, where he raised
a few chickens and was accompanied by a dirty and skeletonlike
brown dog that followed him docilely everywhere and barked at
strangers. . . . He was very rarely seen on the grounds surrounding
the sugar mill, except when he went before the overseer looking for
his provisions.][49]

Leante's novel rewrites Montejo's experiences and *Los guerrilleros negros* also borrows from *The Autobiography of a Runaway
Slave.* There is an intertextual relationship between the ex-slaves
Manzano, Montejo, and Ventura Sánchez and between them and
Francisco regarding Montejo's criticism of passive slaves, as Leante
incorporates passages which appear in Barnet's narration. In response to domestic slaves like Francisco and Manzano, Montejo
says: "If a boy was pretty and lively he was sent inside, to the master's house. And there they started softening him up and . . . well, I
don't know! They used to give the boy a long palm leaf and make
him stand at one end of the table while they ate. And they said,
'Now see that no flies get in the food!' If a fly did, they scolded him
severely and even whipped him. I never did this work because I
never wanted to be on closer terms with the master. I was a runaway
from birth."[50] Similarly, Leante writes:

The boy lived with the rest of the slaves in the barracoons. If he were
a lively boy, flattering, tame, maybe they would have sent him to
serve in the master's house or the sugar mill. They would have put
him to work in the kitchen, in domestic work and above all with a
palm leaf to fan the masters and drive away the flies while they ate
or napped. Ventura saw that that was what boys his age did who
worked in the mansion. But he did not like that. Even though he
would break his back and as an adult was humpback, he preferred to
work with the carts. Without knowing why, he hated being a slave to
the masters.[51]

Sánchez's hatred for the master is equivalent to Montejo's never
wanting to be on closer terms with the master and the slave's rebellious nature.
    But if there appears to be a historical coincidence between Montejo
and Sánchez, other examples suggest even more strongly the pres-

ence of one work in the other. As with Suárez y Romero's work, it appears that Leante relied on them like texts of history for information. Within the context of Leante's novel, Barnet did not go far enough; his testimonial work did not respond to a "true" revolutionary image; Leante reproduces scenes to transcend them. Immediately following the paragraph with the boy who worked in the master's house, Montejo continues with a description of the barracoons.

> Around two hundred slaves of all colours lived in the Flor de Sagua barracoons. This was laid out in rows: two rows facing each other with a door in the middle and a massive padlock to shut the slaves in at night. There were barracoons of wood and barracoons of masonry with tiled roofs. Both types had mud floors and were as dirty as hell. And there was no modern ventilation there! Just a hole in the wall or a small barred window. The result was that the place swarmed with fleas and ticks, which made the inmates ill with infections and evil spells, for those ticks were witches. The only way to get rid of them was with hot wax, and sometimes even that did not work. The masters wanted the barracoons to look clean outside, so they were whitewashed.[52]

Following the same order which appears in Montejo's description, Leante uses almost the same words to narrate a similar account:

> In one of the five rooms of the barracoon where around one hundred and fifty slaves were crowded, he had his straw mattress. Like the rest of the slaves, he got up at four in the morning, when the overseer had rung the bell located at the entrance of the barracoon. He moved the massive padlock which during the night locked the door. . . . Within this one (the barracoon), the gloominess was as intense as the quantity of dirt. It was constructed of masonry with a tile roof. For ventilation, the rooms only had a small barred window above the outside wall. The dirt floors and walls were covered with fleas and ticks; the first fed on Ventura's body while he slept, covering his skin with bumps. The second got underneath his toenails, causing much pain when he walked. There was no way of getting rid of them from within his flesh but with pins or hot wax.[53]

Rewriting memory is not limited to reproducing passages of text from the past but includes transcribing others. Coba's association with historically rebellious leaders establishes a link between *Los guerrilleros negros* and Mackandal and, most importantly, with *The Kingdom of This World*.[54] There is even a spiritual transference from one novel to the other. Leante's Jean-Pierre recalls Carpentier's Ti Noel: Both characters were brought to Cuba by their French masters. And it is through Jean-Pierre that we discover a concern of Carpentier's; that is, the meaning of history and rebellions which the Haitian rebellion symbolizes. Leante uses Carpentier's Monsieur Lenormand de Mezy's emigration to Cuba to form that important connection between the characters, the novels, and history. Jean-Pierre is unmistakably Ti Noel; their stories are practically identical: "His master had taken him out of Haiti by force. He had participated in the first revolts, he fell prisoner and they were going to hang him in the city of Cabo. Monsieur Guizot [who resembles Monsieur Lenormand de Mezy] had prevented it and had brought him to Cuba, not because he cared about the death of another black, but because he did not want to lose a slave" (59–60). After arriving in Cuba, Monsieur Guizot, like Monsieur Lenormand de Mezy, spent most of his life drinking and was usually found in the French coffee-theatre Tivolí in Santiago. And it was through Carpentier's character, Ti Noel/Jean-Pierre, that Ventura was able to find out about the free slaves in Haiti and how they conducted their revolution.

Leante inserts other texts in his. For example, references to the enslavement of blacks by blacks in Africa and the corruption of Africa by whites (18–20) recall a similar scene from Antonio Zambrana's *El negro Francisco* but follow more closely a description already seen in Lino Novás Calvo's *El negrero*. In subsequent pages (22–24), Leante's descriptions of the slave traffic and conditions on board slave ships appear to have been extracted from Novás Calvo's work. Moreover, don Luigi, owner of *Il Corso*, reminds us of Carlo, an Italian who aided both Blanco and Canot in the slave trade. Following the logic of the plot, Leante's Italian trades not with slavers but with fugitive slaves. Like Villaverde, who broke with the chronology of his novel to include the slave hunter Francisco Estévez, Leante does the same to refer to Pedro Blanco. According to Leante, in March 1816 a slave ship arrived from the coast of Gallinas. Although slaves were sold in Gallinas as early as 1813, it did not become an important center until it was developed by Pedro Blanco, who remained there from 1822 to 1839.

As one might suspect, Estévez's diary is also present in Leante's novel. More than a mere reference to the slave hunter, Leante appropriates the voice of the dominant discourse and makes it his as he reproduces parts of Estévez's narration. For example, a "diary" format describing slave attacks (172–173) resembles closely those contained in the *Diario*. If this can be considered a coincidence, some scenes present in one work appear to be repeated in the other. On

October 10, Estévez and his men arrived at a runaway slave community. Estévez tells us that it was a rainy day and smoke was coming from the huts. In order to reach them, they had to climb one at a time a dense, steep, and narrow path. One of his men told Estévez that the Maroons were at the top of a second cliff which measured some fifty yards high. When the slaves realized that the hunters could not find the path to reach them, they attacked by hurling boulders at the hunters. Not finding a place to hide, Estévez fired selectively at the ex-slaves, who then fled. Leante repeats the same descriptions as slave hunters Martínez, Rocha, and Mustelier on March 6 reached the slave community of Sigua. Leante mentions the rainy day, the smoke coming from the huts, the empty village, the narrow path in which the hunters had to walk single file, the second cliff measuring fifty yards high, the sighting of the Maroons, the inability to find the path up to the cliff, the stone attack, the order by Martínez to fire only at visible fugitives, and their fleeing once the hunters found the path. In fact, Leante uses words and constructions similar to those appearing in the diary.[55]

While Leante follows certain patterns and structures of previous works, he includes others that alter, transcend, or introduce new elements. For example, the two Franciscos, Manzano, Sab, Caniquí, and Ti Noel were considered the good and favorite slaves, positioning themselves as house slaves (at one time or another). Sánchez defies that pattern by not becoming the docile house servant. He is the hard-working field slave. After his escape he becomes the assistant, first of Tomás, the captain of the *palenque* of Sigua, and then of Sebastián, of the Gran Palenque de Moa. Unlike the others, Sánchez was a rebel at an early age. Moreover, Mackandal's life is revealed to Coba in a fashion that is consistent with *The Kingdom of This World*, through the words of a possessed sailor. But the religious stage in Carpentier's work is less emphasized and transitory in Leante's novel, though necessary for Coba's final awareness. Significantly, the events of this stage are narrated backward, from the most recent to the most remote; that is, toward a beginning, a movement embodied in Carpentier's "Journey to the Source." Leante, like his character, had to come to terms with Carpentier's text in order to transcend it. In narrating the spiritual scene, Leante chooses to spell Mackandal's name almost as it appears in *The Kingdom of This World*. Carpentier, following the French, spells it Mackandal. Leante drops the *c* but retains the *k*, as Makandal. In Spanish and English, however, the name is spelled with a *c*, as Macandal. The difference and similarity in spelling connote for Leante a need to follow the model Carpentier represents while recognizing his own individuality. Leante's desire to break with Carpentier's influence results in his creative act.[56]

Equally important is the reinterpretation of Henri Christophe. The Kingdom of This World describes Christophe as a ruthless leader who after emancipation "enslaved" his followers and ruled the northern part of Haiti as a European monarch; Los guerrilleros negros shows another interpretation of history. Although Cuban slaves considered the Haitian Revolution a monumental historical transformation, Christophe is depicted as having contributed to the defeat of the French on Saint Domingue, an interpretation consistent with Aponte's (1812) and Estenoz's (1912) beliefs. Regardless of the internal politics of the island, Haiti and the Haitian rebellion were symbols of freedom for slaves in Cuba and throughout the Caribbean.

The Cuban question for Leante necessitated a Cuban answer. Coba could no longer resort to African religions nor believe that dead slaves return to Africa, as Ti Noel, taita Quiala, and Montejo once did. Leante's description reflects policy in the Cuban Revolution, which undermines Afro-Cuban religions. As in the revolution, in the novel historical oppression required a historical solution. The only road to emancipation was through armed revolution: "He had to continue to fight, since that world to which he belonged, to which he felt adhered vertiginously, to which he was a consubstantial part, was a world of struggle, of conflict, of permanent combat" (296–297). Although Coba's realization resembles that of Ti Noel in the ending of Carpentier's novel, their solutions are not the same. Ti Noel's response is nature, Coba's is history.

In spite of a contemporary understanding of religion, Christianity adds a dimension that must be explored as a vehicle for change during the nineteenth century. Sebastián is aware of the historical forces around him, as manifested in the Haitian rebellion and the Aponte Conspiracy; yet one of his closest friends is Father Antonio, a white priest who with Sebastián conspired with Aponte. Much to the surprise of arriving slaves, the priest was a member of the palenque who instructed the slaves in history. He informed them that, some four years before, the Spanish courts had eliminated slavery. Mexican Father Guridi had introduced the proposition, which had been rejected. Nevertheless, Father Antonio saw it necessary to give the fugitive slaves a legal and legitimate base for their rebellion. Levi Marrero states that in the session of March 26, 1811, the deputy Miguel Guridi y Alcócer, within the liberal context of the times, proposed, among other things, an end to the slave trade in the Spanish possessions, freedom for the children of slaves, slave salaries paid by masters, slaves' rights to purchase their freedom, and better treatment for those who remained slaves.[57]

It is historically significant that Leante not only records the aid priests gave to slaves but also transforms Antonio into a religious man, perhaps to underscore the important role some clergy played in the abolition of slavery. The presence of the clergy points directly to Guridi but also to Calcagno's priest of Magarabomba and their reasons for ending slavery. During the nineteenth century it was not uncommon for the clergy and other missionaries to aid slaves. Mary Turner's *Slaves and Missionaries: The Disintegration of Jamaican Slave Society* suggests that missionaries from Britain, particularly Baptist and Wesleyan Methodists, brought to Jamaica a religious fervor which "elaborated the social bases for conflict, sharpened tensions and stimulated new forms of resistance to slavery."[58] The growing abolitionist movement among militant clerics led to the Baptist War of 1831–32.

Although religion and the plantation economy were different in Cuba and Jamaica, Leante nevertheless proposes that the superior organization of the Palenque de Moa over the Palenque de Sigua effectively challenged slave status, created a political consciousness, and placed slave rebellions in a broader context.

But Leante's narration of slavery in the nineteenth century is more than an attempt to develop a plot and story. His novel rescues an important event in Cuban history: the life of the fugitive slaves of the Gran Palenque del Frijol. Recalling fiction, Franco describes the historical slave community in the following manner:

> The Gran Palenque del Frijol contained more than three hundred runaway slaves, both men and women, led by a creole black of Havana called Sebastián. It was well organized and constituted an economic unity of production—according to an official document: National Archives. *Asuntos Políticos* File 109 No. 43—". . . in said Palenque formal establishment of houses, sugar mills, sugarcane fields, banana and tobacco plantations and all species of grains of corn, beans, rice, etc. were found."[59]

Leante rewrites in fiction the history of the nineteenth-century slavery novel in order to establish a communion with the past, not to contemplate it but to actively participate in a collective memory. By closely following the patterns of history, Leante has encountered those works that were based on a similar history. His novel establishes a communion between history and fiction. In basing his text on history, Leante is incorporating factual information into fiction and, therefore, suggesting the fictional characteristics of those works that narrate the same period. Inversely, by containing those past works in his, Leante also acknowledges their history and the historicity of his own work. One implies the other, for both history and fiction are rewritten to uncover a truly American expression. But Leante's attempt to rewrite history seems to clash with some books of history. A reading of fiction and history will lead us to unmask the accepted notions of both and to question the space that separates the two terms. History and fiction do not appear to be in opposition within the context of Cuba and the Caribbean, but can be considered homologous.

Of the books on the subject, Zoila Danger Roll's *Los cimarrones de El Frijol* (1977) documents closely the history of the period narrated in *Los guerrilleros negros*. The affinity between Leante's and Danger Roll's work is noticeable when isolating the Great Expedition's mission to destroy the Gran Palenque. But the narration of this historical event is not without complications, given that one description occurs in a work of fact and the other in a text of fiction. The coincidence between the novel and history is so astonishing that one would assume the fiction is a product of the historical work. This is not possible, since Leante's novel was published one year before Danger Roll's work. However, Danger Roll's use of documents suggests that Leante had access to similar sources. Some resemblances between the two works are as follows: History cites that Alfonso Martínez and Francisco Rocha led the first and unsuccessful attack on the Gran Palenque (47).[60] Both, along with Mustelier, are mentioned in the novel as having participated in the campaign against the Palenque de Sigua (101). Martínez, however, is also singled out for having cooperated in the other campaign (136). Both the novel and the historical account mention that Governor Escudero arrived in Oriente on January 6, 1816 (history, 47; novel, 145). The next date that appears in the historical work is March 16, 1816 (49), the day Escudero requested a set sum of money for the expedition to eliminate the fugitives. The same month and year are mentioned in the novel, which, unlike the factual work, describes the boarding of troops onto two awaiting ships (159). Logic dictates that the latter embarkation would be a result of the money obtained for the expedition. Although both texts mention that the expedition was costly and everyone was well paid, the amounts differ: The novel states 7,000 pesos (160), while the historical account mentions the exorbitant sum of 25,195 pesos (49). Both works, nevertheless, agree that Manuel de Chenard, from the Infantry Regiment of Havana, was to be commander of the expedition (history, 50; novel,

158) and that the northern part of the province would be the best place from which to launch the attack. But the novel states that the trip from Baracoa to the *palenque* lasted two days (165), whereas Danger Roll's work cites nine days (52). During the attack, history reports that the *apalencados* resisted but that the overwhelming forces of the expedition caused the fugitives to flee (52). The novel narrates that Chenard's forces found the *palenque* empty. To save face, a myth was fabricated to convince others of the expedition's success (166, 168–170). The novelistic account coincides with and explains the same success reported in the history. The governor in the novel is aware of Chenard's scheme. In the historical account, the governor learns of the success of the operation by mail. Chenard's report continues to concur with the account reproduced in the novel, further suggesting the use of the same sources. The historical work describes the *palenque*: "The ranches were found in a terrain of more than 1,350 geometric yards not including the terrain that encompassed their cultivated land, where yam and banana trees and other agricultural products were found in the center" (55). In the novel, Chenard writes in a letter he would send to the governor: "In an area of uneven terrain which measured more than 1,350 geometric yards, not comprising the waste that occupied their cultivated land" (167). Other accounts include the forge (history, 57; novel, 167), the inventory of arms that was sent to the governor (history, 57; novel, 167–168), etc.

More precise than a possible coincidence in words is the following account contained in Danger Roll's work:

El jefe de la partida debía ser cuidadoso al asaltar el palenque ya que los fugitivos utilizaban ardides para defenderse de sus enemigos: preparaban veredas falsas, sembraban de estacas puntiagudas o ramas las cañadas profundas y colocaban emboscadas con avanzadas en las crestas de las montañas, para evitar caer en algunas de estas por falta de advertencia. (61)

[The leader of the group had to be careful when overtaking the *palenque*, since the fugitives used artifices to defend themselves from their enemies: They prepared false paths, planted pointed stakes, invisible in many places, disguised deep ravines with fences and branches and placed ambushes with outposts at mountain tops, to avoid falling into some of these traps for lack of warning.]

The written instructions Chenard received in the novel said the following:

Debe ponerse en mayor cuidado en preservarse, al tiempo de asaltar
el palenque, de los ardides de que ordinariamente se sirven los fugitivos, preparando falsas veredas para hacer caer a sus perseguidores
sobre los lugares sembrados de estacas punzantes para inutilizarlos o
cubriendo en falso de empalizadas o ramas algunas cañadas de pro-
fundidad, vigilando no menos sobre las emboscadas que pueda tener
avanzadas en las crestas de las montañas. (164)

[You should be on guard in protecting yourself, when attacking
the *palenque,* against the artifices that the fugitives ordinarily use,
preparing false paths to trap their persecutors over areas planted with
sharp stakes to render them useless or disguising some deep ravines
with fences or branches, watching for ambushes which may have
outposts at mountain tops.]

There were other instructions once in the camp:

Se debía prohibir terminantemente, tocar nada de lo que allí se
encontrase, como: aguas recogidas en estanques o canoas, harina
de maiz, carnes beneficiadas o cualquier alimento, hasta no estar
seguros de que no están mezclados con yerbas o cáscaras mortíferas,
porque los negros que han envejecido en el campo, tienen gran
conocimiento de hacer estas combinaciones. (61)

[It should be absolutely prohibited to touch anything that would
be found there, like: water contained in receptacles or ducts, corn-
meal, slaughtered meats or any type of food, until you are sure that
they are not mixed with herbs or fatal peels, because blacks who
have grown old in the countryside are very knowledgeable in making
these combinations.]

Similarly, Leante provides the following quote:

No probar agua ni alimentos en el palenque hasta estar seguros de
que no están mezcladas con algunas composiciones de yerbas o cáscaras mortíferas, como que de ellas tienen el mayor conocimiento los
negros envejecidos en el campo. (164)

[Do not taste water or food in the *palenque* until being sure that
they are not mixed with some composition of herbs or fatal peels,
since blacks who have grown old in the countryside are very knowledgeable about them.]

The allusion to blacks who deal with poison is a direct reference to Mackandal. The quotations mentioned should eliminate any doubt as to the possibility of there being nothing more than a mere coincidence between the two texts. The last lines of the latter citation point to the use of the same words in both the fiction and the history, although at times arranged differently. We should also note that the same quotations in both texts appear in their same respective pages and in the same order. Furthermore, when narrating the same accounts as Danger Roll, Leante uses letters and quotations, providing authenticity to the fiction by giving it the "objective" value of documents and historical works.

If some of the information provided seems to coincide and reflect a common work, other facts do not. For example, the date on which Governor Escudero receives a gold-handled cane from the "Very Noble and Very Loyal City of Santiago" for eliminating the rebellious blacks is different in fact and fiction. History reports September 1817 as the date, while the novel mentions it as 1816. This discrepancy can be explained in the following manner: Either Leante, conscious of the novel's fictional nature, chose to change the date with a specific purpose in mind, or the difference in dates might have been a copywriter's or printer's error. It is also possible that either Leante or Danger Roll made an unconscious mistake and wrote the wrong date in their respective works. The second discrepancy is more serious. History cites that it was Gallo, Manuel Griñán, and not Coba, Ventura Sánchez, who is surprised by Felipe Fromesta's forces; to escape being captured, Gallo commits suicide. As previously stated, *Los guerrilleros negros* narrates the life of Coba as its protagonist. Therefore, the mentioned suicide corresponds not to Gallo but to Coba's own destiny.

A possible solution to these apparent contradictions would be to consult a prior work that might contain the same information; that is, uncover a text common to both Leante's and Danger Roll's works. For this I chose Franco's "Palenques del Frijol, Bumba y Maluala" (1963).[61] In comparing the relevant sections, one notices that, because of the nature of the disciplines and languages, the writing style of Danger Roll's book is closer to Franco's article. Moreover, Franco states that the ceremony in which the governor received the gold-handled cane took place in September 1817 and not in 1816, as the novel narrates. However, according to Franco it was Coba and not Gallo who plunged into the river Quibiján to avoid being captured by Fromesta's men. Franco's account, from the moment that the Gran Palenque is invaded to Coba's death, parallels closely the accounts narrated in the novel. The same section in Danger Roll's book unfolds very quickly and omits many events contained in the other two texts. The action shifts from the gold-handled cane, to a brief comment on the need for owners to register their fugitive slaves, to measuring the effectiveness of the mentioned attack, to Fromesta's expedition.

Even though Leante's novel parallels Franco's work closely, there are discrepancies. Franco, for example, cites that the lieutenant governor of Baracoa received an order for one hundred men to depart for the river Tao on September 28; another group to depart with fifty men from Tiguabos, whose objective would be the Caujerí *palenque*; and a third with forty-four French naturalized citizens, leaving from the coffee zone, to complete the maneuver. After the attack, Feliciano, the only one accompanying Coba, was taken prisoner and sent to Santiago de Cuba.[62] In the novel, the lieutenant governor of the same city received an order for his men to depart on October 27 and 28. The first group, which contained one hundred men, was to leave from the river Toa and surprise the *palenques* of that region; another, composed of fifty men from Tiguabos, was to attack Caujerí; a third group of military men, sent to combat the Haitian pirates, was to continue down the coast to Barlovento. On September 26, a group of forty French naturalized citizens departed from the nearby hill of Santiago to go north (278–280).

How does one explain that Raimundo and not Feliciano accompanied Coba and was subsequently captured while four of his men escaped? After discovering other discrepancies, the curious reader is left with the unending task of seeking another prior text, and possibly yet another. But there is another path if the other texts are not found: At the prospect of an endless search, the reader must determine for himself what is fact and what is fiction, a process which cannot be based on faith alone. As readers, we may accept the boundaries that separate a work of fact from a text of fiction[63] and are suspicious of texts transgressing these boundaries.

A simultaneous reading of Danger Roll's, Franco's, and Leante's works invariably leads us to question the Western-imposed categories of the novel as fiction and history as fact. Although these observations are applicable to the literatures of other countries, they are evident in the Cuban revolutionary process, that is, in a society which is attempting to rewrite history and fiction. When compared, Franco and Danger Roll affirm the fictionalization of Leante's novel regarding the date Escudero received the gold-handled cane. Leante and Franco show the fictionalization of Danger Roll's work by coinciding in Coba's death. However, Franco's work also reaffirms the historicity of Leante's novel or the fictionalization of Danger Roll's work. The absence of another prior text prevents the reader from confirming further the historicity or fictionalization of either Leante's or Franco's texts. The inability to identify and/or determine that hidden, primary, privileged Ur-text will inevitably lead to an unending quest for the veracity of a historical event, which in any case could be the fictionalization of that act. Thus, even when a privileged reader determines and confirms the historical event by finding the original text, one would still have to question its truthfulness. If we contend that Leante's novel is as factual as Danger Roll's work (if not more so), then we must question whether the "truth" can still be determined, since myth as deception, according to the novel, is characteristic of white society. Escudero's attempt to hide the failure of the Great Expedition is an example of creating myths. Yet Leante's example is in accordance with the "discovery" of America, that is, America as a European invention. The very essence of the language used to discover the region would falsify its reality. As proposed by Vico, the imposition of European languages did not allow a natural institution to emerge or the colonial process to be reversed. The inhabitants experienced their cultural roots not as natives but as foreigners. America would be a world that creates historical fictions.

If facts contain fiction and fiction also contains facts, then where do we draw the thin line that separates a historical work from a novel that is based on history? Leante's text, when read with Franco's, provides the following answer: Franco's article alludes to dissension in the guerrilla ranks. Father Manfugas takes advantage of this division by offering Coba and Feliciano the governor's proposition for the slaves' freedom. Coba receives the priest with great respect, surrounding him with twenty-two *cimarrones* (runaway slaves). Father Manfugas, as in the novel, presents the former slave with necessary documents granting his and Feliciano's freedom. But the governor, alarmed by the enemy ships in the bay, breaks negotiations without prior warning and attacks the fugitive camps. Leante's novel follows the pattern established by history, with two exceptions. In the first case, the novel names Father Izquierdo and not Manfugas. In the second, the obvious interpretive nature of the novel allows it to go beyond the facts seemingly present in history. Father Izquierdo approaches Coba not because the runaway slave has defected but because Coba feels that his delaying tactic, at a time of emotional fervor by whites, would work to the fugitives' advantage as he stalls for time. Coba experiences a moment of introspection and isolation which coincides with Franco's report of self-doubt, but not for the reasons stated in the history. And although Escudero does renounce the treaty with the fugitives, his motive differs from that of Franco. Coba, in spite of his promises, had never intended to keep his word to work for the Spanish forces by capturing other fugitives.

What is clear is that a set of facts or words can generate a series of meanings. For instance, in the novel, Coba's name inevitably suggests an allegorical reading in which the character's given name could allude to fate, fortune, happiness, or even adventure and his nickname to Cuba. Within this interpretation, Coba's life points to the future and means something more than that of one individual— it represents the life of all blacks or all individuals living in Cuba (Coba) during the time of the narration and possibly throughout the nineteenth century. The name may also refer to those individuals who fought during the Cuban Revolution. The novel can go freely beyond "objective" narrative. It can invent its own reality, which will prove to be loyal to historical events without being accountable to them. The history of the Gran Palenque de Moa is extended, in the novel, to the next camp Coba heads, El Frijol. What appear to be two *palenques* in the novel are one and the same in the history. Both Franco's and Danger Roll's texts confirm this assertion. History, on the other hand, cannot pretend to be fiction but fact; whereas history is believed to be attached to a historical referent, fiction is not.

As we continue to demystify the concept of history and fiction, other factors become prevalent. Written in the dominant bourgeois language, the historical work cites and interprets the events contained in history. The historian's aim is to insure that the work coincides with the logic of the historical event. But the text also offers a vision that was present at the time of writing. Such views usually support those of the dominant discourse, in our case that of the Cuban Revolution. All other views are either discredited or nonexistent, for they exist outside the history recorded by the dominant class. For example, little information is available regarding the *palenques* during the first part of the nineteenth century. Those works that do exist must tell their accounts, as we have seen from the information cited by both Leante and Danger Roll, from the slave hunters' point of view. All other accounts, especially those of the *cimarrones* living in slave communities, are not available. For the most part, the slaves did not trust whites and therefore rejected the white concept of history. Montejo, who did not live in a *palenque,* could only relate his experiences through oral tradition and was recorded and transcribed by Barnet, who then appropriated Montejo's story.

But the novel, also written in a dominant language, does not pretend to offer facts, since it is categorized and categorizes itself as fiction. This is precisely the strength of the genre. If the novel at one time presented a marginal yet equally factual point of view, different from the dominant perspective of the existing society, without threatening, transcending, or transgressing the bounds allotted to it, it now comes into direct conflict with other forms of discourse. The tension between reality and invention which gives birth to fiction in the Caribbean and other parts of the New World allows fiction the role of undermining, subverting, and competing with but also complementing history; fiction can question and reinterpret the content of history by infringing on its boundary.[64] The "historical novel" challenges the power and privileged position granted to history. The facade of history has been uncovered. It can no longer show itself and be accepted as total fact. Masks can only exist in the absence of the sacred text. Without it, the novel becomes a part of history and history a part of fiction.

By reinterpreting history, the Cuban Revolution has revealed the subjectivity of this category as it pertains to the function of the dominant discourse. The multiplicity of the signifier is an idea which had already been addressed by fiction. As a novel, *Los guerrilleros negros* provides another interpretation of this genre. Like the Cuban Revolution, this novel establishes itself as a legitimate form of expression of a previously unacceptable reality. If the revolution is at odds with dominant capitalist ideas, so is the Cuban "historical novel" at odds with our understanding of the traditional view of history. But what may be characteristic of the novel in the Cuban Revolution can be found in other literatures. In attempting to rewrite history, the revolutionary government has allowed a politicohistorical and literary interpretation of its fiction. Read alongside history, the novel has shown that one form of discourse can influence the other. In this sense, fiction has liberated history from the artificial constraints placed on it by Western society. Read with fiction, history reveals the intention behind those constraints. Likewise, the historical reality of the revolution has also put demands and constraints on its fiction and, like history, it attempts to limit the novel's signification by forcing it to conform to the strategies of the discourse of power. Both history and fiction live in a state of tension in which they both question and are constantly redefining each other. The ideas put forth serve as a way of reevaluating our notions of history and fiction. More important, they establish a basis from which to explore the native "history" of America, a history that will continue to be rewritten.

# SIX

# Present and Future Antislavery Narratives
## Reinaldo Arenas's *Graveyard of the Angels*

*Un adolescente con un atributo germinativo tan troni-*
*tonante, tenía que tener un destino espantoso, según el*
*dictado de la pitia délfica.*
— JOSÉ LEZAMA LIMA, *PARADISO*

With the Cuban Revolution we arrive at another stage of antislavery narrative, one which corresponds to the society in which the works were written. Within this stage I include another work written during the same revolutionary period published not in Cuba but outside of the island. Reinaldo Arenas's *Graveyard of the Angels* shares common characteristics with works written in the revolution, but, as the most recent antislavery narrative, it also departs from them. Although *The Autobiography of a Runaway Slave*, *Los guerrilleros negros*, and *Graveyard of the Angels* profit from an awareness of the unfolding of history, Arenas's novel does not partake of a revolutionary process but is critical of it. In this regard, *Graveyard of the Angels* proposes a different direction for future antislavery works, one which comes closer to earlier ones that questioned the society in which they were written.

The works of Arenas, Leante, and Barnet engage in the rewriting of history and other texts, but with different results. Considering the theme of slavery and the time in which the works were written, Barnet's and Leante's texts contain both a discourse and counter-discourse. For example, Barnet and Leante reproduce the counter-discourse of Montejo's voice and the earlier antislavery works, respectively, but shape and reshape them to coincide with the revolution's attempt to reinterpret history. In revolutionary Cuba, the past is reproduced in both texts of history and fiction in order for it to conform to the present. From this perspective, the officials of the Castro government are using textual strategies that I have associated with the "fictional" discourse of the antislavery narrative.

*Graveyard of the Angels* is a counter-discourse to the discourse of the Castro government. After its triumph, the revolution sub-stituted the dominant discourse with its own; by affirming its dis-course as "truth," the revolution revealed the subjectivity and ar-bitrariness of the discourse of previous administrations. Similar to what Castro's officials have done, Arenas's novel undermines not only the discourse of the revolution but all discourse, including its own, and shows that discourses are a function of textual authorities. In Arenas's work, the contemporary period in which the novel was written liberates itself from the past of its own narration.

Rewriting history is indeed the goal of the Castro government and is reflected in Leante's novel. The ending of *Los guerrilleros negros* recalls the final moments of *Francisco*. Coba's decision to commit suicide and avoid being captured by slave hunters, though a histori-cal reality, alludes to Francisco's suicide by hanging. Unlike the ro-mantic Francisco, Coba kills himself for political reasons.

Attempting to rewrite aspects of *The Autobiography of a Run-away Slave* and to respond to the society in which the work was written, Leante is less concerned with an accurate religious inter-pretation of his characters' actions than a political one. For example, Montejo denies that blacks threw themselves into rivers, an allusion to Coba's death, but attached to their waists a chain full of magic which returned them to their African land. Seeking a more political response to Coba's death, the protagonist understands that blacks in effect do not return to Africa. Coba preferred death without resur-rection than to return to slavery.

Like *Los guerrilleros negros* and *The Autobiography of a Run-away Slave*, Reinaldo Arenas's *Graveyard of the Angels* is also a rewriting of earlier antislavery images. But, contrary to the works of the revolution, Arenas does not propose a historical continuity which culminates in a radical change in Cuban society. Arenas breaks with the works written under the Castro government and fol-lows more closely the tradition of the early antislavery narrative. Similar to Ramos's *Caniquí,* Novás Calvo's *El negrero,* and others who published their works before 1959 and were critical of the so-ciety in which the works were written, Arenas uses the theme of slavery not only to condemn it, as so many have done, but to de-nounce its manifestation in present-day Cuba.[1] And like the first works, Arenas will attempt to redefine Cuban society and culture.

As the title suggests, *Graveyard of the Angels* is a rewriting of *Cecilia Valdés.* Arenas is conscious of the earlier text. In his preface, Arenas refers to Villaverde's novel: "My re-creation of Villaverde's work is neither a condensation nor a revision of the original. I have taken his general ideas, some of his episodes, a few of his metaphors, and let my own imagination run wild with them. I am not offering the reader the novel Cirilo Villaverde wrote—which is obviously unnecessary—but the novel I would have written if I were in his place."[2]

Arenas attempts to bridge two historical moments; he situates himself in Villaverde's place and writes as if he were the nineteenth-century author living in the late twentieth century; Arenas's novel offers *Cecilia Valdés* a contemporary understanding of the time in which the author lived. Arenas's rewriting of Villaverde's novel recalls Villaverde's own rewriting of his first short story but also of Martín Morúa Delgado's *Sofía,* another version of *Cecilia Valdés.*[3] The numerous rewritings of Villaverde's novel imply that the past must be reshaped in order to conform to the unfolding of events. Yet the repetitions of the different versions also suggest that history repeats itself, but with some important differences which take into account the time in which the authors wrote their works.

Arenas's novel is a contemporary rewriting of Villaverde's *Cecilia Valdés.* Writing or rewriting can produce, as Harold Bloom suggests, an anxiety of influence. Although the Bloomian thesis can be applied to Arenas, there is also a spiritual and even mystical link between Villaverde and Arenas, or between *Cecilia Valdés* and *Graveyard of the Angels.* Both Villaverde and Arenas opposed their respective governments when each lived in Cuba: In the 1840s, Villaverde fought against Spanish colonialism and supported annexation to the United States, a movement which Narciso López championed. Arenas has also been openly critical of the political and cultural policies of the Castro government. For their political beliefs, both Arenas and Villaverde suffered detainment in Cuban prisons and escaped from the island, seeking refuge in the United States. Both authors rewrote and published their versions of *Cecilia Valdés* while in the United States. Arenas completed his novel almost one century after Villaverde published the definitive version of *Cecilia Valdés.* Finally, it is possible that Arenas, like Villaverde, will die an exile in the United States.

Following *Cecilia Valdés, Graveyard of the Angels* describes life in nineteenth-century Cuba and reproduces characters and scenes which have become familiar in Villaverde's novel. In so doing, he reaffirms Villaverde's position regarding the theme of slavery and joins him in denouncing a system of oppression which excludes blacks from the mainstream of society. The problem is generational and is repeated by Arenas's María Alarcón in the following manner: "Granddaughter of a slave grandmother and an unknown white man; daughter of a dark mulatta and an unknown white man; mulatta herself, lover of a white man who is abandoning her, and mother of a baby girl who will also never know her father" (4). Cándido Gamboa's extramarital relations with the mulatto María Alarcón are emblematic of racial and sexual oppression that is continued by Leonardo Gamboa and his half sister Cecilia. Both Villaverde and Arenas use the incestuous relationship between the unsuspecting brother and sister to narrate other cultural and political concerns.

As I proposed in chapter 2, Villaverde's text situates the narration at the time of the corrupt Francisco Dionisio Vives government (1823–1832) but also breaks with it to call attention to the Ladder Conspiracy of 1844. During the alleged conspiracy, hundreds of blacks and mulattoes were killed. Characters such as the tailor Francisco Uribe and poet Gabriel de la Concepción Valdés (Plácido) were incorporated into the narrative to refer to this tragic moment in history. Like Villaverde, Arenas breaks with the chronology of his own novel to recall a contemporary time before and during the Cuban Revolution. The break in the narration is evident with the presence of Lydia Cabrera, José Lezama Lima, and Padre Gastelu, referring the reader to a time one century after the Ladder Conspiracy; that is, to the 1940s and 1950s and to the periodical *Orígenes* (1944–1956), which Lezama edited. During the *Orígenes* years and after the triumph of Castro, Lezama and other group members were accused of stressing the aesthetic over the political.

Aesthetic as well as personal differences led to a split among the ranks of *Orígenes* and to the formation of *Ciclón* (1955–1959), a more socially conscious magazine, edited by José Rodríguez Feo and Virgilio Piñera. In the early years of the revolution, supporters of the literary supplement *Lunes de Revolución* (1959–1961), which was affiliated with *Revolución*, the official newspaper of the 26 of July Movement, continued to criticize Lezama and members of *Orígenes*. The supplement entered into a struggle with the Consejo Nacional de Cultura and the Instituto Cubano de Artes e Industrias Cinematográficos, whose members belonged to the Partido Socialista Popular, to charter the course for the development of culture in revolutionary Cuba. With Castro's shift away from the 26 of July Movement and toward the Cuban Communist party (PSP), the struggle resulted in the closing of *Lunes*. Officials of the Cuban government continued the resistance to Lezama.

Arenas's inclusion of Lezama is an attempt to recall not so much the early years of *Lunes* as the government's attack on Lezama and his monumental *Paradiso* (1966), which was censored but then rescued by Castro himself. The problem pertained to chapter 8, which described in detail heterosexual and homosexual acts. In this regard, just as *Cecilia Valdés* and other antislavery novels were offensive to the Spanish and Cuban governments during the time in which the works were written, *Paradiso* offended supporters of the revolution. In the same spirit, *Graveyard of the Angels* joins *Paradiso* and the early antislavery works insofar as it also tries the sensibility of conservative critics in Cuba. Arenas's reference to Lezama and allusion to homosexuality are a communion of sorts with *Paradiso* and the difficulties it and Lezama encountered in Cuba. Moreover, some writers mentioned in Arenas's novel, including Lydia Cabrera, for political reasons left the country. Lezama and Padre Gastelu were forced to live in internal exile. Arenas confirms this observation when he writes the following: "From 1971 until his death, Lezama was subjected to a rigorous censorship. He was a victim of the official hatred and contempt. In spite of his untiring creative energy and during that fundamental period of his artistic activity, not a word of his was published."[4] In chapter 11, Arenas identifies Lezama as a slave poet, reminding us of Manzano's status during the first third of the nineteenth century, a period in which the antislavery works were censored and could only be published abroad, and continuing an interplay between the past and the present.

The fragmentation in Arenas's chronology allows him to include in his own narration Lezama but also the author of *Cecilia Valdés*. The characters refer to Villaverde's escape in 1848, but also to a time after the publication of the novel. Deviating from Villaverde's biography, the characters visit the author in his native province of Pinar del Río to obtain his interpretation of part 3, chapter 4. Leonardo's girlfriend, Isabel, asks the author what he meant when he said, "Encantadora de Alquízar"; that is, was he referring to Isabel or to her house? Aware of the multiplicity of interpretation, Villaverde responds: "'That's for the curious reader to decide.'" (92). The same words are uttered by Cándido Gamboa, thus also giving him authorial status.

Doña Rosa's anger with the author and her attempt to kill him address a formalist and structuralist concern which would liberate the text from the author. In their "Intentional Fallacy," Wimsatt and Beardsley convincingly show that interpretation is limited when the reader links meaning to author intentionality.[5] The novel supports Wimsatt and Beardsley's position: The death of the author opens the text to multiple interpretations.

Decentralizing Villaverde's authorial voice allows Arenas's text to emerge in some way tied to but also independent of *Cecilia Valdés*.

The multiple interpretations negate any single privileged referentiality, including Arenas's or, for that matter, the one I offer here. Aware of the act of writing, Arenas questions his own authority; Leonardo becomes independent of the author and addresses him as character: "There is absolutely no connection between me and the escapades that syphilitic degenerate who thinks he's Goya himself (I mean Arenas, of course) ascribes to me or those other pranks the other old idiot, who also was just as incapable of accurately depicting my character or anything else" (104). The reference is to Goya, the narrator, and Goya, the painter of the portrait of Fernando VII, as described in the section entitled "The Philharmonic Society Ball."
The narrator is revealed to the reader:

> No doubt some curious and impertinent reader (these are never lacking) might wish to interrupt me at this precise moment—this tense and difficult moment in my story—to ask me how I could possibly give such a faithful and detailed description of the portrait. Very simple, my dear sir: I am the artist, its creator—Francisco de Goya y Lucientes, at your service. . . . I did a perfect piece of work there, and the canvas contains all my fury, all my genius, and all my syphilitic lucidity (an honor conferred on me directly, with no masks, by queen Maria Luisa). When the portrait was finished, Fernando VII ordered it covered with a double canvas, not to protect it but to protect himself. (108)

The narrator, who has been displaced from Villaverde to Arenas and now to Goya, is not Goya but Arenas dressed as Goya. This is revealed by the use of the word "syphilitic," which was first used by Leonardo to address Arenas and is now used to describe Goya. From another point of view, the narrator is Arenas, but he is not Arenas; he is Villaverde, Arenas, or Goya. He is all of them and he is none of them.
The painting has more than one author and refers to more than one subject. The subject in the painting is displaced from one individual to the other only to affirm each one and deny them all. The painting is of Fernando VII, the author of Spanish history during the years in which Saco, Del Monte, and others wanted to make the Literary Commission an independent body of the Sociedad Económica de Amigos del País. However, it is also a portrait of Goya and perhaps Arenas himself. "That portrait of mine" which refers to authorship also alludes to Goya's portrait, but the same words could also have been uttered by Arenas and therefore refers to his authorship and portrait. Covering the characters' eyes is equivalent to covering

those of the readers so that we cannot see the portrait's double or triple referentiality. In this case, the portrait can be of Fernando VII, Goya, or Arenas, that of all of them and none of them. We, as readers, will never be certain of the painting since all the witnesses who did see it have died.

The novel has multiple authors and interpretations. Fernando VII is the author of a certain period of Spanish history; Goya is the author of the paintings of Spanish customs during a time in which the guerrilla became a popular military strategy, thus continuing to refer the reader to a present time in which Castro used the same techniques to overthrow the Batista dictatorship. Villaverde and Arenas are authors of their respective texts; Cándido and Leonardo Gamboa are also authors of their lives and the plot. Let us remember that in certain moments both Cándido and Leonardo repeat the same words which Arenas pronounces.

By undermining the author as the only writer or interpreter of his work, *Graveyard of the Angels* opposes all monolithic and unidimensional understanding of Villaverde's work but also of history. We should recall that Villaverde's and Arenas's works are part of the antislavery narrative tradition, which attempts to rewrite history. Within the context of the time in which Arenas writes his novel, he strives to decentralize an understanding of history in which historians and functionaries of the Castro government are the only authors or interpreters of Cuban history and culture. Likewise, he questions Barnet's and Leante's works as the only representation of the antislavery narrative written in the Cuban revolutionary period.

The negation of the text's authority allows Arenas to question the authority of any text, whether it be literary, political, legal, or otherwise. With regard to *Cecilia Valdés*, Arenas undermines Villaverde's idea of Cuban family and culture that is also repeated in other antislavery works. Villaverde was daring for his time when proposing that the Cuban nationality is composed of the coming together of the white, black, and mulatto races; therefore, the incestuous relationship between Leonardo and Cecilia alludes to the Cuban family. For Arenas, it is that and much more.

Arenas underlines the makeup of the Cuban family by describing scenes in Villaverde's novel and introducing others. Like the early nineteenth-century works, Arenas's text attempts to shock the reader with a different reality. Out of revenge for her husband, Rosa forces her slave Dionisio to impregnate her, thus implying that the Cuban family was not only based on the white male and the black or mulatto female, as proposed in *Cecilia Valdés*, but also on the black male and the white female. In his *La familia Unzúazu*, Martín

Morúa Delgado had described the slave Liberato's rape of his mistress, a theme later repeated by Carpentier in *The Kingdom of This World*, when Ti Noel and his sons rape Monsieur Lenormand de Mezy's second wife. What is new is the mistress's willingness, for whatever reason, to have sex with her slave. In spite of the slave's repulsion, the mistress initiates the action.

Arenas's affirmation, denial, and expansion of the composition of the Cuban family are highlighted in the English translation in chapters 5 and 6, the only two sections without titles. One pertains to Rosa's relation with Dionisio, the other to Bishop Espada and the rest of the Havana population. In history, Bishop Espada was instrumental in promoting culture and education in Cuba. He reformed the prestigious Colegio de San Carlos and chose the best professors; many of its students notable figures, including Saco and Villaverde himself. Bishop Espada was also a member of the Sociedad Económica de Amigos del País and created prizes for distinguished teachers. He absorbed half the cost of the first two free schools founded by the society. Bishop Espada was also responsible for the first teacher's school in Cuba.[6] In fiction, Leonardo Gamboa is also a student there. Bishop Espada was also known for favoring the construction of a cemetery and prohibiting the antisanitary customs of burial in the church, a theme repeated in the novel. Moreover, Bishop Espada promoted vaccination against smallpox. In the novel, the latter two images are combined. The vaccine needle and the bishop's name are transformed into a penis or, rather, a super penis as an instrument of persuasion. To alter the custom of burying the dead in the Cathedral of Havana, Bishop Espada disguises himself as an angel and in the night appears and possesses not only women but men as well. On his death bed he confesses to his successor, Bishop Echerre: "'Yes, brother, I have angelically possessed practically every woman in this city and—oh, I wouldn't dare confess it if I weren't going to expire at any moment—many, many illustrious and highly respectable men who also didn't want to be deprived of that consolation'" (17).

Just as Arenas's novel shows a displacement from one author to the other, it also suggests a change in the concept of the family, from Cándido's relationship with María Alarcón to Rosa's relationship with Dionisio, from Cándido and Leonardo, as fathers of Cuban nationality to Dionisio's fatherhood, but most important to Bishop Espada and Echerre as the real fathers of the Cuban population, a population of "bastards" in which the true father is absent. Here the church is a microcosm of Havana and the island of Cuba. If the Beneficencia is the place where Cecilia and other poor people are provided for, the church is the place of birth and death of the aristocracy. The church is built on a mountain of remains of the buried dead. Within the context of the society in which the work is written, the church and its power are a representation of the Castro government, or the Communist party, and Bishop Espada becomes Castro himself and the control he has over the Cuban people. By deconstructing the figure of the father and fatherhood, Arenas questions not only the presence of Castro as the modern father figure but all Cuban father figures, including that of Martí, the recognized father of Cuban independence.

The concept of the family and of Cubanness, as defined in Villaverde's novel and promoted in today's Cuba, is not based on unity of the people and historical continuity but on rupture with the mother country. The rupture is evident with a discussion of love, another theme presented as a diachronic line in the narration, which gains in intensity toward the end. Explicitly, it is in chapters 9 (José Dolores), 10 (Nemesia), 13 (José Dolores), 22 (Cecilia), 30 (Leonardo), 33 (Cecilia), and 34 (José Dolores). After her downfall and loss of Leonardo, Arenas's Cecilia understands the past and states: "Because a great love is not even the story of a great deception or a cruel betrayal that takes us by surprise and leaves us only the void of our perplexity. No, a great love is the simple story of a self-deception that we impose on ourselves, that we suffer, and that we enjoy. Gestures we know to be circumstantial that we magnify; promises that are forgotten with the same force they are spoken; we treasure things sworn we know will never be done; and we exalt all these things thanks to which and for which we live. Because a great love is not the story of a great love but its invention" (118). Like René Girard's love triangle in his *Deceit, Desire, and the Novel*, love is caused by a desire to possess an object and also the impossibility of a permanent union with it.[7] For Arenas, Girard's mediator has become time and distance.

Love, like fiction or the unity of the Cuban family, as a representation of Cubanness, is questioned and interpreted as an invention. Unity, as a family concept promoted in today's Cuba and associated with the island, exists more in the mind than in reality. It exists within the self and not outside of it. Cuban culture is not a concept which developed and flourished exclusively in nineteenth-century Cuba; it also exists outside of the island. *Necesidad de libertad*, a collection of essays written approximately during the time in which Arenas was writing his novel, is relevant to an understanding of Cuban culture. Arenas states that writers like Martí, Casal, Heredia, Lydia Cabrera, and Guillermo Cabrera Infante had to write in exile. He equates persecution and exile to creation and invention. And, of course, this tradition is continued with Arenas himself. In a letter dated June 10, 1982, Arenas tells Severo Sarduy that the real Cuban literature is written outside of Cuba.[8]

Within the context of the works written in the Cuban revolutionary period, Arenas's novel provides a different understanding of the past and the present of the antislavery narrative. Arenas's novel allows us to understand the contribution Villaverde made in his definition of Cuban culture. Nevertheless, Villaverde concluded and published his work not in Cuba but in exile. Villaverde's ideas are repeated and expanded in Arenas's novel, which like Villaverde's, was written and published in New York. Neither work could have been published in Cuba during the time in which it was written. The works' content undermined and even threatened their respective governments. Exile, which Villaverde and Arenas suffered but which allowed them to write and complete their works abroad, represents a rupture with the mother country and is also part of Cuban culture. Cuban culture is what Cubans carry in their memory; it is the past, the present, and the future. Not unity, but distance and rupture create memory, that Great Love, and a sense of Cubanness.

Arenas's *Graveyard of the Angels* allows us to look at the past, the present, and the future of the antislavery narrative. It returns to a tradition as defined by the first works; that is, to be at the vanguard of reviewing and questioning government policies, whether they be pro–colonial Spain, pro–United States, or pro–Soviet Union. The antislavery works written and published in the revolution do not conform to a tradition of discord with society but offer a unity with it. In contrast, the antislavery narratives written during the same period outside of the island constitute a voice of opposition to a past and a present order and challenge contemporary Cuban society. As representative of the antislavery works to come, Arenas's *Graveyard of the Angels* looks to the present and future in order to recover the past. Slavery as a metaphor of oppression will be a constant in the works to come.

The antislavery narrative and the history of slaves and free blacks are at the foundation of Cuban, Caribbean, and Latin American literature and culture. The antislavery narrative is also at the center of any Latin American literary discord which attempts to question and undermine a dominant element in society. The antislavery narrative has decentralized the dominant discourse and provides another reading of history and fiction to reveal a different truth and reality about the events which unfolded during the time of the narration and the time in which the work was written.

# NOTES

## Introduction: Fiction and Fact

1. Of the stories in *Escenas*, only "Petrona y Rosalía" has been preserved. Although written in 1838, it remained unpublished until 1925. See Max Henríquez Ureña, *Panorama histórico de literatura cubana (1492–1952)* (New York: Las Américas Publishing Company, 1963), Vol. 1, 235–236. Adriana Lewis Galanes tells us that there were three Tanco stories. The other two were "El hombre misterioso," later called "El cura," and "Historia de Francisco," later entitled "El lucumí." See "El album de Domingo del Monte," *Cuadernos Hispanoamericanos* 451–452 (1988): 255–265. Recently, Lewis Galanes discovered "Un niño en la Habana" in the Biblioteca Nacional de Madrid; we believe it also to be a part of Tanco's collection of stories. See Rolando Hernáldez Morelli, "Noticias, lugar y texto de 'Un niño en La Habana' espécimen narrativo inédito de 1837," *Círculo: Revista de Cultura* 15 (1986): 73–84. José Fernández de Castro states that fragments of Tanco's story can be found in *Cuba Contemporánea*. See "Tema negro en letras de Cuba hasta fines del siglo XIX," in *Orbita de José Antonio Fernández de Castro*, ed. Salvador Bueno (Havana: Unión, 1966), 177.

2. For a summary of Del Monte's ideas, see Salvador Bueno, "Domingo del Monte como crítico," in *La crítica literaria cubana del siglo XIX* (Havana: Editorial Letras Cubanas, 1979), 32–50.

3. In a highly recommended article, Antonio Benítez Rojo defines the discourse on sugar as the Spanish Crown, the colonial government of Cuba, slave traders, the sugarocracy, and the sugar mill. For him, Arango y Parreño's text prefigured the change Cuba would undergo to an intense sugar economy. The sugar plantation was a complete system. See his "Azúcar/Poder/Texto: Triada de lo cubano," *Cruz Ansata* 9 (1986): 93–117, and, in particular, 95.

4. For the ideas on discourse and counter-discourse, I am indebted in part to Michel Foucault's work, in particular to his *Language, Counter-Memory, Practice*, trans. Donald F. Bouchard and Sherry Simon (Oxford: Blackwell, 1977) and his *Archaeology of Knowledge*, trans. A. M. Sheridan Smith (New York: Pantheon Books, 1972). After writing this introduction, I became aware of Richard Terdiman's *Discourse/Counter-Discourse* (Ithaca: Cornell Uni-

versity Press, 1985). Although he also uses Foucault's ideas as a point of departure, Terdiman's book and mine develop along different lines.

5. Blacks are present in Spanish literature, but they are represented as marginal characters. See, for example, essays by Sylvia Wynter, Martha Cobb, Howard M. Jason, Carter G. Woodson, and Valaurez B. Spratlin in *Blacks in Hispanic Literature*, ed. Miriam DeCosta (Port Washington, N.Y.: Kennikat Press, 1977), 8–52.

6. For a discussion of these terms, see Seymour Chatman, *Story and Discourse: Narrative Structure in Fiction and Film* (Ithaca, N.Y.: Cornell University Press, 1978).

7. The abolition of slavery began with the law of February 13, 1880, which substituted slavery with a patronage system. This new method of subjugation gave the slave a monthly stipend. The patronage system was finally abolished by the royal decree of October 7, 1886. However, Fernando Ortiz tells us that blacks were not considered free until 1890. See *Los negros esclavos* (1906; enlarged version of *Hampa afro-cubana: Los negros brujos*, Havana: Editorial de Ciencias Sociales, 1975), 353–355, Ortiz's italics. Also see Rebecca Scott, *Slave Emancipation in Cuba* (Princeton, N.J.: Princeton University Press, 1985), 127–197.

8. See Ramiro Guerra, *Azúcar y población en las Antillas* (1930; repr. Havana: Editorial de Ciencias Sociales, 1970), 47. The importance of slavery to sugar is summarized by Rebecca Scott when comparing slaves to laborers: "By tying workers to the workplace, slavery protected planters from the potential competition for labor, wage demands, or even strikes that might result from intense dependence on workers during the harvest. By permitting physical coercion slavery further enabled masters to force workers to perform the demanding tasks required, even at the cost of exhaustion and injury" (Scott, *Slave Emancipation in Cuba*, 24–25).

9. For an analysis of the different versions of Cirilo Villaverde's masterpiece, see my chapter on *Cecilia Valdés*, which is an expansion of my "*Cecilia Valdés:* The Emergence of an Antislavery Novel," *Afro-Hispanic Review* 3, no. 2 (1984): 15–19.

10. See Juan J. Remos's preface to *El negro Francisco* (1873; repr. Havana: Fernández y Compañía, 1953), vi, 3–7; Henríquez Ureña, *Panorama histórico*, vol. 1, 236. Zambrana was born June 19, 1846, two years after the Ladder Conspiracy which kept Domingo del Monte in exile until his death in 1853.

11. See Silvestre de Balboa, *Espejo de paciencia* (Havana: Dirección de Cultura del Ministerio de Educación, 1942).

12. See Lewis Galanes, "El album," 264.

13. Although slavery officially ended in 1886, it was a result of a gradual patronage process which began in 1880. See Fernando Portuondo, *Historia de Cuba: 1492–1898* (Havana: Editorial Pueblo y Educación, 1975), 472–473.

14. Roberto González Echevarría explains the importance of some of these writers within the context of Latin American literature in his *Alejo*

*Carpentier: The Pilgrim at Home* (Ithaca, N.Y.: Cornell University Press, 1977).

15. For other developments of this phenomenon, also see Leslie Wilson, "La Poesía Negra: Its Background, Themes and Significance," in *Blacks in Hispanic Literature*, ed. DeCosta, 90–104, and Gabriel R. Coulthard, *Race and Colour in Caribbean Literature* (London: Oxford University Press, 1962), 27–39.

16. See, for example, Richard Jackson, *The Black Image in Latin America* (Albuquerque: University of New Mexico Press, 1976).

17. See, for example, *Wifredo Lam* (Paris: Amis du Musée d'Art Moderne de la Ville de Paris, 1983); Julia Herzberg, "Afro-Cuban Traditions in the Works of Wifredo Lam," *Review* 37 (1987): 22–30; González Echevarría, *Alejo Carpentier.*

18. For two recent and interesting studies on Ortiz, see Edward Mullen, "*Los negros brujos:* A Reexamination of the Text," in *Cuban Studies 17,* ed. Carmelo Mesa-Lago (Pittsburgh: University of Pittsburgh Press, 1987), 111–129, and Gustavo Pérez Firmat, *Literature and Liminality: Festive Reading in the Hispanic Tradition* (Durham: Duke University Press, 1986).

19. The Puerto Rican Luis Palés Matos has been credited with being one of the initiators of Afro-Caribbean poetry. In 1927 he published "Danza negra" in Cuba, which influenced other writers. See, for example, Oscar Fernández de la Vega and Alberto N. Pamies, *Iniciación a la poesía afro-americana* (Miami: Ediciones Universal, 1973) and Luis Palés Matos, *Poesía,* ed. Raúl Hernández Novás (Havana: Casa de las Américas, 1975). Both Richard Jackson and Lemuel Johnson question the intention of white writers who wrote about blacks. See Jackson, *The Black Image,* and Johnson, "El Tema Negro: The Nature of Primitivism in the Poetry of Luis Palés Matos," in *Blacks in Hispanic Literature,* ed. DeCosta, 123–136.

20. See my "Caribbean Cycles: Displacement and Change," *New England Review and Bread Loaf Quarterly* 7, no. 4 (1985): 425–426. For an exceptional and updated study of Guillén, see *Callaloo No. 31 10,* no. 2 (1987).

21. Preface in Palés Matos, *Poesía,* vi.

22. Janheinz Jahn expresses a similar idea when questioning the ability of the conventional use of language to express accurately and reproduce the life of the Afro-American peasant. See *A History of Neo-African Literature: Writing in Two Continents,* trans. Oliver Coburn and Ursula Lehrburger (London: Faber and Faber Limited, 1968), 229.

23. Coulthard, *Race and Colour,* p. 29.

24. José Antonio Ramos, *Caniquí* (1936; repr. Havana: Consejo Nacional de Cultura, 1963), 7.

25. I have decided to use Elizabeth Sutherland's translation in her *The Youngest Revolution* (New York: Dial Press, 1969), 145.

26. Sutherland goes on to explain that some white Cubans listened to Castro's speech with some reservation. See ibid., 146.

27. Castro's speech commemorated the fifteenth anniversary ceremony

of the Playa Girón victory and discussed Cuban involvement in Angola. See *Foreign Broadcast Information Service, Daily Report,* April 20, 1976, Q1–Q8.

28. According to Rebecca J. Scott, the slave population continued to grow as late as the early 1860s. Because of a conscious immigration policy to increase the numbers of whites, the 1861–62 census shows that the black/white balance had shifted and the white minority became the majority. See her introduction to *Slave Emancipation in Cuba* and in particular tables 1 and 2, pp. 7 and 10, respectively.

29. For a list of uprisings, see José Luciano Franco, *Ensayos históricos* (Havana: Editorial de Ciencias Sociales, 1974), 133–134.

30. According to José Luciano Franco, the black unrest had other explanations. The war between England and Spain (1804) created a drop in prices and the U.S.-British rivalry for dominance in the Caribbean compounded the problem. Slaves were affected the most. The inferiority of some food products and the decomposition of others stored for long periods of time caused sickness among slaves. The scarcity of food created violent protest. See ibid., 138.

31. Bassave, who was known among the poor sectors of Havana, incited the battalion of Milicias Disciplinarias de Pardos y Morenos and other blacks and mulattoes, including Aponte, to rebel against the colonial government. This early movement failed; it was betrayed by Captain Morenos, Isidor Moreno, and the sergeant of Pardos, Pedro Alcántara Pacheco. De la Luz and Bassave were imprisoned in Spain and barred from traveling to America; Aponte and others eluded capture. See ibid., 139–143. For documents regarding the 1810 and 1812 conspiracies, see José Luciano Franco, *Las conspiraciones de 1810 y 1812* (Havana: Editorial de Ciencias Sociales, 1977).

32. Franco, *Ensayos históricos,* 148–149.

33. Ibid., 155, 176–177.

34. For example, in Puerto Príncipe the mulatto slave Rafael Medrano accused black José Miguel González of enlisting him in the uprising. In San Blas, slave Antonio José Vázquez also denounced the conspiracy. In Havana, businessman Pablo Serra betrayed Aponte. Recalling the failed attempt in 1810, Serra wanted to protect his own interests and gave a document he received about the rebellion to Spanish Captain General Someruelos. See ibid., 175.

35. Ibid., 176–177.

36. For an explanation regarding the differences between Cuba and the French and British colonies in the Caribbean, see Manuel Moreno Fraginals, *El ingenio,* vol. 1 (Havana: Editorial de Ciencias Sociales, 1978), 25, note 13.

37. The Sol y Rayos de Bolívar was founded in 1821 with the intention of establishing the Republic of Cubanacán. However, its leaders were captured and detained. For a description of this society, see, for example, Portuondo, *Historia de Cuba,* 284–286.

38. Levi Marrero, *Cuba: Economía y sociedad* (Madrid: Editorial Playor, 1983), 82, my translation.

39. Ramiro Guerra, *Manual de historia de Cuba: Desde su descubrimiento hasta 1868* (Madrid: Ediciones Erre, 1975), 425–434.

40. Ibid., 446–448; Marrero, *Cuba*, 85.

41. For these and other uprisings, see Guerra, *Manual de historia,* 444–448. For an account of the Triunvirato uprising, see José Luciano Franco, *La gesta heróica del Triunvirato* (Havana: Editorial de Ciencias Sociales, 1978).

42. Hugh Thomas, *Cuba: The Pursuit of Freedom* (New York: Harper and Row, 1971), 205.

43. Ibid., 205–206.

44. Franco, *Ensayos históricos,* 198. Marrero provides a different set of figures. He states that of the accused there were more than 4,039 persons which he classifies in the following manner: 2,166 free blacks, 972 slaves, 74 whites, and 827 without classification. Of these, 78 were killed (1 white, 1 woman of color, 39 slaves, and 38 free blacks), 1,292 were jailed, and 435 were exiled from the island. As the figures show, there were a significant number of free blacks accused (93–94). Pedro Deschamp Chapeaux points out that just as there were white slave owners, there were also black masters. He also reproduces newspaper ads seeking help in capturing fugitive slaves. See *El negro en la economía habanera del siglo XIX* (Havana: UNEAC, 1971), 51.

45. See, for example, Marrero, *Cuba,* 93–95; Guerra, *Manual de historia,* 453.

46. Thomas, *Cuba,* 523. Thomas further states that the U.S. secretary of state, Philander Knox, was even willing to use force in Cuba to protect the lives and property of American citizens. On May 31, the U.S. marines landed in Oriente.

47. Carlos Moore, "Le Peuple noir a-t-il sa place dans la révolution cubaine?," *Présence Africaine* 52 (1964): 198. In a note, Moore points out that current research puts the total figure to a minimum of 35,000 deaths.

48. Rafael Conte and José M. Capmany, *Guerra de razas (Negros contra blancos en Cuba)* (Havana: Imp. Militar de Antonio Pérez, 1912), 7–9.

49. See José Luciano Franco, *Las minas de Santiago del Prado y la rebelión de los cobreros: 1530–1800* (Havana: Editorial Ciencias Sociales, 1975).

50. The only documents that I have been able to locate regarding the perspective of the rebel forces are letters contained in Conte and Capmany, *Guerra de razas.* Of particular interest is a letter from Brig. Feliciano Acosta to the chief of the Oriental Province in which he reports taking the town of Palmerito and La Yerba de Guinea, from which the government forces fled. In the same letter, he requests arms. Inadvertently he gives us a glimpse of the other side of the war. If the newspaper reports indicate that the rebels are always on the move, the letter documents that it is the government forces who flee. Furthermore, the letter reminds us of the absence of a body of literature which would put into perspective the war from the other point of view. As in slavery, only the dominant white perspective remains.

51. Thomas, *Cuba,* 524–525.

52. Harry Ring, *How Cuba Uprooted Race Discrimination* (1961; repr. New York: Merit Publishers, 1969), 6. Like Ring, Lourdes Casal points to the improvement in the conditions of blacks but also admits that racial attitudes are difficult to change. See her "Race Relations in Contemporary Cuba," in *The Cuba Reader: The Making of a Revolutionary Society,* ed. Philip Brenner et al. (New York: Grover Press, 1989), pp. 471–486.

53. It is not my intention to defend or criticize policies made by officials in the government but to understand the structures of Cuban history and fiction.

54. Thomas, *Cuba,* 1433. In her *The Youngest Revolution,* Elizabeth Sutherland, although optimistic about the racial situation under the Castro government, admits to racist attitudes among Cubans. See her chapter "Colony within a Colony," 138–168.

55. There are other groups in Cuba which also represent a counterdiscourse to power. Homosexuals are a group that has been more openly persecuted in Cuba than blacks but, unlike blacks, I am not aware of a historically unified presence or a literature about them. For an understanding of the problems homosexuals face in revolutionary Cuba, see Nestor Almendros and Orlando Jiménez-Leal's film script of *Conducta impropia* (Madrid: Editorial Playor, 1984). Also see the issue on gay Latins in *New York Native* 74 (1983) and a response to some of the articles in *Mariel* 2, no. 5 (1983): 8–15.

56. For example, very early in the revolution the literary magazine *Lunes de Revolución,* of the official newspaper of the 26th of July Movement, *Revolución,* dedicated a segment to blacks in North American literature. See *Lunes de Revolución,* March 23, 1959.

57. See Robert Williams, *Crusader* 8, no. 43 (1967) and Eldridge Cleaver, *International Herald Tribune,* June 26, 1969. Also cited by Thomas, *Cuba,* 1434, note 37.

58. Juan René Betancourt, "Castro and the Cuban Negro," trans. Brandon Robinson, *Crisis* (May 1961): 273. Although Betancourt associates Castro with the Communists, he wrote his article before Castro declared himself one. Betancourt's position does not appear to be one-sided. He also criticizes Cuban exiles for not taking into account the plight of blacks. Jan Carew was exposed to racial tension while in Cuba. When inquiring about the lives of blacks in Cuba, an informant responded: "What do you think it's like, my friend? We are still black and a minority and the revolution does not invent soap to wash you white . . . they free us on paper but there is a lot of separateness in our lives still . . . and we're not like the Yankee Negro, we're not trying to be like the white Cuban . . . the white Cuban is one of the most boring human beings God ever made, they're heroic, extreme, they will defy the whole world and you will applaud and admire them but try as you may, you'll never like them . . . my daughter goes to the university . . . she's nineteen . . . she doesn't go out with white Cubans . . . their law says it's all right but it still doesn't happen . . . now I wouldn't want her to get involved with one of those dull, sanctimonious, bearded white idiots, but I'm just telling you that it doesn't happen. The law says we can go anywhere, do any-

thing but that law is a bitch when it comes to making things work."
*Topolski's Chronicle* 11, nos. 17–20 (1963): 16. Also cited partially by
Thomas, *Cuba,* 1433, note 34. Furthermore, reaction to racism in Cuba is
even expressed by some of the young Cubans Sutherland met while in Cuba.
In fact, Arturo makes a distinction between *mestizaje positivo* and *mestizaje negativo.* "The first means a blending of cultures in which there is
equal respect for both. The second means that a minority culture is absorbed—as an inferior culture" (162). Arturo continues: "This [racism] has
to be uprooted before you can have a positive blending of cultures. Until it is
uprooted, we must protect our African culture as separate. Otherwise, we
might as well all take pills to become white." Sutherland, *Youngest Revolution.* Arturo's position is similar to Moore's use of *Weltanschauung.* See "Le
Peuple noir," 226–230.

59. Ibid., 177–230.

60. Ibid., 209, my translation.

61. This observation was made during a trip to Cuba. I was told by
Cuban officials that there was no need for an Afro-Cuban organization since
discrimination had been eradicated in Cuba. Apparently, this may not have
been true for other groups which did have organizations.

62. Moore develops this idea further in his *Were Marx and Engels White
Racists?* (Chicago: Institute of Positive Education, 1972).

63. Walterio Carbonel, in his *Crítica cómo surgió la cultura nacional*
(Havana: 1961), makes similar statements, accusing the present revolutionary officials of being reactionaries and incapable of liberating themselves
from bourgeois ideology. During these early years, Carbonel was detained
and accused of being a counterrevolutionary and an agent of imperialism.
His position is contained in *Crítica.*

64. Moore's ideas are at times convincing and argue for a cyclical structure in Cuban history from which there is no present relief for blacks. However, he omits any consideration that, as in the past, Afro-Cuban religion
and culture have survived as clandestine movements. This is also the case
in Haiti where, under the Duvalier dictatorships, voodoo was outlawed.
Moreover, his presuppositions ignore the conflicts between African and
Western culture which transcend racial concerns. Henri Christophe, who
ruled the northern part of Haiti as a European ruler, is but one example. It is
perhaps in Cuba and the Caribbean and with the coming together of African
and European cultures that the question of race has been transcended.
Moore's startling accusations were answered by René Depestre in his "Let-
tre de Cuba," *Présence Africaine* 56 (1964): 105–142. In spite of his defense of the revolution, Depestre encountered difficulties in Cuba and after
seventeen years of support, in September 1978, he abandoned the island. Depestre objected to a lack of literary freedom in Cuba. He currently lives in
Paris and works for UNESCO. For a synopsis of Depestre's life, see Claud
Couffon, *René Depestre* (Paris: Editions Seghers, 1986), 9–84.

65. Carlos Moore, "Congo or Carabalí? Race Relations in Socialist
Cuba," *Caribbean Review* 15, no. 2 (1986): 12–15, 43.

66. Castro's speech is also mentioned in the editor's introduction to Moore's article.

## 1. The Antislavery Narrative

1. Rebecca Scott proposes different explanations for ending slavery: (1) domestic and international pressures; (2) contradiction between slave labor and the introduction of technology; (3) a shift to free labor with the support of enlightened planters. See *Slave Emancipation in Cuba*, 4–5.

2. Due to literary and administrative differences with Villarino, Del Monte left the magazine in 1830. After Del Monte's departure, the quality of the magazine diminished until it finally closed in 1831. See *Diccionario de la literatura Cubana*, vol. 2 (Havana: Editorial Letras Cubanas, 1984), 625–626.

3. Eduardo Torres-Cuevas and Arturo Sorhegui, eds., *José Antonio Saco: Acerca de la esclavitud y su historia* (Havana: Editorial de Ciencias Sociales, 1982), 25. Antonio Benítez Rojo explores the slavery discourse by dividing the Cuban question into *Cuba grande* and *Cuba pequeña*. For him, the first represents the interest of sugarocrats and a vision toward foreign markets, the second that of creoles and an inward vision to the land, folklore, and tradition. Benítez Rojo situates the "discourse of resistance," beginning with *El Mensajero Semanal*, published by José Antonio Saco and Félix Varela, between 1828 and 1831. However, I feel that Varela's ideas were already present in his "Memorias que demuestra la necesidad de extinguir la esclavitud de los negros en la Isla de Cuba, atendiendo a los intereses de sus propietarios, por el Presbítero don Félix Varela, Diputado a Cortes," which is anterior to Saco and Varela's publication. Since *El Mensajero Semanal* was a New York publication, I agree with Benítez Rojo's subsequent attempt to establish the dialogue in a local publication in 1832 with the liberal takeover of the *Revista Bimestre Cubana*, which belonged to the Comisión de Literatura of the Sociedad Patriótica. See his "Azúcar/Poder/Texto," 93–117.

4. José Antonio Saco, *Colección de papeles científicos, históricos, políticos y de otros ramos sobre la isla de Cuba* (Havana: Editorial Nacional de Cuba, 1963), vol. 3, 442–443. Also cited in Torres-Cuevas and Sorhegui, eds., *José Antonio Saco*, 51. My translation.

5. Torres-Cuevas and Sorhegui, eds., *José Antonio Saco*, 59, 62.

6. Salvador Bueno, *Figuras cubanas del siglo diecinueve* (Havana: UNEAC, 1980), 212; and *La crítica*, 50. Also see Guerra, *Manual de historia*, 340–341 and Francisco Calcagno, *Diccionario biográfico cubano* (New York: N. Ponce de León, 1878), 232–237.

7. See Mario Cabrera Saqui, "Vida, pasión y gloria de Anselmo Suárez y Romero," in *Francisco* (Havana: Biblioteca Básica de Autores Cubanos, 1970), 211–212. This essay appeared as the prologue to the 1947 edition of the novel. My translation. Also see "La tertulia literaria de del Monte," *Revista de la Facultad de Letras y Ciencias* 14, no. 1: 50. Cited in Juan J. Remos, *Historia de la literatura Cubana* (Havana: Cárdenas y Compañía, 1945), vol. 1, 279–280; Bueno, *Figuras cubanas*, 212; and Bueno, *La crítica*, 35.

8. Guerra, *Manual de historia*, 342–343.

9. In his political letters, Del Monte accuses Tacón of being a despot. See, for example, his letter "Al Redactor de *El Correo Nacional* de Madrid," dated June 30, 1838, in his *Escritos*, vol. 1, ed. José A. Fernández de Castro (Havana: Cultural, 1929), 103–109.

10. Del Monte, "Estado de la población blanca y de color de la Isla de Cuba, en 1839," in *Escritos*, 144–159.

11. See José Luciano Franco, *Las minas*.

12. During the fight for colonial independence, Deputy Miguel Guridi y Alcócer was the first to propose an end to slavery. While the new constitution was being debated in the March 26, 1811, session, he proposed the following: An end to the slave trade, salaries for slaves, absolute right for slaves to buy their freedom, and better treatment for those who remained in servitude. One month later, for moral and religious reasons, the liberal deputy Agustín Arguelles offered a less radical approach, limiting himself to the elimination of the slave trade. He believed that once the slave trade ended, masters would treat their slaves better. He also recognized opposition from interest parties. Both Guridi's and Arguelles's propositions were sent for further study to a committee, from which they never emerged. The debates inscribed in the *Diario de las Cortes* were answered by Arango y Parreño, who argued that slavery "pertains to our lives, to all of our future, and that of our descendants." See Levi Marrero, *Cuba*, vol. 9, 28–33, my translation.

13. Ibid., 19, 23–25.

14. See Varela's "Memorias" in *Documentos para la historia de Cuba*, ed. Hortensia Pichardo (Havana: Instituto del Libro, 1971), vol. 1, 269–275.

15. Torres-Cuevas and Sorhegui, eds., *José Antonio Saco*, 23.

16. See Saco's "Análisis por don José Antonio Saco de una obra sobre el Brazil, intitulada, *Notices of Brazil in 1828 and 1829, by Rev. R. Walsh, Author of a Journey from Constantinople, etc.*," in *Colección*, vol. 2, 30–90. In particular, see a reworking of "Mi primera pregunta" in "La supresión del tráfico de esclavos africanos en la isla de Cuba, examinada con relación a su agricultura y a su seguridad, por don José Antonio Saco," in ibid., 90–154.

17. Torres-Cuevas and Sorhegui, eds., *José Antonio Saco*, 44.

18. Saco, *Colección*, vol. 2, 161–162. Also cited in Torres-Cuevas and Sorhegui, eds., *José Antonio Saco*, 39, my translation.

19. Guerra, *Manual de historia*, 380–383.

20. Ibid., 384–391.

21. Although there were economic reasons for ending the slave trade, there were also important moral and religious ones. For example, in the United States the Quakers played an important part in having the Continental Congress declare itself against the slave trade. In Britain, William Wilberforce, an evangelist, for twenty years led the campaign in Parliament to abolish slavery. See Marrero, *Cuba*, 26.

22. Guerra summarizes the treaty between England and Spain as follows: (1) Immediate suppression of the slave traffic north of the equator. (2) Its end south of the equator after April 22, 1821. (3) Great Britain would compensate owners whose ships were captured by British cruisers. For this,

a Mixed Commission would be appointed to determine the amount of the compensation. (4) Within a specified period, British cruisers would not be able to capture or detain Spanish ships which transported slaves south of the equator. (5) The king would dictate the necessary orders to increase the white population of Cuba. (6) If the issues were not resolved, the slave trade would continue (*Manual de historia*, 256).

23. See Leslie B. Rout, *The African Experience in Spanish America* (New York: Cambridge University Press, 1976), 289–290.

24. Guerra, *Manual de historia*, 408. In a letter to Manuel Sanguily dated April 1886, Francisco Jimeno explains the composition of the Mixed Commission in which the British consul in Havana, Mr. Tolme, a businessman living on the island and owner of farms and slaves, was replaced by Mr. David Turnbull, known for his abolitionist ideas. Turnbull was the nightmare of the captain generals interested in contraband slaves. (Biblioteca Nacional José Martí, Clasificación: C.M., Morales, 22, no. 10). Cited in Roberto Friol, *Suite para Juan Francisco Manzano* (Havana: Editorial Arte y Literatura, 1977), 31, note 5.

25. See Richard Robert Madden, *The Memoirs (Chiefly Autobiographical) from 1798 to 1886 of Richard Robert Madden*, ed. Thomas More Madden (London: Ward and Downey, 1891), 76. Cited in Edward J. Mullen, ed., *The Life and Poems* (Hamden, Conn.: Archon Books, 1981), 7.

26. Suárez y Romero started writing his narrative in Puentes Grandes and concluded in the Surinam sugar mill. Del Monte's request is made explicit in a letter to the patrician. See *Centón epistolario de Domingo del Monte* (Havana: Imprenta "El Siglo XX," 1930), vol. 4, 38–39.

27. Adriana Lewis Galanes, "El Album de Domingo del Monte (Cuba, 1838/39)," 263–265.

28. See *The Life and Poems*, 130–131. The interview in Spanish is reproduced in Del Monte, *Escritos*, 133–143.

29. Del Monte, *Centón epistolario*, vol. 4, 83, my emphasis.

30. Ibid., 86.

31. Ibid., vol. 3, 168–169.

32. Esteban Rodríguez Herrera, "Estudio crítico a *Cecilia Valdés*," in *Acerca de Cirilo Villaverde* (Havana: Editorial Letras Cubanas, 1982), 176–177.

33. Del Monte, *Centón epistolario*, vol. 3, 116. Also cited by Salvador Bueno, "La narrativa antiesclavista en Cuba de 1835 a 1839," *Cuadernos Hispanoamericanos*, nos. 451–452 (1988): 178–179. Bueno mentions that there were three stories which made up Tanco's *Escenas de la vida privada en la isla de Cuba:* "Petrona y Rosalía," "El hombre misterioso," and "Historia de Francisco."

34. Although I recognize the importance of *Sab* as an antislavery novel, I have decided not to discuss it here in detail since my primary concern is to analyze the works inspired by Del Monte.

35. Salvador Bueno, *Historia de la literatura cubana* (Havana: Editorial Nacional de Cuba, 1963), 172.

36. Cited by Cruz, "Sab," 43, my translation. Two years later, Tanco would repeat the same idea in a letter dated June 7, 1838.

37. See the letters dated April 14 and May 2, 1836, in González del Valle, *La vida literaria*, 19–27.

38. Echenique's opening paragraph reads as follows: "Man is born naturally free and in entering society he modifies and converts his natural liberty into civil, subject to God and the Laws. It is the principle of law that man presumes himself to be naturally free so long as the opposite is not proven, because slavery is against the natural law." See Marrero, *Cuba*, 42. The solution, according to Marrero, was reached for the following reasons: The Haitian rebellion could be extended to eastern Cuba and the miners could serve as bad examples for slaves arriving at Cuban shores and pose a danger to whites (39–47). This information is also cited by Benítez Rojo, "Azúcar/Poder/Texto," 98–99.

39. Del Monte, *Centón epistolario*, vol. 3, 37–38. In a subsequent letter dated August 18, Padrines answers Del Monte's remarks in two letters of July 27 and August 5 regarding the composition. In it, Padrines recognizes that the blacks are more a part of his imagination than nature and promises to alter the description. He also plans to contrast the beauty of the countryside with the horrors of slavery, thus continuing to imitate nature. Of importance, Padrines states that the sections entitled "La Exposición" and "Súplica" were written two years before, perhaps in 1834, making his work one of the precursors of the antislavery theme (43–44). We are not sure if this composition was ever published. In another letter dated August 27, 1840, Padrines admits not having continued his writings because he needed to make a living selling honey (vol. 4, 176).

40. González del Valle, *La vida literaria*, 152, my translation.

41. "El calesero," in *Tipos y costumbres*, ed. Miguel de Villa (Havana: Imprenta del Avisador Comercial, 1881), 108–110.

42. Anselmo Suárez y Romero, *Francisco* (Havana: Biblioteca Básica de Autores Cubanos, 1970), 37, my translation.

43. Richard L. Jackson, *The Black Image*, 23–31.

44. René Girard, *Deceit, Desire, and the Novel*, trans. Yvonne Freccero (Baltimore: Johns Hopkins Press, 1965), 13.

45. Mario Cabrera Saqui, "Vida, pasión y gloria de Anselmo Suárez y Romero," in Suárez y Romero, *Francisco*, 221.

46. See Rolando Hernáldez Morelli, "Noticias, lugar y texto," 73–84.

47. José Antonio Fernández de Castro, *Tema negro en las letras de Cuba* (Havana: Ediciones Mirador, 1943), 41, my translation.

48. Del Monte, *Centón epistolario*, vol. 3, 118. Also cited in "La narrativa antiesclavista en Cuba de 1835 a 1839," 176. Also see A. M. Eligio de la Puente's introduction to Palma's *Cuentos cubanos* (Havana: Cultura S.A., 1928) and Benítez Rojo, "Azúcar/Poder/Texto," 111.

49. See "Petrona y Rosalía," in *Cuentos cubanos del siglo XIX*, ed. Salvador Bueno (Havana: Editorial de Arte y Literatura, 1977), 103–137.

50. Mary Cruz is mistaken when she suggests that Rosalía and Fernando, as in Villaverde's novel, are brother and sister. See her "Sab," 38.

51. González del Valle, *La vida literaria*, 65–69.
52. Bueno, *Figuras cubanas*, 222.
53. Del Monte, *Centón epistolario*, vol. 4, 83. Although this letter has no date, the editor placed it between letters dated August 20 and September 23, 1839. In the same letter, Madden praises Del Monte for guiding the youth of Cuba and advises him and Luz to put their minor literary differences aside for the sake of the country. Moreover, in defense of the creoles, Madden, unlike his predecessor McCleary, believes that creole proprietors are hostile to the slave trade. Madden ends his letter by offering to help free Manzano, whom I believe was emancipated in 1835 (84).
54. Ibid., 44–45, my translation.
55. González del Valle, *La vida literaria*, 59, my translation.
56. Suárez y Romero, *Francisco*, 49, 70.
57. Zoila Danger Roll, *Los cimarrones de El Frijol* (Santiago de Cuba: Empresa Editorial Oriente, 1979), 16–17. The slave ordinance of 1842 also mentions the twenty-five-lash limit (18–20). Also see Fernando Ortiz, *Los negros esclavos*, 233, 448. The same information is cited in Suárez y Romero, *Francisco*, 183, note 19. In his novel, Antonio Zambrana mentions that said order was never obeyed (*El negro Francisco* [Havana: Fernández y Cía., 1953], 115).
58. See note 15.
59. González del Valle, *La vida literaria*, 91–94; also in Suárez y Romero, *Francisco*, 221–223.
60. See Villaverde's prologue to *Cecilia Valdés* and González del Valle, *La vida literaria*, 139.
61. Coulthard, *Race and Colour*, 9–11.
62. González del Valle, *La vida literaria*, 139.
63. Danger Roll, *Los cimarrones*, 23.
64. Mullen, ed., *Life and Poems*, 89. The brackets contain my translation.
65. This book shows that Madden was also interested in protecting the economy of the West Indies. See Suárez y Romero, *Francisco*, 172–174, note 2.
66. See, for example, Bueno, "La narrativa antiesclavista," 169–186 and in particular 183. Bueno associates slave passivity with reformist attitudes to better the slave condition rather than abolish slavery.
67. Ileana Rodríguez, "Romanticismo literario y liberalismo reformista: El grupo de Domingo Delmonte," *Caribbean Studies* 20, no. 1 (1980): 35–56.
68. Juan Francisco Manzano, *Autobiografía de un esclavo*, ed. Ivan Schulman (Madrid: Ediciones Guadarrama, 1975), 30.
69. Carbonel, *Crítica*.
70. See José Luciano Franco, "La conjura de los negreros," in *Ensayos históricos*.
71. See Turnbull's letter of November 14, 1841, to Del Monte, *Centón epistolario*, vol. 5, 53.
72. For Turnbull's plan, see Guerra, *Manual de historia*, 437–439; for Del Monte's letter to Everett, see 441–444.

73. Marrero, *Cuba*, 83, and Guerra, *Manual de historia*, 437–449.

74. See Gaspar Betancourt Cisneros's letter dated January 29, 1843, to Del Monte. *Centón epistolario*, vol. 5, 90.

75. In a July 31, 1843, letter to Del Monte, Daniel K. Whitaker states that Everett is waiting for information from the patrician to prepare an essay on the political relations of Cuba. In the same letter, Whitaker announces that Del Monte is writing an article for the *Southern Quarterly Review* on Spanish literature. Ibid., 117.

76. Del Monte's position is stated in a letter to Everett dated November 20, 1842. See Marrero, *Cuba*, 83–84, and Thomas, *Cuba*, 207.

77. Del Monte, *Centón epistolario*, vol. 5, 102, 121–122, 130.

78. Saco, *Colección de papeles*, vol. 3, 187. Cited in Torres-Cuevas and Sorhegui, eds., *José Antonio Saco*, 45, my translation. Also see Guerra, *Manual de historia*, 405–406.

79. For a summary of his essay, see Guerra, *Manual de historia*, 295.

80. Gaspar Betancourt Cisneros, El Lugareño, expresses this idea in a letter dated September 24, 1842. See Del Monte, *Centón epistolario*, vol. 5, 85.

81. Ibid., 116.

82. A letter from Miguel de Aldama y Alfonso, ibid., 150.

83. Ibid., 162–164. This letter is dated November 27, 1843. Although it may be difficult to measure, we can presume that the fear worked to the advantage of slavers insofar as it may have brought all whites, in some degree, together.

84. This information is contained in a letter dated December 29, 1843. See ibid., 186. Marrero cites the same information but changes the punctuation and writes November instead of December as the month in question (90).

85. Ibid., 186–187, my translation.

86. Ibid., 181.

87. Ibid., 183–184.

88. Ibid., 92, my translation.

89. Ibid., 92–93, my translation.

90. Fernández de Castro, *Tema negro*, 27–28, my translation.

91. Zambrana, *El negro Francisco*, 152–153, my translation.

92. See his introduction to *El negro Francisco*.

93. For a relationship between Suárez y Romero's novel as fiction and Manzano's work as fact, see César Leante's "Dos obras antiesclavistas cubanas," *Cuadernos Americanos* 4 (1976): 175–188.

94. The request was initiated by don Alonso de Cácerez in 1514 and presented to the municipality of Havana on April 26, 1641. See Danger Roll, *Los cimarrones*, 15–22.

95. Fernández de Castro points out that the lack of a dominant slavery theme among black Cuban writers (and even some white writers) might be attributed to fear of repression by the existing regime. But he also points out that men like Heredia and Domingo del Monte did denounce slavery in their respective works (*Tema negro*, 35–37). Jackson suggests that black

writers have a privileged insight into slavery. See his *Black Writers in Latin America* (Albuquerque: University of New Mexico Press, 1979).

96. My translation. For the sake of clarity, I have chosen to translate from Schulman's edition (*Autobiografía*, 30). This segment is absent in Madden's translation.

97. The second part of Manzano's autobiography was supposed to have been more daring than the first. Writers like Jackson have suggested that it would have been a definitive statement against slavery. We have no way of knowing, since it was lost while in the possession of Ramón de Palma. Jackson speculates the content of part 2 in his *Black Writers*, 32–34.

98. This letter is cited by Friol in his introduction to the diary. See "Cirilo Villaverde: *Diario del rancheador*," *Revista de la Biblioteca Nacional José Martí* 64, no. 1 (1973): 49, my translation. In a subsequent letter to Rosas dated March 20, Villaverde clarifies that the diary covered five years of Estévez's life; that he, Villaverde, copied it in 1843; and that his father was one of the inspectors of the slave hunters.

99. The first part was published in *El Album* in August 1838 and the second in *Faro Industrial de la Habana* in July 1842.

100. For references to these statistics, see, for example, Marrero, *Cuba*, 193–195.

101. Marrero has edited a selection of Cantero and Laplante's 1857 book. See *Los ingenios* (Barcelona: Gráficas M. Pareja, 1984), xxii. Referring to the 1860 statistics, Rebecca Scott agrees that in comparison to other regions, the far-western province of Pinar del Río was not very important for sugar. *Slave Emancipation in Cuba*, 23.

102. See the statistics provided by Marrero in *Cuba*, 216.

103. Estévez, *Diario*, 66, my translation.

104. Ortiz, *Los negros esclavos*, 372, my translation.

105. Ibid.

106. See Friol's introduction, in which he cites a Villaverde letter dated July 17, 1884 (*Diario*, 51).

107. Ortiz, *Los negros esclavos*, 366.

108. José Luciano Franco, "Los cobreros y los palenques de negros cimarrones," *Revista de la Biblioteca Nacional José Martí* 64, no. 1 (1973): 38, my translation.

109. Ortiz, *Los negros esclavos*, 366.

110. Francisco Calcagno, *Romualdo, uno de tantos* (Havana: El Pilar, 1891), 47, my translation. Also cited by Friol in his introduction to the diary, 51, note 5.

111. Estévez, *Diario*, 64, my translation.

112. Ibid., 47–148, and "El rancheador," in *Un siglo de relato latinoamericano* (Havana: Casa de las Américas, 1976), 87–99.

113. Estévez, *Diario*, 86, my translation. References to Estévez's "Diario" will be made by the diary's date of entry, which will be cited in the text.

114. The March 31, 1842, entry provides an example of the discrepancies between Villaverde's copy and Estévez's original text (see *Diario*, 54). Immediately noticeable is that, in one instance, Villaverde states that Estévez re-

turned to his house on the 19th, where he received a letter dated the 16th, which stated that thirteen slaves had rebelled. The "original" informs us that Estévez returned to his house on the 1st, where he received a letter dated the 16th, in which eighteen slaves had rebelled.

115. Estévez, *Diario*, 69, my translation.

116. See my analysis of Manzano's *Autobiografía* in Chapter 2.

117. See quotation on 124 and note 102.

118. See, for example, Del Monte, *Centón epistolario*, vol. 5, 186.

## 2. Textual Multiplications

1. See Fina García Marruz, "De 'estudios delmontinos,'" *Revista de la Biblioteca Nacional José Martí* 11, no. 3 (1969): 29.

2. A list of names and amount of money each individual paid for Manzano's freedom appears in an unpublished manuscript housed in the Yale library. I have been given written permission to publish the notebook and had the opportunity to study it. I believe that it is the one Anselmo Suárez y Romero corrected and the one included in Richard Madden's anti-slavery portfolio. See "Obras completas de Juan Francisco Manzano, esclavo de la Isla de Cuba," copied by Nicolás M. de Ascárate, Madrid, January 15, 1852. After completing this section of Manzano's autobiography, I have been able to verify that many of the changes I have attributed to Madden were made by Suárez y Romero. However, I also believe that Madden made some changes on his own. For a study of Suárez y Romero's intervention in Manzano's autobiography, see my "Autobiografía del esclavo Juan Francisco Manzano: Versión de Suárez y Romero," in *La historia en la literatura iberoamericana*, ed. Raquel Chang-Rodríguez and Gabriella de Beer (Hanover, N.H.: Ediciones del Norte, 1989), 259–268.

3. This information is contained in some letters Manzano wrote to Del Monte. For a selection of these, see Francisco Calcagno, *Poetas de color* (Havana: Imprenta Militar de la V. de Soler y Compañía, 1878), 44. Although many critics cite 1838, Friol has uncovered that the autobiography was written earlier, in 1835. See *Suite*, 29.

4. See José Luciano Franco's edition of *Autobiografía, cartas y versos de Juan Fco. Manzano* (Havana: Municipio de la Habana, 1937). Unless otherwise indicated, all references to the original are from this edition and will appear parenthetically in the text.

5. *Obras, Juan Francisco Manzano* (Havana: Instituto de Libro, 1972).

6. Juan Francisco Manzano, *Autobiografía de un esclavo*, ed. Schulman.

7. Mullen, *Life and Poems*, 90.

8. Friol states that the 1937 edition served as a basis for the one published in Budapest in 1970. See Friol, *Suite*, 45.

9. Vitier, "Dos poetas cubanos Plácido y Manzano," *Bohemia* 65, no. 50 (1973): 21.

10. Frank Kermode, *The Sense of an Ending* (New York: Oxford University Press, 1975).

11. For the sake of expediency and unless otherwise indicated, I have decided to cite from Richard Madden's translation as it appears in Edward J.

Mullen's edition. See 90. References to Madden's English translation of Manzano's autobiography will appear parenthetically in the text.

12. Manzano's original is more explicit and states: "My mother left without money." See Manzano, *Autobiografía*, ed. Franco, 53.

13. For a list of these and other publications, see ibid., 27–28, and Calcagno, *Diccionario*, 43 and note 2.

14. Friol, *Suite*, 34.

15. See the appropriate letters in González del Valle, *La vida literaria*.

16. Manzano, *Autobiografía*, ed. Franco, 83–84, my translation.

17. Friol, *Suite*, 51, note 19.

18. Manzano, *Autobiografía*, ed. Franco, 80.

19. Ibid., 85, my translation.

20. In this comparative analysis, for the sake of clarity I have decided to cite not the work but the editors and the corresponding pages of the English and Spanish editions of Manzano's autobiography. I have translated this and the next quotation from the Spanish since these two sections are missing in the English. I have provided the page where the quotation should have appeared.

21. Friol, *Suite*, 166–167, my translation.

22. Manzano's allusion to freedom suggests that Del Monte's letter had raised the subject, perhaps to offer support and comfort during the time of writing. The first paragraph of the September letter describes Manzano's happiness with regard to the news he received: "My dear and Mr. don Domingo: Today I have received your interesting answer which I have read and reread more than ten times with the same pleasure, each reading heightening my hope which I cannot help but manifest; devouring the sentences, I would like to have in my hands the time to abbreviate my execution for such a lucky day" (Friol, *Suite*, 166–167, my translation).

23. This idea is expressed by Richard Jackson in his "Slavery, Racism and Autobiography in Two Early Black Writers: Juan Francisco Manzano and Martín Morúa Delgado," in *Voices from Under*, ed. William Luis (Westport, Conn.: Greenwood Press, 1984), 56.

24. Manzano, *Autobiografía*, ed. Franco, 83, my translation.

25. Ibid., 84.

26. Danger Roll, *Los cimarrones*, 15–22.

27. Calcagno, *Diccionario*, 41, my translation. Others attest to the same information. In a letter to Del Monte, Suárez y Romero repeats that Palma lost the manuscript and commits himself to copying the manuscript in the event that Manzano wrote it again (Del Monte, *Centón epistolario*, vol. 4, 81–88). This information is also corroborated by Madden, who sheds some light on the matter: "It [the autobiography] was written in two parts—the second part fell into the hands of persons connected with his former master, and I fear it is not likely to be restored to the person to whom I am indebted for the first portion of this manuscript. As far, however, as this portion goes, I have no hesitation in saying, it is the most perfect picture of Cuban slavery that ever has been given to the world, and so full and faithful in its details, that it is difficult to imagine, that the portion which has been suppressed,

can throw any greater light on the evils of this system, than the first part has done" (Mullen, *Life and Poems*, 39). This latter assertion places into question Richard Jackson's statement regarding the militancy of the second part of Manzano's autobiography (see Jackson, "Slavery," 58).

28. See note 2 and Friol, *Suite*, 17, note 3.

29. For information about Manzano's life, see Calcagno, *Diccionario*, 42–44, Friol, *Suite*, 153–212, and Manzano, *Autobiografía*, ed. Franco, 20–32. However, Calcagno is mistaken when he states that Manzano's supporters paid $500 for his liberty (42). For a list of those who contributed to Manzano's freedom, see Azcárate, "Obras completas," 323–325.

30. "Carta a José Luis Alfonso, marqués de Montelo," in *Revista de la Biblioteca Nacional* 2, nos. 1 and 2 (1909): 141–142. Also in García Marruz, "De 'estudios,'" 38, and in Friol, *Suite*, 168–169, my translation. I believe that the copy Calcagno cites is the same one Suárez y Romero corrected and the same one Azcárate copied. The note which I have cited also appears at the end of the Azcárate version. Also see note 2.

31. Calcagno, *Diccionario*, 41.

32. "Declaración de Plácido," fjs. 144, 2nd pieza, Legajo 52, no. 1. Also in García Marruz, "De 'estudios,'" 30.

33. For the most complete study to date on Manzano, see Friol, *Suite*. For additional information about Manzano's life, see Mullen, *Life and Poems*, 39.

34. Friol, *Suite*, 231, my translation.

35. Belkis Cuza Malé states: "The task of the copy writer included taking control of the text, writing, adding, or correcting as he deemed necessary," my translation. See her "Anselmo Suárez y Romero: ¿Esclavista?" *Linden Lane Magazine* 4, no. 1 (1985): 10.

36. For the life and abolitionist activities of Richard Madden, see Mullen, *Life and Poems*, 5–13.

37. Calcagno, *Diccionario*, 31, my translation.

38. David R. Murray, "Richard Robert Madden: His Career as a Slavery Abolitionist," *Studies 61* (1972): 49, cited in Mullen, *Life and Poems*, 8.

39. Ibid., 8.

40. See the *Eclectic Review*, no. 8 (1841): 236, cited in ibid., 11, 12.

41. "The Proceedings of the General Anti-Slavery Convention held in London, 1840," *Eclectic Review*, 233, cited in ibid., 30, note 28.

42. Ibid., 37.

43. Ibid., 38.

44. See ibid., 39. Also in Friol, *Suite*, 36. In a follow-up note, Mullen indicates that the Spaniard was Suárez y Romero. I disagree. Suárez y Romero corrected not the translation but the original; he was not a Spaniard but a Cuban.

45. To illustrate the differences between Franco's edition and the manuscript contained in the library, Friol makes the following comparison. The first paragraph of the 1937 edition reads as follows: "La Sra. Da. Beatriz de Justiz de Sta. Ana, esposa del Sor. Dn Juan Manzano, tenia gusto de cada vez que iva a su famosa asienda el Molino de tomar bonitas criollas, cuando eran

de dies a onse años; las traia consigo y dándoles una educasión conforme a su clase y condision, estaba siempre su casa llena de criadas instruidas en todo lo necesario pa el servisio de ella no asiendose de este notable la falta de tres o cuatro qe no estubiesen aptas pr sus años dolensias o livertad y entre las escojidas fue una Ma. del Pilar Manzano, mi madre, qe del servisio de la mano de la Sra. Marqueza Justiz en su mayor edad, era una de las criadas de distinción o de estimasion o de razon como quiera que se llame." Friol continues: "Original: Enmiendas y tachaduras que aparecen en el mismo párrafo: '. . . su famosa acienda el Molino tomaba las mas bonitas criollas [tachado *ba* y sustituido por *r*; agregado *de* delante del nuevo infinitivo].' '. . . estaba su casa siempre abastecida . . . [tachado *abastecida* y sustituido por llena; tachado *siempre* y cambiado de lugar, ahora precede a *su casa*].' '. . . qe no estubiesen pr. sus edad dolencias o libertad &c. [tachado *edad*]'" (Friol, *Suite*, 43–44).

46. See, for example, *Of Grammatology*, trans. Gayatri Chakravorty Spivak (Baltimore: Johns Hopkins University Press, 1976).

47. See "Cecilia Valdés," *La Siempreviva* 2 (1839): 75–87, 242–254.

48. See *Cecilia Valdés* (Havana: Imprenta Literaria de Lino Valdés, 1839).

49. See *Cecilia Valdés* (New York: Imprenta de El Espejo, 1882).

50. See "El capitalinismo habanero," in Loló de la Torriente, *La Habana de Cecilia Valdés* (Havana: Jesús Montero, 1946), 6. Olga Blondet and Antonio Tudisco confirm that "*Cecilia Valdés* is an antislavery and revolutionary novel in which wc can find the first expression of Cuban life as tragedy." See their edition of *Cecilia Valdés* (Madrid: Anaya, 1971), 18.

51. For example, Loló de la Torriente does not acknowledge that Villaverde made changes in the first volume and believes that the first volume was published in 1839 and the second in 1879. See "Cirilo Villaverde y la novela cubana," in *Acerca de Cirilo Villaverde*, ed. Imeldo Alvarez, 130. Olga Blondet and Antonio Tudisco express the same misconception in an introduction to their edition of *Cecilia Valdés* (17, 20). Enrique Sosa also complains about critics, like Diego Vicente Tejera, who do not acknowledge the publication of the first version. See his "Apreciaciones sobre el plan y método de Cirilo Villaverde para la versión definitiva de *Cecilia Valdés:* Su historisimo consciente," in *Acerca de Cirilo Villaverde*, 382. In his edition of *Cecilia Valdés*, Ivan Schulman's brief introduction coincides with some of the ideas expressed in this study. But unlike my interpretation, Schulman looks for the racial and sociopolitical elements of the last edition in the first two. Although I do agree with Esteban Rodríguez Herrera that Villaverde's early intention was not to write an antislavery novel, I disagree with Schulman, who adds that Villaverde did not do so because the author was forced into silence. Furthermore, I contend that the definitive version is more of an antislavery novel than Schulman would have us believe. This is particularly evident in the second part of the novel, when the Gamboas travel to their sugar estate. See Schulman's prologue in his edition of *Cecilia Valdés* (Caracas: Biblioteca Ayacucho, 1981), xiii–xviii.

52. Del Monte identifies the three censors as the district censor, the

*sota-censor*, a military officer of the palace, and the captain general. Alvarez García, "La obra narrativa de Cirilo Villaverde," in *Cecilia Valdés*, 28.

53. Julio C. Sánchez, *La obra novelística de Cirilo Villaverde* (Madrid: De Orbe Novo, 1973), 20–21, my translation. For additional information about Villaverde's life, see articles in *Acerca de Cirilo Villaverde*.

54. See Villaverde, *El penitente* (Havana: Editorial la Burgalesa, 1925). Also see Juan J. Remos, *Historia de la literatura cubana*, vol. 2, 174–179.

55. De la Torriente, "San Carlos, foco de cultura," in *La Habana de Cecilia Valdés*, 107–112.

56. M. Eligio de la Puente, "Prólogo a *Dos amores*," in *Acerca de Cirilo Villaverde*, 106–107.

57. See Villaverde, *El ave muerta*, *Miscelánea de Util y Agradable Recreo* 1 (August 1837). Also see Eligio de la Puente, "Prólogo a *Dos amores*," 112–113 and Sánchez, *La obra novelística*, 49–50.

58. Ramón de Palma, "La novela," in *Acerca de Cirilo Villaverde*, 15–26.

59. Ramón de Palma, "Crítica del *Espetón de oro*," in ibid., 27–29.

60. Morúa Delgado, *Obras completas*, vol. 5, 15–81.

61. *Cecilia Valdés*, ed. Blondet and Tudisco, 59.

62. *Cecilia Valdes or Angel's Hill*, trans. Sydney G. Gest (New York: Vantage Press, 1962), 16.

63. See María Luz de Nora, "Cartas de Cirilo Villaverde a Julio Rosas," *Bohemia* 57, no. 40 (1965): 100–101, my translation.

64. See Villaverde, *Escursión a Vuelta Abajo* (Havana: Editorial Letras Cubanas, 1981) and Estévez, *Diario de un rancheador*, 47–148. Estévez wrote his diary between 1837 and 1842, about the same time Villaverde wrote his travel book. Estévez was a commissioned slave hunter who distorted the slavery system even further. Villaverde's father was a member of the Junta de Fomento, which formed and inspected slave-hunting groups. The senior Villaverde was one of Estévez's inspectors and had the diary which Villaverde later copied.

65. See Friol's introduction to the *Diario de un rancheador*.

66. See, for example, Eligio de la Puente, "Prólogo," and Remos, *Historia*.

67. Imeldo Alvarez, "La obra narrativa de Cirilo Villaverde," in *Acerca de Cirilo Villaverde*, 303–304.

68. For information about López, see Guerra, *Manual de historia*, 480–494.

69. See Villaverde, *General Lopez, the Cuban Patriot* (New York: 1851).

70. See Villaverde, *El señor Saco con respecto a la revolución de Cuba* (New York: La Verónica, 1852). For a discussion regarding the annexation of Cuba to the United States, see Guerra, *Manual de historia*, 495–565.

71. See, for example, Remos, *Historia*, 168, and Alvarez, *Acerca*, 305–306.

72. See Villaverde, *La revolución de Cuba vista desde Nueva York* (New York: 1869).

73. See Jorge Ibarra, *Aproximaciones a Clío* (Havana: Editorial de Ciencias Sociales, 1979), 51–79.

74. Cited by Sosa, *La economía*, 385, my translation.
75. Remos, *Historia*, 169, and Sánchez, *La obra novelística*, 32–33.
76. See the Havana edition, 48.
77. See Luz de Nora, "Cartas de Cirilo Villaverde," 100.
78. Friol states that "of the 246 pages of *Cecilia Valdés*, of 1839, 195 are dedicated to the 23 of October, 1831, the eve of the Fiesta de San Rafael." "La novela cubana en el siglo XIX," *Unión* 6, no. 4 (1968): 199.
79. I have decided to cite from *Cecilia Valdes or Angel's Hill*. Mariano J. Lorente's translation, *The Quadroon or Cecilia Valdes* (Boston: L. C. Page and Company, 1935), makes important omissions. All references are to Gest's translation and they will appear parenthetically in the text.
80. Some of Sosa's ideas coincide with the ones developed here. He breaks down the structure of the novel by chapters and dates: Part 1, chapter 1, 1812; chapters 2–3, 1823; chapters 4–12, 1828. Part 2, chapters 1–2, 1829; chapters 3–17, 1830. Part 3, chapters 1–9, 1830. Part 4, chapter 1, 1830; chapters 2–7, 1831. Sosa notices that twenty-five of the chapters, approximately half the novel, take place in 1831; between 1812 and 1823 there are three chapters; none between 1828 and 1831; and forty-one between 1828 and 1831. Of the ones which narrate 1830, about 40 percent take place during the months of November and December. Sosa suggests that Villaverde's interest was to describe Cecilia during her most attractive years. Sosa looks for meaning by comparing Cecilia Valdés to Villaverde's own biography. However, he also takes into consideration the history of the period. I disagree with Sosa, who believes that the novel ends in 1831. See his "Apreciaciones sobre el plan y el método de Cirilo Villaverde," 381–409.
81. Critics commenting on the time of the novel claim, as Villaverde does in his prologue, that the novel ends in 1831. See, for example, *Cecilia Valdés*, Blondet and Tudisco, 36, and Sosa, *La economía*, 387–388.
82. Unlike Sosa, Friol considers Cirilo Villaverde's and Cecilia Valdés's coincidence in initials and date of birth as false clues (*Suite*, 200).
83. See, for example, José Luciano Franco, *Las conspiraciones de 1810 y 1812* (Havana: Editorial de Ciencias Sociales, 1977).
84. See Pedro Deschamps Chapeaux, "Francisco Uribe: El sastre de moda," *Contribución a la historia de la gente sin historia* (Havana: Editorial de Ciencias Sociales, 1984), 55–65.
85. Deschamps Chapeaux states that Varona died during an epidemic in 1833. "Los sastres," *El negro en la economía habanera del siglo XIX*, 143. The date I have cited is from his *Contribución a la historia*, which is more precise, accompanied by an endnote: Archivo Nacional, *Escribanía de Junco*, leg. 127, no. 1850, 60 and 65, note 8.
86. For a biography of these and other tailors, see Deschamps Chapeaux, "Francisco Uribe: El sastre de moda" and "Los sastres."
87. Deschamp Chapeaux, "Los sastres," 144–148.
88. Nicolás Guillén, *Brindis de Salas* (Havana: Cuadernos de Historia Habanera, 1936). Also cited by Deschamp Chapeaux, "Los músicos," 107, my translation.
89. Deschamp Chapeaux, "Los músicos," 108–109. Deschamp's dates

do not coincide with those provided by Helio Orovio, who suggests that Brindis de Salas returned to Cuba in 1848, was imprisoned, and received his freedom two years later. See his *Diccionario de la música cubana* (Havana: Editorial Letras Cubanas, 1981), 60.

90. Buelta y Flores, who died in 1851, owned sixteen houses and his wealth was estimated between 45,000 and 50,000. Deschamp Chapeaux, 116–117.

91. Morúa Delgado, *Obras completas*, vol. 5, my translation. In his article, Morúa criticizes Villaverde for his historical aberration and deformation of characters. In particular, he claims that Villaverde presents Uribe as an enemy of whites. From a different perspective, Uribe is described as a man who is aware of the distinction between the races and his own social position within the society. And even if Villaverde imposed certain accusations on Uribe during the Ladder Conspiracy, there is no evidence in the novel that he conspired against whites or that his actions were serious enough to justify the government accusations against him.

92. For information about Plácido, see De la Torriente, *La Habana de Cecilia Valdés*, 139–148 and *Diccionario de la literatura cubana* (Havana: Editorial Letras Cubanas, 1988), vol. 2, 1059–1061.

93. De la Torriente, *La Habana de Cecilia Valdés*, 141.

94. *Diccionario de la literatura cubana*, vol. 2, 1059–1061.

95. Leante, "*Cecilia Valdés*, espejo de la esclavitud," in *El espacio real* (Havana: UNEAC, 1975), 29–42.

96. Freud, *Totem and Taboo*, trans. James Strachey (New York: Norton, 1950), 4–5.

97. Manzano, *Autobiografía de un esclavo*, ed. Schulman.

98. Antonio Zambrana, *El negro Francisco*.

## 3. Time in Fiction

1. See Calcagno, *Diccionario*, 605, my translation.

2. *Romualdo, uno de tantos* is the first antislavery novel published in Cuba before the emancipation of slaves. It was published under the title *Uno de tantos* in 1881, but the government confiscated the edition. In 1884, the author reproduced it as *Sin título* in the *Revista de Cuba*. Not until 1891 was it published as *Romualdo, uno de tantos*. See Remos, *Historia*, vol. 2, 573 and *Diccionario de la literatura cubana*, vol. 1, 172. Of the early antislavery narratives, only two went to print during the time the Del Monte group met and they were published abroad: Juan Francisco Manzano's in England in 1840 and Gertrudis Gómez de Avellaneda's *Sab* in Spain in 1841. Because of its antislavery position, Avellaneda's novel was banished from the island in 1844 but did appear in Cuba in the Havana magazine *El Museo* in numbers 31 to 50 in 1883, two years after Calcagno's novel. See Cruz, "*Sab*," 54.

3. Calcagno tells us that he published two mutilated stories, "El Coburgo" and "Memorias de un síndico," in 1865. See *Los crímenes de Concha* (Havana: Librería e Imprenta de Elías F. Casona, 1887).

4. Villaverde and Calcagno knew each other. They both worked together

and founded the magazine *La Habana* in 1858. See Max Henríquez Ureña, *Panorama histórico*, vol. 1, 286.

5. I disagree with Pedro Barreda, who views the interaction among the characters as a "series of chance occurrences." I believe that there is a conscious intent to create a tragic situation with which the reader can sympathize. See his *The Black Protagonist in the Cuban Novel* (Amherst: University of Massachusetts Press, 1979), 83.

6. *Romualdo, uno de tantos* (Havana: El Pilar de Manuel de Armas, 1891), 94. All citations to this work are my translations and references to it will appear parenthetically in the text.

7. The time of Calcagno's writing is mentioned on page 85.

8. Guerra, *Manual de historia*, 384–392. The year 1836 is also important for Romualdo. There is a coincidence between the dates and his age. Born in 1800, Romualdo was stolen at the age of six and remained in slavery for thirty years. In 1836 Romualdo was thirty-six years old.

9. As compensation for the pacification of Oriente, Tacón was named marqués de la Unión de Cuba and vizconde of Bayamo. See Portuondo, *Historia de Cuba*, 333.

10. Calcagno, *Diccionario*, 610–611, my translation.

11. Portuondo, *Historia de Cuba*, 331.

12. See chapter 11, 117–123 and Calcagno, *Diccionario*, 544, my translation.

13. See Guerra, *Manual de historia*, 712–713.

14. For an account of the War of 1868, see Thomas, *Cuba*, 245–253.

15. A similar relationship between the past and the present is highlighted by José Antonio Saco, who was elected as a representative in the elections of March 25, 1866. Regarding the elections, Guerra writes: "A treinta años de distancia se repetía la victoria de 1836 contra Tacón" (*Manual de historia*, 629).

16. Marrero, *Cuba*, 118, my translation.

17. Thomas, *Cuba*, 252.

18. Remos, *Historia*, vol. 2, 573.

19. I have been unable to document the veracity of Hipólito's story.

20. Francisco Calcagno, *Aponte* (Barcelona: Tipografía de Francisco Costa, 1901), 10. All citations of this work are my translations and references to it will appear parenthetically in the text.

21. Calcagno, *Diccionario*, 40–41, my translation.

22. Mustelier, *La extinción del negro* (Havana: Imprenta dc Rambla, Bouza y Compañía 1912), 49, my translation.

23. Ibid., 49–50, my translation.

24. Ibid., 63, my translation.

25. See Calcagno, *Poetas de color*, 25–46.

26. *En busca del eslabón: Historía de monos* (Barcelona: Imprenta de Salvador Manero, 1888), 189.

27. Ibid., 175, my translation.

28. Ibid., 197.

29. At the end of the novel, the narrator tells us that Sinónimo published

his findings in a series of pamphlets with the following epigraphs: "1. El hombre procede de la transformación secular de un solo individuo placentario, cuya especie ha desaparecido. 2. Los africanos pertenecen a la especie humana, y el eslabón si algún día se halla aparecerá entre estos y los antropomorfos actuales. 3. No hay datos aun para determinar cual sea el antecesor inmediato. 4. Que no es el hombre el único que aparece sin abuelos paleontológicos. 5. Que el hombre de hoy pasará y la *antropoplagia* o humanidad venidera será más perfecta que la actual, como la actual es más perfecta que la *antropopalia* o humanidad pasada" (ibid., 348–349).

30. See Calcagno, *Diccionario*, 40, my translation.

31. Morúa was the son of a Basque father and an African mother from the *gangá longoba* nation. See Pedro Deschamp Chapeaux's prologue to *La familia Unzúazu* (Havana: Editorial Arte y Literatura, 1975), 13. Leopoldo Horrego Estuch states that Morúa's mother was from the *gangá nongova* nation. See *Martín Morúa Delgado* (Havana: Editorial Sánchez, 1957), 7.

32. Morúa Delgado, *Obras completas*, vol. 1, xix.

33. Horrego Estuch, *Martín Morúa Delgado*, 88–92, 105.

34. See Morúa Delgado, "Al Lector" in *Sofía*.

35. Horrego Estuch, *Martín Morúa Delgado*, 105.

36. See Jorge Ibarra's "La Asamblea de Guáimaro" in his *Aproximaciones a Clío* (Havana: Editorial de Ciencias Sociales, 1979), 51–79.

37. See Herrera McElroy's "Martín Morúa Delgado precursor del Afro-Cubanismo," *Afro-Hispanic Review* 2, no. 1 (1983): 20.

38. See Juan Gualberto Gómez, *Por Cuba libre* (Havana: Editorial de Ciencias Sociales, 1974), 19–29.

39. See Thomas, *Cuba*, 267–269.

40. Morúa Delgado, *Obras completas*, vol. 5, 19. Morúa's literary impressions put into doubt Barreda's analysis regarding the influence of Zola's naturalism. See his comments in *The Black Protagonist*.

41. Morúa Delgado, *Obras completas*, vol. 5, 25, my translation.

42. Fernández de Castro, *Tema negro en las letras de Cuba* (Havana: Ediciones Mirador, 1943), 42–43.

43. Morúa Delgado, *Obras completas*, vol. 5, 31, my translation.

44. Ibid., 65–66, my translation; Morúa Delgado, *Obras completas*, vol. 5, 46–47.

45. See García Márquez, *Chronicle of a Death Foretold*, trans. Gregory Rabassa (New York: Knopf, 1983).

46. The latter act will also be repeated by Eladislao Gonzaga and Magdalena in *La familia Unzúazu*. But, unlike Cándido Gamboa, in Morúa's second novel Eladislao assumes the responsibility of rearing his own child, because like María Alarcón, Cecilia's mother, and Contrera, Sofía's mother, Magdalena is not fit to take care of her daughter.

47. See "El Ñáñigo," in *Tipos y costumbres*, 141–145, my translation.

48. For an account of slavery in the city, see Pedro Deschamps Chapeaux's "Cimarrones urbanos" in his and Juan Pérez de la Riva's *Contribución a la historia*, 29–52.

49. Pérez de la Riva, 31–32, my translation.

50. Morúa's attitude toward Maló may even be revealed in her name. If we remove the written accent, her name may suggest her true nature.

51. *La Revolución Cubana y la raza de color (apuntes y datos por un cubano sin odios)* (Key West: Imprenta "La Propaganda," 1895), 13–14.

52. *Contestación a dos desdichados autonomistas de la raza de color* (New York: Alfred Howes, 1898).

53. See Guillén, "Martín Morúa Delgado," in *La familia Unzúazu*, 247, my translation.

54. See Morúa's "Memorias," in *Obras completas*, vol. 5, 170–180. Also see Horrego Estuch, *Martín Morúa Delgado*, 28–32.

55. Richard Jackson has suggested that *La familia Unzúazu* is an autobiographical novel. However, his statement remains unsubstantiated in his book. See "From Antislavery to Antiracism: Martín Morúa Delgado, Black Novelist, Politician, and Critic of Postabolitionist Cuba," in *Black Writers*, 45–52.

56. Morúa Delgado, *Obras completas*, vol. 2, 305. All quotations from this work are my translations and references to it will appear parenthetically in the text.

57. See, for example, ibid., vol. 3, 110, note A.

58. Ibid., vol. 5, 174.

59. Julián González, *Martín Morúa Delgado: Impresiones sobre su última novela* (Havana: Imprenta de Rambla y Bouza, 1902), 29.

60. Ibarra, *Aproximaciones*, 74.

61. Horrego Estuch, *Martín Morúa Delgado*, 93–94.

62. Gonzaga admits that yesterday's slave cannot be today's companion. He prefers to enslave the spirit of those recently emancipated to stop the black conscience from rebelling and maintain old privileges. Here he sees a principle of humanity insofar as the manhood of inferior blacks will not suffer, thus eliminating any possible conflict among the races. Like Morúa, Gonzaga looks toward legislation as a way of preserving democracy without altering the social imbalance. Although such action will not last forever, it will be sufficient to strengthen the ranks of the superior race, which will ensure "moral unity, patriotism, and the completion of the Cuban ideal," Morúa Delgado, *Obras completas*, vol. 2, 168.

63. See "Nota a 'Factores sociales,'" in Ibid., vol. 3, 208.

64. Ibid., 224.

65. See Horrego Estuch, *Martín Morúa Delgado*, 94.

66. Morúa Delgado, "'Factores sociales,'" 233, my translation. Also see 227–228.

67. Horrego Estuch, *Martín Morúa Delgado*, 130.

68. Morúa Delgado, "'Factores sociales,'" 236, my translation.

69. Horrego Estuch, *Martín Morúa Delgado*, 139.

70. Ibid. For a discussion of the Platt Amendment, see 168–179. Also see González, *Martín Morúa Delgado*, 56–57.

71. González, *Martín Morúa Delgado*, 54.

72. Morúa Delgado, "'Factores sociales,'" 235.

73. Horrego Estuch, *Martín Morúa Delgado*, 248, my translation.

74. Jackson, *The Black Image*, 46.

75. For another contrast between Morúa and Gómez, see Guillén, *Brindis de Salas*, 260–265. Like González, Guillén admires Gómez.

76. Morúa Delgado, "'Factores sociales,'" 226, my translation.

77. Federico, whose character is consistent in both works, contrives a plan to extort money from his sister Magdalena and accuses Liberato of kidnapping him. In so doing, he also takes advantage of the slave's fear because the slave had just raped Ana María.

## 4. Historical Fictions

1. See "Henry William Macaulay, Esq. called in; and further Examined," *Committee of the House of Commons*, June 15, 1842, question 5495, 335.

2. See Malcolm Cowley's introduction to Brantz Mayer, *Adventures of an African Slaver* (New York: Albert and Charles Boni, 1928), xi. According to Harry Johnston, Portuguese explorers enslaved Moorish noblemen off the coast of the Sahara. Prince Henry, who desired to colonize Morocco, allowed the Moors to ransom themselves, for which they offered five or six "black Moors" for their freedom. Antam Gonsalvez returned to the Rio de Oro and, in exchange for the noblemen, received ten black Moors, some gold dust, ox hide, and ostrich eggs. The Portuguese learned of the availability of the black Moors, whom they considered to be better slaves than whites or those closest to the white race. See Johnston, *Liberia* (London: Hutchinson and Company, 1906), 104–105.

3. Bartolomé de las Casas, *History of the Indies*, trans. and ed. Andrée M. Collard (New York: Harper and Row, 1971), 257.

4. See Gonzalo Aguirre Beltrán, *La población negra en México*, 2nd ed. (1946; repr. Mexico: Fondo de Cultura Económica, 1972), 15–32.

5. See Instituto de Estudios Africanos, "Facetas del esclavo africano en América Latina," *América Indígena* 29, no. 3 (1969): 677–681.

6. For an account of the Spanish slave trade, see Harry Johnston, *The Negro in the New World* (London: Methuen and Company, 1910), 36–56.

7. Daniel P. Mannix and M. Cowley, *Black Cargoes: A History of the Atlantic Slave Trade* (New York: Viking Press, 1969), 231.

8. For a brief note on Gallinas, see Marrero, *Cuba*, 56–57.

9. See Cowley's introduction to *Adventures of an African Slaver*, xv–xvi. Others, like W. W. F. Ward, attest to the same conditions: "The flogging, the chains, the branding, the stench and disease and the suffocation and death on the overcrowded ships, the women leaping into the shark-infested sea, the living and healthy slaves being thrown overboard in their fetters when the ship was being chased, in order that the naval officer who boarded her should not be able to testify in court that she was carrying slaves when he set foot on her decks." See *The Royal Navy and the Slavers* (New York: Pantheon Books, 1969), 177.

10. Dow, *Slave Ships and Slaving* (Salem, Mass.: Marine Research Society, 1927), 245–246.

11. Cowley, *Adventures*, xiv.

12. Cited in Ortiz, *Los negros esclavos*, 133.

13. Ibid.

14. Lino Novás Calvo, *El negrero* (Madrid: Espasa-Calpe, 1955), 214. Unless otherwise indicated, all translations are mine and references to this work will appear parenthetically in the text.

15. Ward, *Royal Navy*, 132–133.

16. Johnston, *Liberia*, 164.

17. For an account of Canot's life, see Mayer, *Adventures*. Also see Johnston, *Liberia*, 162–178 and Dow, *Slave Ships*, 16.

18. The pamphlet, which narrates a continuation of *El negrero* and Blanco's descendants, was motivated by antislavery articles in a black paper, *El Ciudadano*, written by Fernández de Trava under the pseudonym El Mandinga. Contrary to Morúa's position, the articles exalted the Spanish government and its granting of rights and liberties to blacks.

19. Morúa Delgado, *Obras completas*, vol. 3, 14.

20. Ibid., 14–15.

21. *Enciclopedia universal ilustrada* (Barcelona: Espasa-Calpe, 1930), vol. 8, 1088, my translation.

22. See Johnston, *Negro in the New World*, 41.

23. Marrero, *Cuba*, 56.

24. Canot's account is similar to those of Marrero and Novás Calvo but differs in that Canot and Marrero suggest that Blanco arrived for the first time in Gallinas on board the *Conquistador* (see Mayer, *Adventures*, 295). Moreover, Marrero suggests that the one hundred slaves came from the Lomboko factory (see Marrero, *Cuba*, 56).

25. A more recent and expanded edition indicates that Canot's real name was Theophilus Canneau. See *A Slave's Log Book, or Twenty Years Residence in Africa* (Englewood Cliffs, N.J.: Prentice-Hall, 1976).

26. In 1933, the year in which he wrote *El negrero*, Novás Calvo translated Faulkner's *Sanctuary* and works by Manuel Komroff, Phillip Gosse, Robert Graves, and Walter N. Burns. One year later he also translated Huxley's *Point Counter Point*, D. H. Lawrence's *Kangaroo*, and others. And in 1951, Hemingway requested that Novás Calvo translate *The Old Man and the Sea* for a Spanish edition of *Life*. See Raymond Souza, *Lino Novás Calvo* (Boston: Twayne Publishers, 1981), 11–12, 94.

27. See Mayer, *Adventures*, 296.

28. *Adventures of an African Slaver* is one of the few books cited as a footnote, and it is also listed in Novás Calvo's bibliography, which appears at the end of the novel (see *El negrero*, 74, 270). The sketch that appears in Mayer's and Novás Calvo's books is slightly different from the one in Ortiz, *Los negros esclavos*, fig. 20, which is also cited in *El negrero*'s bibliography.

29. In this comparison between Blanco and Canot, I will cite the pages of the respective works in the text.

30. For a description of Da Souza's life, see Novás Calvo, *El negrero*, 74–75 and Mayer, *Adventures*, 254–255; for an account of Ormond's life, see 131–132 and 78–80. I must point out that in a reference to Da Souza, Novás Calvo suggests Canot's biography (see 74, note 1).

31. Selections of Drake's autobiography were published in Dow, *Slave Ships;* see 189. Like the others, Drake had an uncle, don Ricardo, who initiated him into the slave trade. He got to know and visit with Da Souza and worked for Pedro Blanco.

32. See Drake, 246–247.

33. See "Henry William Macaulay, Esq.," question 5475, June 15, 1842, 354.

34. See Morúa Delgado, *Obras completas,* vol. 5, 15.

35. See Benítez Rojo, "El negrero y el abolicionismo en América," *Linden Lane Magazine* 3, no. 1 (1984): 25. Also see Marrero, *Cuba,* 70. Benítez Rojo spells the slave's name as Sing-gbe, while Marrero writes it as Cinque.

36. Regarding Siacca's presence in Gallinas after Blanco left, see "Correspondence Relative to the Slave Trade at the Gallinas," in *British Sessional Papers, House of Commons,* vol. 31 (1841): 174–190.

37. Johnston, *Liberia,* 169.

38. Ibid., 170. Johnston compares Canot's story with C. B. Wadstrom's *An Essay on Colonization applied to the West Coast of Africa.* However, if we do a similar comparison between Wadstrom's and Johnston's accounts, Johnston's own factual narration is not free of error or fictional discourse. According to Johnston, Wadstrom's book, published in 1795, states that John Ormond was killed by natives in 1792 (*Liberia,* 175). In misreading Wadstrom's book, Johnston confuses Old Ormond with Mongo John. When Wadstrom mentions the death of Ormond's son, he refers not to the slave factor but to Mongo John's son (see Wadstrom, *An Essay on Colonization* [1794; repr. New York: Augustus M. Kelley, 1968], 88–89 and *Liberia,* 170–171). Attempting to justify history, Johnston suggests that either John escaped or had other brothers (*Liberia,* 171).

39. Johnston, *Liberia,* 167.

40. Mayer, *Adventures,* 336.

41. See Marrero, *Cuba,* 56–57.

42. This is the subtitle of the novel.

43. See Souza, *Lino Novás Calvo,* 45.

44. Julio Rodríguez-Luis, "Lino Novás Calvo y la historia de Cuba," *Symposium* 29, no. 4 (1975): 282–283.

45. "Aquella noche salieron los muertos," *Revista de Occidente* 38, no. 114 (1932): 285–322. Also see Lorraine Elena Roses, *Voices of the Storyteller: Cuba's Lino Novás Calvo* (Westport, Conn.: Greenwood Press, 1986), 67–70.

46. The novel establishes a relationship between Blanco and Napoleon. Blanco's independence, determination, and strengths are also patterned after Napoleon, a historical figure present in the text who lived during the early part of Blanco's life. Napoleon's grandeur and fall point to Blanco, who was aware of the activities of one of the world's greatest military leaders. To some extent, Napoleon's activities on the Continent mirror those of Blanco on the high seas and in West Coast Africa. Just as Napoleon excelled in his European battles, Blanco became an emperor of the slave trade. Both men's lives also ended tragically.

47. See Mayer, *Adventures,* 295 and Johnston, *Negro in the New World,* 41.

48. For a synopsis of negritude and *negrismo,* see my "History and Fiction: Black Narrative in Latin America and the Caribbean," in *Voices from Under,* 5–6.

49. Carpentier was one of the first editors of the *Revista de Avance,* and Novás Calvo published several poems in it. The increased interest in Africa during the first third of the century coincided with what was perceived to have been the decline of European civilization. Africa was seen as an exotic place and blacks became a theme of the avant-garde. Europe looked to Africa for an alternative to Western culture. Furthermore, the Surrealists' emphasis on the subconscious made for an easier return to the primitive stage which Africa was assumed to represent.

50. Baroja, *Paradox, Rey* (Buenos Aires: Espasa-Calpe, 1946), 19–20, my translation.

51. Unlike most works, and as we shall see later, Carpentier's *The Kingdom of This World* will stress a similar concern by providing both historical and Afro-religious interpretation of events.

52. Baroja, *Paradox, Rey;* see, for example, 88, 110, 176.

53. Dow, *Slave Ships,* 247.

54. Ward, *Royal Navy,* 176.

55. For the presence of Stedman's narration in Novás Calvo, compare, for example, *Narrative of an Expedition against the Revolted Negroes of Surinam* (Amherst: University of Massachusetts Press, 1972), 252 and Novás Calvo, *El negrero,* 151.

56. See *The Journal of a Slave Trader (John Newton),* ed. Bernard Martin and Mark Spurrell (London: Epworth Press, 1962).

57. Mannix and Cowley, *Black Cargoes,* 237. For the corruption of other British officials during the slave trade, see Marrero, *Cuba,* 77–78.

58. See Owen, *Journal of a Slave Dealer,* Canot, *Adventures,* and Newton, *Journal of a Slave Trader.*

59. Freud, *Totem and Taboo,* 17.

60. See Carpentier, *El reino de este mundo* (repr. 1949; Mexico City: Cía General de Ediciones, 1971), 16. For the sake of expediency, I have used Roberto González Echevarría's translation except for *minuciosa,* his minute, which I translate as detailed. See his *Alejo Carpentier,* 131.

61. For these and other biographical information, see González Echevarría, *Alejo Carpentier,* in particular 101, note 10.

62. The antislavery genre and Surrealism were two distinct literary developments in which blacks and Africa were important components. For a discussion of the antislavery novel, see my "La novela antiesclavista: Texto, contexto y escritura," *Cuadernos Americanos* 236, no. 3 (1981): 103–116, and "The Antislavery Novel and the Concept of Modernity," *Cuban Studies/Estudios Cubanos* 11, no. 1 (1981): 33–47. For an explanation of Surrealism in Carpentier, see González Echevarría, *Alejo Carpentier.*

63. My references are to *The New Science of Giambattista Vico,* trans. Thomas Goddard Bergin and Max Harold Fisch (Ithaca, N.Y.: Cornell Uni-

versity Press, 1984). Carpentier's interest in history motivated me to read Vico. Although I am aware that Vico's cycles refer to centuries and pertain to Greek and Roman civilizations, Carpentier's observations in some ways coincide with Vico's.

64. "La cultura de los pueblos que habitan en las tierras del mar Caribe," in *La novela latinoamericana en víspera de un nuevo siglo y otros ensayos* (Mexico City: Siglo Veintiuno Editores, 1981), 184, my translation.

65. It is not certain whether Carpentier read Vico. I have consulted Roberto González Echevarría and Klaus Müller-Bergh, *Alejo Carpentier: Bibliographical Guide/Guía bibliográfica* (Westport, Conn.: Greenwood Press, 1983) and Araceli García-Carranza, *Bibliografía de Alejo Carpentier* (Havana: Editorial Letras Cubanas, 1984), which I believe to be the most extensive bibliographical tools available, yet they do not contain any entry on Vico. Carpentier's stages in some respects remind me of Vico's ages when studying Greek and Roman civilizations. However, I am aware that there are differences between Vico's and Carpentier's ages. Nevertheless, Vico is present in Carpentier. It is not by chance that González Echevarría notices an opposition between Descartes and Vico when analyzing *Reasons of State*. See *Alejo Carpentier*, 259.

66. Carpentier, "La cultura," 186, my translation.

67. Ibid., 187.

68. For an in-depth historical explanation of "marvelous realism" and "magical realism," the latter a term used by Franz Roh in *Nach-Expressionismus (Magischer Realismus)* (1925), see also González Echevarría, *Alejo Carpentier*, and Frank Janney, *Alejo Carpentier and His Early Works* (London: Tamesis Books Limited, 1981).

69. Emir Rodríguez Monegal suggests that the prologue is an attack on Breton and Surrealism. See his "Lo real y lo maravilloso en *El reino de este mundo*," in *Asedios a Carpentier*, ed. Klaus Müller-Bergh (Santiago de Chile: Editorial Universitaria, 1972), 101–132.

70. See the prologue to the novel in *El reino de este mundo*. Unless otherwise indicated, all quotations of the novel are taken from *The Kingdom of This World*, trans. Harriet de Onis (New York: Collier Books, 1970) and references will appear parenthetically in the text.

71. Carpentier provides another explanation of the marvelous, marvelous realism, and magical realism in Ramón Chao, *Palabras en el tiempo de Alejo Carpentier* (Barcelona: Argos Vergara, 1984), 137–144.

72. For an in-depth study of the African in Carpentier, see Emma Susana Speratti-Piñero, *Los pasos allados en El reino de este mundo* (Mexico City: Colegio de México, 1981).

73. Moreover, the chapter ends with drumbeats in the nearby hills: "There was an evil atmosphere about that twilight of shadow closing in too quickly. It was impossible to know whether the drums were really throbbing in the hills. But at moments a rhythm coming from the distant heights mingled with the *Ave María* the women were saying in the Throne Room, arousing unacknowledged resonances in more than one breast" (Carpentier, *The Kingdom of This World*, 139–140).

74. Also see Speratti-Piñero, *Los pasos allados*, 129.

75. Alfred Metraux, *Voodoo in Haiti*, trans. Hugo Charteris (New York: Schocken Books, 1972), 273. Also cited by Speratti-Piñero, *Los pasos allados*, 130, note 30.

76. See González Echevarría, *Alejo Carpentier*.

77. Both Solimán and Ti Noel are present, though in different chapters, throughout the entire narration. In part 2, chapter 6, the only chapter they share, Ti Noel and Solimán are in two different countries and never meet; Ti Noel is in Cuba and Solimán is in Saint Domingue. I must clarify that part 1, chapter 5, "De Profundis," is the only chapter in which neither Ti Noel nor Solimán is present. Nevertheless, it does narrate Mackandal's use of poison against the white slave masters. The relationship between Ti Noel and Mackandal throughout the novel is obvious.

78. Jean Price-Mars described the possessed state in a similar manner: "Through these different words we are identifying a universal phenomenon in the diversity of religions and one in which the individual, under the influence of ill-determined causes, is plunged into a crisis sometimes manifested by confused movements of chronic agitation (spasmodic convulsions), accompanied by cries or a flood of unintelligible words.

"Other times, the individual is the object of sudden transformation: his body trembles, his face changes for the worse, his eyes protrude, and his foaming lips utter hoarse, inarticulate sounds, or even predictions and prophecies. Finally, oftentimes the subject, without any apparent sign of physical trouble, reveals an abnormal state through the bizarreness of his words, the mysterious air he adopts, the way he views his personality as estranged from his self. In every case, the state of trance, ecstasy, or possession appears as a delirium in which the delirious idea is characterized by a form of hallucination." See his *So Spoke the Uncle*, trans. Magdaline W. Shannon (Washington, D.C.: Three Continents Press, 1983), 116.

79. The African gods indeed punish those who abandon African religion. In *The Beast of the Haitian Hills*, Philippe Thoby-Marcelin and Pierre Marcelin explain a similar circumstance to what occurred to Solimán and Christophe: "I knew a poor woman once. Assefi was her name. One day . . . she joined the Adventist Church. She rejected the loas. But three months later, what do you think happened? A spirit entered her head and asked the family why it was that Assefi no longer left food for him. They told him that she had become a Protestant. —Aha, so that's it—the spirit said, in a rage. —So she did that without even asking my permission? —He had hardly finished speaking through her own mouth, that spirit, than he threw the woman violently to the ground. Then he took her head and bashed it against the walls of the house. And when he left the body, Assefi was dead, her skull crushed and her blood streaming out of her body like a river" (*The Beast of the Haitian Hills*, trans. Peter C. Rhodes [New York: Times, 1946], 43).

80. Vico did think of American Indians when he proposed that "in the new world the American Indians would now be following this course of human institutions if they had not been discovered by the Europeans" (*The New Science*, 414, also xxxviii).

The structures I am proposing are by no means the only ones present in *The Kingdom of This World*. González Echevarría has shown that the novel adheres to other cycles. For example, he sees an alternation between Sunday and Monday, between ritual and action. For him, the "pendular movement between Sundays and Mondays, as well as that between December and January . . . is the ritualistic repetition to which Carpentier has submitted history and his text" (*Alejo Carpentier*, 141). Moreover, he notices another structure that pertains to the twenty-six chapters, in which the thirteenth chapter, the numerical center, divides the novel into two cycles. Ti Noel's stay in Santiago de Cuba occurs in the novel at the center of both the set of chapters and the chronology. "In this same chapter, in Santiago, a city famous for its carnivals, there is a series of carnivallike scenes, theatrical performances, the surrender to the summons of the flesh on the part of M. Lenormand de Mezy and his fellow colonists. In chapter 26 we have the apocalypse, the 'green wind' that razes everything after a series of omens that are taken directly from the Apocalypse in the Bible. Is it not significant then that chapter 13 is the fifth of part II ($5+2=7$) and that chapter 26 ($2+6=8$) is the fourth of part IV ($4+4=8$)? That 7 and that 8, that Sunday and that Monday—Carnival and Apocalypse—are the two poles between which the action of the story stands suspended. It is an action divided into two perfect cycles of twelve chapters each . . . And in view of this, could it be dismissed as purely accidental that counting consecutively, the Sunday of Macandal's apparition occurs in the seventh chapter of the first cycle; while Bre[i]lle's apparition on Ascension Sunday happens in the seventh chapter of the second cycle? And also that Macandal's and Christophe's deaths occur in parallel chapters?" (143). González Echevarría's study does not contradict my own. In my reading of his two cycles, the first pertains to Mackandal and African culture and the second to European culture. Chapters 13 and 26 are pivotal chapters, as the last, chapter 26, suggests a return to the first cycle, thus pointing to an endless repetition between Africa and Europe. Ti Noel realizes that he, like Mackandal and Bouckman before him, must continue to fight against the New Masters. González Echevarría concludes his study by proposing that Carpentier's usage of Christian religious references is his attempt to make the action fit into a liturgical cycle (144–147). Needless to say, this is the same religious cycle the slaves were forced to accept. In Afro-Cuban religion, for their religion to survive, the descendants of Africans appeared to accept Christian religion but gave Christian saints the names and characteristics of their own gods. Although they prayed to a white figure, they were paying homage to their own spiritual protectors. Therefore, the same liturgical cycle had a double referent, both Christian and African.

81. Although there is no direct evidence that Carpentier read Price-Mars, not in González Echevarría and Müller-Bergh, *Alejo Carpentier: Bibliographical Guide/Guía bibliográfica* or in García-Carranza, *Bibliografía de Alejo Carpentier*, they both cite Moreau de Saint-Méry, *Description topographique*, as a common source. See, for example, *Alejo Carpentier: Bibliographical Guide/Guía bibliográfica*, 109.

82. For Price-Mars, voodoo, a Haitian word, is a syncretic of Dahomean,

Congolese, Sudanese, and other beliefs. Unlike other Africologists who view voodoo as a derivative of the Vaudois sect created by Pierre de Vaux or Valdo, Price-Mars suggests that it comes from the Bantu people of Dahomey, who called certain spirits Vodoun (see *So Spoke the Uncle*, 50–52). By the 1790s, Moreau de Saint-Méry analyzes for the first time a religion in Haiti by the name Vodou (*Description topographique*, 109–112).

83. Price-Mars, *So Spoke the Uncle*, 97. This information also recalls Carpentier's "La cultura de los pueblos que habitan en las tierras del mar Caribe." Within the context of Price-Mars, Carpentier's statement that Cuba breaks a past cycle suggests that its history is only a continuation of that structure. But even if the Cuban Revolution is presently viewed as breaking with the cycle, I wonder whether in the future it will conform to past cycles. Nevertheless, what Carpentier interprets as a historical solution in the essay, Price-Mars and *The Kingdom of This World* view as religious structure.

84. Ibid., 97–98.

85. Ibid., 48, note 22. Also compare the similarity between Carpentier's and Price-Mars's description of Mackandal's death: "We all know the story of Mackandal, executed in 1758. He was the most famous of the leaders who exercised a genuine fascination over his associates. Revolt was the objective of every one of them. They did not recoil from any means to realize their purpose, and if by chance they were taken and delivered to the executioner, they accepted their torture with the proud faith of the martyr. The masters multiplied the punishments in vain: castration, quartering, the stake, the wheel, but nothing could check the mystical fervor of the mutinous rebels. 'They suffer without uttering a word,' writes M. (Monsieur) de Machult, a colonial administrator, and M. de Sezellan adds: 'They endure the cruelest torments with a steadfastness that has been unequalled, appearing on the scaffolds and the funeral pyres with fierce tranquility and courage'" (Letter of M. de Sezellan of Le Cap, June 7, 1763 [Documents of Saint Domingue, Carton 15], 53–54).

86. See Price-Mars, *So Spoke the Uncle*, 104–105.

## 5. The Politics of Memory

1. Manzano's slave narration ends at the moment of his escape. The second part of his autobiography, which would have described his life as a fugitive slave, was lost while in the hands of Ramón de Palma.

2. Although Cuba was the last country to emancipate slaves in the Caribbean, Brazil was the last country to do the same in the New World in 1888.

3. See my "Caribbean Cycles: Displacement and Change," *New England Review and Bread Loaf Quarterly* 7, no. 4 (1985): 412–430.

4. *The Autobiography of a Runaway Slave*, trans. Jocasta Inness (New York: Pantheon Books, 1968), 63–64. Unless otherwise indicated, all quotations are from this edition.

5. There are other common points between Carpentier's and Barnet's works. As in *The Kingdom of This World*, African religion, which is associ-

ated with nature, subverts Western history. For Mackandal, Ti Noel, and now Montejo, the African gods are in complete control of man and his destiny. Because of Cuban syncretism, for Montejo the gods are both Christian and African, while recognizing that, as in Carpentier's novel, those of African origin are the strongest. Man and his society are part of a larger design. For Montejo, the course that nations follow is already present in nature.

6. For Eugene Vance, the commemorative process is part of oral culture. See his "Roland and the Poetics of Memory," in *Textual Strategies*, ed. Josué Harari (Ithaca, N.Y.: Cornell University Press, 1979), 379.

7. See García Márquez, *Chronicle of a Death Foretold*, and Fuentes, *Distant Relations*.

8. Montejo's recollections suggest a synthesis of European, African, and Cuban myths and ideas. Jean-Pierre Tardieu's "Religions et croyances populaires dans *Biografía de un cimarrón* de M. Barnet: Du refus à la tolérance," *UTIEH/Caravelle* 43 (1984): 43–67, analyzes the cultural and religious mixture. In particular, Tardieu notices that Montejo's descriptions of the mermaids during the festival of San Juan responds to Greek but also African heritage. The legend of *mamiwata* (mammy water) is well known on the West Coast of Africa (57).

9. Other works suggest that slaves did commit suicide. As we shall see with César Leante's *Los guerrilleros negros*, the protagonist, Coba, in order to escape from the slave hunters, jumps to his death. See Leante, *Los guerrilleros negros* (Havana: UNEAC, 1976).

10. References to working women serve as another example. Montejo states: "Women in those days were worth as much as men. They worked hard and they had no patience with feckless drifters" (Barnet, *Autobiography*, 71–72). He later repeats: "They washed the men's clothes, mended and sewed. Women worked harder in those days than they do now" (97).

11. Vance, "Roland," 374–375.

12. Ibid., 381.

13. For an insightful essay on the importance of this genre, see Roberto González Echevarría, "*Biografía de un cimarrón* and the Novel of the Cuban Revolution," *Novel* 13, no. 3 (1980): 249–263.

14. See "La novela testimonio: Socio-literatura," *Unión*, año 6, no. 4 (1969): 99–122. The same essay also appears in *La canción de Rachel* (Barcelona: Estela, 1970). For the sake of expediency, I have quoted González Echevarría's translation in his "*Biografía de un cimarrón*," 260. The quoted information is rehashed in Barnet, "The Documentary Novel," *Cuban Studies/Estudios Cubanos* 11, no. 1 (1981): 29.

15. Barnet, *Biografía de un cimarrón* (Mexico City: Siglo Veintiuno, 1975), 9, my translation.

16. Emilio Bejel, "Entrevista: Miguel Barnet," *Hispamérica* 10, no. 29 (1981): 41.

17. González Echevarría writes: "He shares more with them: their epic-like wanderings, their authorial propensities, their more or less obvious association with Christ (once removed, since they hark back to Saint Stephen,

born the day after Christ's birthday; the first martyr after Him). Furthermore, according to Barnet, Montejo may be a corruption of the French 'mont haut' (high mountain). It is the same of Esteban's mother, who was a descendant from Haitian slaves (his link with the past is matrilineal, thus sharing a feminine quality with the protagonists of the second trend of the documentary novel). The Christian symbolism of the mountain is clear. What is not so clear is that *monte*, both 'mountain' and 'wild' or 'bush,' are charged with implications in Afro-Cuban religion and lore" (*"Biografía de un cimarrón,"* 258–259).

18. Bejel, "Entrevista," 44, my translation. Later on in the same interview, Barnet takes a different point of view and describes his close identification with his protagonists to the extent that he becomes the other (49).

19. Barnet, "The Documentary Novel," 25.

20. Ibid., 23.

21. Barnet, *Biografía de un cimarrón*, 12, my translation.

22. Bejel, "Entrevista," 46, my translation. Like many others, José Soler Puig attributes his success as a writer to the Cuban Revolution. See "José Soler Puig: 'Sin la Revolución no hubiera podido llegar a ser escritor,'" *América Latina*, no. 4 (1979): 145–153.

23. El Caimán Barbudo, under the direction of Jesús Díaz, was another group of the second generation of writers. This group was more politically committed than those belonging to El Puente.

24. For an understanding of homosexuals and other "undesirables" in Cuba, see the transcript of the film *Conducta impropia* by Néstor Almendros and Orlando Jiménez-Leal (Madrid: Editorial Playor, 1984). The transcript includes interviews with José Mario and Ana María Simó, editors of *El Puente*, and pertinent sections of the penal code as it relates to "improper conduct."

25. Bejel, "Entrevista," 43.

26. A brief review of the success appeared under "Triunfo en Europa de El cimarrón" in *La Gaceta de Cuba*, no. 87 (1970): 31.

27. For a temporal and spatial connection between Montejo and Rachel, see Angel L. Fernández Guerra, "Cimarrón y Rachel: Un continuum," in *Nuevos críticos cubanos*, ed. José Prats Sariol (Havana: Editorial Letras Cubanas, 1983), 530–537.

28. Barnet, *La canción de Rachel* (Barcelona: Editorial Estela, 1970), 58–60, my translation. Part of Montejo's response to Rachel is cited in Ernesto Méndez y Soto, *Panorama de la novela cubana de la revolución (1959–1970)* (Miami: Ediciones Universal, 1977), 114.

29. Barnet, *La canción de Rachel*, 57.

30. See Carpentier, "La cultura," 177–189.

31. We must note that throughout the narration, Montejo compares the present to the past. This is evident by the presence of the word "today" in the text. For example, Montejo states that "today's festivals do not compare to previous ones" (Barnet, *Autobiography*, 72); "women then were harder workers than today" (90); "women in the past had less trouble giving birth than today's women" (97); etc.

32. See Foucault, "What Is an Author?" in *Textual Strategies*, 141–160.

33. My conclusion coincides with González Echevarría when he states that the narration is a fusion between Barnet and Montejo, whom he identifies as "Bartejo." However, I prefer to use "Montenet."

34. In his "Congo or Carabalí," Carlos Moore accuses José Luciano Franco, among others, of representing black struggles as "natural calamities" (15).

35. For a historical account of this event, see José Luciano Franco, *Las minas*.

36. A survey of the rebellions in the New World are compiled by José Luciano Franco in his "Cimarrones en las Antillas y América continental," in *Los palenques de los negros cimarrones* (Havana: Departamento de Orientación Revolucionaria del Comité Central del Partido Comunista de Cuba, 1973), 17–48. Also see Franco's "Esquema de los movimientos populares de liberación nacional (1511–1868)," in *Ensayos históricos*, 11–44. The problem of runaway slaves is reflected in the number of laws that were passed to contain and recover the slave. See "El cimarrón en las leyes de Indias," in *Los palenques*, 7–16.

37. José Luciano Franco, "Los cobreros," 38.

38. Ibid., 39, my translation.

39. Ibid., 39–40.

40. See Lourdes Casal, "Images of Cuban Society among Pre- and Post-Revolutionary Novelists," Ph.D. diss., The New School for Social Research, 1975, 209–213.

41. For an account of Padilla's problems, see Lourdes Casal, ed., *El caso Padilla* (Miami: Ediciones Universal, 1971).

42. Leante left Cuba in September 1981. Since then, he has reedited *Los guerrilleros negros* under the title *Capitán de cimarrones*. The change in title may be due to Leante's desire to distance himself and his works from a revolutionary context. This is most noticeable by eliminating the word *guerrilleros*, an allusion to the Castro forces. A comparison between *Los guerrilleros negros* and *Capitán de cimarrones* shows no substantive changes other than the one expressed in the title.

43. See Barnet, *Autobiography*, 208–209.

44. Portuondo, *Historia de Cuba*, 438, author's italics.

45. Ibid., 475. The term *guerrilla*, applied to a small band of men, originated during the Spanish war for independence against the French (1808–1814).

46. Ernesto Ché Guevara, *Guerrilla Warfare* (London: Penguin Books, 1969), 240.

47. Franco, *Los palenques*, 54, my translation.

48. Anselmo Suárez y Romero, *Francisco*, ed. Eduardo Castaneda (1800; repr. Havana: Biblioteca Básica de Autores Cubanos, 1970), 78–79. Unless indicated otherwise, all translations are mine.

49. *Los guerrilleros negros*, 17–18. Unless indicated otherwise, references are to this edition and all translations are mine.

50. Barnet, *Autobiography*, 21.

51. Leante, *Los guerrilleros negros*, 12–13.

52. Barnet, *Autobiography*, 22.

53. Leante, *Los guerrilleros negros*, 13–14. These two are not isolated incidents. For example, a similar description is repeated with the *maní* and *yuca* dances. Again, Leante organizes his information in the same manner and uses the same words contained in Barnet's text. See Barnet, *Biografía de de un cimarrón*, 28–29, and Leante, *Los guerrilleros negros*, 15.

54. For the importance of this novel in Leante's works, see his "*El reino de este mundo*," *Revolución*, October 5, 1959, 2.

55. Let us compare. Leante states: "Perpendicular como un muro, el farallón no parecía ofrecer sitio alguno por donde treparlo. Entonces, viendo el desconcierto en que se encontraban, los cimarrones empezaron a derribar peñascos sobre ellos. Una lluvia de piedras se les vino encima" (*Los guerrilleros negros*, 103). Estévez writes: "Perpendicularmente arriba de nosotros; tratamos de buscar la subida . . . empezaron a derribar peñascos sobre nosotros, y viendo que estábamos en bastante peligro, y que no había recurso de escaparnos de la lluvia de piedras, que nos venían encima, determiné hacer fuego a discreción," (*Diario*, 91).

56. This act, for Harold Bloom, would have the effect of a "misreading." The anxiety Bloom wishes to see, by recognizing what belongs to the precursor in one's own work, does not exist in Leante's case. What is present is a feeling of communion and transcendence. See *The Anxiety of Influence: A Theory of Poetry* (New York: Oxford University Press, 1975).

57. See Marrero, *Cuba*, 30. This and a less radical proposal by Agustín Arguelles, which did not call for the manumission of slaves, were sent to an ad hoc committee, where they remained without an opinion (30–32).

58. Mary Turner, *Slaves and the Missionaries: The Disintegration of Jamaican Slave Society, 1784–1834* (Urbana: University of Illinois Press, 1982), 80.

59. Franco, "Los cobreros," 43, my translation.

60. The page reference to the comparison between these two works will appear parenthetically in the text. In this analysis I am aware of Barthes's distinctions between a work and a text. See his "From Work to Text," in *Textual Strategies*, 73–81.

61. Franco, "Palenques del Frijol, Bumba y Maluala," *Universidad de La Habana*, no. 160 (1963): 167–179. Some of this information also appears in Franco, "Los cobreros."

62. Franco, "Palenques," 178–179.

63. For an explanation of this type of reader, see Julio Cortázar's distinctions between "lector hembra" and "lector complice" in his *Hopscotch*.

64. For Octavio Paz, Latin American literature has to invent its past. See his "A Literature of Foundations," trans. Lysander Kemp, *Tri-Quarterly* E, nos. 13–14 (1968): 7–12.

## 6. Present and Future Antislavery Narratives

1. In *Necesidad de libertad* (Mexico City: Kosmos-Editorial, S.A., 1986), 203, Arenas writes: "Cubanos esclavisados."

2. *Graveyard of the Angels*, trans. Alfred J. MacAdam (New York: Avon Books, 1987), 1. Unless otherwise indicated, all references are to this edition and the pages to the quotations will appear parenthetically in the text.

3. For the rewritings of *Cecilia Valdés*, see my chapters 2, part 2, and 3, part 2.

4. Arenas, *Necesidad de libertad*, 205, my translation.

5. See Wimsatt and Beardsley, "The Intentional Fallacy," in *Problems in Aesthetics*, ed. Morris Weitz (New York: Macmillan Company, 1970), 437–460.

6. For the importance of this figure, see, for example, Portuondo, *Historia de Cuba*, 304–305, 309–310.

7. For a discussion of *Deceit, Desire and the Novel* and how it pertains to the antislavery literature, see my chapter 1, part 2.

8. Arenas, *Necesidad de libertad*, 167.

# BIBLIOGRAPHY

Aimes, Hubert H. S. "Coartación: A Spanish Institution for the Advancement of Slaves into Freedom." *Yale Review* 17 (1909): 412–431.

Alexandre-Debray, Janine. *Victor Schoelcher.* Paris: Librairie Académique Perrin, 1983.

Almendros, Néstor, and Orlando Jiménez-Leal, eds. *Conducta impropria.* Madrid: Editorial Playor, 1984.

Alvarez García, Imeldo, ed. *Acerca de Cirilo Villaverde.* Havana: Editorial Letras Cubanas, 1982.

*América Indigena* 29, no. 3 (1969).

Angulo y Heredia, José Miguel. "Carta a José Luis Alfonso, marqués de Montelo." *Revista de la Biblioteca Nacional* 2, nos. 1 and 2 (1909): 141–142.

Arango y Parreño, Francisco de. *Obras completas.* 2 vols. Havana: Ministerio de Educación, 1952.

Arenas, Reinaldo. *Graveyard of the Angels.* Trans. Alfred J. MacAdam. New York: Avon Books, 1987.

———. *La loma del Angel.* New York: Mariel, 1987.

———. *Necesidad de libertad.* Mexico City: Kosmos Editorial, S.A., 1986.

Azcárate Rosell, Rafael. *Nicolás Azcárate el reformista.* Havana: Editorial Trópico, 1939.

Bachiller y Morales, Antonio. *Los negros.* Barcelona: Gorgas y Compañía, n.d.

Balboa, Silvestre de. *Espejo de paciencia.* Havana: Dirección de Cultura del Ministerio de Educación, 1942.

Barnet, Miguel. *The Autobiography of a Run Away Slave.* Trans. Jocasta Inness. London: Bodley Head, 1966.

———. *The Autobiography of a Runaway Slave.* Trans. Jocasta Inness. New York: Pantheon Books, 1968.

———. *Biografía de un cimarrón.* Mexico City: Siglo Veintiuno, 1975.

———. *La canción de Rachel.* Barcelona: Editorial Estela, 1970.

———. "The Documentary Novel." *Cuban Studies/Estudios Cubanos* 11, no. 1 (1981): 19–32.

———. "La novela testimonio: Socio-literatura." *Unión* 6, no. 4 (1969): 99–122.

Baroja, Pío. *Paradox Rey.* Buenos Aires: Espasa-Calpe, 1946.

Barreda, Pedro. *The Black Protagonist in the Cuban Novel.* Amherst: University of Massachusetts Press, 1979.

Barthes, Roland. *Mythologies.* Trans. Annette Lavers. New York: Hill and Wang, 1972.

Bejel, Emilio. "Entrevista: Miguel Barnet." *Hispamérica* 10, no. 29 (1981): 41–52.

Beltrán, Gonzalo Aguirre. *La población negra en México.* Mexico City: Fondo de Cultura Económica, 1972.

Benítez Rojo, Antonio. "Azúcar/Poder/Texto: Triada de lo cubano." *Cruz Ansata* 9 (1986): 93–117.

———. "La cultura caribeña en Cuba: Continuidad versus ruptura." *Cuban Studies/Estudios Cubanos* 14, no. 1 (1984): 1–15.

———. "*El negrero* y el abolicionismo en América." *Linden Lane Magazine* 3, no. 1 (1984): 25.

Betancourt, Juan René. "Castro and the Cuban Negro." Trans. Brandon Robinson. *Crisis* (May 1961): 270–275.

Blanchet, Emilio. "La tertulia literaria de del Monte." *Revista de la Facultad de Letras y Ciencias* 14, no. 1: 50.

Bloom, Harold. *The Anxiety of Influence: A Theory of Poetry.* New York: Oxford University Press, 1975.

Brenner, Philip, William M. LeoGrand, Donna Rich, and Daniel Siegel, eds. *The Cuba Reader: The Making of a Revolutionary Society.* New York: Grove Press, 1989.

Bueno, Salvador. *La crítica literaria cubana del siglo XIX.* Havana: Editorial Letras Cubanas, 1979.

———. *Figuras cubanas del siglo diecinueve.* Havana: UNEAC, 1980.

———. *Historia de la literatura cubana.* Havana: Editorial Nacional de Cuba, 1963.

———. "Ideología y literatura: La novela antiesclavista cubana." In *Pensamiento y literatura en América Latina.* Ed. Matyas Horanyi, 65–71. Budapest: Departamento de Español de la Universidad Eotovos Lorand de Budapest, 1982.

———. "La narrativa antiesclavista en Cuba de 1835 a 1839." *Cuadernos Hispanoamericanos,* nos. 451–452 (1988): 169–186.

———. "La primitiva narración antiesclavista en Cuba (1835–1839)." *Universidad de La Habana,* no. 207 (1978): 143–165.

Cabrera Saqui, Mario. "Vida, pasión y gloria de Anselmo Suárez y Romero." In Anselmo Suárez y Romero, *Francisco,* 201–226. Havana: Biblioteca Básica de Autores Cubanos, 1970.

Calcagno, Francisco. *Aponte.* Barcelona: Tipografía de Francisco Costa, 1901.

———. *Los crímenes de Concha.* Havana: Librería e Imprenta de Elías F. Casona, 1887.

———. *Diccionario biográfico cubano.* New York: N. Ponce de León, 1878.

———. *En busca del eslabón: Historia de monos.* Barcelona: Imprenta de Salvador Manero, 1888.

———. *Poetas de color.* Havana: Imp. Militar de la V. de Soler y Compañía, 1878.

———. *Romualdo, uno de tantos.* Havana: El Pilar de Manuel de Armas, 1891.

Canneau, Theophilus. *A Slave's Log Book; or, Twenty Years Residence in Africa.* Englewood Cliffs, N.J.: Prentice-Hall, 1976.

Cantero, J. G., and E. Laplante. *Los Ingenios de Cuba.* Ed. Levi Marrero. Barcelona: Gráficas M. Pareja, 1984.

Carbonel, Walterio. *Crítica cómo surgió la cultura nacional.* Havana: 1961.

Carew, Jan. *Topolski's Chronicle* 11, nos. 17–20 (1963).

Carpentier, Alejo. *¡Ecue Yamba-O!* Buenos Aires: Editorial Xanandú, 1968.

———. "Los fugitivos." *Narrativa de la revolución.* Ed. José M. Caballero Bonald, 25–37. Madrid: Alianza, 1968.

———. *Guerra del tiempo.* Mexico City: Cía General de Ediciones, 1958.

———. *The Kingdom of This World.* Trans. Harriet de Onís. New York: Knopf, 1957.

———. *La novela latinoamericana en víspera de un nuevo siglo y otros ensayos.* Mexico City: Siglo Veintiuno Editores, 1981.

Carrera y Jústiz, Francisco. *El Municipio y la cuestión de razas.* Havana: Librería e Imprenta "La Moderna Poesía," 1904.

Casal, Lourdes. "Images of Cuban Society among Pre- and Post-Revolutionary Novelists." Ph.D. diss., The New School for Social Research, 1975.

———, ed. *El caso Padilla.* Miami: Ediciones Universal, 1971.

Castañeda, Eduardo. "Francisco: El héroe bueno y el abolicionista reformista." In Anselmo Suárez y Romero, *Francisco,* 9–27. Havana: Biblioteca Básica de Autores Cubanos.

Castro, Fidel. "Address to the 3rd Congress of the Communist Party of Cuba." *Granma* 21, no. 7 (February 16, 1986): 15.

———. "Speech Commemorating the 15th Anniversary Ceremony of the Playa Girón Victory." *Foreign Broadcast Information Service, Daily Report* 6, no. 77 (April 20, 1976): Q1–Q8.

Cepero Bonilla, Raúl. *Azúcar y abolición.* Havana: Editorial de Ciencias Sociales, 1971.

Céspedes Casado, Emilio. *La cuestión social cubana.* Havana: La Propagandista, 1906.

Chao, Ramón. *Palabras en el tiempo de Alejo Carpentier.* Barcelona: Argos Vergara, 1984.

Chatman, Seymour. *Story and Discourse: Narrative Structure in Fiction and Film.* Ithaca, N.Y.: Cornell University Press, 1978.

Cleaver, Eldridge. *International Herald Tribune,* June 26, 1969.

Clytus, John. *Black Man in Red Cuba.* Coral Gables: University of Miami Press, 1970.

Cobb, Martha. *Harlem, Haiti and Havana.* Washington, D.C.: Three Continents Press, 1979.

Cohen, David W., and Jack P. Greene, eds. *Neither Slave nor Free.* Baltimore: Johns Hopkins University Press, 1972.

Conte, Rafael, and José M. Capmany. *Guerra de razas: Negros contra blancos en Cuba.* Havana: Imp. Militar de Antonio Pérez, 1912.

*Contestación a dos desdichados autonomistas de la raza de color.* New York: Alfred Howes, 1898.

"Correspondence Relative to the Slave Trade at the Gallinas." *British Sessional Papers, House of Commons* 31 (1841): 174–190.

*Correspondence Relative to the Slave Trade at the Gallinas.* London: Clowes and Sons, 1841.

Cortázar, Julio. *Hopscotch.* Trans. Gregory Rabassa. New York: Pantheon Books, 1966.

Corwin, Arthur F. *Spain and the Abolition of Slavery in Cuba, 1817–1886.* Austin: University of Texas Press, 1967.

Couffon, Claud. *René Depestre.* Paris: Editions Seghers, 1986.

Coulthard, Gabriel R. *Race and Colour in Caribbean Literature.* New York: Oxford University Press, 1962.

Coupland, Sir Reginald. *The British Anti-Slavery Movement.* New York: Barnes and Noble, 1933.

Courlander, Harold. *The Drum and the Hoe.* Berkeley and Los Angeles: University of California Press, 1960.

Cruz, Mary. "Sab, su texto y su contexto." In Gertrudis Gómez de Avellaneda, *Sab,* 7–123. Havana: Instituto Cubano del Libro, 1973.

Cudjoe, Selwyn R. *Resistance and Caribbean Literature.* Athens: Ohio University Press, 1980.

Curtin, Philip D. *The Atlantic Slave Trade.* Madison: University of Wisconsin Press, 1969.

Cuza Malé, Belkis. "Anselmo Suárez y Romero: ¿Esclavista?" *Linden Lane Magazine* 4, no. 1 (1985): 10.

Dallas, R. C. *Historia de los cimarrones.* Trans. Gilberto Hernández Santana. Havana: Casa de las Américas, 1980.

Dana, Jr., Richard Henry. *To Cuba and Back.* Carbondale and Edwardsville: Southern Illinois University Press, 1966.

Danger Roll, Zoila. *Los cimarrones de El Frijol.* Santiago de Cuba: Empresa Editorial Oriente, 1979.

DeCosta Willis, Miriam. "Self and Society in the Afro-Cuban Slave Narrative." *Latin American Literary Review* 16, no. 32 (1988): 6–15.

———, ed. *Blacks in Hispanic Literature.* Port Washington, N.Y.: Kennikat Press, 1977.

De la Cruz, Manuel. *Sobre literatura cubana.* Ed. Ana Cairo. Havana: Editorial Letras Cubanas, 1981.

De la Torriente, Loló. *La Habana de Cecilia Valdés.* Havana: Jesús Montero, 1946.

Del Castillo, Adolfo. *En la paz y en la guerra.* Havana: Editorial "Hermes," 1922.

Del Monte, Domingo. *Centón epistolario de Domingo del Monte.* 7 vols. Havana: Imprenta "El Siglo XX," 1930.

———. *Escritos.* 2 vols. Ed. José A. Fernández de Castro. Havana: Cultural, 1929.

DeMan, Paul. *Blindness and Insight: Essays in the Rhetoric of Contemporary Criticism.* New York: Oxford University Press, 1971.

De Nora, María Luz. "Cartas de Cirilo Villaverde a Julio Rosas." *Bohemia* 57, no. 40 (1965): 100.

De Palma, Ramón. "Crítica del *Espetón de oro.*" In *Acerca de Cirilo Villaverde.* Ed. Imeldo Alvarez, 27–29. Havana: Editorial Letras Cubanas, 1982.

———. "La novela." In *Acerca de Cirilo Villaverde.* Ed. Imeldo Alvarez, 15–26. Havana: Editorial Letras Cubanas, 1982.

De Villa, Miguel, ed. *Tipos y costumbres.* Havana: Imprenta del Avisador Comercial, 1881.

Derrida, Jacques. *Of Grammatology.* Trans. Gayatri Chakravorty Spivak. Baltimore: Johns Hopkins University Press, 1977.

Deschamp Chapeaux, Pedro. "Autenticidad de algunos negros y mulatos de *Cecilia Valdés.*" *Gaceta de Cuba,* no. 81 (1970): 24–27.

———. *El negro en la economía habanera del siglo XIX.* Havana: UNEAC, 1971.

Deschamp Chapeaux, Pedro, and Juan Pérez de la Riva. *Contribución a la historia de la gente sin historia.* Havana: Editorial de Ciencias Sociales, 1974.

*Diccionario de la literatura cubana.* 2 vols. Havana: Editorial Letras Cubanas, 1980.

Domínguez, Jorge I. *Cuba: Order and Revolution.* Cambridge, Mass.: Belknap Press,1978.

Dow, George Francis. *Slave Ships and Slaving.* Salem, Mass.: Marine Research Society, 1927.

Eligio de la Puente, A. M. "Prólogo a *Dos amores.* In *Acerca de Cirilo Villaverde.* Ed. Imeldo Alvarez, 106–113. Havana: Letras Cubanas, 1982.

*Enciclopedia Universal Ilustrada.* Vol. 8. Barcelona: Espasa-Calpe, 1930.

Entralgo, Elías. *Domingo Delmonte.* Havana: Cultural, 1940.

Estévez, Francisco. *Diario de un rancheador.* Ed. Roberto Friol. *Revista de la Biblioteca Nacional José Martí* 64, no. 1 (1973): 47–148.

Fanon, Franz. *The Wretched of the Earth.* Trans. Constance Farrington. New York: Grove Press, 1968.

Fernández de Castro, José Antonio. *Orbita de José Antonio Fernández de Castro.* Ed. Salvador Bueno. Havana: Unión, 1966.

———. *Tema negro en la literatura cubana.* Havana: El Mirador, 1943.

Fernández de la Vega, Oscar, and Alberto M. Pamies. *Iniciación a la poesía afro-americana.* Miami: Ediciones Universal, 1973.

Fernández Retamar, Roberto. *Calibán: Apuntes sobre la cultura en nuestra América.* Mexico City: Editorial Diógenes, 1972.

———. *Para una teoría de la literatura hispanoamericana y otras aproximaciones.* Havana: Casa de las Américas, 1975.

Foucault, Michel. *Archaeology of Knowledge.* Trans. A. M. Sheridan Smith. New York: Pantheon Books, 1972.

———. *Language, Counter-Memory, Practice.* Trans. Donald F. Bouchard and Sherry Simon. Oxford: Blackwell, 1977.

————. *The Order of Things: An Archeology of the Human Science.* New York: Random House, 1973.

Franco, José Luciano. "Los cobreros y los palenques de negros cimarrones." *Revista de la Biblioteca Nacional José Martí* 64, no. 1 (1973): 37–46.

————. *Las conspiraciones de 1810 y 1812.* Havana: Editorial de Ciencias Sociales, 1977.

————. "Cuatro siglos de lucha por la libertad: Los Palenques." *Revista de la Biblioteca Nacional José Martí* 58, no. 1 (1967): 5–44.

————. *La diáspora africana en el Nuevo Mundo.* Havana: Editorial de Ciencias Sociales, 1975.

————. *Ensayos históricos.* Havana: Editorial de Ciencias Sociales, 1974.

————. *La gesta heroica del Triumvirato.* Havana: Editorial de Ciencias Sociales, 1978.

————. *Las minas de Santiago del Prado y la rebelión de los cobreros, 1530–1800.* Havana: Editorial de Ciencias Sociales, 1975.

————. "Palenques del Frijol, Bumba y Maluala." *Universidad de la Habana,* no. 160 (1963): 167–179.

————. *Los palenques de los negros cimarrones.* Havana: Departamento de Orientación Revolucionaria del Comité Central del Partido Comunista de Cuba, 1973.

Freud, Sigmund. *Totem and Taboo.* Trans. James Strachey. New York: Norton, 1950.

Friol, Roberto. "La novela cubana en el siglo XIX." *Unión* 6, no. 4 (1968): 179–207.

————. *Suite para Juan Francisco Manzano.* Havana: Editorial Arte y Literatura, 1977.

Fuentes, Carlos. *Distant Relations.* Trans. Margaret Sayers Peden. New York: Farrar, Straus and Giroux, 1982.

García-Carranza, Araceli. *Bibliografía de Alejo Carpentier.* Havana: Editorial Letras Cubanas, 1984.

García Márquez, Gabriel. *Chronicle of a Death Foretold.* Trans. Gregory Rabassa. New York: Knopf, 1983.

García Marruz, Fina. "De 'estudios delmontinos.'" *Revista de la Biblioteca Nacional José Martí* 11, no. 3 (1969): 23–49.

Gates, Henry Louis, Jr., ed. *Black Literature and Literary Theory.* New York: Methuen, 1984.

"Gay Latins." *New York Native* 74 (1983).

Girard, René. *Deceit, Desire, and the Novel.* Trans. Yvonne Freccero. Baltimore: Johns Hopkins Press, 1965.

Gobineau, M. A. de. *The Inequality of the Human Race.* Trans. Adrian Collins. New York: Howard Fertig, 1967.

Gómez, Juan Gualberto. *Por Cuba libre.* Havana: Editorial de Ciencias Sociales, 1974.

Gómez de Avellaneda, Gertrudis. *Sab.* Ed. Mary Cruz. Havana: Instituto Cubano del Libro, 1973.

González, Julián. *Martín Morúa Delgado: Impresiones sobre su última novela.* Havana: Imprenta de Rambla y Bouza, 1902.

González del Valle, José Zacarías. *La vida literaria en Cuba.* Havana: Publicaciones de la Secretaría de Educación, 1938.

González Echevarría, Roberto. *Alejo Carpentier: The Pilgrim at Home.* Ithaca, N.Y.: Cornell University Press, 1977.

———. "*Biografía de un cimarrón* and the Novel of the Cuban Revolution." *Novel* 13, no. 3 (1980): 249–263.

González Echevarría, Roberto, and Klaus Müller-Bergh. *Alejo Carpentier: Bibliographical Guide/Guía bibliográfica.* Westport, Conn.: Greenwood Press, 1983.

Guerra, Ramiro. *Azúcar y población en las Antillas.* 1930; repr. Havana: Editorial de Ciencias Sociales, 1970.

———. *Manual de historia de Cuba.* Madrid: Ediciones Erre, 1975.

Guevara, Ernesto. *Guerrilla Warfare.* London: Penguin Books, 1969.

Guillén, Nicolás. *Brindis de Salas.* Havana: Cuadernos de Historia Habanera, 1936.

———. "Martín Morúa Delgado." In *La familia Unzúazu.* Havana: Editorial Arte y Literatura, 1975.

———. "Nicolás Guillén: A Special Issue." Ed. Vera M. Kutzinski. *Callaloo* No. 31 10, no. 2 (1987).

Gutiérrez de la Solana, Alberto. "Novás Calvo: Precursor y renovador." *Symposium* 29, no. 3 (1975): 243–254.

Harari, Josué. *Textual Strategies: Perspectives in Post-Structuralist Criticism.* Ithaca: Cornell University Press, 1979.

Hegel, Georg. *The Philosophy of History.* Trans. J. Sibree. New York: Wiley Book Company, 1944.

———. *Reason in History.* Trans. R. Hartman. Indianapolis: Bobbs-Merrill, 1959.

Heinl, Jr., Roberto Debs, and Nancy Gordon Heinl. *Written in Blood.* Boston: Houghton Mifflin, 1978.

Henríquez Ureña, Max. *Panorama histórico de literatura cubana (1492–1952).* 2 vols. New York: Las Américas Publishing Company, 1963.

Herzberg, Julia. "Afro-Cuban Traditions in the Works of Wifredo Lam." *Review,* no. 37 (1987): 22–30.

Higman, B. W. *Slave Population of the British Caribbean, 1807–1834.* Baltimore: Johns Hopkins University Press, 1984.

Horrego Estuch, Leopoldo. *Martín Morúa Delgado, vida y mensaje.* Havana: Editorial Sánchez, 1957.

Ibarra, Jorge. *Aproximaciones a Clío.* Havana: Editorial de Ciencias Sociales, 1979.

Instituto de Estudios Africanos. "Facetas del esclavo africano en América Latina." *América Indígena* 29, no. 3 (1969): 667–697.

Jackson, Richard L. *The Afro-Spanish American Author.* New York: Garland Publishing, 1980.

———. *The Black Image in Latin American Literature.* Albuquerque: University of New Mexico Press, 1976.

———. *Black Writers in Latin America.* Albuquerque: University of New Mexico Press, 1979.

———. "Slavery, Racism and Autobiography in Two Early Black Writers: Juan Francisco Manzano and Martín Morúa Delgado." In *Voices from Under*, ed. William Luis, 55–64. Westport, Conn.: Greenwood Press, 1984.

Jackson, Shirley. *La novela negrista en Hispanoamérica*. Madrid: Editorial Pliegos, 1986.

Jahn, Janheinz. *A History of Neo-African Literature: Writing in Two Continents*. Trans. Oliver Coburn and Ursula Lehrburger. London: Faber and Faber Ltd., 1968.

Jameson, Fredric. *The Prison-House of Language: A Critical Account of Structuralism and Russian Formalism*. Princeton: Princeton University Press, 1972.

Janney, Frank. *Alejo Carpentier and His Early Works*. London: Tamesis Books Ltd., 1981.

Johnson, Lemuel. *The Devil, the Gargoyle and the Buffoon: The Negro as a Metaphor in Western Literature*. Port Washington, N.Y.: Kennikat Press, 1969.

Johnston, Harry. *Liberia*. London: Hutchinson and Company, 1906.

———. *The Negro in the New World*. London: Methuen and Company Ltd., 1910.

———. *Pioneers in West Africa*. London: Blackie and Son Ltd., 1912.

Kermode, Frank. *The Sense of an Ending*. New York: Oxford University Press, 1975.

Knight, Franklin W. *Slave Society in Cuba in the Nineteenth Century*. Madison: University of Wisconsin Press, 1970.

Lagardere, Rodolfo de. *Blancos y negros: Refutación al libro "La prostitución" del Dr. Céspedes*. Havana: La Universal, 1889.

Lam, Wifredo. *Wifredo Lam*. Paris: Amis du Musée d'Art Moderne de la Ville de Paris, 1983.

*La Revolución Cubana y la raza de color (Apuntes y datos por un cubano sin odios)*. Key West: Imprenta "La Propaganda," 1895.

Las Casas, Bartolomé de. *History of the Indies*. Trans. and ed. Andrée M. Collard. New York: Harper and Row, 1971.

Leal, Luis. "The Pursued Hero: 'La noche de Ramón Yendía.'" *Symposium* 29, no. 3 (1975): 255–260.

Leante, César. *Capitán de cimarrones*. Barcelona: Argos Vergara, 1982.

———. "Dos obras antiesclavistas cubanas." *Cuadernos Americanos* 207, no. 4 (1976): 175–188.

———. *El espacio real*. Havana: UNEAC, 1975.

———. *Los guerrilleros negros*. Havana: UNEAC, 1977.

———. "El reino de este mundo." *Revolución*, October 5, 1959, 2.

Lévi-Strauss, Claude. *Tristes tropiques*. Trans. John and Dreen Weightman. New York: Atheneum, 1975.

Lewis Galanes, Adriana. "El album de Domingo del Monte." *Cuadernos Hispanoamericanos*, nos. 451–452 (1988): 255–265.

Lezama Lima, José. *Paradiso*. Mexico City: Ediciones Era, 1968.

Luis, William. "The Antislavery Novel and the Concept of Modernity." *Cuban Studies/Estudios Cubanos* 11, no. 1 (1981): 33–47.

———. "Autobiografía del esclavo Juan Francisco Manzano: Versión de Suárez y Romero." In *La historia en la literatura iberoamericana*, edited by Raquel Chang-Rodríguez and Gabriella de Beer. Hanover, N.H.: Ediciones del Norte, 1989.

———. "Caribbean Cycles: Displacement and Change." *New England Review and Bread Loaf Quarterly* 7, no. 4 (1985): 412–430.

———. "César Leante: The Politics of Fiction." Ph.D. diss., Cornell University, 1980.

———. "La novela antiesclavista: Texto, contexto y escritura." *Cuadernos Americanos* 234, no. 3 (1981): 103–116.

———. "La novelística de César Leante." *Cuadernos Americanos* 246, no. 5 (1982): 226–236.

———. "The Politics of Memory and Miguel Barnet's *The Autobiography of a Run Away Slave.*" *Modern Language Notes* 104, no. 2 (1989): 475–491.

———. "Re-Writing History: César Leante's *Los guerrilleros negros.*" *Journal of Caribbean Studies* 2, nos. 2–3 (1981): 250–265.

———. "Time in Fiction: Lino Novás Calvo's *El negrero.*" *Linden Lane Magazine* 3, no. 1 (1984): 27.

———, ed. *Voices from Under: Black Narrative in Latin America and the Caribbean.* Westport, Conn.: Greenwood Press, 1984.

Macaulay, Henry William. "Henry William Macaulay, Esq. called in; and further Examined." *Committee of the House of Commons*, question 5475, June 15, 1842.

McElroy, Herrera. "Martín Morúa Delgado, precursor del Afro-Cubanismo." *Afro-Hispanic Review* 2, no. 1 (1983): 19–24.

Madden, Richard Robert. *The Island of Cuba. Its Resources, Progress, etc., in Relation Especially to the Influence of its Prosperity on the Interests of the British West India Colonies.* London: C. Gilpin, 1849.

———. *The Memoirs (Chiefly Autobiographical) from 1798 to 1886 of Richard Robert Madden.* Ed. Thomas More Madden. London: Ward and Downey, 1891.

Mannix, Daniel P., and M. Cowley. *Black Cargoes: A History of the Atlantic Slave Trade.* New York: Viking Press, 1969.

Manzano, Juan Francisco. *Autobiografía, cartas y versos de Juan Francisco Manzano.* Ed. José Luciano Franco. Havana: Municipio de La Habana, 1937.

———. *Autobiografía de un esclavo.* Ed. Ivan Schulman. Madrid: Ediciones Guadarrama, 1975.

———. *Obras completas de Juan Francisco Manzano, esclavo de la Isla de Cuba.* Ms. Copied by Nicolás M. de Azcárate. Madrid, January 15, 1852.

———. *Obras, Juan Francisco Manzano.* Havana: Instituto de Libro, 1972.

———. *Poems by a Slave in the Island of Cuba.* Ed. and trans. Richard Madden. London: Ward, 1840.

Marrero, Levi. *Cuba: Economía y sociedad.* Madrid: Editorial Playor, 1983.

Martínez Furé, R. Diálogos imaginarios. Havana: Editorial Arte y Literatura, 1979.

Mayer, Brantz. Adventures of an African Slaver. New York: Albert and Charles Boni, 1928.

Mellafe, Rolando. La esclavitud en Hispanoamérica. Buenos Aires: Editorial Universitaria de Buenos Aires, 1964.

Méndez y Soto, Ernesto. Panorama de la novela cubana de la revolución (1959–1970). Miami: Ediciones Universal, 1977.

Metraux, Alfred. Voodoo in Haiti. Trans. Hugo Charteris. New York: Schocken Books, 1972.

Millet, Gabriel, Manuel Ruiz de Quevedo, and Agustín Sarda, eds. La raza de color de Cuba. Madrid: Establecimiento Tipográfico de Fortanet, 1894.

Mintz, Sidney W. "The Caribbean as a Socio-Cultural Area." Cahiers d'Histoire Mondiale 9, no. 4 (1966): 912–937.

———. Caribbean Transformations. Chicago: Aldine Publishing Company, 1974.

Molloy, Sylvia. "From Serf to Self: The Autobiography of Juan Francisco Manzano." Modern Language Notes 104, no. 2 (1989): 393–417.

Moore, Carlos. "Congo o Carabalí? Race Relations in Socialist Cuba." Caribbean Review 15, no. 2 (1986): 12–15, 43.

———. "Le Peuple noir a-t-il sa place dans la revolution cubaine?" Présence Africaine, no. 52 (1964): 226–230.

———. Were Marx and Engels White Racists? Chicago: Institute of Positive Education, 1972.

Moreau de Saint-Méry. Description topographique, physique, civile, politique et historique de la partie française de l'Isle de Saint-Domingue. 3 vols. Ed. Blanche Maurel and Etienne Taillemite. 1797; repr. Paris: Société de l'Histoire des Colonies Française, 1958.

Moreno Fraginals, Manuel. El ingenio. 3 vols. Havana: Editorial de Ciencias Sociales, 1978.

———. The Sugarmill. The Socioeconomic Complex of Sugar in Cuba, 1760–1860. Trans. Cederic Belfarge. New York: Monthly Review Press, 1976.

Morilla, José. "El ranchador." In Un siglo de relato latinoamericano. Ed. Mario Benedetti and Antonio Benítez Rojo, 85–99. Havana: Casa de las Américas, 1976.

Morúa Delgado, Martín. Obras completas. 5 vols. Havana: Ediciones de la Comisión Nacional del Centenario de Martín Morúa Delgado, 1957.

Mullen, Edward J., ed. The Life and Poems of a Cuban Slave. Hamden, Conn.: Archon Books, 1981.

———. "Los negros brujos: A Reexamination of the Text." In Cuban Studies 17. Ed. Carmelo Mesa-Lago, 111–129. Pittsburgh: University of Pittsburgh Press, 1987.

Müller-Bergh, Klaus, ed. Asedios a Carpentier. Santiago de Chile: Editorial Universitaria, 1972.

Murray, David R. "Richard Robert Madden: His Career as a Slavery Abolitionist." Studies 61 (1972): 41–53.

Mustelier, Gustavo Enrique. *La extinción del negro.* Havana: Imprenta de Rambla, Bouza y Compañía, 1912.

Netchinsky, Jill Ann. "Engendering a Cuban Literature: Nineteenth-Century Antislavery Narrative (Manzano, Suárez y Romero, Gómez de Avellaneda, Antonio Zambrana)." Ph.D. diss., Yale University, 1986.

Newton, John. *The Journal of a Slave Trader.* Ed. Bernard Martin and Mark Spurrell. London: Epworth Press, 1962.

Novás Calvo, Lino. "Aquella noche salieron los muertos." *Revista de Occidente* 38, no. 114 (1932): 285–322.

———. *El negrero.* Madrid: Espasa-Calpe, 1955.

———. "La noche de Ramón Yendía." In *El cuento hispanoamericano.* Ed. Seymour Menton, vol. 2, 244–279. Mexico City: Fondo de Cultura Económica, 1965.

O'Brien, George Dennis. *Hegel on Reason and History.* Chicago: University of Chicago Press, 1975.

O'Gorman, Edmundo. *La invención de América.* Mexico City: Fondo de Cultura Económica, 1958.

Orovio, Helio. *Diccionario de la música cubana.* Havana: Editorial Letras Cubanas, 1981.

Ortega y Gasset, José. *The Dehumanization of Art, and Other Essays on Art, Culture, and Literature.* Princeton: Princeton University Press, 1968.

Ortiz, Fernando. *Los cabildos africanos.* Havana: "La Universal," 1921.

———. *Contrapunteo cubano del tabaco y el azúcar.* Havana: J. Montero, 1940.

———. *Cuban Counterpoint: Tobacco and Sugar.* Trans. Harriet de Onis. New York: Vintage, 1970.

———. *El engaño de las razas.* Havana: Editorial Páginas, 1946.

———. *Los negros esclavos.* Havana: Editorial de Ciencias Sociales, 1975.

Owen, Nicholas. *Journal of a Slave Dealer.* Ed. Eveline Martin. London: George Routledge and Sons, Ltd., 1930.

———. *Orbita de Fernando Ortiz.* Ed. Julio Le Riverend. Havana: UNEAC, 1973.

Palés Matos, Luis. *Poesía.* Ed. Raúl Hernández Novas. Havana: Casa de las Américas, 1975.

Palmer, Colin A. *Human Cargoes.* Urbana: University of Illinois Press, 1981.

Paquette, Robert Louis. "The Conspiracy of La Escalera: Colonial Society and Politics in Cuba in the Age of Revolution." Ph.D. diss., University of Rochester, 1982.

Paz, Octavio. *Los hijos del limo.* Barcelona: Editorial Seix Barral, 1974.

———. "A Literature of Foundations." Trans. Lysander Kemp. *Tri-Quarterly* E, nos. 13–14 (1968): 7–12.

Pérez de la Riva, Juan. *El barracón y otros ensayos.* Havana: Editorial de Ciencias Sociales, 1975.

———. *Para la historia de la gente sin historia.* Barcelona: Ariel, 1976.

Pérez Firmat, Gustavo. *Literature and Liminality: Festive Reading in the Hispanic Tradition.* Durham: Duke University Press, 1986.

Pichardo, Hortensia, ed. *Documentos para la historia de Cuba.* 2 vols. Havana: Instituto del Libro, 1971.

Portuondo, Fernando. *Historia de Cuba: 1492–1898.* Havana: Editorial Pueblo y Educación, 1965.

Portuondo, José Antonio. "Corrientes literarias en Cuba." *Cuadernos Americanos* 26, no. 4 (1967): 193–213.

———. *Crítica de la época y otros ensayos.* Las Villas, Cuba: Universidad Central de Las Villas, 1965.

Prats Sariol, José, ed. *Nuevos críticos cubanos.* Havana: Editorial Letras Cubanas, 1983.

Price, Richard, ed. *Maroon Society: Rebel Slave Communities in the Americas.* 2nd ed. Baltimore: Johns Hopkins University Press, 1979.

Price-Mars, Jean. *So Spoke the Uncle.* Trans. Magdaline W. Shannon. Washington, D.C.: Three Continents Press, 1983.

"Proceedings of the General Anti-Slavery Convention Held in London, 1840." *Eclectic Review* 8 (July–December 1841): 227–247.

Ramos, José Antonio. *Caniquí.* Havana: Consejo Nacional de Cultura, 1963.

Remos, Juan J. "Algunas consideraciones sobre 'El negro Francisco.'" In Antonio Zambrana, *El negro Francisco,* v–vii. Havana: Imprenta de P. Fernández y Cía., 1953.

———. *Historia de la literatura cubana.* 2 vols. Havana: Cárdenas y Compañía, 1945.

Renan, Ernast. *Caliban.* Trans. Elenoir Grant Vickery. New York: Shakespeare Press, 1896.

Reynolds, Edward. *Stand the Storm.* New York: Allison and Busby Ltd., 1985.

Ring, Harry. *How Cuba Uprooted Race Discrimination.* 1961; repr. New York: Merit Publishers, 1969.

Ripoll, Carlos. *Indice de la Revista de Avance (Cuba 1927–1930).* New York: Las Américas, 1967.

———. "La Revista de Avance (1927–30) vocero del vanguardismo y pórtico de revolución." *Revista Iberoamericana* 30, no. 58 (1964): 261–282.

Rodríguez, Ileana. "Romanticismo literario y liberalismo reformista: El grupo de Domingo Delmonte." *Caribbean Studies* 20, no. 1 (1980): 35–56.

Rodríguez-Luis, Julio. "Lino Novás Calvo y la historia de Cuba." *Symposium* 29, no. 4 (1975): 281–293.

*Romances cubanos del siglo XIX.* Ed. Samuel Feijoó. Havana: Editorial Arte y Literatura, 1977.

Romero Fivel-Démaret, Sharon. "The Production and Consumption of Propaganda Literature: The Cuban Anti-Slavery Novel." *Bulletin of Hispanic Studies* 66, no. 1 (1989): 1–12.

Roses, Lorraine Elena. *Voices of the Storyteller: Cuba's Lino Novás Calvo.* Westport, Conn.: Greenwood Press, 1986.

Rout, Leslie B. *The African Experience in Spanish America.* New York: Cambridge University Press, 1976.

Rubin, Vera, and Arthur Tuden, eds. *Comparative Perspectives on Slavery in New World Plantation Societies.* New York: New York Academy of Science, 1977.

Saco, José Antonio. *Colección de papeles científicos, históricos, políticos y de otros ramos sobre la Isla de Cuba.* 3 vols. Havana: Editorial Nacional de Cuba, 1963.

————. *Contra la anexión.* Ed. Fernando Ortiz. Havana: Editorial de Ciencias Sociales, 1974.

————. *Historia de la esclavitud de la raza africana en el Nuevo Mundo.* 4 vols. Havana: Colección de Libros Cubanos Cultural, 1938.

————. *Memoria sobre la vagancia en la Isla de Cuba.* Santiago de Cuba: Instituto Cubano del Libro, 1974.

————. *La supresión del tráfico de esclavos africanos en la Isla de Cuba.* Paris: Imprenta de Panckoucke, 1845.

Said, Edward. *Beginnings: Intention and Method.* New York: Basic Books, 1975.

————. *Orientalism.* New York: Pantheon Books, 1979.

Saiz de la Mora, Jesús. *Domingo del Monte.* Havana: 1930.

Salky, Andrew. *Writing in Cuba since the Revolution.* London: Bogle-l'Overture Publications Ltd., 1977.

Sánchez, Julio C. *La obra novelística de Cirilo Villaverde.* Madrid: De Orbe Novo, 1973.

Sarmiento, Domingo Faustino. *Facundo: Civilización y barbarie.* Buenos Aires: Editorial Sopena Argentina, 1949.

Scarano, Francisco. *Sugar and Slavery in Puerto Rico: The Plantation Economy of Ponce, 1800–1850.* Madison: University of Wisconsin Press, 1984.

Scott, Rebecca. *Slave Emancipation in Cuba.* Princeton, N.J.: Princeton University Press, 1985.

Soler Puig, José. "José Soler Puig: 'Sin la Revolución no hubiera podido llegar a ser escritor.'" *América Latina,* no. 4 (1979): 145–153.

Sosa, Enrique. *La economía en la novela cubana del siglo XIX.* Havana: Editorial Letras Cubanas, 1978.

Soto Paz, Rafael. *La falsa cubanidad de Saco, Luz y del Monte.* Havana: Editorial "Alfa," 1941.

Souza, Raymond. *Lino Novás Calvo.* Boston: Twayne Publishers, 1981.

Spengler, Oswald. *The Decline of the West.* Vol. 1. Trans. Charles Francis Atkinson. New York: Knopf, 1926.

Speratti-Piñero, Emma Susana. *Los pasos ayados.* Mexico City: Colegio de México, 1981.

Stedman, William. *Narrative of an Expedition against the Revolted Negroes of Surinam.* Amherst: University of Massachusetts Press, 1972.

Suárez y Romero, Anselmo. *Francisco.* Ed. Eduardo Castañeda. Havana: Biblioteca Básica de Autores Cubanos, 1970.

Sutherland, Elizabeth. *The Youngest Revolution.* New York: Dial Press, 1969.

Tagliacozzo, Giorgio, Michael Mooney, and Donald Phillip Verne, eds. *Vico and Contemporary Thought.* Atlantic Highlands, N.J.: Humanities Press, 1979.

———. ed. *Vico: Past and Present.* Atlantic Highlands, N.J.: Humanities Press, 1981.

Tanco y Bosmeniel, Félix. "Un niño en la Habana." Ed. Rolando Hernáldez Morelli. *Círculo: Revista de Cultura* 15 (1986): 73–84.

———. "Petrona y Rosalía." In *Cuentos cubanos del siglo XIX.* Ed. Salvador Bueno, 103–137. Havana: Editorial de Arte y Literatura, 1977.

Tardieu, Jean-Pierre. "Religions et croyances populaire dans *Biografía de un cimarrón* de M. Barnet: Du refus à la tolérance." *UTIEH/Caravelle* 43 (1984): 43–67.

Terdiman, Richard. *Discourse/Counter-Discourse.* Ithaca, N.Y.: Cornell University Press, 1985.

Thoby-Marcelin, Phillippe, and Pierre Marcelin. *The Beast of the Haitian Hills.* Trans. Peter C. Rhodes. New York: Times, 1946.

Thomas, Hugh. *Cuba: The Pursuit of Freedom.* New York: Harper and Row, 1971.

Torres-Cuevas, Eduardo, and Arturo Sorhegui, eds. *José Antonio Saco: Acerca de la esclavitud y su historia.* Havana: Editorial de Ciencias Sociales, 1982.

Turner, Mary. *Slaves and the Missionaries: The Disintegration of Jamaican Slave Society, 1784–1834.* Urbana: University of Illinois Press, 1982.

Vico, Giambattista. *The Autobiography of Giambattista Vico.* Trans. Max Harold Fisch and Thomas Goddard Bergin. London: Cornell University Press, 1975.

———. *The New Science.* Trans. Thomas Goddard Bergin and Max Harold Fisch. Ithaca: Cornell University Press, 1984.

Villaverde, Cirilo. *El ave muerta. Miscelánea de Util y Agradable Recreo,* 1 (August 1837).

———. *Apuntes biográficos de Emilia Casanova de Villaverde.* New York: 1874.

———. "Cecilia Valdés." *La Siempreviva* 2 (1839): 75–87, 242–254.

———. *Cecilia Valdés.* Havana: Imprenta Literaria, 1839.

———. *Cecilia Valdés.* New York: El Espejo, 1882.

———. *Cecilia Valdés.* Ed. Olga Blondet and Antonio Tudisco. Madrid: Anaya, 1971.

———. *Cecilia Valdés.* Ed. Raimundo Lazo. Mexico City: Editorial Porrúa, 1972.

———. *Cecilia Valdés.* Ed. Ivan Schulman. Caracas: Biblioteca Ayacucho, 1981.

———. *Cecilia Valdés.* Ed. Imeldo Alvárez García. Havana: Editorial Letras Cubanas, 1982.

———. *Cecilia Valdes or Angel's Hill.* Trans. Sydney G. Gest. New York: Vantage Press, 1956.

———. *Dos amores.* Havana: Imp. de Próspero Massana, 1858.

———. *Escursión a Vuelta Abajo.* Havana: Editorial Letras Cubanas, 1981.

———. *El espetón de oro.* Havana: Imp. de Oliva, 1838.

————. *General Lopez, the Cuban Patriot.* New York: 1951.

————. *La joven de la flecha de oro.* Havana: Imp. de R. de Oliva, 1841.

————. *El penitente.* Havana: Editorial la Burgalesa, 1925.

————. *The Quadroon or Cecilia Valdes.* Trans. Mariano J. Lorente. Boston: L. C. Page and Company, 1935.

————. *La revolución de Cuba vista desde Nueva York.* New York: 1869.

————. *El señor Saco con respecto a la revolución de Cuba.* New York: La Verdad, 1852.

Vitier, Cintio. "Dos poetas cubanos Plácido y Manzano." *Bohemia* 65, no. 50 (1973): 21.

Wadstrom, C. B. *An Essay on Colonization.* New York: Augustus M. Kelley, 1968.

Ward, W. E. F. *The Royal Navy and the Slavers.* New York: Pantheon Books, 1969.

Weitz, Morris. *Problems in Aesthetics.* New York: Macmillan Company, 1970.

White, Hayden. *Metahistory.* Baltimore: Johns Hopkins University Press, 1973.

Williams, Robert. *Crusader* 8, no. 43 (1967).

Zambrana, Antonio. *El negro Francisco.* Havana: Imprenta P. Fernández y Compañía, 1953.

# INDEX